Buffett & Munger

UNSCRIPTED

TSOH INVESTMENT RESEARCH

IN APRIL 2021, AFTER A DECADE WORKING IN THE FINANCE INDUSTRY AS A BUYSIDE equities analyst, I launched the TSOH Investment Research service. The pitch to subscribers is comprehensive access to my equity research: I provide 100% transparency on my investment philosophy, research process, portfolio decision-making, and outcomes (quarterly portfolio returns).

Complete transparency as a cornerstone of the service was informed by what I witnessed during my time in the finance industry. To quote Warren G. Harding, many discussions about stocks can be best described as "the art of speaking for as long as the occasion warrants, and saying nothing".

A notable example is on position sizing. When somebody says that they own a stock, that in itself isn't a particularly insightful comment; that changes as they explain if their portfolio weighting for that security is 0.1%, 1%, or 10%, along with the rationale for that sizing relative to other positions. These decisions are revealing in terms of the thought process and investment approach/philosophy being employed by a given investor; in addition, I believe they are an integral part of learning and improving as an investor.

TSOH subscribers receive full transparency on all investment decisions (prior disclosure of all changes), along with quarterly portfolio return updates. I naturally cannot make any guarantees on my future performance, but I can promise subscribers will always have complete knowledge on what I'm thinking, along with how it is impacting my decision-making within my investment portfolio.

You can save 20% on a subscription to TSOH Investment Research by scanning the QR code or visiting thescienceofhitting.com/unscripted. Thank you for your time, and I hope you enjoy *Buffett and Munger Unscripted.*

Buffett & Munger

UNSCRIPTED

Three Decades of Investment and Business Insights from the Berkshire Hathaway Annual Shareholder Meetings

SELECTED AND ARRANGED BY

Alex W. Morris

HARRIMAN HOUSE LTD
3 Viceroy Court
Bedford Road
Petersfield
Hampshire
GU32 3LJ
GREAT BRITAIN
Tel: +44 (0)1730 233870

Email: enquiries@harriman-house.com
Website: harriman.house

First published in 2025.

Hardback: 978-1-80409-067-1
Paperback: 978-1-80409-141-8
eBook: 978-1-80409-068-8

British Library Cataloguing in Publication Data
A CIP catalogue record for this book can be obtained from the British Library.

Printed and bound in India by Replika Press Pvt. Ltd.

10 9 8 7 6 5 4

CONTENTS

To Mom, Dad, and my sister Amanda—For giving me the greatest gift in life, a loving family.

To my wife Jessica—From lifelong road trips to raising our family, I'll always be by your side.

To my son Jack—I will do my best as a dad to try and live up to the high bar Papa set for me.

INTRODUCTION

FOR ONE OF THE FINANCIAL WORLD'S MOST STORIED EVENTS, THE Berkshire Hathaway annual meetings were long available to just a relatively small group. For decades, it was an in-person event held each spring in Omaha, Nebraska, with no video recordings. (In the 2000s and 2010s, value investors like myself waited anxiously for notes taken by meeting attendees to be shared online.) That changed in 2018 when Berkshire Hathaway released the annual meeting videos dating back to 1994. While this precious resource was now widely available for all to access, it still presented a daunting task for an individual who hoped to derive valuable insights on a particular topic of interest.

This book will hopefully be a useful resource for those in search of a solution to that problem. As Warren Buffett noted at the 1998 Berkshire Hathaway annual meeting, he believed that Larry Cunningham's *The Essays of Warren Buffett: Lessons For Corporate America*—a synthesis of Buffett's annual shareholder letters, organized by theme—was the book that did the best job of conveying the lessons that he hoped to share with investors and business owners. (Buffett: "He has done a first-class job of organizing, by topic, all these things that I've written ... If I were picking one thing to read, that would probably be the one.") I have a dog-eared copy of Cunningham's book on my desk and consider it a must read for people who are interested in business and investing.

This book was inspired by Cunningham's work, and seeks to perform a similar act of synthesis for the countless unscripted insights delivered by Warren Buffett and Charlie Munger at Berkshire Hathaway annual meetings since the early 1990s. I have reviewed every Berkshire Hathaway annual meeting from 1994 to 2024, covering more than 1,700 questions over 31 years. Buffett and Munger's answers represent a treasure trove of investment and business wisdom; the goal of this book is to unlock that trove and to make it accessible to all.

Over the past five years, I listened to each of those 31 annual meetings. I then organized all of the questions by topic, and selected roughly 500 answers that offered the most valuable insights for business people and fellow investors. This is the output from that exercise.

To that end, I have organized this book based on a number of important investment and business themes, including the skills and temperament required to be a successful long-term investor, the art of business valuation, living with uncertainty and market volatility, defining your circle of competence, thinking about opportunity costs, navigating macroeconomic uncertainty, and many more. While Buffett and Munger have said many insightful things about politics, life lessons, etc., that is not the focus of this book.

As you might imagine, Buffett and Munger covered similar ground at multiple meetings over the years, as their investment approach has largely remained unchanged for decades. For that reason, when an answer was largely comparable to a prior year, I've only kept the most useful phrasing. In addition, when the wording wasn't additive to the heart of the answer, I've edited it for clarity and conciseness. Any changes to direct quotes were made with deep respect and admiration for Buffett and Munger, with the goal being to fairly and fully present their ideas to the reader.

Much of what I've learned about investing and business came from Buffett and Munger. For that, I will be forever grateful. Hopefully this book will help pass that wisdom to the next generation of investors. It's my attempt to thank Buffett and Munger for all that they have given to the investment community.

One final note: I will donate 50% of my net proceeds (after-tax) from this book to GLIDE, a charitable organization that Buffett has supported for years. While Warren's philanthropic endeavors are not the focus of this book, that is another part of life where he has proven to be a leader and a role model.

ALEX MORRIS
Davie, Florida
2024

PART ONE:
Value Investing

"We're trying to buy businesses we want to own forever, and if you're thinking that way you might as well look back a way and see what it's been like to own them forever."

"The growth aspects overall of a market are not a big factor with us; it's really a question of figuring out who's going to win what game, and who's going to lose what game."

"Time is the enemy of the poor business, and it's the friend of the great business."

"I think you would better understand any presentation using the word EBITDA, if every time you saw that word, you just substituted the phrase, 'bullshit earnings.'"

"You're a better doctor if you drop by the pathology department occasionally."

INTRODUCTION

THE PRIMARY OBJECTIVE IN INVESTING, WHETHER BUYING A SINGLE share of a stock or acquiring 100% of a company, is straightforward: to get more than what you pay for. Or, as Buffett puts it, "Value is getting a lot for the expectable future cash flows in terms of what you're laying out today."

As we think about the art of intelligently applying a framework for assessing value and making investment decisions *in practice*, a number of pertinent considerations arise, including our time horizon, our ability and willingness to bear risk, and position sizing / diversification, among others. Those topics, the foundation of a sound investment philosophy, are the focus of part one.

While many investors start their journey in search of a magic formula with mathematical precision, that is ultimately a fool's errand. In investing, to paraphrase Keynes, it's sufficient to be roughly right, especially if it helps to avoid the risk of being precisely wrong. As Munger notes, the broader objective is continual learning and improvement, to wake up slightly wiser each day: "If you have a passionate interest in knowing why things are happening, and you are always trying to figure out the world in terms of why is this happening or not happening—that cast of mind, over long periods, gradually improves your ability to cope with reality. If you don't have that cast of mind, I think you're destined, probably, for failure, even with a pretty high IQ."

SUBJECTS AND MEETINGS FEATURED

VALUE INVESTING

2009 MEETING (02:48:46)

WARREN BUFFETT: "Charlie and I think there is no other kind of investment than a value investment. In other words, we don't know how anybody would invest in a *non*-value investment. We've always been puzzled by the term 'value,' suggesting it contrasts with growth. Value is getting a lot for the expectable future cash flows in terms of what you're laying out today. Every time somebody characterizes us as value investors, we ask: What other kind could there be?"

2012 MEETING (00:47:33)

WB: "Probably the silliest stuff we've seen taught at major business schools has been in the investment area. It is astounding how they've focused on one fad after another in finance theory, and it's usually been very mathematically based ... Investing is really not that complicated. I would have two courses: one on how to value a business, and another on how to think about markets. If people grasped the basic principles in those two courses, they would be far better off than if they were exposed to a lot of things like modern portfolio theory or options pricing. Who needs options pricing to be an investor?

"The teaching of investments has totally drifted away. I look at the books that are sometimes used, and there's really nothing in there about valuing businesses—but that's what investing is all about. If you buy businesses for less than they're worth, you're going to make money. And if you know the difference between the businesses that you can value and the ones you can't, you're going to make money. But they've tried to make it a lot more difficult. That's what the high priests in any particular arena do; they have to convince the laity that the priests need to be listened to."

CHARLIE MUNGER: "The folly creeps into the accounting, too. The optimal way to price a very long-term option on the stock of a big business you understand—or even a stock market index—is not by using Black-Scholes. And yet the accounting profession does that. They want some kind of a standardized solution that requires them not to think too hard, and they found one."

2015 MEETING (04:37:26)

WB: "We basically look for companies where we think we could understand what the future will look like in five, ten, or fifteen years. That doesn't mean we calculate it to four decimal places—but we need to have a feel for it, and we know our limitations. We stay away from a lot of things ... We just keep reading and thinking and looking at things that come along; as Charlie describes it, comparing Opportunity A with Opportunity B. When we were capital-constrained, we usually had to sell something if we were going to buy something else. And that always makes for an interesting challenge, when you're measuring something you hold against something that has come along, to see which is more attractive. We probably leaned very much toward things where we felt we were certain to get a decent result, as opposed to where we were hopeful of getting a brilliant result. We went with our instincts and kept putting one foot in front of the other."

CM: "We had some good fortune. Warren says he was lucky to go find GEICO, but not every twenty-year-old was going down to Washington DC, and knocking on the doors of empty buildings to try and find something out that he was curious about. So we also made our own luck by being curious and seeking wisdom—and we certainly recommend that to anybody else. There's nothing that produces wisdom more thoroughly than really getting your own nose whacked hard when you make a mistake—and we had a fair amount of that, didn't we?"

WB: "We had plenty. We thought we knew the department store business in Baltimore [with Hoschild-Kohn] and we thought we knew about the trading stamp business [with Blue Chip Stamps]. We've had a lot of experience with bad businesses, and that really makes you appreciate a good business. To some extent, it sharpens your ability to make distinctions between the good ones and bad ones. And we've had a lot of fun along the way. That helps too. If you enjoy what you're doing, you are likely to get a better result than if you go to work with your teeth clenched every morning."

CM: "I think we were helped because we came from families where there were some admirable people, and we tended to identify other admirable people better than we would if we had come from a different background. My deceased wife used to say, 'You can't accomplish much in one generation.' We owe a considerable amount, both of us, to the families that we were raised in."

2016 MEETING (03:19:48)

WB: "I owe a great deal to Ben Graham in terms of learning about investing. And I owe a great deal to Charlie, in terms of learning a lot about business. I've also spent a lifetime looking at businesses, seeing why some work and why some don't. As Yogi Berra said, 'You can see a lot just by observing.' That's pretty much what Charlie and I have been doing for a long time.

"It's also important to recognize what you can't do. We may have tried the department store business and a few things, but we've generally tried to only swing at things in our strike zone [within our circle of competence]. It really hasn't been much more complicated than that.

"You don't need the IQ in the investment business that you need in certain activities in life, but you do have to have emotional control. We see very smart people do very stupid things; it's fascinating. Just take the people who get very rich and then leverage themselves up in some way that they lose everything. They are risking something important for something that isn't important. Well, you could figure that out in first grade, but people do it time after time."

CM: "There are a few simple tricks that work well, particularly if you have a temperament that has a combination of patience and opportunism in it. And I think that's largely inherited, although I suppose it can be learned to some extent. Then I think there's another factor that accounts for why Berkshire has done as well as it has: We're really trying to behave well.

"I had a great-grandfather; when he died, the preacher gave the talk, and he said, 'None envied this man's success, so fairly won and wisely used.' That's a very simple idea, but it's exactly what Berkshire's trying to do. There are people who make a lot of money and everybody hates them; they don't admire the way that they earned the money. I do not particularly admire making money running gambling casinos. We don't own any. And we've turned down certain businesses, including a big tobacco business. I don't think Berkshire would work as well if we had just been terribly shrewd and didn't have a little bit of what the preacher said about my grandfather. We want to have people think of us as having won fairly, and used wisely."

2019 MEETING (01:27:59)

WB: "As Charlie has said, all investing is value investing. You're putting money out now to get more later on, and you're making a calculation as to the probabilities of getting that money, when you'll get it, and what interest rates will be in between. The same calculation goes into it, whether you're buying a bank at 70% of book value or if you're buying Amazon at a very high multiple of reported earnings. Our investment managers [Todd Combs and Ted Weschler] making the Amazon investment decision are absolutely as much value investors as I was when I was looking around for all these things selling below working capital many years ago … They are looking for things where they feel they understand how the business will develop between now and Judgment Day, in cash. Current sales and current profit margins make some difference. The level of tangible assets, whether the business has excess cash or excess debt, it all goes into the calculation as to whether they should buy A, B, or C. They are absolutely following value principles … The considerations are identical.

"In the end, it all goes back to Aesop, who said in 600 B.C. that a bird in the hand is worth two in the bush. When we buy Amazon, we try and figure out whether there's three or four birds in the bush and how long it will take to get to the bush, how certain it is that we're going to get to the bush, and then who else is going to come and try and take the bush away. Despite a lot of equations you learn in business school, that's the basic equation … That will guide me, and that will guide my successors in investment management at Berkshire."

CM: "I don't mind not having caught Amazon early. Jeff Bezos is kind of a miracle worker. It's very peculiar. I give myself a pass on that one. But I feel like a horse's ass for not identifying Google [Alphabet] better. I think Warren feels the same way. We screwed up."

WB: "He's saying we blew it. We had some insights, because we were using Google ads at GEICO, and we were seeing the results produced. We were paying $10 a click for something that had a marginal cost to Google of exactly zero. And we saw that the ads were working for us."

CM: "We could see at GEICO how well Google advertising worked—and we sat there sucking our thumbs. So, we're ashamed and we're trying to atone. Maybe Apple was atonement."

2023 MEETING (00:43:24)

CM: "I think value investors are going to have a harder time now that there's so many of them competing for a diminished bunch of opportunities. My advice is to get used to making less."

WB: "Charlie has been telling me the same thing the whole time we've known each other."

CM: "But we *are* making less. We did better when we were younger."

WB: "That's mostly, I think, because we never thought that we would be managing $500 billion. But I would argue that there's going to be plenty of opportunities ... What gives you opportunities is other people doing dumb things. And I'd say that in the fifty-eight years that we've been running Berkshire, there's been a great increase in the number of people doing dumb things.

"They do big, dumb things. And the reason they do it, to some extent, is because they can get money from other people so much easier than when we started. You could start ten or fifteen dumb insurance companies in the last ten years, and you could become rich if you were adroit at it. Whether the business succeeds or not, the underwriters and the lawyers got paid. It couldn't be done fifty-eight years ago; you couldn't get the money to do some of the dumb things that we wanted to do, fortunately.

"The big money now is in selling other people's ideas. It isn't in outperforming. If you run small amounts of money, I think the opportunities will be greater. But Charlie and I have always differed on this subject. He likes to tell me how gloomy the world is. I like to tell him, 'We'll find something.' So far, we've both been kind of right. Charlie, will you budge an inch or not?"

CM: "There is so much money now in the hands of so many smart people all trying to outsmart one another and out promote one another, getting more money out of other people. It's radically different from the world we started in. I suppose it will have its opportunities, but it's also going to have some unpleasant episodes."

WB: "But they're trying to outsmart each other in arenas that you don't have to play in.

"The world is overwhelmingly short-term-focused. If you go to a quarterly call, they're all trying to figure out how to fill out a sheet to show earnings for the current year, and the management team is interested in feeding them expectations that will be slightly beaten. That is a world that is made to order for anybody just trying to think about what you can do that should work over five, ten, or twenty years. I would love to be born today, to go out with not too much money and—hopefully—turn it into a lot of money. Charlie would, too, actually. He would find something to do, I guarantee you. It wouldn't be exactly the same as before, but he would end up with a big, big, big pile."

CM: "I would not like the thrill of losing my big pile. I like my big pile the way it is."

WB: "We agree on that incidentally."

STOCK SELECTION

1998 MEETING (03:02:34)

WB: "The criteria for selecting a stock is really the criteria for looking at a business. We are looking for a business we can understand. They sell a product that we think we understand, or we understand the nature of the competition and what could go wrong with it over time. And then we try to figure out whether the economics, the earnings power, over the next five, ten, or fifteen years is likely to be good and getting better, or poor and getting worse. Then we try to decide whether we're getting in with people that we feel comfortable being in with. And then we try to decide what's an appropriate price for what we've seen up to that point in the business.

"What we do is simple, but it is not necessarily easy. The checklist that we go through in our minds is not very complicated. Knowing what you don't know is important; knowing the future is impossible in many cases, and difficult in others. We're looking for the ones that are relatively easy. Then you have to find it at a price that's interesting to you, and that's very difficult for us now (although there have been periods in the past where it's been a total cinch).

"That's what goes through our mind. If you were thinking of buying a gas station, dry cleaner, or convenience store to invest your life savings in and to run as a business, you'd think about the competitive position and what it would look like five to ten years from now, and how you were going to run it, or who was going to run it for you, and how much you had to pay. That's what we think of when we look at a stock, because a stock is nothing other than a piece of a business."

CM: "When finance is properly taught, it should be taught from cases where the investment decision is easy. I always cite the early history of National Cash Register (NCR); it was created by a fanatic who bought all the patents, had the best salesforce, and had the best production plants. He was a very intelligent man and passionately dedicated to the cash register business. And it was a godsend to retailing when cash registers were invented. Cash registers were the pharmaceuticals of a former age. If you read an early annual report prepared by John Henry Patterson, who was CEO of National Cash Register, any idiot could see this was a talented fanatic who was very favorably located—and, therefore, the investment decision was easy. If I taught finance, I'd collect a hundred cases like that. That's the way I would teach students."

WB: "We have that NCR annual report from 1904. It's really a classic because Patterson not only tells you why his cash register is worth to people about twenty times what he's selling it for, but he also tells you that you're an idiot if you want to go into competition with him."

2012 MEETING (02:54:55)

WB: "We try and stay away from things that we don't understand. And when I say understand, I mean we'll have a reasonable fix on what the earnings power and competitive position will look like in five or ten years. So, I've got some notion of how the industry will develop and where the company will stand within the industry. That eliminates a whole bunch of things.

"Beyond that, if the price is crazy, even though I understand it, that eliminates another bunch of companies. You get down to a very small universe, and then you get down to a particularly small universe when we're working with lots of money, as we are now ... There's industries we know that may have a wonderful future, but we don't have the faintest idea who the winners will be. So there's a whole lot of things we don't think about.

"Charlie and I have a number of filters that companies have to get through very quickly before we're willing to think about them. Sometimes we are thought of as rude—probably Charlie a little more often than me—because people will call and start explaining some idea, and it just doesn't make it through the first filter or two. We think we're saving their time if we just politely say we have no interest, and we don't want to have you finish the sentence.

"We don't have to do very many things that work. That's the beauty of this business. You don't have to be able to spell five hundred words to get to the end of the spelling bee and beat everybody else."

CM: "There are a couple of little rules of thumb. If it's got a really large commission on it, don't read it, because the chance that somebody who is paying a very high commission will give you a big advantage is very low. The other thing that is helpful in reverse is to look at what other smart people are buying. That is not a crazy search method as a way to sort opportunities to consider."

WB: "I used to grab the updated Graham-Newman reports as fast as they would come out. If Graham-Newman was doing something, it was certainly worth my time to look at it."

BUSINESS QUALITY

2003 MEETING (04:10:30)

WB: "The ideal business is one that earns very high returns on capital and can keep using lots of capital at those high returns. That becomes a compounding machine. If you can put $100 million into a business that earns 20% on capital, ideally it would be able to earn 20% on $120 million the following year, $144 million the following year, and so on. You could keep redeploying capital at these same returns over time. But there are very, very, very few businesses like that.

"Unfortunately, good businesses like Coca-Cola or See's Candies don't require much capital. And the incremental capital doesn't produce anything like the returns produced by some great intangible [asset]. We would love a business that could redeploy all of its earnings, or even well beyond the earnings: We'd love to have a business earning 20% on $100 million where, if we put another $1 billion in, it would earn 20% on that $1 billion. But those businesses are so rare ...

"Most of the great businesses generate a lot of money; they do not generate lots of opportunities to earn high returns on incremental capital. We can deploy X at See's and earn a lot of money, but if we put 5× in we don't earn any more money to speak of. We can earn high returns on X at *The Buffalo News*, but if we try to make it 5× we don't earn any more money. They just don't have the opportunities to use incremental capital. We look for them, but they don't exist ...

"We've largely bought businesses that earn good returns on capital, but which have limited opportunities to earn anything like the returns on their base business with incremental capital.

"The good thing about our structure at Berkshire is that we can take businesses that earn good returns on capital, but which don't have the opportunity for returns of a similar magnitude on incremental money, and move that money around to buy other businesses. Take the newspaper publishing business, which has been a fantastic business over the years: You earned terrific returns on your own invested capital, but if you went out to buy other newspapers, you had to pay a very fancy price, and you didn't get great returns on incremental capital. But the people in that business felt the only thing they knew was newspaper publishing or media, so their options were limited. We can move money any place that it makes sense, and that's an advantage of our structure … See's has produced probably $1 billion of pre-tax earnings for us. If we tried to employ that in the candy business we would have gotten terrible returns over time. But because we moved it around, it enabled us to buy some other businesses over time."

CM: "A good but not fabulous business tends to fall into two categories. One is the business where the whole reported profit just sits there in surplus cash at the end of the year, and you can take it out of the business and it will do just as well without it as it would if that cash stayed in the business. The second business is one that reports the 12% return on capital but there's never any cash. It reminds me of the used construction equipment business. My old friend, John Anderson, used to say, 'In my business, every year you make a profit, and there it is, sitting in the yard.' There are an awful lot of businesses like that; the money is needed just to keep going, to stay in place, so there's never any excess cash. That business doesn't enable headquarters to drag out all the cash and invest it elsewhere. We hate that kind of business."

WB: "It would be terrific if every one of our great businesses had ways to deploy additional capital at great rates, but it doesn't happen. Gillette has a great razor and blade business, but there's no way they can keep putting those profits back into the razor and blade business. It just doesn't take that kind of capital. They have to deploy some money, but it's peanuts compared to the razor and blade profits. The temptation then is to go out and buy other businesses—but we don't think that the batting average of American industry in redeploying capital has been great … In a sense, we sort of knock the very procedure that has got us to where we are."

SUCCESS IN BUSINESS AND INVESTING

1998 MEETING (03:10:53)

WB: "If you're interested in business, you ought to learn all the accounting you can. It is the language of business. That doesn't mean it's perfect, so you have to know the limitations.

"I would also advise you to work at a number of businesses. There's nothing like seeing how business operates to build your future judgment about businesses. When you understand which businesses are very competitive and which are less competitive, and why that works that way, it adds to your knowledge. I would take accounting courses, I would do a lot of reading about investments, and I would get business experience. I would talk with people that are in business to find out what they think makes their operation tick, or to see where they have problems and why.

"Sop it up every place you can. And if it turns you on, you'll do well in it. Certain activities grab different people. If you understand business, you understand investments. Investments are simply business decisions in terms of capital allocation."

CM: "There's also the little matter of underspending your income year after year after year. That really works if you keep at it."

WB: "Any $1 you save before you get out and start having a family is probably worth $10 later on simply because you can save it and invest it. The time to save is when you're young; you'll never have a better time to save, because the expenditures come along whether you like them or not. Work for yourself first, and put the money aside. I was lucky that way, I didn't have to pay for my own college. I probably wouldn't have gone to college if I'd had to pay for it. I was able to save everything I made in my teens, and those dollars got magnified quite a bit. Whereas when I started selling securities, the money I made then was taken up by family needs to quite an extent. So start saving early. A lot of that is a habit anyway; it's a great habit to have."

1999 MEETING (03:46:30)

WB: "Compound interest behaves like a snowball on sticky snow. The trick is to have a very long hill, which means starting very young or living to be very old. If I were getting out of school today and had $10,000 to invest, I'd start with the As and go right through all of the companies. And I probably would focus on smaller companies, because I would be working with smaller sums and there's more of a chance that something is overlooked in that arena. It wouldn't be like doing that in 1951 when you could leaf through and find all kinds of things that just leapt off the page. But that's the only way to do it. You have to buy businesses, and you have to buy them at attractive prices, and you have to buy into good businesses. That advice will be the same 100 years from now. That's what it's all about.

"You can't expect anybody else to do it for you. People will not tell you about wonderful little investments. It's not the way the investment business is set up. When I first visited GEICO in January 1951, I went back to Columbia. And the rest of that year, I went down to Blythe and Company and to one other firm, Geyer & Co., which was a leading insurance analyst. I thought that I had discovered this wonderful thing, so I'd see what these great investment houses that specialized in insurance stocks said; they told me I didn't know what I was talking about. It wasn't of interest to them. You've got to learn what you know and what you don't know. Within the arena of what you know, you have to pursue it very vigorously and act when you find it. You can't look around for people to agree with you. You can't look around for people to even know what you're talking about. You have to think for yourself. And if you do, you'll find things."

CM: "The hard part of the process for most people is the first $100,000. If you start at $0, getting to $100,000 is a long struggle for most people. And I would argue that people who get there relatively quickly are helped if they're passionate about being rational, very eager, opportunistic, and if they steadily underspend their income grossly. Those factors are very helpful."

2002 MEETING (01:53:48)

WB: "I don't know to what extent it's innate or to what extent it's learned, but an ability to detach yourself from the crowd is a quality you need. A great IQ is not needed. You do not have to be terrifically smart to do well as an investor.

"I first learned from Ben Graham in a very big way; I learned something additionally from Phil Fisher; and I learned a lot from Charlie. And the proof is in my record, actually. From eleven to nineteen, I read every book there was on investments, and I didn't do well at all. I had no real investment philosophy. I tried a lot of things and I was having a lot of fun, but I wasn't making any money. Then I read Ben Graham's book in 1949 [*The Intelligent Investor*] when I was at the University of Nebraska, and it changed my whole view of investing. Basically, it told me to think about a stock as a part of a business. Now, that seems so obvious ... but once you crank into your mental apparatus that you're not looking at things that wiggle up and down on charts, but instead you're buying a business, you've set a foundation for thinking rationally about investing.

"There's no reason you need a high IQ ... Temperament, however, is enormously important; it may be innate, it may be learned, it may be intensified by experience or reinforced in various ways. You have to be realistic. You have to define your circle of competence accurately. You have to know what you don't know, and not get enticed by it. You have to have an interest in money, I think, or you won't be good at investing. But if you're very greedy, it'll be a disaster, because that will overcome rationality.

"The books I read that really molded how I thought about businesses and investing are just as valid now. I've seen nothing to improve on Graham and Fisher in terms of the basic approach of investing, which is to think about stocks as businesses, and then to think about what makes a good business. That's all there is to investing, and having a margin of safety, which Ben talks about. It's not complicated, but it definitely requires discipline. It requires insulating yourself from popular opinion. Listening to lots of people telling you things is just a waste of time. You're better off sitting and thinking. You have to think about stocks in terms of their business characteristics and what they can earn on capital employed.

"I would read Graham and Fisher, and then read a lot of annual reports, think about businesses, and try and think about which businesses you understand and which you don't. You don't have to understand them all. Just forget about the ones that you don't understand."

CM: "If you have a passionate interest in knowing why things are happening, and you are always trying to figure out the world in terms of why is this happening or not happening—that cast of mind, over long periods, gradually improves your ability to cope with reality. If you don't have that cast of mind, I think you're destined, probably, for failure, even with a pretty high IQ."

WB: "We've seen relatively little correlation between investment results and IQ. Not that there are a whole bunch of people out there with 80 IQs knocking the cover off the ball. But there are all kinds of people with high IQs that get no place. It's more interesting to look at why people with high IQs don't succeed, and then see if you can cast those factors out of yourself, and leave a residual that will work.

"It's like Charlie says: 'All I want to know is where I'm going to die, so I'll never go there.' If you study people who 'die,' financially, with high IQs and ask why, you'll see certain overwhelming characteristics present in most cases. You have to make sure that you don't possess them, or if you do possess them, that you can get rid of them or control them in some manner."

2003 MEETING (01:55:19)

CM: "There's a lot to be said for developing a temperament that can own securities without fretting. The fretful disposition is an enemy of long-term performance."

WB: "It's almost impossible to do well in equities over a period of time if you go to bed every night thinking about the price of them. We think about the value of them; if they closed the stock exchange tomorrow, it wouldn't bother me and Charlie at all ... A lot of people have private companies and they never get a quote on them. We bought See's Candies in 1972, we haven't had a quote on it since; does that make us wonder about how we're doing with See's Candies? No, we look to the company's results.

"Focusing on the price of a stock is dynamite; it really means that you think that the stock market knows more than you do. The stock market *may* know more than you do—but then you shouldn't be in stocks. The stock market is there to serve you, not to instruct you. You need to formulate your own ideas on value, and if the price gets cheaper and you have funds, you should buy more ... Where we make our mistakes, frankly, is when we focus on price and value and we start buying, and the price goes up a little and we quit, like we almost did on See's Candies. A mistake like that cost us $8 billion in the case of Walmart stock a few years ago, because it went up in price and we stopped buying. We are not happy when things we're buying go up in price. We want them to go down and down and down."

2004 MEETING (01:21:13)

CM: "I don't know anybody who is wise who doesn't read a lot. On the other hand, that alone won't do it. You have to have a temperament which grabs the correct ideas and does something with those ideas."

WB: "Temperament is all important. If you can't control yourself, no matter what intellect you bring to the process, you're going to have disasters. Investing is not a business that requires extraordinary intellect. It does require extraordinary discipline. That shouldn't be so difficult, but as I look around the world sometimes, apparently it is quite difficult. The whole world went a little mad a few years back in terms of investments. And you say, 'How could that happen? Don't they learn anything from the earlier ones?' But what we learn from history is that people don't learn from history. You certainly see that in financial markets all the time."

2004 MEETING (04:33:03)

CM: "I've watched Warren through all these decades, and he has learned a hell of a lot, even in the last twenty or thirty years … It's a lifelong game, and if you don't keep learning, other people will pass you by."

WB: "But you don't have to have any blinding insights or a high IQ. Look at PetroChina, for example … If you're buying something like that at maybe one-third of what comparable oil companies are selling for, that's not high-level stuff. You have to be willing to read the reports, but I enjoy doing that. You wouldn't say that requires any high-level insights or anything."

CM: "When you were buying that block of stock, nobody else to speak of was buying. So, the insights can't have been all that common. No, I think that takes a certain amount of what an old Omaha friend used to call 'uncommon sense.' He used to say, 'There is no common sense. When people say common sense, they mean uncommon sense.' Part of it, I think, is being able to tune out folly as distinguished from recognizing wisdom. If you just have whole categories of things you bat away, so your brain isn't cluttered with them, then you're better able to pick up a few sensible things to do."

WB: "We don't consider many stupid things, we get rid of them fast … There was a great article in *The New Yorker* when the Fischer/Spassky chess matches were going on [in 1972]. It got into this speculation of whether humans would be able to take on computers in chess. They said, 'How can the human mind, when all you're really looking at is the results from various moves in the future, deal with a computer that's thinking at unbelievable speeds?' They examined the subject and found a Fischer or a Spassky, essentially, was eliminating 99.99% of the possibilities without even thinking about it. It wasn't that they could outthink the computer in terms of speed, but they had this ability in what you might call grouping, or exclusion, where they just got right down to the few possibilities out of the zillions of possibilities that really had any chance of success. Getting rid of the nonsense—Charlie and I are pretty good at that. We can hang up fast."

CM: "There you have it. All you have to do is go at it in the way that Vasily Smyslov did when he was the world champion of chess."

2007 MEETING (01:39:54)

CM: "When you're trying to determine intrinsic value, the margin of safety, and so on, there isn't one easy method that could simply be mechanically applied by a computer that would make anybody who could punch the buttons rich. By definition, this is a game which you play with multiple techniques and multiple models, and a lot of experience is very helpful. I don't think you can become a great investor very rapidly, any more than you could become a great bone tumor pathologist very rapidly. It takes some experience, and that's why it's helpful to get a very early start … The other thing you should recognize is that we've never had any system for being able to make correct judgments on the values of all businesses. We throw almost all decisions into the too-hard pile, and we just sift for a few decisions that we can make that are easy … If you're looking for an ability to correctly value all investments at all times, we can't help you."

WB: "We don't know how to jump over seven-foot bars. But we do know how to recognize, occasionally, a one-foot bar. And we know enough to stay away from the seven-foot bars, too."

2009 MEETING (00:58:32)

WB: "If you're in the investment business and you have an IQ of 150, sell thirty points to somebody else because you don't need it. You need to be reasonably intelligent. But you do not need to be a genius, at all. In fact, it can hurt. You do have to have an emotional stability. You have to have sort of an inner peace about your decisions. It is a game where you get subjected to minute-by-minute stimuli, where people are offering opinions all the time. You have to be able to think for yourself. I don't know how much of that's innate and how much can be taught. But if you have that quality, you'll do very well in investing if you spend some time at it."

CM: "If you think your IQ is 160 and it's 150, you're a disaster. It's much better to be a guy with a 130 IQ that's operating well within himself."

2010 MEETING (03:42:57)

WB: "We've seen a few periods of great opportunities that scream at us, and we've seen a few periods of overvaluation that scream at us. And then 90% of the time we're somewhere in between. In terms of being scared, I don't know what you can do about that. If you have a temperament that when others are fearful you're going to get scared yourself, you are not going to make a lot of money in securities over time, in all probability ... People look at quotations, and more than that, do something based on small changes in quotations. Think how much more rational investing in a farm is than the way many people buy stocks. If you buy a farm, do you get a quote next month? No, you look at the farm and say, 'I expect it to produce so many bushels of corn, and if it does that, it meets my expectations.' Many people buy a stock and think that if it goes up it's wonderful, and if it goes down it's bad. We think just the opposite. When it goes down we love it, because we'll buy more. And if it goes up, it kills us to buy more. But if you can't get yourself into that mental attitude, you're going to be scared whenever everybody else is scared. If somebody else tells you when to buy, a week later somebody else will tell you the world is coming to an end. You're a broker's friend, but you won't make a lot of money."

CM: "I think I developed more courage after I learned I could handle hardship. So maybe you should get your feet wet with a little more failure."

WB: "Some people really do not have the temperament, emotional stability, or whatever it may be, to invest in securities. They'd be much better off if there were no quotations at all ... In the end, what counts is buying a good business at a decent price, and then forgetting about it for a long, long, long time. Some people can do it and some people can't."

2010 MEETING (04:10:51)

WB: "In my own case, I started out without knowing anything about valuing companies. And Ben Graham taught me a way to value a certain type of company that would prove successful, except the universe of those companies dried up. It was almost a guarantee against failure, but it was not a guarantee that these things would continue to be available. Charlie taught me a lot about the value of a durable competitive advantage and a first-class business. Over time, I've learned more about various types of businesses, but you'd be amazed how many businesses I don't feel that I understand well.

"The biggest thing is not how big your circle of competence is, but knowing where the perimeter is. You don't have to be an expert on 90% of businesses, or 80%, 70%, or even 50%. But you do have to know something about the ones that you actually put your money into—and if that's a very small part of the universe, that still is not a killer.

"Think about the businesses in your own hometown. Which would you like to buy into? Which do you think you could understand their economics? Which do you think will be around ten or twenty years from now? Which do you think it would be very tough to compete with? Just keep asking yourself questions about businesses and talk with other people about them. You will extend your knowledge over time.

"Always remember that margin of safety, and recognize your limitations. That's enormously important in this business. You will find things to do. Six or seven years ago, when I was looking at Korean stocks, I never had any idea Korean stocks would be something I would buy. But I looked, and I could see that there were a number of businesses that met the margin of safety test. And there I diversified, because I didn't know that much about any specific one, but I knew that a package of twenty of them was going to work out very well because they were so cheap. And that was sort of the old Graham approach. You will find opportunities from time to time, and the beauty of it is you don't have to find very many of them."

CM: "Obviously, if you want to get good at something which is competitive, you have to think about it a lot, learn a lot, and practice doing it a lot. You have to keep learning, because the world keeps changing and your competitors keep learning. You have to get up each morning and try and go to bed that night a little wiser than you were when you got up. If you keep doing that for a long time—and accumulate some experience, good and bad, as you try and master what you're trying to do—people who do that almost never utterly fail. They may have a bad period when luck goes against them, but very few people have ever failed with that. If you have the right temperament, you may rise slowly but you're sure to rise.

"It's hard to get anywhere near the top, and it's hard to hold any position once you've attained it. But I think you could have predicted that Pete Kiewit [leader of the Omaha-based construction company Kiewit Corporation from 1924 to 1979], for example, was likely to win. They cared more about doing it right, they cared more about avoiding trouble, and they put more discipline on themselves ... I would have bet on Pete Kiewit."

WB: "If you'd followed Pete Kiewit around for ten years, you never would have seen him do anything dumb. It's avoiding the dumb things. You really don't have to be brilliant, but you have to avoid obvious mistakes. When he practiced law, Charlie would think about any client's business as if he owned it. I remember talking to Charlie fifty years ago, and he would start talking about a Caterpillar dealership in Bakersfield or something. He was incapable of looking at a business without thinking about the fundamental economics of it."

READING ANNUAL REPORTS

1998 MEETING (01:30:00)

WB: "We've read a lot of annual reports. We start by looking at the annual reports of companies we think we can understand. And I read hundreds every year. We hope to be reading reports of businesses that are understandable to us. And then we see from that report whether management is telling us about the things that we would want to know about if we owned 100% of the company. When we find a management that does tell us about those things, and that is candid in the same way that a manager of a subsidiary would be candid with us, and talks in language that we can understand, it definitely improves our feeling about investing in such a business.

"The reverse turns us off, to some extent. If we read a bunch of public relations gobbledygook, and we see lots of pictures and no facts, it has some effect on our attitude toward a business. We want to understand the business better when we get through with the annual report than when we picked it up. And that is not difficult for a management to do if they want to do it. If they don't want to do it, we think that is a factor in whether we want to be their partners over a ten-year period or so. We've learned a lot from annual reports."

CM: "If you've got a standardized bunch of popular jargon that looks like it came out of some consulting firm, I do think it's a big turnoff. That's not to say that some of the consulting mantras aren't right—but I think there's a lot to be said for a sort of candid, simple, coherent prose."

WB: "Almost every business has problems, and we'd just assume the manager would tell us about them. We would like that in the businesses we run. We give very little advice to our managers, but one thing we always do say is to tell us the bad news immediately. And I don't see why that isn't good advice for the manager of a public company. Over time, I'm positive it's the best policy. But a lot of companies, for example, have IR [investor relations] people, and they are dying just to pump out what they think is good news all the time. They have this attitude that you've got a bunch of animals out there to be fed and that they're going to feed them what they want to eat all the time. Over time, the animals learn. So, we've tried to stay away from businesses like that."

CM: "What you seldom see in an annual report is a sentence like this: 'This is a very serious problem and we haven't quite figured out yet how to handle it.' But believe me, that is an accurate statement much of the time."

WHEN TO SELL

2009 MEETING (01:52:53)

WB: "If we lose confidence in management or in the durability of the competitive advantage, or if we recognize that we made a mistake, we sell. On the other hand, if you really get a wonderful business with outstanding management—mostly the wonderful business part—when in doubt, keep holding. But it's not an inviolable rule.

"On the wholly-owned businesses, we have an attitude that, when we buy, it's for keeps. We make only two exceptions: when they promise to start losing money indefinitely, or if we have major labor problems. But, otherwise, we are not going to sell something just because we get offered more money for it, even if it's more than it's worth.

"That's a peculiarity we have, and we want our partners to know about that. We do think it helps in terms of buying businesses over time. It's also the way we want to run our business. With stocks, we sell them, but we're often more reluctant to sell than most people. If we made the right decision, we like to ride that a very long time. We've owned some stocks for decades. But if the competitive advantage disappears, if we really lose faith in the management, or if we were wrong in the original analysis, we sell."

OWNING BUSINESSES

1999 MEETING (03:19:43)

CM: "Generally speaking, trying to dance in and out of the companies that you really love on a long-term basis has not been a good idea for most investors. We're quite content to sit with our best holdings."

WB: "People have tried to do that with Berkshire over the years. I've had some friends that thought it was getting a little ahead of itself from time to time; they thought they'd sell and buy it back cheaper. It's pretty tough to do. You have to make two decisions right—you have to sell it right and then you have to buy it right later on, and usually you have to pay some tax in between.

"If you get into a wonderful business, the best thing to do is usually to stick with it. Coca-Cola and Gillette both experienced disappointments, below what they anticipated twelve to eighteen months ago and below what we anticipated. But that will happen. It happens with some of our wholly-owned businesses from time to time. Sometimes they do better than we anticipate, too.

"It's not the nature of things that everything goes in a nice, straight, smooth line upward … It's a competitive world. Your competitor's correct moves, your own incorrect moves, the world environment—all of those things can interrupt trend lines."

2002 MEETING (00:35:31)

WB: "It's not our natural inclination to sell. We have held Washington Post stock since 1973. I've never sold a share of Berkshire, having bought the first shares in 1962. We've held Coca-Cola stock since 1988. We've held Gillette stock since 1989. We've held American Express stock since 1991 … We would sell if we needed money for something else, but that has not been the problem the last ten or fifteen years.

"Forty years ago my sales were all because I found something I liked even better. I hated to sell, but I also didn't want to borrow money, so I would reluctantly sell something that I thought was terribly cheap to buy something that was even cheaper. Those were the times when I had more ideas than money. Now I've got more money than ideas, and that's a different equation. So now we sell when we're re-evaluating the economic characteristics of the business. In other words, we had one view of the long-term competitive advantage of the company at the time we bought it, and we may have modified that. That doesn't mean we think that the company is going into some disastrous period or anything remotely like that. We think McDonald's has a fine future and we think Disney has a fine future, but we probably don't think that their competitive advantage is as strong as we thought it was when we initially made the decision. That may mean that we were wrong when we made the original decision. It may mean that we're wrong now, and that their strengths are every bit as what they were before. But, for one reason or another, we think that the strengths may have been eroded to some degree.

"A classic case of that would be the newspaper industry, generally. In 1970, when Charlie and I were looking at the newspaper business, we felt it was about as impregnable a franchise as could be found. We still think it's quite a business, but we do not think the franchise in 2002 is the same as it was in 1970. We do not think the franchise of a network television station in 2002 is the same as it was in 1965. Those beliefs change quite gradually. And who knows whether they're right, even. But that is the reason, in general, that we sell now. If we got into some terribly cheap market, we might sell some things that we thought were cheap to buy something even cheaper, after we'd bought lots and lots of equities. But that's not the occasion right now."

AVOIDING DIFFICULT DECISIONS

1994 MEETING (01:20:08)

WB: "Some businesses are a lot easier to understand than others, and Charlie and I don't like difficult problems. We'd rather multiply by three than by pi. It's just easier for us."

CM: "That is such an obvious point. And yet so many people think if they just hire somebody with the appropriate labels, they can do something very difficult. That is one of the most dangerous ideas a human being can have. All kinds of things just intrinsically create problems. The other day I was dealing with a problem, and I said, this new building has three things I've learned to fear: an architect, a contractor, and a hill. And if you go at life like that, I think you will, at least, make fewer mistakes than people who think they can do anything by just hiring somebody with a label. You don't have to hire out your thinking if you keep it simple."

WB: "You don't have to do exceptional things to get exceptional results. You can do very ordinary things. What is complicated about [Coca-Cola]? But we're $3 billion pre-tax better off than a few years ago because of it. There's nothing I know about that product, its distribution system, its finances, or anything really, that hundreds of thousands or millions of people don't already know. They just don't do anything about it. Similarly, if you get into some complicated business, you can get a report that's a thousand pages thick and have PhDs working on it, but it doesn't mean anything. What you've got is a report but you won't understand what that business is going to look like in ten or fifteen years. The big thing to do is avoid being wrong."

CM: "There are some things that are so intrinsically dangerous. Another of my heroes is Mark Twain, who looked at the promoters of his day and said, 'A mine is a hole in the ground owned by a liar.' That's the way I've come to look at projections. Warren and I were offered $2 million worth of projections once in the course of buying a business and the book was [a foot] thick. And we wouldn't open it."

WB: "We almost paid $2 million not to look at it. It's ridiculous. I do not understand why any buyer of a business looks at a bunch of projections put together by a seller or his agent. You can almost say that it's naive to think that that has any utility whatsoever. We just are not interested. If we don't have some idea ourselves of what we think the future is, to sit there and listen to some other guy who's trying to sell us the business or get a commission on it, tell us what the future's going to be, it's very naive. We had a line in the report one time, 'Don't ask the barber whether you need a haircut.' It's quite applicable to the projections of sellers of businesses."

DECLINING BUSINESSES

2012 MEETING (02:49:31)

CM: "Declining businesses are not worth nearly as much as growing businesses, but they can still be quite valuable if a lot of cash is going to come out of them."

WB: "Generally speaking, it pays to stay away from declining businesses. If you really think a business is declining, most of the time you should avoid it. Now, we are in several declining businesses … but that is not where we're going to make the real money at Berkshire. The real money is going to be made in the growing businesses, and that's where the focus should be.

"I would never spend a lot of time trying to value a declining business—what I call the cigar-butt approach—where you get one free puff out of the cigar butt that you find. The same amount of energy and intelligence brought to other types of businesses is just going to work out better. So, our general reaction, unless there's some special case, is to avoid declining businesses."

DUE DILIGENCE

2014 MEETING (03:19:30)

WB: "When I was twenty-three, if I got interested in the coal business, I would go out and see the CEOs of eight or ten coal companies … I'd ask them a lot of questions, but there were two questions I'd always ask at the end: If they had to put all of their money into any coal company except their own, and go away for ten years and couldn't change it, which one would it be and why? After I got an answer to that, I would ask, if they had to sell short in the equivalent amount one coal company, which would it be and why? If I went around and talked to everybody in the coal business about that, I would know more about the coal companies from an economic standpoint than any one of those managers probably would."

CM: "You might try a version of the trick that Larry Bird [former basketball player and coach] used. When he wanted an agent to negotiate his new contract, he asked every agent why he should be selected—and if he was not going be selected, whom the agent would recommend. Since everybody recommended the same number-two choice, Larry Bird just hired him and negotiated the best contract in history. There are a lot of tricks that people use."

PUBLIC AND PRIVATE MARKETS

1994 MEETING (01:44:52)

WB: "We very seldom find something to buy on a negotiated basis for an entire business … A big limiting factor is it has to be something we can understand; that eliminates 95% of businesses. We get lots of proposals for things that are totally outside the boundaries of what we're interested in. We prefer to buy entire businesses, or an 80% or greater interest, partly for tax reasons, and frankly, we like it better …

"We can usually get more for our money in wonderful businesses, in terms of buying little pieces of them in the stock market, because the market is far more inefficient in pricing businesses than in the negotiated market … In the stock market, you get a chance to buy businesses at foolish prices, and that is why we end up with a lot of money in marketable securities. If we absolutely had our choice, we would own three times the number of businesses we own outright … You'll never get a chance to buy all of Coca-Cola or Gillette. Businesses like that, sensational businesses, are just not available. But sometimes you get a chance to make a sensible purchase in the market of such businesses."

CM: "If you stop to think about it, if 100% of a business is for sale, the average corporate buyer is being run by people who have the mindset of buying with somebody else's money. We have the mindset of buying with our own money. There's also a class of buyers for 100% of businesses who are basically able and shrewd financial promoters; I'm talking about leveraged buyout (LBO) funds and so on. And those people tend to have the upside, but not the downside, in the private arrangements they've made with their investors. And naturally, they tend to be somewhat optimistic. So, we have formidable competition when we try and buy 100% of businesses."

WB: "If you can pay for it with other people's money, that gets pretty attractive. Let's say you're a baseball fan—how much would you pay to own the Yankees? You might pay more if you were writing a check on someone else's bank account than if on your own bank account. And in corporate America, animal spirits are there. Those are our competitors when buying entire businesses. In terms of buying publicly traded securities, most managers don't think about it. It's very interesting to me, because they'll have somebody else manage their money in terms of a portfolio of securities; well, that's a portfolio of businesses. I'll say, 'Why don't you pick out your own portfolio?' And they'll say, 'That's much too difficult.' Then some guy will come along with some business they never heard of a week before and give them some figures and a few projections, and he thinks he knows enough to buy that business. It's very puzzling to me."

TIME HORIZONS AND RISK

1994 MEETING (01:54:34)

WB: "We define risk as the possibility of harm or injury. And in that respect, we think it's inextricably wound up in your time horizon for holding an asset. If you intend to buy XYZ Corporation at 11:30 this morning and sell it out before the close today, that is, in our view, a very risky transaction … We think the risk of buying something like Coca-Cola at the price we bought it at a few years ago is essentially so close to nil, in terms of our perspective holding period. But if you asked me the risk of buying Coca-Cola this morning, and you're going to sell it tomorrow morning, I'd say that is a very risky transaction.

"It became very fashionable in the academic world—and then that spilled over into the financial markets—to define risk in terms of volatility, of which beta became a measure. But that is no measure of risk to us. The risk, in terms of our super-cat business [exposure to very large insurance losses from earthquakes, hurricanes, etc.], is not that we will lose money in any given year. We know we're going to lose money on some given day, that is for certain. And we're extremely likely to lose money in a given year. Our time horizon of writing that business would be at least a decade. And we think the probability of losing money over a decade is low. So, we feel that, in terms of our horizon of investment, that is not a risky business. And it's a whole lot less risky than writing something that's much more predictable.

"The interesting thing is that, using conventional measures of risk, something whose return varies from year to year between +20% and +80% is riskier, as defined, than something whose return is +5% a year every year. We just think the financial world has gone haywire in terms of measures of risk. We are perfectly willing to lose money on a given transaction—arbitrage being an example, any given insurance policy being another example. We are not willing to enter into transactions in which we think the probability of doing a number of mutually independent events, but of a similar type, has an expectancy of loss. And we hope that we are entering into transactions where our calculations of those probabilities have validity. To do so, we try to narrow it down; there are a whole bunch of things we just won't do because we don't think we can write the equation on them.

"If we knew it was an honest coin, and someone wanted to give us seven-to-five on one flip, how much of Berkshire's net worth would we put on that flip? It would sound like a big number to you—it would not be a huge percentage of our net worth, but it would be a significant number. We will do things when probabilities favor us."

CM: "We try and think like Fermat and Pascal, as if we had never heard of modern finance theory. I really think that a lot of modern finance theory can only be described as disgusting."

VOLATILITY AND RISK

1998 MEETING (04:34:37)

WB: "We don't worry about risk in the traditional sense. We look at riskiness, essentially, as being a go/no-go valve in terms of looking at the future businesses. In other words, if we think we don't know what's going to happen in the future, that doesn't mean it's necessarily risky, it just means we don't know. It means it's risky for us. It might not be risky for someone else who understands the business. In that case, we just give up. We don't try to predict those things.

"We don't say, 'Well, we don't know what's going to happen, so therefore we'll discount it at 9% instead of 7%.' That is not our way to approach it. We feel that, once it passes a threshold test of being something about which we feel quite certain, the same discount factor tends to apply to everything. And we try to only do things about which we are quite certain when we buy into the businesses.

"The capital asset pricing model (CAPM) type reasoning, with different rates of risk-adjusted return and all that, we think it's nonsense. But we think it's also nonsense to get into situations, or to try and evaluate situations, where we don't have any conviction as to what the future is going to look like. And we don't think you can compensate for that by having a higher discount rate and saying it's riskier ... That just is not our way of approaching things."

CM: "The great emphasis on volatility in corporate finance we just regard as nonsense. Put it this way: As long as the odds are in our favor and we're not risking the whole company on one throw, or anything close to it, we don't mind volatility in results. What we want is the favorable odds. We figure the volatility, over time, will take care of itself at Berkshire."

WB: "If we have a business about which we're extremely confident as to the business results, we would prefer that it had higher volatility rather than lower. We will make more money out of a business where we know where the endgame is going to be if it bounces around a lot ... When we see a business about which we're very certain, but the world thinks that its fortunes are going up and down, and therefore it behaves with great volatility, we love it. That's way better than having a lower beta. We actually would prefer what other people would call risk. When we bought The Washington Post it went down 50% in a matter of a few months. That was the best thing that could've happened; it doesn't get any better than that. The business was fundamentally very nonvolatile in nature—TV stations and a strong, dominant newspaper, that's a nonvolatile business—but it was a volatile stock. That is a great combination from our standpoint."

2001 MEETING (03:43:27)

WB: "We regard volatility as a measure of risk to be nuts. The reason it's used is because the people who are teaching want to talk about risk, and the truth is, they don't know how to measure it in business. That would be part of our course on how to value a business, understanding the riskiness of the business. Risk with us relates to several possibilities. One is the risk of a permanent capital loss. The other risk is just an inadequate return on the kind of capital we put in. It does not relate to volatility at all ... You can find all kinds of wonderful businesses that have great volatility in their results, but it does not make them bad businesses. And you can find some terrible businesses that are very smooth ... It just doesn't make any sense to translate volatility into risk ... If somebody starts talking to you about beta, zip up your pocketbook."

CYCLICALITY AND LUMPY EARNINGS

2011 MEETING (04:58:46)

WB: "When we made the decision to buy the leading manufacturer of brick in Alabama [Jenkins Brick & Tile for $50 million, as discussed in the 2010 Berkshire Hathaway shareholder letter], it was not because I thought brick was going to turn in two months, six months, or a year. I thought that, over time, being a very important brick manufacturer and distributor in Alabama, adjacent to our strong operation in Texas, would be a good investment at the price we paid. I feel good about the decision, but I won't feel good about our brick results over the next six months."

CM: "One advantage of buying these very cyclical businesses is a lot of people don't like them. What difference does it make to us if the earnings which average, say, $300 million a year, come in in a very lumpy fashion? In the big scheme of things, what do we care if it's lumpy, as long as it's a good business? We have an advantage on that stuff. Nobody else was bidding for a brick plant in Alabama with no current customers to speak of."

WB: "See's Candies, a wonderful business, loses money roughly eight months of the year. We know the seasonal pattern, so we don't worry in July that somehow Christmas won't come. We've got a couple thousand years on our side. But that's easy to see. If you just looked at one quarter of See's earnings, you'd think, 'What are these guys doing in this business?' Now, obviously, cyclical businesses are not going to behave exactly the same as seasonal businesses, but why look at it any differently? If you take the next twenty years, there will be a few terrible years for residential housing, there will be a lot of them that are pretty good, and there will be a few that are terrific. I don't know the order in which they're going to appear, but I know if I buy the assets cheap enough to participate in those twenty years, we'll do OK over that time."

HOLDING CASH

1994 MEETING (02:10:36)

WB: "The question is, do we get into asset allocation by maintaining given cash levels, depending on some kind of outlook? We don't really think that way. If we have cash, it's because we haven't found anything intelligent to do with it that day, in the way of buying the kind of businesses we like. When we can't find anything for a while, the cash piles up. That's not through choice; it's because we're failing at what we want to do, which is to find things to buy.

"We make no attempt to guess whether cash is going to be worth more three months, six months, or a year from now. We would never have an asset allocation meeting. We're looking for things to buy that meet our tests, and if we showed no cash at year-end, we would love it, because it would mean that we'd found ways to employ the money in ways that we like ... If we have a lot of money around, we are a little dumber than usual; it tends to make you careless. I would say that the best purchases are usually made when you have to sell something to raise the money to get them, because it just raises the bar a little bit that you jump over in the mental decisions."

1995 MEETING (02:36:57)

WB: "Cash at Berkshire is a residual; we would like to have no cash at all times. We also don't want to owe a lot of money at any time. If we have cash around, it's simply because we haven't found anything we like to do, and we hope to deploy it as soon as possible. We never think about whether the market's going to go down or something of the sort, or whether we might buy something even cheaper. If we like something, we'll buy it. And when you see cash on our balance sheet of any size, that's an acknowledgment by Charlie and me that we have not found anything, in size anyway, attractive at that point. It's never a policy of ours to hold a lot of cash."

2004 MEETING (01:43:49)

WB: "We think the best way to minimize risk is to think. And the idea that you say, 'I've got 60% in stocks and 40% in bonds,' and then have a big announcement, 'Now we're moving to 65% in stocks and 35% in bonds,' as some strategists or whatever they call them on Wall Street do, that is pure nonsense. What you ought to do is have your default position be short-term instruments, and whenever you see anything intelligent to do, you should do it ... So much of what you see about asset allocation is just merchandising. It's a way to make you think that if you don't know how to determine whether it should be 60%/40% or 65%/35% that you need these people. You don't need them at all in investing."

CM: "People have always had this craving to know the future. The king used to hire the magician or the forecaster, and he'd look at sheep guts or something for an answer as to how to handle the next war. There's always been a market for people who purport to know the future based on their expertise, and there's a lot of that still going on. People have an economic incentive to sell some nostrum. It can be sold over and over and over again ... I think it's disgusting. It's much better to make a living by being part of a system that delivers value to the people who are buying the product. But nobody refrains from creating gambling casinos or something on my theory. If it'll work to make money, we tend to do it in this country."

2006 MEETING (01:43:19)

WB: "You might consider a normal level of cash at Berkshire as being about $10 billion, although there could be circumstances where we'd go below that [at the 2012 meeting, that minimum was increased to about $20 billion]. But because of the catastrophe insurance business we're in and all of that, we do not scrape the bottom of the barrel—but we also don't need anything like $40 billion like we have now. We would be much happier if we had $10 billion of cash and all the balance in things we liked very much. We work toward that end at all times.

"There is nothing even about the way businesses come to us ... We don't like having excess cash around—but we like even less doing dumb deals, because we do them for forever. If we make a dumb deal, it just sits there. We don't resell it three months later by having an IPO or something. So, we should be very uncomfortable about the fact that we've got all that cash. But it's also important that we not be so uncomfortable that we go out and do something just to be doing something. I would say it's likely, but far from certain, that three years from now we have significantly less cash and significantly more earning power. The goal is to translate that cash into permanent earning power over time ... That's our job."

CM: "I think you may get some perspective on what bothers you if you go back to the annual report of Berkshire ten years ago and then compare it with the last annual report. Despite the great difficulties of deploying cash, we managed to put an awful lot of wonderful stuff into Berkshire in the last ten years. So, we aren't altogether gloomy about that process continuing."

2019 MEETING (03:34:01)

WB: "On balance, I would rather own an index fund than carry Treasury bills. That said, if we'd instituted that policy in 2007 or 2008, we might have been in a different position in terms of our ability to act in late 2008. It also has certain execution problems with hundreds of billions of dollars than a similar policy with $1 billion. But it's a perfectly rational observation. And looking back on ten years of a bull market, it really jumps out at you. I would argue that if you were working with smaller numbers, it would make a lot of sense. And if you're working with large numbers, it might well make sense in the future for Berkshire to operate that way. We committed $10 billion a week ago. And there are conditions under which—although they're not likely in any given week or month—we could spend $100 billion very, very quickly. And if those conditions existed, it would be capital very well deployed, much better than in an index fund. So, we've been operating on the basis that we will get chances to deploy capital. They will come in clumps in all likelihood, and when other people don't want to allocate capital."

CM: "I plead guilty to being a little more conservative with the cash than other people. But I think that's all right. We could have put all the money into a lot of securities that would've done better than the S&P 500 with twenty-twenty hindsight. Remember, we had all that extra cash all that period, if something had come along in the way of opportunities and so on. I don't think it's a sin to be a little strong on cash when you're as big of a company as we are. I watched Harvard use the last ounce of their cash, including all their prepaid tuition from the parents, and plunge it into the market at exactly the wrong moment and make a lot of forward commitments to private equity. They suffered two or three years of absolute agony. We don't want to be like Harvard. We're not going to change."

WB: "We do like having a lot of money to be able to operate very fast and very big. We know we won't get those opportunities frequently. Certainly, in the next twenty or thirty years, there'll be two or three times when it'll be raining gold and all you have to do is go outside. But we don't know when they will happen. And we have a lot of money to commit ... The one thing you should very definitely understand about Berkshire is that we run the business in a way that we think is consistent with serving shareholders who have virtually all of their net worth in Berkshire. I happen to be in that position myself, but I would do it that way under any circumstances.

"We have a lot of people who trust us, who really have disproportionate amounts of Berkshire compared to their net worth, if you were to follow standard investment procedures. We want to make money for everybody, but we want to make very, very sure that we don't lose, permanently, money for anybody who buys our stock somewhere around intrinsic business value to begin with. We just have an aversion to having a million-plus shareholders, having a lot of them ever really lose money, if they're willing to stay with us for a while. And we know how people behave when the world, generally, is upset. I think they want to be with something they feel is like the Rock of Gibraltar. We have a real disposition toward that group."

BUFFETT'S RESEARCH PROCESS

1994 MEETING (02:15:45)

WB: "The speed of information really doesn't make any difference to us. It's the processing and finally coming to some judgment that has some utility. It's a judgment about the price of a business or a part of a business, a security, versus what it's worth. And none of that involves anything to do with quick information. It involves getting *good* information.

"Virtually everything we've done has been reading public reports, and then maybe asking questions to ascertain trade positions or product strengths or something of that sort. But we can make decisions very fast. We get called on a business, and we can make up our mind whether we're interested in two or three minutes. That takes no time. We may have to do a little checking on a few things subsequently. But I can't think of anything where we really needed lots of price data or things like that to make any decisions ... You could be in someplace where the mail and quotations were delayed three weeks, and I think you could do just fine in investing."

1998 MEETING (01:40:05)

WB: "If I were teaching a course on investments, there would be one valuation study after another, with the students trying to identify the key variables in that particular business, and evaluating how predictable they were, because that is the first step. If something is not very predictable, forget it. You don't have to be right about every company. You have to make a few good decisions in your lifetime. The important thing is to know when you find one where you really do know which variables are important, and you think you've got a fix on them.

"Charlie and I made a dozen or so very big decisions relative to net worth, but not as big as they should have been. We knew we were right on those going in; they just weren't that complicated. We knew we were focusing on the right variables and they were dominant. And we knew that even though we couldn't take it out to five decimal places or anything like that, we knew that in a general way we were right. That's what we look for: the fat pitch. And that's what I would be trying to teach. I would not try to teach students to think they can do the impossible."

CM: "If you're planning to teach business valuation the way people teach real estate appraising—so your students, after studying your course, will be able to give you an appraisal of any company, indicating its future prospects compared to its price—I think you're attempting the impossible."

WB: "On the final exam I would take an internet company, and I would say the only question is, 'How much is this worth?' Anybody that gave me an answer, I would flunk."

INVESTING STYLES

1994 MEETING (02:22:56)

WB: "Peter Lynch likes to diversify a lot more than I do. He owns more stocks than the names of companies I can remember. But that's Peter. I've said on investing, there's more than one way to get to heaven. There isn't a true religion in this, but there's some very useful religions. Peter's got one, and I think we've got one that's useful, too. And there is a lot of overlap. But I would not do as well if I tried to do it the way Peter does it, and he probably wouldn't do as well if he tried to do it exactly the way I do it."

POSITION SIZING AND DIVERSIFICATION/ CONCENTRATION

1994 MEETING (02:55:31)

WB: "We are willing to put a lot of money into a single security. When I ran the partnership, the limit I got up to was about 40% in a single stock. I think Charlie, when you ran your partnership, you had more than 40%."

CM: "Sure."

WB: "And we would do the same thing if we were running smaller partnerships, or if our own capital were smaller and we were running that ourselves. We're not going to do that unless we think we understand the business very well, and we think the nature of the business—what we're paying for it, the people running it, and all of that—lead to virtually no risk. But you find those things, occasionally. And assuming it were that much more attractive than the second, third, and fourth choices, we would put a big percentage of our net worth in it ... It's not crazy, if you understand the business well, and if the price is sufficiently attractive, to put a very significant percentage of your net worth in. If you don't understand businesses, then you're better off diversifying—and fairly widely diversifying."

CM: "Berkshire has a substantial shareholder whose father accumulated the original position, and when he died, he left a very large estate, practically all of which was in two securities: Berkshire and one other outstanding company. A bank was a co-trustee, and the bank trust officer said, 'You've got to diversify this.' It was a very large estate. And the young man, who was co-trustee with the bank said, 'Well, you know, if my father believed the way you do, he might have been a trust officer in a bank instead of leaving this large estate.' That young man holds the Berkshire to this day, and I suppose the bank is still giving the same advice."

1996 MEETING (02:43:36)

WB: "We like to put a lot of money in things we feel strongly about. Diversification, as practiced generally, makes very little sense for anyone that knows what they're doing. Diversification is protection against ignorance; if you want to make sure that nothing bad happens to you relative to the market, you own everything. There's nothing wrong with that. That is a perfectly sound approach for somebody who does not feel they know how to analyze businesses. But if you know to analyze and value businesses, it's crazy to own thirty, forty, or fifty stocks, because there aren't that many wonderful businesses that are understandable to a single human being in all likelihood. And to have some super-wonderful business, and then put money in number thirty-five on your list of attractiveness and forego putting more money into number one, it just strikes us as madness. It's conventional practice; if all you have to achieve is the average, it may preserve your job. But it's a confession, in our view, that you don't really understand the businesses that you own.

"On a personal portfolio basis, I own one stock [Berkshire]. It's a business I know and it leaves me very comfortable. Do I need to own twenty-eight stocks to have proper diversification? It'd be nonsense. Within Berkshire, I could pick out three businesses, and I would be very happy if they were the only businesses we owned and I had all my money in Berkshire. Three wonderful businesses is more than you need in this life to do very well ... If you look at how the fortunes were built in this country, they weren't built out of a portfolio of fifty companies. They were built by someone who identified a wonderful business. Coca-Cola's a great example. A lot of fortunes have been built on that. There aren't fifty Coca-Cola's. If there were, we could all go out and diversify like crazy among that group and get results that would be equal to owning that really wonderful one—but you're not going to find it. And the truth is, you don't need it.

"A really wonderful business is very well protected against the vicissitudes of the economy over time, and competition. We're talking about businesses that are resistant to effective competition. Three of those will be better than a hundred average businesses. And they'll be safer, incidentally. There is less risk in owning three easy-to-identify, wonderful businesses than there is in owning fifty well-known, big businesses. It's amazing what has been taught, over the years, in finance classes about that. If I had to bet the fortunes of my family on the next thirty years, I would rather pick three businesses from those we own than own a diversified group of fifty."

CM: "He's saying that much of what is taught in modern corporate finance courses is twaddle."

WB: "It has no utility. It will tell you how to do average, but anybody can figure out how to do average in fifth grade. It's just not that difficult. It's elaborate. There's little Greek letters and all kinds of things to make you feel that you're in the big leagues, but there is no value added."

CM: "I have great difficulty with it because I am something of a student of dementia. But modern portfolio theory, it involves a type of dementia I just can't classify. Something very strange is going on."

WB: "If you find three wonderful businesses in your life, you'll get very rich. Bad things aren't going to happen to those three. I mean, that's the characteristic of it."

CM: "By the way, maybe that's the reason there's so much dementia: If you believed what Warren just said, you could teach the whole course in about a week."

WB: "And the high priests wouldn't have any edge over the laypeople; that never sells well."

2001 MEETING (03:48:55)

WB: "We've had relatively few big ideas, good ideas, over the years. I don't know how many you think we've had, maybe twenty-five each?"

CM: "If you took the top fifteen out of Berkshire Hathaway, most of you people wouldn't be here. So, roughly one every two years."

WB: "And sometimes there'll be a bunch of them, like in 1973 and 1974. But the problem for us is that big really means *big*. It has to be billions of dollars to move the needle at Berkshire. But I would say that when I would turn those pages fifty years ago in the *Moody's Manuals*, I would know when I hit a big idea ... When I met Lorimer Davidson, in January 1951, and he spent five hours with me explaining GEICO, I knew it was a big idea. Later, I wrote an article for *The Commercial and Financial Chronicle* on 'The Security I Like Best.' It was a big idea. When I found Western Insurance Securities, I knew it was a big idea."

CM: "The game in our kind of life is being able to recognize a good idea when it is (rarely) presented to you. I think that's something you have to prepare for over a long period. What is the old saying? 'Opportunity comes to the prepared mind.' I don't think you can teach people in two minutes how to have a prepared mind. But that's the game ... On opportunity costs, the current freshman economics text, which is sweeping the country, says, 'All intelligent people should think primarily in terms of opportunity cost.' And that's obviously correct. But it's very hard to teach business based on opportunity cost. It's much easier to teach a capital asset pricing model where you could just punch in numbers and the answers come out. And people teach what is easy to teach, instead of what is correct to teach. It reminds me of Einstein's famous saying: 'Everything should be made as simple as possible, but no more simple.'"

2003 MEETING (02:36:36)

WB: "The beauty of the investment game, what really makes it great, is that you don't have to be right on everything. You don't have to be right on 20%, 10%, or even 5% of the companies in the world. You only have to get one good idea every year or two. I used to be very interested in horse handicapping, and the old story was you could beat a race but you can't beat the races ... If somebody gave me all five hundred stocks in the S&P and I had to make some prediction about how they would behave relative to the market over the next couple years, I don't know how I would do. But maybe I could find one where I'm 90% sure I'm right. It's an enormous advantage in stocks: You only have to be right on a very, very few things as long as you never make big mistakes."

CM: "What's interesting is that at least 90% of the professional investment management operations don't think the way we do at all. They just think, if they hire enough people, they can be better at determining whether Pfizer or Merck is going to do better over the next twenty years. And they think that they can do that, stock by stock, all through the S&P 500 and have wide diversification, and at the end of ten years they'll be way ahead of other people. Of course, they won't. Very few people have this idea of searching for just a few opportunities."

WB: "You wait for the fat pitch. Ted Williams wrote about it in a book called *The Science of Hitting*. The most important thing in being a good hitter is to wait for a pitch in the sweet spot."

2003 MEETING (04:54:51)

CM: "We ordinarily don't like small positions."

WB: "We like to go in heavy. If we want to invest in a business through the stock market, we want to put a lot of money in. We do not believe in a little of this and a little of that. So, at our present size, we're limited primarily by the availability of the quantity we want, rather than restricting ourselves based on some percentage of a total portfolio. It's very hard for me to think of a stock we quit on, in terms of buying, except because we were going to run into some 10% limit where we would get liable for short-swing profits or become insiders or that sort of thing. We almost never want to quit."

CM: "Unless the price goes up."

WB: "Of course, that's where I've made the big mistakes. There have been a couple of things that we knew enough to buy, that were in our circle of competence, where we could have bought lots of stock, except it went up a little bit, and then we faded because of price. We didn't fade because we didn't want to put more than X dollars in. If we find an idea that we want to put $500 million in, we probably would be even happier if we could put $3 billion or $4 billion in. Good ideas are too scarce to be parsimonious with once you find them."

CM: "Having narrowly averted the mistake of being unwilling to pay up at See's Candies, we've gone on and made the same damn mistake several times, with respect to marketable securities. We evidently learn very slowly."

WB: "It's cost us many, many, many billions of dollars, too."

CM: "Those are opportunity costs. They don't show up on the financial statements, but the amount of money blown by dumb decisions at headquarters at Berkshire is awesome."

2004 MEETING (01:36:43)

CM: "I would say that the chief lesson would be that you're unlikely to find very many great investments in a whole lifetime. And when you find one in which you really have thought it out and have confidence, for God's sakes, don't do it in a niggardly fashion. The idea that very smart people with investment skills should have hugely diversified portfolios is madness. It's a very conventional madness. It's taught in all of the business schools. But they're wrong."

WB: "You will occasionally see something that you should load up on; as Charlie says, that's what you really have to do. Some of the people in this room loaded up on Berkshire many years ago. The truth was, they didn't need diversification. I loaded up on it. Charlie did. And you'll see opportunities occasionally, but you're not going to see them every day or every week. If you think you're going to see an opportunity every week, you're going to lose a lot of money because people will come around and tell you that they've got them."

2008 MEETING (02:01:33)

WB: "If Charlie and I were only running our own net worth over the past fifty years, I'm certain there would have been a significant number of times we would have put at least 75% of our net worth into an idea; we've seen all kinds of ideas we would've put 75% of our net worth in."

CM: "Warren, there have been times in my life when I've had more than 100% of my net worth invested in things."

WB: "Several times I had 75% of my net worth in one situation ... If you're working with smaller sums, you will see things that it would be a mistake to not have half of your net worth in. Sometimes in securities, you really do see things that are lead-pipe cinches. You're not going to see them often, and they're not going to be talking about them on television or anything of the sort, but there will be some extraordinary things that happen in a lifetime where you can put 75% of your net worth in a given situation. The problem has been the guys who have put 500% of their net worth in. Take LTCM. Very smart and very decent guys. But they put, maybe, twenty-five times their net worth into things that were a cinch if they hadn't gone in that heavily. They were in things that had to converge, but they didn't get to play out the hand. If they had 200% of their net worth in it, it would have worked fine. But they went to 2,500% or something like that.

"There's quite a few people in this room that have close to 100% of their net worth in Berkshire, and some of them have had it for forty or more years. Berkshire was not in a cinch category. It was in the strong probability category, I think. But I saw things in 2002 in the junk bond field. I saw things in equity markets. If you bought Cap Cities with Tom Murphy running it in 1974, it was selling at a third or a fourth of what the properties were worth and you had the best manager in the world running the place, and you had a business that was pretty damn good even if the manager wasn't. You could have put 100% of your net worth in there and not worried. You could have put 100% of your net worth in Coca-Cola, earlier than when we bought it, but certainly around the time we bought it, and that would not have been a dangerous position. It would be far more dangerous to do a whole bunch of other things that brokers were recommending to people."

CM: "Students of America go to elite business schools and law schools, and they learn corporate finance the way it's now taught, and investment management the way it's now taught. And some of these people write articles in the newspaper and other places and they say, 'The whole secret of investment is diversification.' That's the mantra—and they've got it exactly backwards. The whole secret of investment is to find places where it's safe and wise to not diversify. It's just that simple. Diversification is for the know-nothing investor; it's not for the professional."

WB: "There's nothing wrong with the know-nothing investor practicing it. It's exactly what they should practice. It's exactly what a good professional investor should *not* practice. There's no contradiction in that. A know-nothing investor will get decent results as long as they know they're a know-nothing investor, diversify as to the time they purchase their equities, and as to the equities they purchase. That's crazy for somebody who really knows what they're doing. You will find opportunities that, if you put 20% of your net worth in it, you'll have wasted the opportunity of a lifetime, in terms of not really loading up."

2012 MEETING (01:51:04)

CM: "Basically the Munger family is in two or three things only. Diversification is not something I have practically any interest in, except as it happens automatically in a big place like Berkshire Hathaway. I rejoiced the day I got rid of a stock-quoting machine. I like this buy-and-hold investing. It's a lovely way to live a life; you deal with a better class of people and it's worked pretty well for all of us."

2019 MEETING (04:47:25)

WB: "Personally, my estate will have basically nothing but Berkshire in it for some time as it gets disbursed to philanthropies. And I have a section in there which says to the trustees, in effect, that they are exempt, from my standpoint, from the law that trustees normally should diversify. I want the entire amount to be kept in Berkshire as they distribute it over time to the philanthropies. I would like to have a very large sum go to the philanthropies, and I don't worry about the fact that it essentially will all be in Berkshire. I'm willing to make that decision while I'm alive, which will continue for some years after I die. So, I have a lot of confidence in the ability of the Berkshire culture to endure and that we have the right people to make sure that that happens. I'm betting my entire net worth on that. That doesn't give me pause at all. I rewrite my will every few years, and write it the same way in respect to the Berkshire holdings."

CM: "I have always been willing to own just two or three stocks, and I have not minded that everybody who teaches finance in business school teaches that what

I'm doing is wrong. It isn't wrong. It's worked beautifully. I don't think you need a portfolio of fifty stocks if you know what you're doing. I hope my heirs will just sit."

2023 MEETING (02:02:15)

WB: "Apple is not 35% of Berkshire's portfolio. Berkshire's portfolio includes the railroad, the energy business, you name it. They're all businesses. And the good thing about Apple is that we can go up when they buy in their stock. We can't own more than 100% of the BNSF or See's Candies. We'd love to own 200%, but it just isn't doable. They're good businesses. Apple just happens to be a better business than any we own. And we put a fair amount of money in, but we haven't got more money than we've got in the railroad—and Apple is a better business. Apple has a position with consumers where maybe they pay $1,500, or whatever, for a phone. These same people pay $35,000 for a second car. And if they had to give up a second car or give up their iPhone, they'd give up their second car. We probably don't have anything like that, that we own 100% of, but we're very, very, very happy to have 5.6%, or whatever it may be. And we're delighted every one tenth of a per cent that goes up. That's like adding $100 million to our share of the earnings. They use their earnings to buy out our partners; we're glad to see them sell out, too … I made a mistake a couple of years ago when I sold some Apple shares when I had certain reasons why gains were useful to take that year from a tax standpoint. Having heard me say that, it was a dumb decision. But we do not have 35% of Berkshire's portfolio in Apple."

REQUIRED GROWTH RATES

1994 MEETING (03:21:48)

WB: "We are willing to buy companies that aren't going to grow at all, assuming we get enough for our money when we do it. We are looking to project numbers out, as to what kind of cash we think we'll get back over time. If you're going to put $1 million in a savings account, would you rather have something that paid you 10% a year and never changed, or would you rather have something that paid you 2% a year and increased at 10% a year? You can work out the math to answer those questions.

"You can certainly have a situation where there's absolutely no growth in a business, and it's a much better investment than some company that's going to grow at very substantial rates, particularly if they're going to need capital in order to grow. There's a huge difference in the business that grows and requires a lot of capital to do so, and the business that grows and doesn't require capital. Generally, financial analysts do not give adequate weight to the difference between those two. In fact, it's amazing how little attention is paid to that. If you're investing, you should pay a lot of attention to it … Some of the best businesses we own outright don't grow. But they throw off lots of money, which we can use to buy something else. And therefore, our capital is growing, without physical growth being in the business. We are much better off being in that kind of situation than being in some business that itself is growing, but that takes up all the money in order to grow and doesn't produce high returns as we go along. A lot of managements don't understand that very well, actually."

RECOVERING FROM POOR INVESTMENTS

1995 MEETING (01:01:17)

WB: "A very important principle in investing is that you don't have to make it back the way you lost it. In fact, it's usually a mistake to try and make it back the way that you lost it."

CM: "That's the reason so many people are ruined by gambling; they get behind and then they feel they have to get it back the way they lost it. It's a deep part of human nature. It's very smart just to lick it by will; little phrases like that are very useful."

WB: "One of the important things in stocks is that the stock does not know you own it. You have all these feelings about it; you remember what you paid and you remember who told you about it, all these little things. And it doesn't give a damn, it just sits there. If a stock is at $50 when somebody's paid $100, they feel terrible. Meanwhile, somebody else who paid $10 feels wonderful. It has no impact whatsoever. As Charlie says, gambling is the classic example. Someone goes out and gets into a mathematically disadvantageous game. They start losing it, and they think they've got to make it back, not only the way they lost it, but that night. It's a great mistake."

PATIENCE (WATCHING FOR THE FAT PITCH)

1995 MEETING (01:45:15)

WB: "We have sat through some dry spells; that's true in both the stock market and the acquisition business. I closed up the partnership in 1969 because there was nothing that made sense to do, and I'm glad I did because that situation prevailed in 1971 and 1972, but in 1973 and 1974 there were all kinds of things to do. That will happen from time to time. People will behave, particularly in markets, just as foolishly in the future as they have in the past. It'll come at unexpected times. But we will get a chance to do something … We will try to think about big things. We may not find them. But the larger something is, the more interested we are."

FIRST QUESTION ON AN INVESTMENT

1995 MEETING (02:21:45)

WB: "The first question is, 'Can I understand it?' Unless I think I can understand it, there's no sense looking at it. I won't kid myself into thinking I'm going to understand some software company or some biotech company. What am I going to know about it? So, that's the first question. The second question is, 'Does it look like it has good economics?' Has it earned high returns on capital? Does it strike me as something that's likely to do that? I go from there."

CM: "We tend to judge by the past record; by and large, if the thing has a lousy past record and a bright future, we're going to miss that opportunity."

BEN GRAHAM AND PHIL FISHER

1995 MEETING (02:44:01)

WB: "I don't know what my percentage would be between Ben Graham and Phil Fisher ... I was very influenced by Phil Fisher when I first read his two books, back around 1960. I think Phil is a terrific guy. But I'd rather think of myself as being 100% Ben Graham and 100% Phil Fisher. They really don't contradict each other, it's just that they had a vastly different emphasis.

"Ben would not have disagreed with the proposition that, if you can find a business with a high rate of return on capital that can keep using more capital, that's the best business in the world. He made most of his money out of GEICO, which was precisely that sort of business. He recognized it, it's just that he felt that the other system of buying things that were statistically very cheap, and buying a large number of them, was an easier policy to apply and more teachable. He would've felt that Fisher's approach was less teachable than his, but his had a more limited value because it was not workable with really large sums of money. Graham-Newman Corp had $6 million of net worth, and Newman and Graham, the partnership that was affiliated with it, had $6 million. So, a total pool of $12 million. Well, you could go around buying stocks in machine tool companies, whatever it might be, all statistically cheap. That was a very good group operation.

"If you own a lousy business, you have to sell it at some point. If you own a group of lousy businesses, you better hope some of them get taken over or something happens. You need turnover. If you own a wonderful business, you don't want turnover, basically."

CM: "What was interesting to me about the Phil Fisher businesses is that a very great many of them didn't last as wonderful businesses. One was Title

Insurance and Trust Company, which dominated the state of California. It had the biggest title plant, which was maintained by hand, and it had great fiscal solvency, integrity, and so forth. It just dominated a lucrative field. And along came the computer, and now you could create, for a few million dollars, a title plant and keep it up without an army of clerks. Pretty soon, we had twenty different title companies, and they would go to big lenders and big real estate brokers and pay them outlandish commissions by the standards of yore, and bid away huge blocks of business. In due course, the aggregate earnings of all the title insurance companies in California went below zero, starting with a virtual monopoly for Title Insurance and Trust Company. So, very few companies are so safe that you can just look ahead twenty years. Technology is sometimes your friend, and sometimes your bitter enemy. If Title Insurance and Trust Company had been smart, they would've looked at that computer, which they saw as a cost reducer, as one of the worst curses that ever came to man."

WB: "To some degree, it probably takes more business experience and insights to apply Fisher's approach than Graham's. The only problem is, you may be shut out of doing anything for a long time with Ben's approach, and you may have a lot of difficulty in doing it with big money. But if you strictly apply, for example, his working capital test to securities, it will work. It just may not work on a very big scale, and there may be periods when you're not doing much.

"Ben really was more of a teacher. He had no urge to make a lot of money. It did not interest him. He really wanted something that he thought was teachable as a cornerstone of his philosophy and approach. You could read his books sitting out here in Omaha and apply them—by buying things that were statistically cheap—and you didn't have to have any special insights about business or consumer behavior, anything of the sort. I don't think there's any question about that being true, but I also don't think you can manage lots of money in accord with it."

THE ROLE OF MATH IN INVESTING

1995 MEETING (03:51:29)

WB: "Advanced math is of no use in the investment process. An understanding of mathematical relationships, an ability to quantify—a numeracy—that's generally helpful in investments; something that tells you when things make sense or don't make sense, or how an item in one area relates to something someplace else. But that doesn't really require any great mathematical ability. It really requires sort of a mathematical awareness and a numeracy ... Charlie and I, when we read about one business, we're always thinking of it against a screen of dozens of businesses—it's just sort of automatic—but that's just like a scout in baseball thinking about one baseball player against an alternative. You only have a given number on the squad, one guy may be a little faster, one guy can hit a little better, that sort of thing. And always in your mind, you are prioritizing and selecting in some manner. My own feeling about the best way to apply that is just to read everything in sight. If you're reading a few hundred annual reports a year, and you've read Graham, Fisher, and a few things, you'll soon see whether it falls into place or not."

HISTORIC FINANCIAL DATA

1995 MEETING (03:54:41)

CM: "I think the one set of numbers that are the best quick guide to measuring one business against another are the *Value Line* numbers. That stuff on the log scale paper going back fifteen years, that is the best one-shot description of a lot of big businesses that exists. I can't imagine anybody being in the investment business involving common stocks without that on their shelf."

WB: "And, if you have in your head how all of that looks in different businesses and industries, then you've got a backdrop against which to measure. If you'd never watched a baseball game and never seen a statistic on it, you wouldn't know whether a .300 hitter was a good hitter or not. You have to have some kind of a mosaic there that you're thinking is implanted against, in effect. And the *Value Line* figures, if you ripple through that, you'll have a pretty good idea of what's happened over time in American business."

CM: "I would like to have that material going all the way back; they cut it off at fifteen years back. I wish I had that in the office, but I don't."

WB: "I saved the old ones. We tend to go back. If I'm buying Coca-Cola, I'll go back and read the *Fortune* articles from the 1930s on it. I like a lot of historical background on things, just to get it in my head how the business has evolved over time, and what's been permanent and what hasn't been permanent, and all of that. I probably do that more for fun than for actual decision-making. We're trying to buy businesses we want to own forever, and if you're thinking that way you might as well look back a way and see what it's been like to own them forever."

ASSESSING COMPETITIVE ADVANTAGES

1995 MEETING (04:03:48)

WB: "The growth aspects overall of a market are not a big factor with us; it's really a question of figuring out who's going to win what game, and who's going to lose what game."

OPPORTUNITY COSTS

1995 MEETING (04:18:03)

WB: "We bought more Coca-Cola last year, and it's not a bad measuring stick for other things. I don't have any plans to do it right now, but I wouldn't rule out buying more because if I look at another business I will say, 'Why would I rather have this than more Coca-Cola?'"

CM: "For an ordinary individual, the best thing you have easily available is your measuring stick. If the new thing isn't better than what you already know is available, it hasn't met your threshold, then that screens out 99% of what you see, and it's an enormous thought conserver. That is not taught in the business schools, by and large."

WB: "That's why we think it's slightly nuts when big institutions decide, because everybody else is doing it, to put 4% of their money in international equities or 3% in emerging growth countries; the only reason to put the money there is if they've measured against what they're already doing. And if they measure it against what they're already doing, and they think it's a screamingly good idea to leave 97% in the other place and put 3% in, it just doesn't make any sense. But it's what committees are talked to about, and what keeps investment managers going to conferences and everything."

CM: "They're deliberately using a technique that takes away the best mental tool they have. You can say that's nuts, and you're right. Nietzsche said it pretty well when he said he laughed at the man who thought he could walk better because he had a lame leg. They literally are blinding themselves and then they're teaching our children how to do this in our own business schools. Very interesting, don't you think? All Warren says is, when deciding whether to do something, compare it with the best opportunity you have. If that one is better and you're not taking it, why would you do this just because somebody tells you that you need 2% in international equities?"

2003 MEETING (05:04:30)

WB: "We don't want to buy equities where our real expectancy [expected rate of return] is below 10%. That's true whether short rates are 6% or 1%. We just feel that it would get very sloppy to start dipping below that. And we feel that we will get opportunities that are at least at that level, and perhaps substantially above. There's just a point at which we drop out of the game. And it's arbitrary. There's no scientific studies or anything. But I will bet you that a lot of years in the future we will be able to find equities that we understand, and that have the probability of returns at 10% or greater. Once we find a group of equities in that range, we just buy the ones that are most attractive. That usually means the ones we feel surest about as a practical matter. There's some businesses that possess economic characteristics that make their future prospects far more predictable than others ... We have, over time, become very partial to the businesses where we think the predictability is high. We still want a threshold return of 10%, which is not that great after-tax, anyway."

CM: "I think, in the last analysis, everything we do comes back to opportunity cost. But to some considerable extent we are guessing at our future opportunity cost. Warren is basically saying that he's guessing that he'll have opportunities in due course to put out money at pretty attractive rates of return, and, therefore, he's not going to waste a lot of firepower now at lower returns. But that's an opportunity cost calculation. And if interest rates were to more or less permanently settle at 1% or something like that, and Warren were to reappraise his notions of future opportunity cost, he would change the numbers. It's like [economist John Maynard] Keynes said, 'When the facts change, I change my mind. What do you do, sir?' But, so far at least, we have hurdles in our mind that involve, implicitly, future opportunity cost."

WB: "Right now, with $16 billion getting 1.25% pre-tax, that's $200 million a year. We could easily buy governments due in twenty years and get 5%, or $800 million a year of pre-tax income. We're making a decision, as Charlie says, that it's better to take $200 million for a while, on the theory that we'll find something that gives us 10% or better, than to commit to the $800 million a year and then find that, in a year or so, when the better opportunities come along, that what we have committed to has a big principal loss in it. But that's not terribly scientific. All I can tell you is, in practice, it seems to work pretty well ... We do go into insurance transactions with huge volatility, which could mean that a big chunk of money could go out in a very short period of time. And we won't give up a lot in expectable return for smoothness. But if you give us a choice of having money come in every week, and the same present value of money coming in in very lumpy ways that we wouldn't know about, we would choose the smooth. If you give us a choice of a higher present value for the lumpiness, we will take the lumpiness ... Other people value smoothness so highly that we do get a spread for lumpy returns."

CM: "Once you're talking about an opportunity cost that's personal to yourself, your own situation and your own abilities, you've departed from modern finance, totally. And that's what we've done. We're intelligently making these guesses, as best we can, based on our own circumstances and our own abilities. I think it's crazy to do it based on somebody else's circumstances and somebody else's abilities."

READING ANNUAL REPORTS

1996 MEETING (02:19:16)

WB: "I really like to know as much as I can about the person running a business, how they think about the business, and what's really going on in the business. In other words, if I owned half of a company but was away for a year, and I had a partner who owned the other half, when I came back, I would like to have a report that would tell me about what had taken place during the past year, what he foresaw coming up, and all of that. That is what I think the purpose of the report is. There's an intent behind the report. If it's a sales document, I'm less interested.

"I like to understand what's generally going on in all kinds of businesses. If we own stock in a company, and there are eight other companies in the industry, I want to be on the mailing list for the reports for the other eight, because I can't understand how my company is doing unless I understand what the other eight are doing. I want to have perspective in terms of market share, their margins, the trend of margins, all kinds of things. I can't be an intelligent owner of a business unless I know what all the other businesses in that industry are doing. So, I try to get that information out of a report.

"If I'm thinking about investing in a specific company, I try to size up their business and the people running it. Over the years, I have found reading a lot of reports to be quite useful in terms of making business decisions at Berkshire. If we own all of a business, I want to own shares in all of the competitors just to keep track of what's going on. I want to be able to intelligently evaluate how our managers are doing, and I can't do that unless I know the industry backdrop against which they're working. It's amazing how well you can do in investing, really, with what I would call outside information ... You don't have to understand all of them; you just have to understand the ones you're thinking about getting in. You can do it, but nobody will do it for you. In my view, you can't read Wall Street reports and get anything out of them. You have to do it yourself and get your arms around it. I don't think we've ever gotten an idea, in forty years, from a Wall Street report. But we've gotten a lot of ideas from annual reports."

CM: "What I find is that it takes a long time to read the annual report even if it's a comparatively simple business, because if you really are trying to understand it, it's not a bit easy."

WB: "On average, in a business we're really interested in, even though we know what to skip and what to read, it's going to be forty-five minutes or an hour on a report. And if there are six or eight companies in the industry, that's six or eight hours, perhaps, and then their quarterly reports and a lot of other things.

The way you learn about businesses is by absorbing information about them, thinking, deciding what counts and what doesn't count, relating one thing to another. That's the job. And you can't get that by looking at a bunch of little numbers on a chart bobbing up and down or reading market commentary and periodicals or anything of the sort. That just won't do it. You've got to understand the businesses. That's where it begins and ends."

OWNING GREAT COMPANIES

1996 MEETING (03:21:17)

WB: "A great company is one that's going to remain great for thirty years. If it's only going to be a great company for three years, it isn't a great company. You really want to go along with the idea that, if you were going to take a trip for twenty years, you wouldn't feel bad leaving it with no orders at your broker and no power of attorney or anything; when you come back, you know it's going to be a terribly strong company. I think it's better just to own them. We could attempt to buy and sell some of the things we own that we think are fine businesses, but they're too hard to find. We found See's Candies in 1972; here and there, we get the opportunity to do something. But they're too hard to find.

"To sit there and hope you buy them in the throes of some panic, you sort of take the attitude of a mortician, waiting for a flu epidemic. I'm not sure that will be a great technique ... I think the main thing to do is find wonderful businesses ... Phil [Carret] has done awfully well by finding businesses he likes, sticking with them, and not worrying too much about what they do day to day ... Say there was no stock market, and the owner of the best business in your hometown came to you and said, 'My brother died and he owned 20% of the business. I want somebody to go in with me to buy that 20%. And the price looks a little high, maybe, but this is what I think I can get for it. Do you want to buy in?' If you like the business and you like the person coming to you, and the price sounds reasonable, and you really know the business, I think the thing to do is to take it and don't worry too much about how it's quoted. It won't be quoted tomorrow, next week, or next month. I think people's investment would be more intelligent if stocks were quoted about once a year ... We did well in 1964 because American Express ran into a crook. We did well in 1976 because GEICO's managers and auditors didn't know what their loss reserves should've been the previous couple of years. So we've had our share of flu epidemics, but you don't want to spend your life waiting around for them."

BUSINESS RISK, INVESTMENT RISK, AND MR. MARKET

1997 MEETING (00:37:16)

WB: "We think first in terms of business risk. The key to Ben Graham's approach to investing is not to think of stocks as part of a stock market; stocks are part of a business. People in this room own a piece of a business. If the business does well, they're going to do all right as long as they don't pay way too much to join that business. So, we're thinking about business risk. Now, business risk can arise in various ways. It can arise from a capital structure where somebody sticks a ton of debt on some business, so if there's a hiccup in the business then the lenders can foreclose. It can come about by the nature of the business; certain businesses are just very risky.

"When there were more commercial aircraft manufacturers, Charlie and I would think of making a big commercial airplane as sort of a bet-your-company risk because you would shove hundreds and hundreds of millions of dollars into the pot before you really had customers. If you had a problem with the plane that company could go out of business. There are certain businesses that inherently—because of long lead times and heavy capital investment—have a lot of risk. Commodity businesses have risk unless you're the low-cost producer, because the low-cost producer can put you out of business. Our textile business was not the low-cost producer; we had a fine management, everybody worked hard, we had cooperative unions, all kinds of things, but we weren't the low-cost producer, so it was a risky business. The guy who could sell it cheaper than we could made it risky for us. So, there's a lot of ways businesses can be risky.

"We tend to go into businesses that are inherently low risk, and are capitalized in a way such that the low risk of the business is transformed into a low risk to the enterprise. The risk beyond that is when you pay too much for them; that is usually a risk of time rather than loss of principal, unless you get into a really extravagant situation. Then the risk becomes the risk of you yourself, whether you can retain your belief in the real fundamentals of the business and not get too concerned about the stock market. The stock market is there to serve you, not to instruct you. That's key to owning a good business and getting rid of the risk that would otherwise exist in the market. It doesn't make any difference to us whether the volatility of the market averages 0.5% a day or 5% a day. In fact, we'd make a lot more money if volatility were higher, because it would create more mistakes in the market; volatility is a huge plus to the real investor.

"Ben Graham used the example of 'Mr Market.' Ben said, 'When you buy a stock, imagine that, in effect, you bought into a business where you have an obliging partner who comes around every day and offers you a price at which you'll either buy or sell. And the price is identical.' No one ever gets that in a private business, a daily buy/sell offer from the other party, but you do in the stock market. That's a huge advantage—and it's a bigger advantage if this partner of yours is a heavy-drinking manic depressive. The crazier he is, the more money you're going to make. So, as an investor, you love volatility. Not if you're on margin; but if you're an investor you aren't on margin. If you're an investor, you love the idea of wild swings because it means more things get mispriced ... Volatility was much higher many years ago than it is now. The amplitude of the swings was really wild, and that gave you more opportunity."

CM: "It got to be the occasion in corporate finance departments of universities where they developed the notion of risk-adjusted returns. My best advice to all of you would be to totally ignore it. Risk had a very good colloquial meaning, meaning a substantial chance that something would go horribly wrong. The finance professors got volatility mixed up with a lot of foolish mathematics. To me, it's less rational than what we do, and I don't think we're going to change."

WB: "Finance departments teach that volatility equals risk. They want to measure risk and they don't know any other way. So, they say volatility measures risk. I've often used the example of The Washington Post: when we first bought in 1973 it had gone down almost 50%; the valuation of the whole company was $175 million, down to maybe $80 or $90 million. And because it happened very fast, the beta of the stock increased. A professor would have told you that the company was riskier if you bought it for $80 million than if you bought it for $170 million. I've thought about that ever since they told me that twenty-five years ago, and I still haven't figured it out."

ACTIVE MANAGEMENT AND PROFESSIONAL INVESTORS

1997 MEETING (01:21:40)

WB: "Money managers, in aggregate, have underperformed index funds. It's the nature of the game. They simply cannot overperform, in aggregate. There are too many of them managing too big a portion of the pool. It's for the same reason that the crowd could not come out here to Ak-Sar-Ben [racetrack] and make money, in aggregate, because there's a bite taken out of every dollar that was invested in the pari-mutuel machines. People who invest their dollars elsewhere through money managers in aggregate cannot do as well as they could do by themselves in an index fund. They say you can't get something for nothing. But the truth is money managers, in aggregate, have gotten something for nothing; they've gotten a lot for nothing. And the corollary is investors have paid something for nothing. That doesn't mean people are evil.

It doesn't mean they're charlatans or anything. It's the nature of things: If you have a $7 trillion equity market, and you have a very significant percentage of it managed by professionals, and they charge you significant fees to invest with them, and they have costs when they change around, they cannot do as well as unmanaged money, in aggregate.

"It's the only field in the world that I can think of where the amateur, as long as he recognizes he's an amateur, will do better than the professional ... Charlie and I would be glad to take any money management organization in the world managing $10 billion or more, and we'd be willing to bet their aggregate investment experience over the next five or ten years for the group they advise will be poorer than that achieved by a no-load, very low-cost, index fund. We'd put up a lot of money to make that wager with anybody who would care to step forward..."

CM: "I certainly agree with you. I always say that exactly one-fifth have to be in the bottom 20%. There are certain fundamental forces at work here ... I think we know investment managers who add value. But it's a comparatively rare and small percentage."

WB: "We have identified, in the past ... on a prospective basis, not retrospective, managers who have added value. You can do it. But you can't do it with unlimited amounts of money, and a good record tends to attract money. Even a mediocre record presented by a good salesperson tends to attract money. But there are people working with smaller amounts of money, where the probabilities are that they will do better than average—but they're very rare."

2006 MEETING (02:24:08)

WB: "It is an interesting business in that the activities of the professionals are self-neutralizing. If your wife is going to have a baby, you're probably better off calling an obstetrician than doing it yourself. And if your pipes are clogged, you're probably better off calling a plumber. Most professions have value added to them above what the laymen can accomplish themselves. In aggregate, the investment profession does not do that. You have a huge group of people making a lot of money—I put the estimate at $140 billion a year—that, in aggregate, can only accomplish what somebody can do in ten minutes a year by themselves. And it's hard to think of another business like that, Charlie."

CM: "I can't think of any."

WB: "But it's become a bigger and bigger business. The main thing that's been learned is that the more you charge, at least temporarily, the more money you bring in; people have this idea that price equals value. It's useful to get into a business like that. Sometimes, if I'm talking to a business school, I ask them to name me a great business—and, of course, one of the great businesses is a business school because, basically, the more you charge, the more prestige you have, to some extent. People think that a business school that charges $50,000 a year tuition is going to be better than one that charges $10,000 a year. Well, there's a lot of that that has got into the investment field recently, and you now have certain large portions of investment management that are charging fees that, in aggregate, cannot work out for investors …

"Then the question that you will have is, 'How do I pick out the few exceptions?' Everyone that calls upon you to sell to you will tell you that they are an exception. I am willing to bet a significant sum of money—we'll put it up—to anybody who wants to name ten partnerships that are $500 million or more of management and pit those, after fees, against the S&P 500 over a ten-year period … It isn't going to happen … If you know enough about the person, how they've done it in the past, their personality, honesty, and a whole bunch of things, I think that occasionally you can make a very intelligent choice in picking an investment manager. But I don't think you can do it if you're running a pension fund in some state and you have fifty people calling you. You're going to go with the ones who are the best salespeople, not the ones who are the best investors."

CM: "On that subject, I think it ought to be a crime to entertain, in any way, a state pension fund official; and it ought to be a crime, if you are a pension fund official, to accept the entertainment. It's not a pretty scene, a lot of investment management. And, human nature being what it is, and the amounts of money being what they are, I don't think much is going to be improved."

THE FIVE-MINUTE TEST

1997 MEETING (02:03:48)

WB: "Charlie and I are familiar with virtually every company of a size that would interest us in the country. If you've been looking at businesses for forty years, it's just like if you were studying baseball players; you get to know all the players after a while. Then we have a bunch of filters we've developed in our minds. We don't say they're perfect filters; we don't say that those filters don't occasionally leave things out that should get through. But they're efficient. And they work just as well as if we spent months and hired experts and did all kinds of things. So we really can tell you in five minutes whether we're interested in something. We had never owned shares in FlightSafety, but we'd been familiar with the company for at least twenty years, wouldn't you say?"

CM: "Sure, I had a partner who bought a lot of it twenty years ago."

WB: "That's true of almost any business. We've got a fix on what we don't understand, and then we don't care to know any more about them, although maybe we'll pick up a little as we go along. And then the ones we're capable of understanding, we've probably gotten about as far as we'll get already. So we do know in five minutes … FlightSafety has forty or so training centers around the world. I've never set foot on one of them. I've never been to their headquarters. We never looked at a lease. We never look at the title of the properties. We don't do any of those things. To date, that's never cost us a penny. What costs us money is when we do not properly assess the fundamental economic characteristics of the business. But that is something we would not learn by what people generally consider due diligence. We could have lawyers look over all kinds of things, but that isn't what makes it a good deal or a bad deal. And we don't kid ourselves by having lots of studies and reports. They're going to support whatever they think the guy that pays them wants anyways, so they don't mean anything. They're nonsense. But we do care about being right about the economic characteristics of the business, and that's one thing we think we've got certain filters that tell us in certain cases that we know enough to assess."

CM: "People underrate the importance of a few simple big ideas. To the extent Berkshire is a didactic enterprise teaching the right systems of thought, I think the chief lesson is that a few big ideas really work. These filters of ours have worked pretty well because they're so simple."

WB: "I think most of the people in this room, if they just focused on what made a good business and thought about it a little while, they could develop a set of filters that would let them, in five minutes, figure out pretty well what made sense or didn't make sense. Another thing you can usually tell, at least in the extreme cases, is whether you've got the kind of manager you want to have. If you've got somebody that's been batting .400 all their life in terms of business performance—and fortunately age doesn't change that picture—and they love what they do, it's going to work. If the seller cares a lot about the money, you're probably not going to make a very good deal. If their real interest is what they're going to do with the money, they may fall out of love or have less interest in their business subsequently. We love working with people who are just plain nuts about their businesses. It works very well, and you can usually spot that."

MARGIN OF SAFETY

1997 MEETING (03:15:20)

WB: "If you understood the future of a business perfectly, you would need very little in the way of a margin of safety. The more volatile the business is—or the possibility of it is—the larger the margin of safety. In that first edition of Graham and Dodd—I think it was J.I. Case—he said maybe it was worth between $30 and $110. How much good does it do for you to know that it's worth between $30 and $110? Well, it does you some good if it's selling for below $30 or above

$110. If you're driving a truck across a bridge that holds 10,000 pounds and you've got a 9,800-pound vehicle, if the bridge is about six inches above the crevice that it covers, you may feel OK. But if it's over the Grand Canyon, you may feel you want a little larger margin of safety, in terms of only driving a 4,000-pound truck across. So, it depends on the nature of the underlying risk.

"The biggest thing to do is to understand the business and to get into the kind of businesses where, by their nature, surprises are few. And we think we're largely in that type of business. I've talked about learning from your mistakes; the best thing to do is learn from other guys' mistakes. George Patton used to say, 'It's an honor to die for your country. Make sure the other guy gets the honor.' Our approach is to try and learn vicariously. But there's a lot of mistakes that I've repeated, I can tell you that. The biggest category over time has been being reluctant to pay up a little for a business I knew was really outstanding, or to continue to buy it at higher prices when I knew it was outstanding. The cost of that has been many, many billions. And I'll probably keep making that mistake. The mistakes are made when there are businesses you can understand and they're attractive and you don't do something about it. I don't worry at all about the mistakes that come about because, when I met Bill Gates, I didn't buy Microsoft or something. That's not my game. Most of our mistakes have been mistakes of omission rather than commission."

CM: "I think that most people get very few, what I call, no-brainer opportunities, where it's just so damned obvious that the investment is going to work. And since they are very few and they may be separated by periods of years, I think people have to learn to have the courage and the intelligence to step up in a major way when those rare opportunities come by."

WB: "You've got to be willing to take a really big bite; it's crazy if you don't. And it's crazy if you dabble around at the edges so you're not prepared to take a big bite when the time comes."

2007 MEETING (01:09:24)

WB: "We favor the businesses where we really think we know the answer. If a business gets to the point where we think the industry in which it operates, or its competitive position or anything, is so chancy that we can't really come up with a figure, we don't try to compensate for that by having some extra large margin of safety. We really want to go in on something that we understand better. So if we buy See's Candies as a business or Coca-Cola as a stock, we don't think we need a huge margin of safety because we don't think we're going to be wrong about our assumptions in any material way.

"What we really want to do is buy a great business, which means it's going to earn a high return on capital employed for a very long period of time, and where we think the management will treat us right. We don't have to mark those down a lot when we find those factors ... It's like if you see somebody walk in the door; you don't know whether they weigh three hundred pounds or three hundred and twenty-five pounds, but you still know they're fat, right? And so if we see something we know is fat, financially, we don't worry about being precise ... You should always feel you're getting a little more than what it's worth, and there are times we've been able to buy wonderful businesses at 25% of what they're worth—but you don't see those sorts of things very often. Does that mean you should sit around and wait ten or fifteen years? That's not the way we do it. If we can buy good businesses at a reasonable valuation, we're going to keep doing it."

LEVERAGE AND OPTIONS

1997 MEETING (04:18:26)

WB: "[In relation to] futures, call options, or whatever they may be, I think investors should stick to buying ownership in businesses. It's not that you can't come up with a theoretical argument—if you think Coca-Cola's attractive, you can say, well, I'd rather buy a five-year option than buy the stock directly, because it introduces leverage without the risk of going broke—but I think that's a dangerous path to start down. It's dynamite to start playing with things that can expire and become worthless, or can be bought with very low margin, as with the options you were talking about.

"Borrowed money frequently leads to trouble—and it's not necessary ... You really ought to figure out how you can be happy with the present amount of money you've got, and then figure that everything else is all to the good as you go along. I think that once people start focusing on short-term price behavior—which is the nature of buying calls, LEAPS, or speculating in futures—they're very likely to take their eyes off the main ball, which is just valuing businesses. I don't recommend it."

CM: "This is a group of affluent investors—and I don't think many of them did it in LEAPS."

WB: "If we'd operated Berkshire with considerable borrowed money over the years, it would've done much better than it has. But nobody knew what that appropriate level of borrowed money was, and it wouldn't have made any difference to us. We have had just as much fun doing what we've done than if we'd owned it on leverage and had it been twice as much. It's just not the way we approach it ... If you can make 12% a year or 15% a year, and you desire to save, and you like piling it up, it will all come in time. Why risk losing what you need and have, for what you don't need and don't have? It's never made a lot of sense to us."

2004 MEETING (02:25:01)

WB: "We believe almost anything can happen in financial markets—and the only way smart people can get clobbered, really, is through leverage. If you can hold them, you have no real problems. So, we have a great aversion to leverage, and we would predict that a very high percentage of the smart people operating in Wall Street, at one time or another, are likely to get clobbered through the use of leverage. It's the one thing that can prevent you from playing out your hand. All of the hands we enter into look pretty good to us, but you do have to be able to play them out ... The big thing you want, at a minimum, is to protect yourself against that insanity in market prices/volatility wiping you out."

2005 MEETING (03:47:34)

CM: "It wasn't even controversial in this country when we came to introduce single-stock futures and commonly traded puts and calls. Ordinary people got in trouble. If I'd been running the country, I never would have allowed that. I don't know what good it does for the country to have a lot of trading in puts and calls. One of my children knew a man who had a $2.5 million house and $5 million worth of securities. But he couldn't live as comfortably as he liked on the income from his securities, so he got in the habit of picking up easy money. He kept selling naked puts secured by his account, including on a whole lot of internet stocks. And, in due time, he didn't have the $5 million of securities and he didn't have the house, and he now works in a restaurant. That kind of self-destruction wasn't possible before we created all these wonderful trading opportunities involving credit. It was not a smart thing for this country to do, to legalize gambling everywhere and to bring it in a more facile form into our investment practices."

2008 MEETING (00:21:56)

WB: "There was one time we sold a put on Coca-Cola with the idea that, if it got exercised, we were very happy to own more Coca-Cola. It didn't get exercised, and we would have been better off if we just bought the stock. If you want to buy or sell a stock, you should buy or sell the stock. Using an option technique to buy a call instead of buying the stock outright, with the idea that you'll get it a little cheaper, means about four times out of five you'll be right—and the fifth time the stock will move and you'll miss the transaction you wanted. So, we have virtually never used options as a way to enter or exit a position ... If we want to buy something, we'll just buy it. And if we want to get out of it, we'll sell it. We won't get involved in any fancy techniques."

CIGAR BUTT INVESTING

1998 MEETING (00:16:29)

WB: "It's extremely difficult to get rich by owning a business that earns low returns on equity. We always look at what a business does in terms of what it earns on capital. We want to be in good businesses. Where you really want to be is in businesses that are going to be good and better businesses ten years from now. And we want to buy them at a reasonable price.

"But many years ago, we gave up what I've labeled the 'cigar butt' approach to investing, which is where you try and find a kind of pathetic company, but it sells so cheap that you think there's one good free puff left in it. We used to pick up a lot of soggy cigar butts. I had a portfolio full of them, there were free puffs in them, and I made money out of that. But it doesn't work with big money, and we don't find many cigar butts around that we would be attracted to.

"Those companies had low returns on equity. If you have a business that's earning 5–6% on equity, and you hold it for a long time, you are not going to do well, even if you buy it cheap to start with. Time is the enemy of the poor business, and it's the friend of the great business. If you have a business earning 20–25% on equity, and it does that for a long time, time is your friend. Time is your enemy in a low-return business. You may be lucky enough to pick the exact moment when it gets taken over by someone else, but we like to think, when we buy a stock, that we're going to own it for a very long time—and therefore we have to stay away from businesses with low ROEs."

CM: "It's not that much fun to buy a business where you really hope the sucker liquidates before it goes broke."

WB: "I've owned stock in an anthracite company. There are probably people in this room that don't know what anthracite is. Street railway companies, windmill manufacturers, textiles. Berkshire was a mistake, believe it or not. We went into Berkshire because it was cheap statistically in the early 1960s, and it was a company that in the previous ten years earned less than nothing; it had a significant net loss over the previous ten years. It was selling well below working capital, so it was a cigar butt. We could have done things that we've done subsequently from a neutral base rather than a negative base, and it would have worked out better."

2001 MEETING (04:48:55)

WB: "If you found a group [of ten to twenty stocks trading at a sizable discount to net current asset value]—and you won't, I don't think—you'd probably do all right buying the group. Not because the businesses themselves worked out that well, but because there would probably be a reasonable amount of corporate activity in that group—managements taking them private, takeovers, that sort of thing. But those sub-working capital stocks are just almost impossible to find now. And if you got into a market where a lot of them existed, you'd probably find wonderful businesses selling a lot cheaper, too. And our inclination would be to go with a cheap, wonderful business … Ben Graham always emphasized a group operation because, when you're dealing with lousy companies but you expect a certain number to be taken over and all that, you'd better have a group of them. Whereas if you deal with wonderful companies, you only need a couple."

CM: "There's another change. In the old days, if the business stopped working, you could take the working capital and stick it in the shareholders' pockets. Nowadays, when things really go to hell in a bucket, somebody else owns a lot of the working capital. The whole culture has changed. If you have a business in France and you get tired of it, the French say, 'What the hell do you mean you're trying to take your capital back from France? There're French workers in this business.' They don't care. They don't say, 'It's your working capital, take it back,' when the business no longer works for you. They say, 'It's our working capital.' The whole culture has changed on that one. Not completely, but a lot from Ben Graham's day. There are a lot of reasons why the investment idiosyncrasies of one era don't translate that perfectly into another."

EBITDA

1998 MEETING (02:56:54)

WB: "The best business is one that gives you more and more money every year without putting up anything to get it, or putting up very little to get it. The second-best business is one that takes more money [required reinvestment to grow], but the rate at which you reinvest for that growth is a very satisfactory rate. The worst business of all is the one that grows a lot, and where you're forced, in effect, to grow to stay in the game at all, and where you're reinvesting the capital at a very low rate of return. Sometimes people are in those businesses without knowing it."

CM: "There is a class of businesses where the eventual cash back part of the equation tends to be an illusion. I think there are businesses where you just keep pouring it in and pouring it in, and then all of a sudden it doesn't work, and no cash comes back. And what makes our life interesting is trying to avoid those and get in the alternative kind that drowns you in cash."

WB: "The one figure we regard as utter nonsense is EBITDA. The idea of looking at a figure before the cash requirements of merely staying in the same place … any business with significant fixed assets almost always has with it a concomitant requirement that major cash be reinvested in order simply to stay in the same place competitively and in terms of unit sales. To look at some figure that is stated before those cash requirements is absolute folly—and it's been misused by lots of people to sell lots of merchandise in recent years."

CM: "It's not to the credit of the investment banking fraternity that it has learned to speak in terms of EBITDA. The idea of using a measure that you know is nonsense, and then piling additional reasoning on that false assumption, is not creditable intellectual performance. And once everybody is talking in terms of nonsense, why, it gets to be standard."

2002 MEETING (01:21:11)

CM: "I think you're asking for a lot if you want some simple way of not being taken in by the frauds of the world. Enormously talented people deliberately go into fraud, [or] drift gradually into it because the culture carries them there, and the frauds get very sophisticated and they're very slickly done. I think it's part of the business of getting wisdom in life that you avoid getting taken by the frauds ... There are whole fields that you can just quit playing because it looks like there's too much fraud in it. And I think we do a lot of that ... I've always said that the guy who takes us is going to have a modest little office and a modest demeanor. The kind of people who defraud us are not going to be the kind of people who are defrauding everybody else."

WB: "I would say the number of times we're going to buy into a company, whether a stock or the entire company, where people are talking about EBITDA, is going to be about zero. If we take all the people in the world that talk about EBITDA, and all the people in the world who haven't talked about EBITDA, there are more frauds in the first group, percentage-wise, by a substantial margin. Very substantial. It's very interesting to me: If you look at some enormously successful companies—Walmart, General Electric, and Microsoft—I don't think that term has ever appeared in their annual reports. So when people start talking about that sort of thing, either they're trying to con you in some way, or they've conned themselves, to a great degree."

CM: "Or both."

WB: "That often happens. If you set out to con somebody, after a while you con yourself ... If somebody thinks you're focusing on EBITDA, they may arrange things so that that number looks bigger than it really is ... It just amazes me how widespread the usage of EBITDA has become. I would say there have been people who have tried to dress up financial statements in a way to appeal to people who are impressed by such a number. Charlie and I have found that many of the crooks look like crooks."

2003 MEETING (03:44:35)

WB: "Not thinking of depreciation as an expense strikes us as absolutely crazy. I can think of very few businesses where depreciation is not a real expense. Depreciation is real and it's the worst kind of expense. It's reverse float; you lay out the money before you get any revenues. Any management that doesn't regard depreciation as an expense is living in a dream world. They're encouraged to do that by investment bankers, and certain people have built fortunes on misleading investors by convincing them EBITDA was a big deal ... people want to send me books with EBITDA in it, and I tell them I'll look at that figure when they tell me they'll pay all the capital expenditures ... There's very few businesses where I think I can spend a whole lot less than depreciation year after year and maintain the economic strength of the business. EBITDA has been a term that has cost a lot of investors a lot of money; you saw it in the telecom field. They were spending money so damn fast, they couldn't have it coming in the door fast enough from investors. And then they pretended depreciation was not a real expense. That's nonsense."

CM: "I think you would better understand any presentation using the word EBITDA, if every time you saw that word, you just substituted the phrase, 'bullshit earnings.'"

2017 MEETING (04:59:06)

WB: "In respect to EBITDA, depreciation is an expense, and it's the worst kind of an expense. We love to talk about float, where we get the money first and have the expense later. Depreciation is where you spend the money first, and, then, record the expense later. It's reverse float, and it's not a good thing. It's much better to buy a business that has, everything else being equal, no depreciation because it has, essentially, no investment and fixed assets that makes X, than it is to buy a company where there's a lot of depreciation in getting to X. Of course, it's enormously in the interests of Wall Street to focus on EBITDA because it results in higher borrowing power, higher valuations, and all that sort of thing. So it's become very popular in the last twenty years, but it's a very misleading statistic that can be used in very pernicious ways."

CM: "I think you've understated the horrors of the subject and the disgusting nature of the people that brought that term into the valuation of business. It would be like a leasing broker of real estate who has a 1,000 square-foot new suite to be leased, and he says it's 2,000 feet. That's not honorable behavior. And that's the way that term got into common usage. Nobody in his right mind would think that depreciation is not an expense."

WB: "But it's very much in the interest of Wall Street."

CM: "That's why they did it. It made the multiple seem lower."

WB: "What's amazing is the way it's accepted. It just illustrates how people use language and sell concepts that work to their own use ... As long as it can get sold, it will get sold."

CM: "Now they use it in the business schools. It's bad enough that a bunch of thieves start using a term. But when it gets so common that the business schools copy it, that is not a good result."

MAINTENANCE CAPEX AND BUSINESS QUALITY

1998 MEETING (04:05:22)

WB: "In airlines, you have to keep spending money like crazy. You have to spend money like crazy if it's attractive to spend money, and you have to spend it the same way if it's unattractive. It's part of the game. Even in our textile business, to stay competitive we would've needed to spend substantial money without any clear prospects of making any money when we got through spending it. Those are real traps, those kinds of businesses. They make out one way or another, but they're dangerous.

"In See's Candies, we would love to be able to spend $10 million, $100 million, or $500 million and get anything like the returns we've got in the past. But there aren't good ways to do it, unfortunately. We'll keep looking, but it's not a business where capital produces the profits ... At Coca-Cola, particularly when new markets come along, they would frequently make the investments needed to build up the bottling infrastructure to rapidly capitalize on those markets. Those are expenditures you don't even make the calculation on; you just know you have to do it. You have a wonderful business, you want to have it spread worldwide, and you want to capitalize on it to its fullest. And you can make a return on investment calculation, but as far as I'm concerned it's a waste of time because you're going to do it anyway. You know you want to dominate those markets over time."

CM: "I've heard Warren say since very early in his life that the difference between a good business and a bad business is usually the good business just throws up one easy decision after another, whereas the bad business gives you a horrible choice where the decision is hard to make. Is this really going to work? Is it worth the money? If you want a system for determining which is a good business and which is a bad business, just see which one is throwing the management easy decisions time after time after time. It's not very hard for us to decide to open a new See's store in a new shopping center in California that's obviously going to succeed. On the other hand, there are plenty of businesses where the decisions that come across your desk are just awful. And those businesses, by and large, don't work very well."

WB: "I've been on the board of Coca-Cola for ten years, and we've had project after project come up, and there's always an ROI. But it doesn't really make much difference to me, because in the end almost any decision you make that solidifies and extends the dominance of Coke around the world, in an industry that's growing by a significant percentage, and which has great inherent underlying profitability, the decisions are going to be right and you've got people to execute them well.

"Then Charlie and I sat on the USAir board, and the decisions would come along … they're agony because you don't have any real choice, but you also don't have any real conviction that those choices—or lack of choices—are going to translate themselves into real money later on. One game is just forcing you to push more money onto the table with no idea of what kind of a hand you hold, and the other one you get a chance to push more money in knowing that you've got a winning hand all the way."

SCUTTLEBUTT (ON-THE-GROUND RESEARCH)

1998 MEETING (04:27:09)

WB: "One advantage of allocating capital is that an awful lot of what you do is cumulative in nature, so you get continuing benefits out of things you've done earlier. By now, I'm fairly familiar with most of the businesses that might qualify for investment at Berkshire. But when I started out, and for a long time, I used to do a lot of what Phil Fisher described, the scuttlebutt method …

"The general premise of why you're interested in something should be 80% of it. You don't want to be chasing down every idea that way; you should have a strong presumption. You should be like a basketball coach who runs into a seven-footer on the street. You're interested to start with; now you have to find out if you can keep him in school, if he's coordinated, and all that sort of thing. That's the scuttlebutt aspect of it. But as you're acquiring knowledge about industries in general, and companies specifically, there really isn't anything like first doing some reading about them, and then getting out and talking to competitors, customers, suppliers, ex-employees, current employees, whatever it may be. You will learn a lot. But it should be the last 10% or 20%. You don't want to get too impressed by that, because you really want to start with a business where you think the economics are good, where they look like seven-footers, and then you want to go out with a scuttlebutt approach to possibly reject your original hypothesis. Or maybe, if you confirm it, do it even more strongly.

"I did that with American Express back in the 1960s; essentially the scuttlebutt approach so reinforced my feeling about it that I kept buying more and more as I went along. If you talk to a bunch of people in an industry and you ask them what competitor they fear the most, and why they fear them, who they would use the silver bullet on, you're going to learn a lot about it. You'll probably know more about the industry than most of the people in it when you get through, because you'll bring an independent perspective to it, and you'll be listening to everything everyone says rather than coming in with these preconceived notions and just sort of listening to your own truths after a while. I advise it …

"That was really what I was doing back in 1951 when I visited Lorimer Davidson down in Washington, because I was trying to figure out why people would insure with GEICO rather than with the companies that they were already insuring with, and how permanent that advantage was. What other things could you do with that advantage? There were a lot of questions I wanted to ask him, and he was terrific in giving me the answers. It changed my life in a major way."

EVALUATING DECISIONS (POSTMORTEMS)

1999 MEETING (04:50:18)

WB: "We believe in postmortems at Berkshire. One thing I used to do when I ran the partnership was I contrasted all sale decisions versus all purchase decisions. It wasn't enough that the purchase decisions worked out well, they had to work out better than the sale. And managers tend to be reluctant to look at the results of the capital projects or the acquisitions that they proposed with great detail a year or two earlier to a board. They don't want to actually stick the figures up there as to how the reality worked out against the projections. That's human nature. But I think you're a better doctor if you drop by the pathology department, occasionally. And I think you're a better manager or investor if you look at every one of the decisions you've made, of importance, and see which ones worked and which ones didn't and, what is your batting average. And if your batting average gets too bad, you better hand the decision-making over to someone else."

INVESTMENT RESEARCH AND THE SILVER BULLET

1999 MEETING (04:54:53)

CM: "I think both of us learn more from the great business magazines than we do anywhere else. It's such an easy, shorthand way of getting a vast variety of business experience, just to riffle through issue after issue, covering a great variety of businesses. If you get the mental habit of relating what you're reading to the basic structure of the underlying ideas being demonstrated, you gradually accumulate some wisdom about investing. I don't think you can get to be a really good investor over a broad range without doing a massive amount of reading."

WB: "You might think about picking out five to ten companies where you feel quite familiar with their products, but maybe not necessarily so familiar with their financials and all of that. If you understand their products, you know what's going on in the business itself. And then get lots of annual reports, all the magazine articles written on those companies for the past ten years, just sort of immerse yourself as if you were either going to work for the company, or they'd hired you as the CEO, or you're going to buy the whole business.

"Back many years ago, I would go around and I would talk to competitors, always. I'd talk to employees ... If I were interested in the ABC Company, I would go to the XYZ Company and try and learn a lot about it. There's spin on what you get, but you learn to discern it. Essentially, you're being a reporter. It's very much like journalism.

"Andy Grove talked in his book about the silver bullet. You talk to the competitor and you say, 'If you had a silver bullet and you could only put it through the head of one of your competitors, which one would it be and why?' You learn a lot if you ask questions like that over time. And you ask somebody in some industry and you say, 'If you were going to go away for ten years and you had to put all of your money into the stock of one of your competitors, not your own, which one would it be and why?' Just keep asking, asking, and asking. You'll have to discount the answers you get in certain ways, but you will be getting things poured into your head that then you can use to reformulate and do your own thinking.

"The biggest thing is to find out how businesses operate. If we're running GEICO, who do we worry about and why do we worry about them? Who would we like to put that silver bullet through? Keep asking those questions. Then you go to the guy they want to put the silver bullet through and find out who he wants to put the silver bullet through. That's the way you approach it, learning all the time. You can talk to current employees, ex-employees, vendors, suppliers, distributors, retailers, customers, all kinds of people. It's an investigative and journalistic process. And, in the end, you want to write the story; six months later, you want to say, 'The XYZ Company is worth this amount because...' and you write the story. Some companies are easy to write stories about, and other companies are much tougher to write stories about. We try to look for the ones that are easy."

CM: "For the histories of the thousand biggest corporations laid out in digest form, *Value Line* is in a class by itself. That one volume really tells a lot about the histories of our best companies."

WB: "If you look at each page and what's happened in terms of ROE, sales growth, all kinds of things, and then you say, 'Why did this happen? Who let it happen? What's that chart going to look like the next ten years?' That's what you're really trying to figure out—not the price chart, but the chart about business operation. You're trying to print the next ten years of *Value Line* in your head. There are some companies that you can do a reasonable job with, and there are others that are just too tough. But that's what the game is about. If you have some predilection toward it, it can be a lot of fun. I mean, the process is as much fun as the conclusion that you come to."

CM: "What Warren's saying there, when he talks about 'why,' that's the most important question of all. And it doesn't apply just to investment, it applies to the whole human experience. If you want to get smart, the question you've got to keep asking is: 'Why?' And you have to relate the answers to a structure of deep theory. And you've got to know the main theories. It's mildly laborious, but it's also a lot of fun."

MISTAKES OF OMISSION

2001 MEETING (00:22:58)

CM: "The mistakes that have been most extreme in Berkshire's history are mistakes of omission. They don't show up in our figures; they show up in opportunity costs. In other words, we have an opportunity and we almost do it. In retrospect, we can tell that we were very much mistaken not to do it. In terms of the shareholders, those are the ones that really cost the most. And very few managements do much thinking or talking about opportunity costs. I don't like mentioning specific companies, because we may, in due course, want to buy them again and have an opportunity to do so at our price. But practically everywhere in life, and in corporate life too, what really costs, in comparison with what easily might have been, are the blown opportunities. It's just an awesome amount of money.

"When I was somewhat younger, I was offered three hundred shares of Belridge Oil. Any idiot could've told there was no possibility of losing money and a large possibility of making money. I bought it. The guy called me back three days later and offered me 1,500 more shares. But this time, I had to sell something to buy the damn Belridge. That mistake [not buying more shares], if you traced it through, has cost me $200 million. And it was all because I had to go to a slight inconvenience and sell something. Berkshire does that kind of thing, too. We never get over it."

WB: "When we speak of errors of omission, of which we've had plenty and some very big ones, we don't mean not buying some stock where a friend runs it or we know the name and it went from one to a hundred. That doesn't mean anything. We only regard errors as being things that are within our circle of competence. So if somebody knows how to make money in cocoa beans or a software company and we miss that, that is not an error as far as we're concerned. What's an error is when it's something we understand, and we stand there and stare at it, and we don't do anything. Or worse yet, what really gets me is when we do something very small with it. We do an eyedropper's worth when we could do it very big. Charlie refers to that elegantly as sucking your thumb. We have been thumb suckers at times with businesses that we understood well. And it may have been because we started buying and the price moved up a little and we waited around hoping we would get more at the price we originally started. Those are huge mistakes. Conventional accounting, of course, does not pick those up at all. But they're in our scorebook."

SIZE CONSTRAINTS

2007 MEETING (02:18:06)

WB: "If I were working with very small sums, I would be doing almost entirely different things than I do currently. Your universe expands. If you're looking, there are thousands and thousands and thousands of times as many options if you're investing $10,000 than if you're investing $100 billion. You've got all the options you have with $100 billion, except buying entire businesses, and you've got all of these other options. So, you can earn very high returns with very small amounts of money, and it will always be such.

"I don't mean that everybody can do it, but if you know something about values and investments, you will find opportunities with small sums, and it will not be with the portfolio that Berkshire owns. We can't earn phenomenal returns putting $3 billion in a stock. It won't work that way. It won't even come close to working that way. But if Charlie or I were in a position of working with $1 million, we would find little things here and there where we would earn very high returns on capital—and it wouldn't always be stocks."

2008 MEETING (00:38:16)

WB: "We would be very happy if we could buy common stocks where our expectation over a long period, from a combination of dividends and capital gains, was going to be 10%, pre-tax; and we would probably settle for a little less than that. There's absolutely no question that returns from owning Berkshire will be less in the future than they have been in the past ... We operate now in a universe of marketable stocks in companies with market caps of at least $10 billion; to have a meaningful impact on Berkshire, we're talking much bigger than that, maybe $50 billion and up. That is not as profitable a universe to operate in as if you have the entire universe of thousands and thousands of companies ... Our universe has shrunk enormously, and we will not do remotely as well in that universe as we would if we were operating in a much wider universe and could do all kinds of things ... We're going to get decent results over time, but we're not going to get indecent results. We prefer indecent, but we're not going to get them."

CM: "You can take Warren's promises to the bank. We are very happy making money at a rate in the future that is way less than the rate at which we made money in the past. And I suggest that you adopt the same attitude."

WB: "Well, I wouldn't condemn them to that. If you're working with small amounts of money you may have something very much better to do with your money than to buy Berkshire. I mean, if you're working with small amounts of money and you want to put in significant amounts of time, and examine thousands of securities, you will find things that are more intelligent to buy than Berkshire. We still think Berkshire is an attractive investment over a long period of time. We think it stacks up reasonably well with other very large companies. But we don't think it's the most attractive investment in the world, in terms of what you can find if you're willing to go through those thousands of possibilities, which is what Charlie and I used to do many years ago. It's not feasible for us to do it now, and wouldn't have any impact on Berkshire.

"What we really like at Berkshire is finding and buying large to very large first-class businesses with first-class management and just sitting there. The nice thing is you don't have to go from flower to flower. You can just sit there and watch them produce more and more every year, and give you capital, and you can buy more businesses. That's a nice formula. It's a formula that will work, I think, for us—but it won't produce returns like the past."

PART TWO:
Valuation and Intrinsic Value

"The first investment primer that I know of, and it was pretty good advice, was delivered in about 600 B.C. by Aesop: 'A bird in the hand is worth two in the bush.'"

"The investing where you find a few great companies and just sit on your ass because you've correctly predicted the future, that is what it's very nice to be good at."

"Somebody once subpoenaed our staffing papers on some acquisition; not only did we not have any staffing papers, we also didn't have any staff."

"It's the old story: don't ask the barber whether you need a haircut. You do not want to ask an investment banker what he thinks earnings are going to be in five years for a company he's trying to sell."

"A business with something glorious underneath, disguised by terrible numbers that cause cutoff points in other people's minds, is ideal for us, if we can figure it out."

INTRODUCTION

THE DETERMINATION OF THE PROPER PRICE FOR A BUSINESS—ITS intrinsic value—is the focal point of the investment research process. If you can properly assess value, you are on the path to attractive investment returns over the long run. But while this question can be answered with pinpoint accuracy in hindsight, tweaking the underlying assumptions will lead to widely varying estimates when running the calculation before the inputs have been settled. And as it relates to intangibles like management quality, there's a lot of guesswork in thinking about how to weigh those variables—for example, what was the proper adjustment in the valuation of Berkshire at any point over the past six decades to account for the CEO (Buffett) being a one-of-a-kind investor and capital allocator?

As you will read in part two, that can lead to interesting thoughts on the "right" way to think about intrinsic value. As an example, Buffett and Munger became more willing over time to be somewhat price agnostic in owning great businesses; that worked to their benefit in certain cases, but also led to periodic mistakes. (2006 meeting: "Coca-Cola strikes us as a really wonderful business that sold at a very silly price some years back. You can definitely fault me for not selling.") As with many things in investing, I think the main takeaway relates to the trade-offs inherent in any approach. In theory, the role of valuation in investing is impartial and definitive. In practice, it is painted by personal preference—the risk you're willing to bear. A reasonable marrying of those two ideas will provide a path to sensible long-term portfolio management.

SUBJECTS AND MEETINGS FEATURED

INTRINSIC VALUE

1994 MEETING (03:18:11)

WARREN BUFFETT: "The economic value of any asset is the present value, at the appropriate interest rate, of all future streams of cash going in or out of the business. There are all kinds of businesses that Charlie and I don't think we have the faintest idea what those future streams will look like. And if we don't have the faintest idea what the future stream is going to look like, we don't have the faintest idea what it's worth now. If you think you know what the price of a stock should be today, but you don't think you have any idea what the stream of cash will be over the next twenty years, you've got cognitive dissonance. We are looking for things where we feel—with a fairly high degree of probability—that we can come within a range of those numbers over a period of time, and then we discount them back. And we are more concerned with the certainty of those numbers than we are with getting the one that looks absolutely the cheapest, but based upon numbers we don't have great confidence in.

"The numbers in any accounting report mean nothing, per se, as to economic value. They are guidelines to tell you something about how to get at economic value. But there are no answers in the financial statements; there are guidelines to enable you to figure out the answer. To figure out that answer, you have to understand something about business. You don't have to understand a lot about mathematics; the math isn't complicated. But you do have to understand something about the business. That's the same thing you would do if you were going to buy an apartment house, farm, or any small business. You would try to figure out what you are laying out currently, what you were likely to get back over time, how certain you felt about getting it, and how it compared to other alternatives. That's all we do, just with large businesses.

"The accounting figures are very helpful, in the sense that they generally guide us to what we should be thinking about. And, of course, if we find numbers where it looks like they're taking the most optimistic interpretation of things that they can under GAAP, we get very worried. We worry about people who look like they massage the numbers in any way—and there are plenty of people that do."

1997 MEETING (02:33:27)

WB: "Looking at any business, if we could see its future cash inflows or outflows to or from the owners over the next, call it one hundred years, or until the business is extinct, and then could discount that back at the appropriate interest rate, that would give us a number for intrinsic value. In other words, it would be like looking at a bond that had a whole bunch of coupons on it that was due in a hundred years. If you could see what those coupons are, you could figure out the value of that bond compared to government bonds, if you wanted to stick an appropriate risk rate in. Or you could compare a government bond with 5% coupons to another government bond with 7% coupons. Each one of those bonds has a different value because they have different coupons. Businesses have coupons that are going to develop in the future, too. The only problem is that they aren't printed on the instrument—it's up to the investor to try to estimate what those coupons are going to be over time. In high-tech businesses or something like that, we don't have the faintest idea what the coupons are going to be. When we get into businesses where we think we can understand them reasonably well, we try to print the coupons out. We are trying to figure out what businesses will be worth in ten or twenty years.

"When we bought See's Candies in 1972, we had to come to a judgment as to whether we could figure out the competitive forces that would operate, the strengths and weaknesses of the company, and how that would look over ten, twenty, or thirty years. And if you attempt to assess intrinsic value, it all relates to cash flows. The only reason for putting cash into any kind of investment now is because you expect to take cash out in the future, not by selling it to somebody else—because that's just a game of who beats who—but by what the asset produces over time. That's true if you're buying a farm, an apartment house, or a business. There are a number of filters which say to us we don't know what that business is going to be worth in ten or twenty years; we can't even make an educated guess. Obviously, we don't think we know to two or three decimal places, anything like that, precisely what's going to be produced. But we have a high degree of confidence that we're in the ballpark with certain kinds of businesses. The filters are designed to make sure we're in those kinds of businesses.

"We basically use long-term, risk-free/government bond-type interest rates to think back in terms of what we should discount future cash flows at. And that's what the game of investing is all about. Investment is putting out money to get more back later from the asset; not by selling it to somebody else, but by what the asset itself will produce. If you're an investor, you're looking at what the asset (business) is going to do. If you're a speculator, you're primarily focusing on what the price is going to do independent of the business. That's not our game. If we're right about the business, we're going to make a lot of money. And if we're wrong about the business, we don't expect to make money."

CHARLIE MUNGER: "One filter that's useful in investing is the simple idea of opportunity costs. If you already have one opportunity available in large quantity, and you like it better than 98% of the other things you see, you can just screen out the other 98%—you already know something better. So, people who have a lot of opportunities tend to make better investments than people that don't.

And people who have very good opportunities, using the concept of opportunity costs, can make better decisions about what to buy. With this attitude, you get a concentrated portfolio, which we don't mind. That practice of ours, which is so simple, is not widely copied. I do not know why. It's not the standard in investment management, even at great universities and other intellectual institutions. If we're right, why are so many eminent places so wrong?"

WB: "If somebody shows us a business, the first thing that goes through our head is would we rather own this business than more Coca-Cola or more Gillette? It's crazy not to compare it to things you're very certain of. There are very few businesses we'll find where we're as certain about the future as we are with Coca-Cola or Gillette. We will want companies where the certainty gets close to that. And then we'll want to figure that we're better off than just buying more of those. ... They tend not to measure against what we regard as close to perfection."

1998 MEETING (2:19:31)

WB: "By definition, intrinsic value is the present value of the stream of cash that's going to be generated by any financial asset between now and doomsday. That's easy to say and impossible to figure, but it's the kind of thing that we're thinking about when we look at Coca-Cola, where we think it's much easier to evaluate the stream of cash that will come in the future than it is in a company such as Intel, marvelous as it may be. It's easier for us. ... Berkshire is complicated by the fact that we have no business that naturally employs all of the capital that flows to us, so it is dependent, to some extent, on the opportunities available and the ingenuity used when that cash pours in. In relation to the resources available, we have to come up with new ways to use cash. That makes for a more difficult valuation job. ... Sometimes we have good ideas for that cash and sometimes we don't. That makes your job more difficult, in terms of computing Berkshire's intrinsic value."

GROWTH AND VALUE

2000 MEETING (00:11:56)

WB: "Growth and value are not two distinct categories of business. If you knew what a business was going to be able to disgorge in cash between now and Judgment Day, you could come to a precise figure as to what it is worth. Elements of that can be the ability to use additional capital at good rates, and most companies that are characterized as growth companies have that as a characteristic. But there is no distinction, in our minds, between growth and value. We look at every business as being a value proposition. The potential for growth, and the likelihood of good economics being attached to that growth, are part of the equation. But they're all value decisions. ... You have to decide how much value you're going to get.

"The first investment primer that I know of, and it was pretty good advice, was delivered in about 600 B.C. by Aesop: 'A bird in the hand is worth two in the bush.' Incidentally, Aesop did not know it was 600 B.C.—he was smart, but not that smart. Aesop was onto something, but he didn't finish it, because there's a couple of other questions that go along with it. He forgot to say exactly when you were going to get the two from the bush, and he forgot to say what the interest rates were that you had to measure this against. But if he'd given those two factors, he would have defined investment for the next 2,600 years.

"You will trade a bird in the hand, which is investing—you lay out cash today; then ... you have to evaluate how many birds are in the bush, and when they're going to come out. Now, if interest rates are 5%, and you're going to get two birds from the bush in five years, that's much better than a bird in the hand now. If you get them in five years, that's roughly 14% compounded annually and interest rates are only 5%. But if interest rates were 20%, you would decline to take the two birds in the bush five years from now. It's not good enough, because at 20%, if I just keep this bird in my hand and compound it, I'll have more birds in five years.

"What's all that got to do with growth? Well, usually people associate growth with a lot more birds in the bush, but you still have to decide when you're going to get them, you have to measure that against interest rates, and you have to measure it against other bushes (opportunity costs). And that's all investing is: It's a value decision based on what something is worth, how many birds are in the bush, when you're going to get them, and what interest rates are.

"When we buy a stock, we always think in terms of buying the whole enterprise; it enables us to think as businessmen, rather than stock speculators. Let's take a company that has marvelous prospects, but it is paying you nothing now and you buy it today at a valuation of $500 billion. If you feel 10% is the appropriate rate of return, that means that if it pays you nothing this year, but starts next year, it has to be able to pay $55 billion in perpetuity, each year. But if it's not going to pay until the third year, then it has to pay you $60.5 billion in perpetuity to justify the present price. Every year that you wait to take a bird out of the bush, you have to take out more birds later on. It's that simple.

"I question sometimes whether people who pay $500 billion implicitly for a business by buying ten shares of stock at some price, are really thinking of the mathematics implicit in what they are doing. Let's just assume there's only going to be a one-year delay before the business starts paying out, and you want to get a 10% return on a valuation of $500 billion. That means they have to be able to disgorge $55 billion of cash, year after year after year. To do that, they have to make perhaps $80 billion pre-tax. Look around at the universe of businesses in this world and see how many are earning $80 billion pre-tax, or $70 billion, $60 billion, $50 billion, $40 billion, or even $30 billion. You won't find many. So, it requires a rather extraordinary change in profitability to give you enough birds out of that particular bush to make it worthwhile to give up the one you have in your hand."

CM: "I agree that all intelligent investing is value investing. You have to acquire more than you pay for, and that's a value judgment. But you can look for more than you're paying for in a lot of different ways. You can use filters to sift the investment universe. If you stick with stocks that can't just be put away in your safe deposit box for forty years, but which are underpriced, then you have to keep moving around all the time; as they get closer to what you think the real value is, you have to sell them, and then find others. It's an active kind of investing. The investing where you find a few great companies and just sit on your ass because you've correctly predicted the future, that is what it's very nice to be good at."

2001 MEETING (00:55:02)

WB: "Growth and value, they're indistinguishable. Growth is part of the value equation. There is no such thing as growth stocks or value stocks, the way Wall Street generally portrays them as being contrasting asset classes. Growth, usually, is a positive for value, but only when it means that by adding capital now, you add more cash availability later on at a rate that's considerably higher than the current rate of interest. We calculate into any business we buy what we expect to happen, in terms of the cash that's going to come out of it or the cash that's going to go into it.

"At FlightSafety, we're going to buy $200 million of simulators this year. Our depreciation will probably be $70 million, so we're putting $130 million above depreciation into that business. Now, that can be good or bad. It's growth, there's no question. But whether that's good or bad depends on what we earn on that incremental $130 million over time. So if you tell me that you own a business that's going to grow to the sky, I don't know whether it's wonderful or not until I know what the economics are of that growth. How much you have to put in today, and how much you will reap from putting that in today, later on.

"The classic case is the airline business. The airline business has been a growth business ever since Orville Wright took off. But the growth has been the worst thing that happened to it. It's been great for the American public, but growth has been a curse in the airline business because more and more capital has been put in at inadequate returns. Now, growth is wonderful at See's Candies, because it requires relatively little incremental investment to sell more pounds of candy. Growth is part of the equation, but anybody that tells you, 'You should have your money in growth stocks or value stocks,' really does not understand investing."

CM: "I think it's fair to say that at Berkshire, with a very limited headquarters staff—and that staff is pretty old—we are especially partial to laying out large sums of money under circumstances where we won't have to be smart again. In other words, if we buy good businesses run by good people at reasonable prices, there's a good chance we will prosper for many decades without more intelligence at headquarters. And you can say, in a sense, that's growth stock investing."

WB: "If you had asked Wall Street to classify Berkshire since 1965—year by year, 'Is this a growth stock or value stock?'—who knows what they would have said. But the real point is that we're trying to put out cash now to get more cash back later on. If you do that, the business grows. You can call that value or growth, but they're not two different categories."

MODELING AND VALUATION

1995 MEETING (01:41:56)

WB: "We are looking at businesses in terms of what kind of cash they can produce, if we're buying all of them, or they will produce, if we're buying part of them—and there's a difference. Then at what discount rate do we bring it back? How far out do we look and all that? Despite the fact that we can define it in a simple and direct equation, we've never actually sat down and written out a set of numbers to relate to that equation. We do it in our heads, in a way.

"There is no piece of paper. There wasn't a piece of paper that showed our calculation on Helzberg, See's Candies, or The Buffalo News. It would be attaching a little more scientific quality to our analysis than there really is, if I gave you some gobbledygook about, 'We do it for eighteen years and stick a terminal value and do all of this.' We are sitting in the office thinking about that question with each investment. And we have discount rates, in a general way, in mind. But we really like the decision to be obvious enough to us that it doesn't require making a detailed calculation. That's the framework, but it's not applied in the sense that we actually fill in all of the variables."

CM: "Berkshire is being run the way Thomas Hunt Morgan, the great Nobel laureate, ran the biology department at Caltech. He banned the Friden calculator, the computer of that era. And people said, 'How can you do this? Every other place in Caltech has Friden calculators.' And he said, 'Well, we're picking up these great nuggets of gold just by organized common sense, resources are short, and we're not going to resort to any damn placer mining as long as we can pick up these major aggregations of gold.' That's the way Berkshire works. And I hope the placer mining era will never come. Somebody once subpoenaed our staffing papers on some acquisition; not only did we not have any staffing papers, we also didn't have any staff."

2011 MEETING (04:14:13)

WB: "Growth is part of the investment equation, and obviously, we love profitable growth. ... When we look at a business and we're looking out in the future, obviously, if we see growth in that picture and it's growth which produces a high return on incremental capital involved, we love it. But we do not rule out companies where we think there will be little or no growth, if the price is attractive relative to the earning power. ... It's a factor in every investment decision, because we're looking out to the future earning power, but also future capital requirements. And we think plenty about whether any business we go into is likely to grow profitably ... but we don't rule out companies that have very slow growth or no-growth possibilities."

CM: "The interesting thing is that, in our country, the business schools teach people to make these projections way in the future, and they program computers to grind these projections out. And then they use them in their business decision-making. I've always regarded those projections as doing more harm than good. Warren has never prepared one that I know of, and where an investment banker prepares one, we tend to throw them aside without reading them. I think an enormous false precision gets into things when you program computers to make forward projections for a long period of time. We make rough projections in our head all the time. We don't do any of those formal projections, because the fact that they're there on paper and came out of a computer makes some people think they must be significant. I really think they do more harm than good."

WB: "When we bought The Scott & Fetzer Company (Scott Fetzer) in 1986, it had been shopped by First Boston to more than thirty parties. They never got around to calling us. ... I'd read about it in the paper, so I sent a letter to Ralph Schey. I'd never met or talked to the guy, but I figured I'd gamble twenty-one cents, or whatever the first-class rate for a stamp was. I said, 'We'll pay $60 a share. If you like the idea, I'll meet you in Chicago on Sunday, and if you don't like the idea, tear up this letter.'

"Ralph met me, we made the deal, and we paid the $60 per share. Charlie and I went to sign the deal, and the fellow from First Boston was there; he was a little abashed since he had not contacted us at all when they were looking for a buyer. But naturally he had a contract that called for a few million dollars of commission even though we made the deal by ourselves. So, in a moment of exuberance while he was collecting his few million dollars, he said to Charlie, 'We prepared this book in connection with Scott Fetzer, and since you're paying us a couple million dollars and have gotten nothing so far, maybe you would like to have it.' Charlie, with his usual tact, said 'I'll pay you $2 million if you don't show me the book.'

"With [specialty chemicals firm] Lubrizol, Dave Sokol met James Hambrick, and Lubrizol had already made projections publicly out to 2013. Dave told me James had also given him some projections out to 2015; did I want to see them? I told him no. I don't want to look at the other fellow's projections. I've never seen a projection from an investment banker that didn't show the earnings going up over time—and believe me, they don't always go up over time. It's the old story: don't ask the barber whether you need a haircut. You do not want to ask an investment banker what he thinks earnings are going to be in five years for a company he's trying to sell. I pay no attention to that sort of thing.

"But as Charlie says, we are doing projections in our head when we look at a business. When we look at any company or stock to buy, we have a model in our mind of what that place is likely to look like over some period of years. And then we also have some model in our mind of how far off we can be. There's some things we can be way off on, and there are other things we're likely to be in a fairly narrow range on. All that is taking place—but we sure don't want to listen to anybody else's projections."

CM: "Those of you about to enter business school, or who are there, I recommend you learn to do it our way, but at least until you're out of school you have to pretend to do it their way."

DISCOUNTED CASH FLOW (DCF) MODELS

1996 MEETING (04:18:46)

CM: "Warren talks about these discounted cash flows, but I've never seen him do one. If it isn't obvious that it's going to work well unless you do the calculation, he tends to go on to the next idea."

WB: "It's true: If you have to actually do it with pencil and paper, it's too close to think about. It ought to just kind of scream at you that you've got this huge margin of safety."

EARNINGS GROWTH AND VALUATIONS

2001 MEETING (02:10:28)

WB: "I think it's a mistake for any company to predict 15% a year earnings growth, but plenty do. For one thing, unless the U.S. economy grows at 15% a year, eventually any 15% number catches up with you. It just doesn't make sense. Very, very few large companies can compound their earnings at 15%. It isn't going to happen. Look at the Fortune 500—if you pick a company that currently has record earnings, and you want to pick ten that over the next twenty years will average 15% or greater, I will bet you that more than half of your list will not make it. So, I think it's a mistake; it leads people to stretch on accounting, it tends to make them change trade practices. If you look at the companies that have done it, you will find plenty of examples of people who have made those sorts of mistakes."

CM: "That kind of stuff happens all the time. It will continue to happen. It's just built into the system. I see more predictions of future earnings growth at a high rate, not less. A few people have sort of taken an abstinence pledge, but it's very few. It's what the analysts want to hear."

WB: "It's what the investor relations departments want management to say. It makes their life easier. But they don't have to be there five to ten years from now doing the same thing. If we predicted 15% from Berkshire, that means in five years, $200 billion. In ten years, $400 billion. Fifteen years, $800 billion. In twenty years, $1.6 trillion. The values get to be crazy. And if you have a business with a market value of $500 billion—and you had a few not so long ago—just think of what it takes to deliver, in the way of future cash, at a 15% discount rate to justify that. A business selling at $500 billion delivering you no cash today, to get 15% on your money, it would have to give you $75 billion this year. But if it doesn't give you $75 billion this year, it has to give you $86.25 billion next year. And if it doesn't do it next year, it has to give you almost $100 billion in the third year. Those numbers are staggering.

"The implications involved in certain market valuations really belong in *Gulliver's Travels*. But people take them very seriously. People were valuing certain businesses at $500 billion a year ago; there's almost no mathematical calculation you could make that would possibly lead you to justify those valuations if you demanded something like 15% on your money."

CM: "To some extent, stocks sell like Rembrandts. ... They sell based on the fact that Rembrandts have gone up in value in the past. When you get that kind of valuation in stocks, some crazy things can happen. Bonds are way more rational, because nobody can believe a bond paying a fixed rate of modest interest can go to the sky, but stocks behave partly like Rembrandts.

"Suppose you filled every pension fund in America with nothing but Rembrandts? Of course, Rembrandts would keep going up and up as people bought more Rembrandts, or pieces of Rembrandts, at higher and higher prices. Wouldn't that create a hell of a mess after twenty years of buying Rembrandts? And to the extent stock prices generally become sort of irrational, isn't it sort of like filling half the pension funds with Rembrandts? I think those are good questions."

BOOK VALUE

1994 MEETING (02:14:59)

WB: "Book value is virtually not a consideration at all in how we analyze securities. The best businesses, by definition, are going to be businesses that earn very high returns on capital employed over time. So, by nature, if we want to own good businesses, we're going to own things that have relatively little capital employed compared to our purchase price. That would not have been Ben Graham's approach, but Ben was not working with very large sums of money. And he would not have argued with this approach, he just would've said his approach was easier. And it is easier, perhaps, when you're working with small amounts of money.

"My friend Walter Schloss has an absolutely sensational record and he has hewed much more toward the kind of securities that Ben would've selected, but he's worked with smaller amounts of money. It's not surprising to me at all; when Walter left Graham-Newman, I would've expected him to do well. But I don't look at the primary message of Graham as anything to do with formulas. There are three important aspects to it. One is your attitude toward the stock market. That's covered in chapter eight of *The Intelligent Investor.* If you've got the right attitude toward the market, you start ahead of 99% of people operating in the market. You have an enormous advantage. Second principle is the margin of safety, which again, gives you an enormous edge, and actually has applicability far beyond the investment world. And then third is looking at stocks as businesses, which gives you an entirely different view than most people in the market. With those three philosophical benchmarks, the exact evaluation technique you use is not really that important because you're not going to go way off track."

CM: "To the extent that estimating future cash flows requires projections, I would say projections, while they're logically required by the circumstances, on average do more harm than good. Most of them are put together by people with an interest in a particular outcome. The subconscious bias that goes into the process, and its apparent precision, makes it fatuous, dishonorable, foolish, or what have you. Mark Twain used to say a mine is a hole in the ground owned by a liar. And a projection prepared in America by anybody with a commission, or an executive trying to justify a particular course of action, will frequently be a lie. It's not a deliberate lie in most cases; the man has gotten to believe it himself, and that's the worst kind. Projections are to be handled with great care, particular when somebody has an interest in misleading you."

WB: "Charlie and I, I think it's fair to say, have never looked at a projection in connection with either a security or a business we've bought. We've had them offered to us, and we voluntarily turn them away when people try to thrust them upon us. The very fact that they are prepared so meticulously by the people selling the business, or by the executives who are presenting them to their boards and all of that sort of thing, either we're wrong or they're wrong.

"It's a ritual that managers go through to justify doing what they want to do in the first place in nine cases out of ten. I have never met an executive who wanted to buy something that said, 'Well, I had to turn it down because the projections didn't work.' It never happens. There will always be somebody who comes up with projections that will satisfy the guy who's signing his paycheck or will sign the deal that provides the commissions. And they will pass those along to whomever else they need, the bankers or the board, to approve it. It is total nonsense. I was recently involved in a situation where projections were a part of the presentation. I asked that the record of the people who made the projections, that their past projections also be presented at the same time. It was a very rude act, but believe me, it proved the point."

1998 MEETING (03:52:48)

WB: "Earnings are what determine value, not book value. Book value is not a factor we consider. Future earnings are a factor we consider. And earnings have been poor for a great many Japanese companies. Now, if you think that the ROE of Japanese business is going to increase dramatically, and you're correct, you're going to make a lot of money in Japanese stocks. But the ROE for Japanese businesses has been quite low, and that makes a low price-to-book ratio very appropriate because earnings are measured against book. If a company's earning 5% on book value, I don't want to buy it at book value if I think it's going to keep earning 5% on book value. So, a low price-to-book ratio means nothing to us. It does not intrigue us. In fact, if anything, we are less likely to look at something that sells at a low relationship to book than something that sells at a high relationship to book, because the chances are we're looking at a poor business in the first case and a good business in the second case."

MINIMUM FCF YIELD

1994 MEETING (00:19:02)

WB: "I don't think we'd be likely to, but we could conceivably buy a business with no current after-tax cash flow; we would have to think it had a tremendous future. The current figures, particularly for the kind of businesses we buy, tend to be representative, we think, of what's going to happen in the future. But that would not necessarily have to be the case. We bought GEICO when it was losing significant money. We didn't expect it to continue to lose significant money. If we think the present value of the future earning power is attractive enough compared to the purchase price, we would not be overwhelmed by what the first year's figure would be."

CM: "We don't care what we report in the first year or two after buying anything."

WB: "I would say that in a world of 7% long-term bond rates, we would certainly want to think we were discounting future after-tax streams of cash at a rate of at least 10%. But that will depend on the certainty we feel about the business. The more certain we feel, the closer we are willing to play it. We have to feel pretty certain about any business before we're interested at all. But there are still degrees of certainty. If we thought we were getting a stream of cash over the next thirty years that we felt extremely certain about, we would use a discount rate that would be somewhat less than one where we thought we might get some surprises in five or ten years."

VALUING BERKSHIRE'S INSURANCE BUSINESSES

1994 MEETING (00:22:03)

WB: "It's very hard to quantify, as we've said many times in the report. But I think it's clear, even with fairly pessimistic assumptions, that the excess of intrinsic value over carrying value [book value] is higher, by some margin, for our insurance business. And I think that the table in the report that shows our [attractive] cost to float over the years, and also what the trend of float has been over the years, would—unless you thought that table had no validity for the future—tend to point you in the direction of saying the insurance businesses have a very significant excess of intrinsic value over carrying value. We started with $20 million of float and now we're close to $3 billion. And that float has come to us at a cost that's extremely attractive, on average, over the years. Just to pick an example, last year, when we had an underwriting profit, the value of that float was something over $200 million. And that figure was a lot bigger than it was ten or twenty years ago. That's a very significant stream of earnings, and it's one we feel we have reasonably good prospects in. So, we feel very good about the insurance business."

PUBLIC OPINION AND ANALYST COMMENTARIES

1994 MEETING (00:50:30)

WB: "Every day somebody sells a few shares of Berkshire and somebody buys a few shares of Berkshire, and they are probably coming to differing opinions on the valuation. ... It really doesn't make any difference to us. We don't pay any attention to what people say about Coca-Cola or Gillette either. On any given day, two million shares of Coca-Cola trade. That's a lot of people selling and buying. You really should not make decisions in securities based on what other people think. If you're doing that, you should think about doing something else. A public opinion poll will not get you rich on Wall Street. You want to stick with businesses that you feel you can evaluate yourself. We don't read anything about what the economy or the market is going to do. Anytime I see an article that says these analysts say this or that about some business, it just doesn't mean anything to us. You cannot get rich with a weathervane."

INTEREST RATES AND VALUATION

1994 MEETING (02:04:19)

WB: "The value of a business, farm, apartment house, or any economic asset, is 100% sensitive to interest rates, because all you are doing in investing is transferring some money to somebody now in exchange for what you expect the stream of money to be over a period of time. The higher interest rates are, the less that present value is going to be. The intrinsic valuation of every business is, by its nature, 100% sensitive to interest rates."

2010 MEETING (04:07:00)

WB: "Very low interest rates are very tough for anybody who has their investments in short-term money. If you're getting 0.1% on some money market fund that you started investing in when Columbus landed in 1492, and didn't pay any taxes, you'd have almost doubled your money by now.

"People talk about easy money policies, but it isn't so easy on the people who have the money. It won't go on forever, but it may seem like forever to people who are on fixed income. I'm very sympathetic with them. Many of them became fearful when the world was looking like it was collapsing in late 2008. The price they pay is really terrible in terms of returns, and their purchasing power will be eaten away. I don't know how, but this will end at some point. It won't work forever to run huge budget deficits and to try and have very easy monetary policy. If we do run into trouble, the blame should go to Congress, not the Fed."

CM: "In some sense, the reality of our situation is almost amusingly depressing. Stocks are up because the return from loaning your money out at interest in a safe way is so lousy. Of course, one answer is that it can't last. In which case, stocks won't be as pronounced a value, relatively speaking. And if it does last, as it has in Japan, we won't like that either because it will mean we're mired in some horrible stagnation. This is a very cheery message."

WB: "It's hard to overestimate the pressure exerted by extremely low short-term interest rates on the value of everything else. The reason people have their money out at 0.1% is that they're afraid of everything else. But as their being afraid of everything else abates, as it has over the last couple of years, the pressure to push stock prices and real estate prices back up is enormous. And, of course, that's understood by people who have something to do with those matters. But I don't think you should underestimate the degree to which the last year of stock prices has been a result of the agony people are being put through that kept their funds in short-term money instruments. Unless they're terrified of the world, they will get pushed into other investments, and I think we've seen a lot of that. We'll see what happens when those money rates do go up, if they do."

MVA, EVA, AND CAPM

1995 MEETING (01:06:29)

CM: "If Warren is using economic value added (EVA) exactly the way they're now teaching it in the business schools, he hasn't told me. Obviously, the concept has some merit in it. But the exact formal methods, I do not believe we use them. Warren, are you using this stuff secretly?"

WB: "In a sense, they're trying to get at the same thing we do, but I think it has some flaws in it. Although I think it generally comes out with the right answers, it sort of forces itself to come out with the right answers. I really don't think you need that sort of thing. I do not think it's that complicated to figure out where it makes sense to put money; in terms of the mental manipulations you go through, I don't think it's a very complicated subject. The people marketing one fad or another in management tend to make them a little more complicated than needed, so that you have to call in the high priest. If all that really counts is the Ten Commandments, it's very tough on religious counselors; it just doesn't make it complicated enough. There's quite a bit of that in management consulting, and in the books that you see."

CM: "It's way less silly than the capital assets pricing model (CAPM). So, at least academia's improving."

WB: "CAPM had these great waves of popularity. You get that in management and investing. ... You can read *Pensions & Investment*, which is a pretty good magazine, but you see these fads going through. Then they have seminars and everything; the investment bankers create product to satisfy the demand. There are these fads in management. Obviously, listening to your customers and things like that—but it's hard to write a three-hundred-page book that just says, 'Listen to your customer.' That's one of the things I liked about Graham's book. Everything he wrote sort of made sense. He didn't try and make it more complicated than it is."

VALUING BANKS

1995 MEETING (02:23:31)

WB: "There's no difference in the criteria we apply to banks compared to other businesses. We don't have any sector allocation theories whatsoever. We simply apply the same criteria when looking at banks that we would at any other business. ... We bought a bank for Berkshire in 1969, the Illinois National Bank and Trust of Rockford. We've had an interest in the banking business. We feel it falls within our circle of competence to evaluate. That doesn't mean we'll be right every time, but we don't think it's beyond us to understand the banking business."

P/E RATIOS

1995 MEETING (04:27:46)

WB: "A multiple of today's earnings is not primarily determinative of things. We bought Coca-Cola, for example, in 1988 and 1989 at $11 a share—as low as $9, as high as $13, but it averaged about $11. Most estimates are for earnings between $2.30 and $2.40 this year. So, that's under five times this year's earnings, but it was a pretty good size multiple back when we bought it. It's the future that counts. It's like what Wayne Gretzky says, to skate to where the puck is going, not where it is. The current multiple interacts with the reinvestment of capital and the rate at which that capital's invested, to determine the attractiveness of something now.

"We are affected in that valuation process to a considerable degree by interest rates, but not by whether they're 7.3%, 7.0%, 7.5%. We'll be thinking much differently if long-term rates are 11% versus 5%. But we don't have any magic multiples in mind. We want to be in the business that ten years from now is earning a whole lot more money than it is now, and where we will still feel good about the prospects of the business at that time. That's the kind of business we're trying to buy all of, and that's the kind of business that we try and buy part of."

CM: "We don't do any of that rigid formulaic stuff."

WB: "There's a general framework, that you can call a formula, in our mind. But we don't kid ourselves that we know so much about the specifics that we would actually make a calculation, in terms of an equation. When we bought Coke in 1988 and 1989, we had an idea about what we thought the business would do over time, but we never reduced it to making a calculation. Maybe we should, but we don't think there's that kind of precision to it. We think it's the right way to think in a general way, but we also think if you think that you can do it to pinpoint it, you're kidding yourself. Therefore, we think that when we make a decision, there ought to be such a margin of safety—it ought to be so attractive—that you don't have to carry it out to three decimal places."

2000 MEETING (01:08:09)

WB: "We have no cutoff whatsoever. We don't think in terms of absolutes that way because we are trying to think of how many birds are in the bush. And sometimes the number currently being shown could be negative.

"One of the best buys we ever made was in 1976 when we bought what became, through repurchases, 50% of GEICO—at a time when the company was losing a lot of money, and was destined to lose a lot of money in the immediate future. The fact they were losing money was not lost on us, but we thought we saw a future there that was significantly different than the current situation. So, it would not bother us in the least to buy into a business that currently was losing money for some reason that we understood, and where we thought that the future was going to be significantly different. There's no P/E ratio that we have in mind as being a cutoff point at all. You could have some business making a sliver of money on which you would pay a very, very high P/E ratio. We look at all of these as businesses. For example, at [private jet company] NetJets, we're losing money in Europe. We expect to lose money in Europe getting established. Does that mean it's a bad thing to buy it? No.

"There are all kinds of decisions that involve the future looking different, in some important way, to the present. Most of our decisions relate to things where we expect the future not to change much. American Express was a good example. When we bought it in 1964, a fellow named Tino De Angelis had caused them incredible trouble; it looked for a time as if it could break the company. If you'd been charging what Tino had stolen from the company against the income account that year, or the legal costs that were going to be attached to it, you were looking at a significant loss. But the question was, what was American Express going to look like ten or twenty years later? We felt very good about that.

"So there are no arbitrary cutoff points. But there is that focus on, how much cash will this business deliver, between now and Kingdom Come? As a practical matter, if you estimate it for twenty years or so, the terminal values get less important. But you do want to have, in your mind, a stream of cash that will be thrown off over, say, a twenty-year period, that makes sense discounted at a proper interest rate, compared to what you're paying today."

CM: "The answer is almost the exact reverse of what you were pointing toward. A business with something glorious underneath, disguised by terrible numbers that cause cutoff points in other people's minds, is ideal for us, if we can figure it out."

WB: "And we've had a couple of those in our history that have made us a lot of money."

DISCOUNT RATES

1996 MEETING (02:07:37)

WB: "We basically think in terms of the long-term government rate. And there may be times when we might use a little higher rate, probably during a period of what would seem like very low rates. But we don't put a risk factor in, per se, because essentially, the purity of the idea is that you're discounting future cash. And it doesn't make any difference whether cash comes from a risky business or a so-called safe business. The value of the cash delivered by a water company, which is going to be around for a hundred years, is not different than the value of the cash derived from some high-tech company. It may be harder for you to make the estimate. And you may, therefore, want a bigger discount when you get through with the calculation.

"But we believe in using a government bond-type interest rate. We believe in trying to stick with businesses where we think we can see the future reasonably well—you never see it perfectly, obviously—but where we think we have a reasonable handle on it. We don't want to go below a certain threshold of understanding. We want to stick with businesses we think we understand quite well, and not try to have the whole panoply with all different kinds of risk rates, because, frankly, we think that'd just be playing games with numbers. I don't think you can stick numbers on a highly speculative business, where the whole industry's going to change in five years, and have it mean anything when you get through. If you say I'm going to stick an extra 6% in on the interest rate to allow for the fact, I tend to think that's nonsense. It may look mathematical, but it's mathematical gibberish in my view. You're better off sticking with businesses that you can understand, using the government bond rate. And when you can buy something you understand well at a significant discount, then, you should start getting excited."

1997 MEETING (03:20:25)

WB: "The risk-free rate is used merely to equate one item to another. In other words, we're looking for whatever's the most attractive. But in terms of present-valuing anything, we're going to use a number. We can always buy government bonds so that becomes the yardstick rate. ... It's the appropriate yardstick, in our view, to use to compare across all kinds of investment opportunities: oil wells, farms, whatever it may be. Now, it gets into degree of certainty, too. But it's the yardstick rate. It serves as a constant throughout the valuation process."

CM: "One opportunity cost of buying stock is to compare it with a bond. You may find that half the stocks in America, you're so fearful about or know so little about or think so poorly of, that you'd rather have the government bond. So, on an opportunity cost basis, they're taken out of the filter. Now, you start finding corporations where you like the stocks way better than government bonds. You have to compare one against the other. And when you find one that you regard as the best opportunity, that you can understand as the best opportunity, now you've got one to buy. It's a very simple idea. It uses nothing but the most elementary ideas from economics or game theory. It's hard to make the business appraisals, but the mental process is a cinch."

WB: "If Charlie and I had the choice of buying stock A, B, C, or D for all stocks listed on the NYSE, or buying a ten-year government bond, and we had to hold the stock or the bond for ten years, probably in at least 80% of the cases, we'd take the government bond. In many cases because we didn't understand the business well enough, or secondly, we may understand it and still prefer the 10% government bond. But we would measure everything that way."

CM: "Life is a whole series of opportunity costs. You've got to marry the best person who is convenient to find who will have you. Investment is much the same sort of a process."

2007 MEETING (03:15:14)

WB: "We don't have formal discount rates. Every time I start talking about this stuff, Charlie reminds me that I've never prepared a spreadsheet. But, in effect, I do it in my mind. We are going to want to get a significantly higher return, obviously, in terms of cash produced relative to the amount we're outlaying now for a business, than from a government bond. That has to be the yardstick at a base. How much more do we want? Well, if government bond rates were 2%, we're not going to buy a business to earn 3.5% expectancy over the years. We just don't want to commit our money that way; we'd rather sit around and wait a little while. If they're 4.75%, what do we hope to get over time? We want to get a fair amount more than that. But I don't sit down every morning, call Charlie, and say, 'What's our hurdle rate today?' We've never used the term. We want enough so we feel very comfortable that if they closed down the stock market for a couple years, or if interest rates go up another hundred or two hundred basis points, we're still happy with what we've bought. Beyond that, I know it sounds kind of fuzzy, but it is fuzzy."

CM: "The concept of a hurdle rate makes nothing but sense, and yet a lot of terrible errors are made by people talking about hurdle rates. Just because you can measure something and guess at it, doesn't mean it should be the controlling variable in dealing with a messy world. I don't think there's any substitute for thinking about a whole lot of investment options, and thinking about why one is better than another and what the likely returns are from each. The trouble with the hurdle rate concept—not that we don't have one, in a sense—is that it doesn't work as well as a system of comparing things. In other words, if I have something available that I think will give me 8% for sure and I can buy all I want of it, and you've got a perfectly good investment that I think will earn 7%, I don't have to waste five minutes with you … I can go on to some different subject. … In the real world, opportunity costs are what you want to make decisions based on."

PERMANENT HOLDINGS/NEVER SELL?

1996 MEETING (04:42:59)

WB: "There are things we think there's no price for. We've been tested sometimes, and haven't sold them. Bill Gates says it has to be illogical at some point to hold. At some price, you have to be willing to sell a marketable security, forgetting about a controlled business. But I doubt if we ever get tested … there's only a couple in that category. We really have a great reluctance to sell when we like the business and the people. I don't think I'd count on seeing many sales. But if you ever attend a meeting here and they're at sixty or seventy times earnings, keep an eye on me."

CM: "If you're right about the companies, you can hold them at pretty high values."

WB: "You can really hold them at extraordinary levels … they're too hard to find. You're not going to find businesses that are as good. So then you have to say, 'Am I going to get a chance to buy back the same business at a lot lower price? Or am I going to buy something that's almost as good at a lot lower price?' We don't think we're very good at doing that. We'd rather just sit and hold the business and pretend the stock market doesn't exist. That actually has worked out way better for us than I would've predicted twenty years ago. There's been a fair amount of good fortune that's flowed out of that that I really wouldn't have predicted."

1997 MEETING (00:14:16)

WB: "I talked in the annual report about Coca-Cola and Gillette as being 'The Inevitables,' and what wonderful businesses they were. I thought it was appropriate to discuss them so that people would not take that as an unqualified 'buy' recommendation; they're absolutely wonderful companies run by outstanding managers, but you can pay too much, at least in the short run, for businesses like that.

"No matter how wonderful a business it is, there is always a risk that you will pay a price where it will take a few years for the business to catch up with the stock. The stock can get ahead of the business. And I don't know where that point is with those companies or any other companies, but I did say that I thought that the risks were fairly high that that situation existed with most securities in the market, including companies such as 'The Inevitables.' I wanted to make sure that people did not take the remarks I made about those companies as an unqualified buy recommendation regardless of price. We have no intention of selling those two stocks; we wouldn't sell them if they were selling at prices considerably higher than they are now. But I didn't want relatively unsophisticated people to see those names there and then think, 'This guy is touting these as a wonderful buy.'

"Generally speaking, I think if you're sure enough about a business being wonderful, it's more important to be certain about the business being a wonderful business than it is to be certain that the price is 5% or 10% too high. And that's a philosophy I came slowly to.

"I originally was incredibly price conscious. We used to have prayer meetings before we would raise our bid an eighth. But that was a mistake. And in some cases, a huge mistake; we've missed things because of that. We never try to predict the stock market. We do try to price securities. We try to price businesses. And we find it hard to find wonderful, good, average, or substandard businesses that look to us like they're cheap right now. But you don't always get a chance to buy things cheap."

CM: "The one thing we can confidently guarantee is real, inflation-adjusted returns from investing in a standard collection of stocks will be lower in the long-term future than they've been in the last fifteen years or so. This has been an unprecedented period, and there will be some regression toward the mean in average returns from investing in the stock market."

WB: "American business has done extraordinarily well in the last decade-plus. Interest rates have fallen over the last fifteen years, and that's a big plus for stocks. Anytime interest rates go down, the value of every financial asset goes up, in a rational calculation. Those factors have combined in recent years to produce conditions that enhance the true value of American businesses—but those are widely recognized now.

"Ben Graham used to say you can get in more trouble in investments with a good premise than with a bad premise, because the bad premise will shout out to you immediately as being fallacious, whereas a good premise will work for a while. Businesses are worth more money if interest rates fall; but eventually the market action of the securities themselves creates its own rationale for a large crop of buyers, and people forget about the reasons and the mathematical limitations implied in what got them excited in the first place. And after a while, rising prices alone will keep people excited and cause more people to enter the game. The good premise, after a while, is forgotten except for the fact that it produced these rising prices. And the prices themselves take over.

"In 1924 Edgar Lawrence Smith wrote a fine book on why stocks were better than bonds, and that was sort of the bible of the bull market of the 1920s; it made sense if you paid attention to a couple of the caveats in his book, which related to price. But people tend to forget about the importance of the price they pay as the experience of a bull market just sort of dulls the senses generally."

1997 MEETING (05:05:59)

WB: "I think it's usually a bad mistake to sell your interest in wonderful businesses. I don't think people find them that often. And I think they get hung up, if they've sold them at X, that they then want to buy them back at 90% of X, or 85% of X, so they'll never go back in at 105% of X. I think, on balance, if you are in a business that you understand and you think it's a really outstanding business, the presumption should be that you just hold it and don't worry. And if it goes down 25% or 30% in price, if you have more money available, buy more. And if you don't, so what? Just look at the business and judge how it's doing."

1998 MEETING (00:25:50)

WB: "The best thing to do is buy a stock that you don't ever want to sell—and that's what we're trying to do. That's true when we buy an entire business like GEICO, See's Candies, or The Buffalo News. We're not buying those to resell.

What we're trying to do is buy a business that we will be happy with if we own it the rest of our lives, and we expect to with those.

"The same principle applies to stocks. You get extra options with marketable securities: You can add to holdings. We can never own more than 100% of a business, but if we own 2% of a publicly traded business and we like it at a given price, we can take our ownership interest to 4% or 5%. So that's an advantage. ... We think they're wonderful businesses or we wouldn't own them at all. ... The real thing to do with a great business is to just hang on for dear life."

CM: "Sales that do happen, the ideal way is when you've found something you like immensely better. Isn't it obvious that that's the ideal way to sell?"

WB: "And, incidentally, the ideal purchase is to have something you already like to be selling at a price where you feel like buying more of it. We probably should have done more of that in the past in some situations. But that's the beauty of marketable securities. If you're in a wonderful business, you do get a chance, periodically, maybe to double up in it, or something. If the stock market were to sell a lot cheaper than it is now, we would probably buy more of the businesses we already own. They would certainly be the first ones that we would think about. They're the businesses we like best."

PAYING UP FOR QUALITY

1998 MEETING (04:43:24)

CM: "The investment game always involves considering both quality and price. The trick is to get more quality than you're paying for in the price. It's just that simple—but it's not easy."

PART THREE:
Capital Allocation

"It's a little bit like getting to Carnegie Hall playing the violin and then you walk out on the stage and they hand you a piano. Berkshire would not do well if somebody was put in who had a lot of skills in other areas but really did not have capital allocation abilities."

"We want to buy easy things. We do not have to prove our manhood by doing something terribly difficult. And I think a lot of managements feel that necessity."

"You don't want to keep accumulating so much money that it burns a hole in your pocket. It's been said that a full wallet is a little like a full bladder, that you may get an urge fairly quickly to pee it away, and we don't want that to happen."

INTRODUCTION

Capital allocation, particularly as it relates inorganic growth (M&A) and capital returns to shareholders (dividends and share repurchases), is a topic that attracts the attention of various stakeholders, including politicians. Unfortunately, their perception on the rationale for certain capital allocation decisions, most notably share repurchases, is often misunderstood. In many cases, that misunderstanding also applies to management teams: the track record for corporate America on share repurchases has historically been poor, which reflects the deleterious impact of short-term pressures, misaligned incentives, and an insufficient understanding of how to weigh the various available options. This can result in significant value destruction. For that reason, this has been a frequent topic of discussion for Buffett and Munger at the meetings over the decades.

This comment, from Munger at the 2018 annual meeting, strikes at the heart of the matter: "People want to find some formula. It's what I call 'physics envy.' These academics want the world to be like physics. But the world isn't like physics, outside of physics. And that false precision does nothing but get you in trouble. I would say you need to master the general ideas, and you have got to work to improve your judgment slowly, the way all the rest of us had to."

SUBJECTS AND MEETINGS FEATURED

in mind the possibilities of repurchases. But it should be determined by whether a dollar left in the business is worth more to the shareholder than a dollar paid out."

2000 MEETING (01:34:25)

WB: "If we can keep $1 and it becomes, on a present-value basis, worth more than $1, it's foolish to pay it out. To date, we have felt that if we keep $1 and use it in buying other businesses, or whatever it may be, it becomes worth more than $1 on a present-value basis. That's subjective, but any given decision like that is subjective. Over time, you get an objective test as to whether we do indeed create more value for each $1 of retained earnings. If that changed—and it could change—then we would give the money to shareholders. It might be done through repurchases or dividends, but there's no reason to keep $1 in the business that's worth $0.90 if you keep it in the business ...

"I think we would be fairly objective about figuring out whether we are indeed creating or destroying value by retaining earnings. We would never have a conventional dividend policy. The idea of paying out 20% or 30% of earnings in dividends strikes us as nuts. You may get yourself in a position where you have to do it because you build these expectations in people's minds, but there is no logic to it whatsoever. If you create more than $1 of value for $1 retained, why in the world would you pay it out? The people who want to get $1 as a dividend can instead get a $1.10 by selling the stock for the value that was retained.

"So, it's a very simple dividend philosophy, and I see nothing that would change in terms of the principles of it. ... Obviously, we aren't going to decide every week or every month whether we can employ money that week at a higher rate of return. But in terms of a reasonable expectancy over a couple-year period, whether we think we can use retained earnings advantageously, that's our yardstick."

CM: "What's interesting about what Warren is saying about logical dividend policy is that if you went to all the leading business schools of the United States, all the leading economics departments and all the professors of corporate finance, this wouldn't be the way they teach the subject. In other words, we're basically saying we're right and all the rest of academia is wrong."

M&A AT GREAT BUSINESSES

2002 MEETING (02:16:42)

WB: "Gillette has not done as well with acquisitions, which is clear. The acquisition of Duracell resulted in giving twenty-odd per cent of the business for another business, and that business has not done nearly as well as management or the investment bankers thought it was going to do."

CM: "I would say that's the normal result. When you've got a wonderful business and you issue shares in it to buy another business, at least two times out of three, it's a terrible idea."

WB: "In the last twenty years GEICO went into at least three other insurance businesses I can think of ... they were all disasters. I don't know why in the hell they would go into them. They had a great, great insurance business, and there aren't that many great insurance businesses. Why, when you have an absolutely wonderful business, would you start buying others that are obviously mediocre, where you bring nothing to the party? But it's very human to want to do that ... we see it happen time after time after time.

"I can tell you this: Charlie and I have no urges like that. We want to buy easy things. We do not have to prove our manhood by doing something terribly difficult. And I think a lot of managements feel that necessity. The cigarette companies did that; they had these great businesses, and it irritated them. They liked to think they were business geniuses, so they would go out and buy other businesses; generally, that did not go well. I'm not saying they should've been in the cigarette business, but they were not business geniuses because they had made a lot of money selling an addictive product. So they wanted to prove it other ways—and they fell on their faces in many cases."

CM: "I think a lot of the people who rise to the top in public companies, who come up in sales or engineering or drug development or what have you, it's natural to assume once you're sitting in the top chair that now you know pretty much everything. Or, at least, you'll know how to get wisdom out of this wonderful staff and all these outside advisors available to you. And so it's very natural that perfectly terrible acquisition decisions get made more often than not."

SHARE REPURCHASES

2015 MEETING (03:56:26)

WB: "There's been more stupid stuff written, and stupid stuff done, on such a simple activity as stock repurchases. It's a very simple decision, in my view, as to whether you repurchase your shares: You do it if you're taking care of the needs of the business and if your stock is selling for less than it's intrinsically worth. I don't see how anything could be more simple.

"If you had a partnership and the partner wanted to sell out to you at 120% of what the business was worth, you'd say forget it. And if he wanted to sell out at 80% of what it was worth, you'd take it. It's not complicated. But so many other motivations have entered into people's minds when deciding whether to repurchase shares. It's gotten to be a very contorted and kind of silly discussion in many cases.

"If you look at the history of share repurchases, they fall off like crazy when stocks are cheap and tend to go up dramatically when stocks get fully priced. That's not what we'll do at Berkshire. We would love to buy it at 120% of book, because we know it's worth a lot more than that; we don't know how much more, but we know it's a lot more. We don't get a chance to do that very often, but if we do get a chance, we'll do it, big time. But we won't buy it in at 200% of book, because it isn't worth it. It's not a complicated question, but I've been around a lot of managements that announce they're going to buy X worth and then they buy it regardless of price. A lot of times the price makes sense—but if it doesn't, they don't seem to stop, and nobody seems to want to stop them."

2023 MEETING (02:35:56)

WB: "Share repurchases can be the dumbest thing you can do or it can be the smartest thing you can do. Obviously, do what the business needs to do when the opportunities are there. Grow your present business, buy additional businesses, whatever it may be. Then you make the decision on dividends. But that decision becomes pretty irrevocable because you don't cut dividends without having major effects on your shareholder base and a lot of things. If you have ample capital and if your stock is attractive such that repurchases will enhance the intrinsic value for remaining shareholders, it's a no-brainer to repurchase shares. And if it's above the price of intrinsic value, it's a no-brainer not to do it."

REPURCHASES AT BERKSHIRE HATHAWAY

1994 MEETING (02:18:36)

WB: "We generally have felt market conditions that would make Berkshire attractively priced are probably going to make other things even more attractively priced, because we think our shareholders are more rational than those of many companies. It's more likely we will find some wonderful business at a silly price than we will find Berkshire at a silly price. That tends to eliminate repurchases. It doesn't rule them out, but it explains why circumstances will not arise very often where repurchases make good sense."

1995 MEETING (02:57:50)

WB: "We actually repurchased a few shares in the 1960s, but we basically have never bought back shares, although there were plenty of times when we thought it would be quite attractive to do it. But we've also felt that if we could create more than a dollar of market value—and maybe well over a dollar of market value—by retaining a dollar, that on balance would work better over time. As long as we can find ways to use the cash, to turn dollar bills into something larger than dollar bills, we'll retain the money. We won't measure that on whether we can find anything this week or this month, but we'll certainly measure it based on whether we can find anything in a couple of years.

"We've had dry spells a lot of times over a twenty-odd year period. I wound up the partnership during one dry spell. So, it's measured partly on what's going on now, and it's measured partly on the expectancy. Whether our stock is selling at 100% of X or 75% of X right now wouldn't make a lot of difference. But it would make a difference if we thought we couldn't find things to do with the money externally."

1997 MEETING (02:51:26)

WB: "If the market went in the tank, Berkshire stock would go in the tank, too. There shouldn't be anybody in this room who would not find it palatable, if not become positively enthusiastic, about Berkshire stock going down 50%. It would not bother Charlie or me, because we would have very intelligent things to do with whatever capital we came into. ... One of the intelligent things, possibly, could be to buy in our own stock. But that would imply our own stock was cheaper relative to value than anything else we could find among possible opportunities—and the chances are we could find things that were more attractive.

"Back in 1973 or 1974, when we were buying The Washington Post at a fraction of what it was worth, Berkshire stock may have been cheap, but it wasn't as cheap as The Washington Post. In 1988 and 1989, Berkshire stock may have been cheap, but it wasn't as cheap as Coca-Cola. It's unlikely among thousands of possible investments that Berkshire will be the most attractive at any time. But if it were, obviously, we would buy in our own stock. But if the Dow went down 50%, we would have plenty of interesting things to do—and we would not be unhappy."

CM: "We don't have any rule against it. Opportunity cost is the game around here."

1998 MEETING (02:00:01)

WB: "I think it's a valid criticism to say we have missed the boat at various times in not repurchasing shares. We'll see what we do in the future. If it looks like the best thing to do with money, it's what we should be doing. In the past, I probably wasn't optimistic enough on Berkshire compared to other things we were doing with money.

"We've never wanted to leverage up. That's just not our game. We've never wanted to borrow a lot of money to repurchase shares. We might advise other people to do it, but it's not our style ourselves. ... We have never wanted to leverage up this company like it was just one of a portfolio of a hundred stocks. But it's a valid criticism to say we have not repurchased shares when we should have. And it's also a valid criticism to say we've issued some shares we shouldn't have issued."

CM: "I'd agree with both comments."

1999 MEETING (04:04:25)

WB: "At times in the past when Berkshire seemed inefficiently priced, it always seemed to us that there were other securities that were even less efficiently priced—but we were incorrect in some cases. In 1974, when Berkshire sold at $50 a share, I might have thought it was cheap—but I was looking at the whole Washington Post Company selling for $80 million when I thought it was clearly worth $400 million. There have been times when I thought Berkshire was underpriced, even significantly underpriced, but at the same time I was finding other things I felt were even more attractive. And like I said, many times I was wrong. We would have been better off buying our own stock instead of the things that I was buying …

"I think it's difficult for most companies in this market, even though repurchases are close to or at an all-time high, to have a repurchase of shares that makes a whole lot of sense. I do not think they're getting much for their money, because we don't want to buy those shares ourselves. And I'm talking about the stock of various companies in America. And yet, companies are much more enthusiastic about repurchasing shares now than they were twenty years ago when they were getting far, far greater returns. … We're unlikely to repurchase our shares unless we think they're fairly dramatically underpriced because we would want a big margin for error in making that kind of a decision. We would not want to buy a dollar bill for $0.95, $0.94, or $0.93. But there is some level where we would get excited if we didn't have other uses for the money."

2012 MEETING (00:29:19)

WB: "Repurchases at 1.1× book value is a figure that we feel very comfortable with. We would probably feel comfortable with a figure somewhat higher than that, but we want it to be very significantly undervalued to do buybacks, and we want to be very sure that every shareholder that sells to us knows that we think that it's significantly undervalued when we do it. … If we get the chance to do it, as long as we don't take our cash position below $20 billion, we would buy very aggressively at 1.1× book. We know we're making significant money for remaining shareholders at that level. The value per share goes up when we buy at 110% of book, and it's so obvious to us, that we would do it on a big scale if given the chance to. … We will only do it for one reason, and that's to increase the per-share value the day after we've done it. If we get a chance to do that in a big way, we'll do it. Strictly operating as a financial guy, I would hope we get a chance to do a lot of it. Operating as a fiduciary for thousands of people, I don't want to see them sell."

CM: "We hope the opportunity never comes."

WB: "Yes—but if it does, we'll grab it."

2016 MEETING (02:41:47)

WB: "Clearly in my view, Charlie's view, and the board's view, the stock is worth significantly more than 1.2× book value, but it should be worth significantly more, or we wouldn't have the repurchase limit set at that level. On the other hand, we did move it up from 1.1× to 1.2× because we had acquired more businesses over time where the differential between our carrying value and book value—the intrinsic value of Berkshire—had widened from when we set the 1.1×.

"I have mixed emotions on the whole thing. From a strictly financial standpoint, and from the standpoint of the continuing shareholders, I love the idea of buying it at 1.2×, which means I probably would love the idea of buying it a little higher than 1.2×. It's the surest way of making money per share; if you can buy dollar bills for anything less than a dollar, there's no more certain way of making money.

"On the other hand, I don't particularly enjoy the actual act of buying out people who are my partners at a price that is well below what I think the stock is worth. But we will buy stock, almost certainly ... Would we increase the multiple of book value? Perhaps. If we run out of ideas—I don't mean day by day—but if it really becomes apparent that we can't use capital effectively within the company, in the quantities with which it's being generated, then at some point the threshold might be moved up a little because it could still be attractive to buy it. You don't want to keep accumulating so much money that it burns a hole in your pocket. It's been said that a full wallet is a little like a full bladder, that you may get an urge fairly quickly to pee it away, and we don't want that to happen. But so far that hasn't happened.

"If it ever gets to where we have $100 billion or $120 billion around, we might have to increase the price. Anytime you can buy stock in for less than it's worth, it's advantageous to the continuing shareholders, but it should be by a demonstrable margin. Intrinsic value can't be that finely calculated that you can figure it out to four decimal places or anything of the sort."

CM: "You'll notice that elsewhere in corporate America these buyback plans get a life of their own, and it's become quite common to buy back stock at very high prices that really don't do the shareholders any good at all. I don't know why people are doing it. I think it gets to be fashionable."

WB: "It's fashionable and they get sold on it by advisors. Can you imagine somebody saying we're going to buy a business and we don't care what the price is? But that's what companies do when they don't attach some kind of a metric to buybacks. To say we're going to buy back $5 billion of stock—maybe they don't want to publicize the metric, but certainly they should say we're going to buy back $5 billion of stock if it's advantageous to buy it back. If they say we're going to buy the XYZ Company, they say, we'll buy it at this price, but we won't buy it at 120% of that price.

"Jamie Dimon at J.P. Morgan is very explicit about saying he's going to buy back the stock when he thinks it's below intrinsic value. But I have seen hundreds of buyback notices, and I've sat on boards of directors where they have voted buybacks and basically said they were doing it to prevent dilution or something like that. It's got nothing to do with preventing dilution. Dilution by itself is a negative—and buying back your stock at too high a price is another negative. It has to be related to valuation. And, as I say, you will not find a lot of press releases about buybacks that say a word about valuation."

CM: "We're always behaving a lot like what some might call the Episcopal prayer. We prayerfully thank the Lord that we're not like these other religions who are inferior. I'm afraid there's probably too much of that in Berkshire, but we can't help it."

2019 MEETING (00:42:03)

WB: "We have the money to buy $100 billion worth of stock. And bear in mind, if we're buying in $100 billion stock, it probably would be that the company wasn't selling at $500 billion. So, it might buy well over 20%. We will spend a lot of money. We've been involved in companies where the number of shares was reduced 70% or 80% over time. And we like the idea of buying shares at a discount. We do feel, if we're going to be repurchasing shares from shareholders who are partners, and we think it's cheap, we ought to be very sure that they have the facts available to evaluate what they own. ... It's very important that our disclosure be the same sort of disclosure that I would give to my sisters—they're the shareholders to whom I address the annual report every year. Because I do feel that you, if you're going to sell your stock, should have the same information that's important to me and to Charlie. But if our stock gets cheap, relative to intrinsic value, we will not hesitate. We wouldn't be able to buy that much in a very short period of time, in all likelihood. But we would certainly be willing to spend $100 billion."

CM: "I think when it gets really obvious, we'll be very good at it."

WB: "We don't have any trouble being decisive. ... If you and I are partners, and our business is worth $1 million, and you say you'll sell your half for $300,000, you'll have your $300,000 very quickly."

2023 MEETING (04:05:49)

WB: "If Berkshire shares are selling for less than we think they're worth, that could be a big way to distribute cash. What we really like to do is buy great businesses. If we could buy a company for $50 billion or $100 billion, we could do it. But it's difficult with a public company because, in effect, if you make a bid on a company, then their shareholders vote months later—you're giving them an option. Now another guy has a way to top your offer, all kinds of things. If they get out of it, then you get paid a 2% fee or whatever, which is not an appropriate price. ... It's easier to do with a private company, but there are not very many which are that big. On the other hand, there's nobody else that can quite make a deal like we can under the right circumstances. And there could be a situation where a number of very decent companies have a very uncomfortable borrowing structure and money comes due to them at the exact wrong time. That's when they pick up the phone, as Harley-Davidson and a whole bunch of other companies did in 2008.

"That sort of thing will happen again; and the number of phone calls you can make (as the borrower) at a time like that is very, very limited, and they can be good companies. They may not want to sell the company necessarily, but they may need $5 billion, $10 billion, or $20 billion, depending on the company you're talking about. Our own shareholders can sell the stock too cheap—and we'll never do anything to make them sell cheap, but if market circumstances result in us being able to buy in $50 billion of our own stock, we'll buy it. So, we'll see what the world holds. We don't have the opportunities we used to have, but we're making money. It isn't killing us to hold $130 billion of T-bills at 5%+ bond equivalent yields. I don't have the faintest idea what yields will do in the future. The prime rate was 21.5% in 1981, and people were worried that it was going to go totally out of control. If Volcker hadn't been in there, who would know what would happen. But we're running Berkshire so that we'll do OK, and maybe we'll do a little bit better than OK."

REPURCHASES AT WONDERFUL BUSINESSES

1997 MEETING (02:01:20)

WB: "Gillette hasn't repurchased its shares in any significant quantity for many years. Coca-Cola consistently repurchases its shares. We generally like the policy of companies with really wonderful businesses repurchasing shares. There aren't that many super businesses in the world, and the idea of owning more and more of a company like that over time has an appeal to us, and almost an appeal regardless of price. The problem is that most companies that repurchase their shares are frequently so-so businesses. They're being done for motivations other than intensifying the interests of the shareholders in a wonderful business. But when you really know you have a wonderful business—and we think most of the ones we own are anywhere from extremely good to wonderful—it usually makes a lot of sense."

1997 MEETING (03:28:30)

WB: "Someplace like Coca-Cola, if they paid no dividends and simply repurchased shares and developed the bottling system and did the things that they have done, the shareholders probably would've been even better off. They've been sensationally well off as it is. But they probably would've been even better off than they have been with the dividend policy they have had. And that's true for Gillette and Disney and the companies of that sort that have got these terrific opportunities to use capital within the business or to repurchase shares of a company that simply can't be replaced. That's usually the best use of capital. It's probably better than dividends."

1998 MEETING (01:04:55)

WB: "It sounds like a very high price in terms of a [40×] P/E to buy back stock at that sort of number. But Coca-Cola's been around 112 years, and there are very few times in that 112 years, if any, when it would not have been smart for Coca-Cola to be repurchasing its shares. Among businesses that I can understand, Coca-Cola is in my view the best large business in the world. It is a fantastic business. And we love it when Coke repurchases shares and our interest goes up. We owned 6.3% of Coca-Cola in 1988 when we bought in. We actually increased that a little bit a few years later. But if they had not repurchased shares, we would own about 6.7% or 6.8% of Coke now. As it is, we own a little over 8.0% through repurchases. There are going to be about one billion eight-ounce servings of Coca-Cola products sold around the world today. And 8% is 80 million and 6.8% is 68 million. So, there are 12 million extra servings for the account of Berkshire Hathaway being sold around the world. And they're making a little over a penny a serving, so that gets me kind of excited. All I can tell you is I approve of Coke repurchasing shares. I would much rather have them repurchasing shares at 15× earnings, but when I look at other ways to use capital, I still think it's a very good use of capital. Maybe the day will come when they can buy it at 20× earnings—and if they can, I hope they go out and borrow a lot of money to buy a ton of it at those prices.

"I think we will be better off 20 years from now if Coke follows a consistent repurchase approach. I do not think that is true for many companies. I think repurchases have become *en vogue* and done for a lot of silly reasons. I don't think everybody's repurchases are well reasoned at all. We see companies issue options by the ton and then they repurchase shares much higher. I started reading about investments when I was six, and the first thing that I read was buy low, sell high. But these companies, through options, sell low and buy high. They've got a different formula than I was taught. So, there are a number that we don't approve of. When we own stock in a wonderful business, we like the idea of repurchases, even at prices that may give you nose bleeds. It generally turns out to be a pretty good policy."

CM: "I think the answer is that in any company the stock could get to a price so high it would be foolish for the corporation to repurchase its shares. And you can even get into gross abuse. Before the 1929 Crash, Sam Insull's utilities were madly buying their own shares as a way of promoting the stock higher. It was like a giant Ponzi scheme at the end. All kinds of excess is possible, but the really great companies that buy at high P/Es—that can be wise."

WB: "Our interest in GEICO went from 33% to 50% without us laying out a dime, because GEICO was repurchasing its shares. And we've benefited substantially. But we benefitted a lot more, obviously, when prices were lower. Our interest in The Washington Post went from 9% to 17% over the years without us buying a single share. But The Post, Coca-Cola, or any number of companies, don't get the bargain in repurchasing their shares that they used to. We still think it's probably the best use of many in many cases."

REPURCHASES AT BANKS

1994 MEETING (00:52:40)

WB: "There's much more repurchasing going on [at banks], and that's simply a judgment call by management as to the level of capital needed going forward, and what level of capital enables them to earn the return on equity (ROE) they think appropriate, and what they feel like paying for their own shares. So, I think you have to look at that case by case. If we own shares in a bank, we certainly like the idea of them repurchasing stock at a price we think is attractive. We would think that they probably knew more about their own bank than some other bank they were going to buy, and if the numbers are right, it's an attractive way to use capital."

1996 MEETING (04:33:23)

WB: "Wells Fargo should repurchase their shares if they feel that they're below intrinsic business value. ... That will determine whether the repurchase program makes good sense or not."

REPURCHASES AT COCA-COLA

1995 MEETING (00:04:04)

WB: "I commend managements that have a wonderful business for utilizing cash in those wonderful businesses, or in businesses they understand that will also have wonderful economics, and for giving the rest of the money back to the shareholders. Coca-Cola, in my book, is doing exactly the right thing with its cash when it uses all it can, effectively, in the business to expand in new markets and all of that sort of thing—but then beyond that, it pays a dividend which distributes cash to shareholders, and then it repurchases shares in a big way, which returns cash on a selective basis to shareholders, but in a way that benefits all of them."

1996 MEETING (01:24:41)

WB: "If you're repurchasing shares above a rationally calculated intrinsic value, you are harming your shareholders, just as if you issue shares beneath that figure, you are harming your shareholders. That's a truism. Now, the tough part of that, of course, is coming up with the intrinsic value. A good example might be Coca-Cola.

"I think a number of people might have thought Coca-Cola was repurchasing shares at a very high price, because they'll look at book value or P/E ratios. But there's a lot more to intrinsic value than book value and P/E ratios. … The management has been very forthright over the years, saying that by repurchasing their shares, they are adding to the value per share for remaining shareholders. People who didn't understand Coca-Cola, or who thought mechanistic methods of valuation should take precedence, really misjudged the value of those repurchases.

"When you have a wonderful business, we favor using funds that are generated out of that business to make the business even more wonderful. And we favor repurchasing shares if they are below intrinsic value. And I would say that if it's a really wonderful business, we probably come up with higher intrinsic values than most people do. Charlie and I—and I think it's developed over the years—have enormous respect for the power of a really outstanding business. And we recognize how scarce they are. And if a management wishes to further intensify our ownership by repurchasing shares, we applaud it. … Our percentage interest in Coca-Cola has gone up significantly through their repurchases. And we are better off because they have bought those shares at what looked like, to some people, perhaps, high prices. We thought [the critics] were wrong at the time, and I think now it's been proven. If you're trying to decide on the wisdom of repurchases, you don't think in terms of book value. You don't think in terms of specific P/Es. You don't think in terms of any little model. You think in terms of what you really would pay to be in those businesses. That's what counts over time, whether the repurchases are made at a discount from that figure."

1997 MEETING (02:01:20)

WB: "Coca-Cola has been very intelligent about using their capital to fortify and improve their bottler network around the world. They've done a terrific job. That was a neglected area for a long time. ... But there's only so far you can go with that. When we bought our first Coca-Cola shares in 1988, we bought about 6.2% of the company. And at that time, there may have been 600 million servings a day. So we had an interest in 37 million servings. Now we have 8% of 900 million-plus servings. So, we have an interest in 75 million or so servings a day ... And the profit's gone up a little per serving. That gets pretty attractive. ... They used capital beyond [bottler network investments] to repurchase shares in a big way, and it's been very smart. They are repurchasing shares, probably, as we talk—and that's fine with me."

PART FOUR:
Management and Board of Directors

"If you hire somebody without integrity, you really want them to be dumb and lazy, don't you? The last thing in the world you want from someone who lacks integrity is for them to be smart and energetic."

"We have no human relations department, no legal department, no investor relations, no public relations, we don't have any of that. We've got a bunch of all-stars out there running businesses. We ask them to mail the money to Omaha. But beyond that, it would be foolish."

"The important thing we do with managers, generally, is to find the .400 hitters and then not tell them how to swing."

"We have a number of people working for us that have no financial need to work at all. And they probably outwork 95% or more of the people in the world, and they do it because they just love smacking the ball."

"A lot of the corporate compensation plans of the modern era work just about the way things would work for a farmer if you put a rat colony in the granary."

INTRODUCTION

In a similar vein to how Buffett and Munger have preached the importance of business quality as an input to long-term investment success, they have also opined on the impact that management plays in that outcome. With time, the interplay between the two draws them closer together; said differently, best-in-class managers have a knack for positioning their companies well over time (discarding/minimizing their exposure to undesirable businesses while growing/maximizing their exposure to desirable businesses). As with many of the key investment and business lessons in this book, there are few examples that show this more clearly than Berkshire itself: What started as a loss-making textile manufacturer that was destined for failure, in due time evolved over six decades into a thriving conglomerate that has eclipsed a $1 trillion market capitalization.

Given that they've observed this relationship from various angles—as minority shareholders dealing with public company CEOs, as board members at various companies over the decades, in dealing with the CEOs of Berkshire's subsidiaries, and in being CEOs themselves—Buffett and Munger are unique in their personal experience of the incentives and other considerations that factor into the principal-agent problem that can arise between owners and managers. In this section, they discuss the key lessons learned over time about how to best deal with that issue.

SUBJECTS AND MEETINGS FEATURED

JUDGING MANAGEMENT

1994 MEETING (00:28:30)

WARREN BUFFETT: "I think you judge management by two yardsticks. One is how well they run the business. You can learn a lot about that by reading about what they've accomplished and what their competitors have accomplished, and seeing how they have allocated capital over time.

"You have to have some understanding of the hand they were dealt when they got a chance to play the hand. But, if you understand something about the business they're in—and you can't understand it in every business, but you can find industries or companies where you can understand it—then you simply want to look at how well they have played the hand they've been dealt.

"The second thing you want to figure out is how well they treat their owners. I think you can get a handle on that oftentimes, but a lot of times you can't. There are many companies somewhere in the 20th to 80th percentile, and it's a little hard to pick out where they fall. But it's not hard to figure out that, say, Bill Gates [at Microsoft], Tom Murphy [at Capital Cities], Don Keough [at Coca-Cola], people like that, are really outstanding managers. And it's not hard to figure out who they're working for.

"I can give you some cases on the other end of the spectrum, too. It's interesting how often the ones that, in my view, are poor managers also turn out to be the ones that really don't think that much about shareholders; the two often go hand in hand. By reading competitors' reports, you'll get a fix on that in some cases. You don't have to make fifty or a hundred correct judgments in this business; you only have to make a few. And that's all we try to do. Generally speaking, the conclusions I've come to about managers have really come about the same way you can make yours. They come by reading reports rather than any intimate personal knowledge of the managers. Read the proxy statements, see how they treat themselves versus how they treat shareholders, look at what they have accomplished, and consider what hand they were dealt when they took over compared to what is going on in the industry. You can figure it out sometimes. You don't have to figure it out very often."

2005 MEETING (00:16:54)

WB: "We want to buy from somebody who doesn't really want to sell. If we hand somebody $1 billion for their business, they have no financial need to work. They have to want to work, and we can't stand there with a whip. We don't have any contracts at Berkshire; as far as I'm concerned, they don't work. We hope they love their business, and then we do everything possible to avoid extinguishing, or in any way dampening, that love.

"What we're looking for beyond this passion is intelligence, energy, and integrity—and if they don't have the last one, the first two will kill you. If you hire somebody without integrity, you really want them to be dumb and lazy, don't you? The last thing in the world you want from someone who lacks integrity is for them to be smart and energetic ..."

MANAGING BERKSHIRE'S SUBSIDIARIES

1998 MEETING (02:51:33)

WB: "We may meet with some of our managers annually or semiannually, but we have no formal system whatsoever, and we will never have a formal system. We don't demand any meetings of our managers. We have no operating plan submitted to headquarters. They are all run by people who have terrific records, and they have different batting styles. We're not about to tinker with somebody that's batting .375 just because somebody else holds the bat a little differently or uses a different weight bat. We believe in letting them do, currently and in the future, what has been successful for them in the past. And different people have very different styles. We have managers that like to talk things over, we have other managers that like to go their own way. We have managers that have a by-the-book approach which works well, we have other managers who wouldn't dream of that. Most managers probably have monthly statements of financials, others don't. That really isn't a problem.

"What we want to have is good managers. There's more than one way to get to business heaven, and we have a number that have found different ways to get there. We have certain requirements because we're a public company; SEC requirements and IRS coordination. But we've never imposed anything from the top on the operating managements. We have MBAs running companies; we have people who never saw a business school. Talent is the scarce commodity, and when you find talent and they've got their own way of doing things, we're delighted to have them do it. We want them to do it their way."

CHARLIE MUNGER: "The truth of the matter is that we have decentralized power in the operating businesses to a point just short of total abdication. We don't think our system is right for everybody. It has suited us and the kind of people that have joined us. But we don't have criticism for people who have operating plans, and compare performance quarterly against plan, and all sorts of things. It's just not our style."

WB: "We centralize money. Everything else we decentralize, pretty much. ... Our managers know their businesses and they know how to run them. And if they didn't, we'd do something about the manager, we wouldn't try and build a bunch of systems."

1998 MEETING (03:32:27)

WB: "We tell each subsidiary to run their business in the way that they think is best for their operation. Borsheims takes American Express, See's takes American Express, the Furniture Mart doesn't. But that'll be true in other areas, too ... We will never tell a subsidiary manager which vendor to patronize or anything of that sort. Once we start making decisions for our managers in that respect then we become responsible for the operation, and they are no longer responsible for the operation. They are responsible for their operations, and that means they get to call the decisions. They should do what is best for their subsidiary, and it's up to any other company that wants to do business with them to prove why that is best for them. That's the Berkshire approach to things. And I think, on balance, our managers like it that way. They're not getting second-guessed and somebody can't go over their head. I get letters all the time from people who are trying to jump over the heads of our managers. It doesn't work at Berkshire. They deal with the managers of the businesses and they're not going to get around them."

2011 MEETING (02:15:19)

CM: "If you look at the greatest institutions in the world, they select very trustworthy people, and they trust them a lot. It's so much fun to be trusted. There's so much self-respect you get from it when you are trusted and are worthy of the trust, that I think your best compliance cultures are the ones which have this attitude of trust. Some of the ones with the biggest compliance departments, like Wall Street, have the most scandals. So, it's not so simple that you can make your behavior better automatically just by making the compliance department bigger and bigger and bigger. This general culture of trust is what works. Berkshire hasn't had that many scandals of consequence, and I don't think we're going to get huge numbers, either."

RETAINING GREAT MANAGERS

1994 MEETING (00:31:47)

WB: "If [Ajit Jain] gets offered $200 million, we may not compete too vigorously at that level. Charlie and I have two jobs: We have to identify, and then keep, good managers interested after we've figured out who they are. That often is a little different here, because I would say a majority of our managers are financially independent, so that they don't go to work because they are worried about putting kids through school or putting food on the table. They need some reason to go to work aside from that. They have to be treated fairly in terms of compensation, but they also have to figure it is better than playing golf every day or whatever it may be. So that's one of the jobs we have. And we look at what they do the same way we look at what we do.

"Before I ran this, I had a partnership. I had a great group of partners. And, essentially, I liked to be left alone to do what I did. I liked to be judged on the scorecard at the end of the year rather than on every stroke—and not second-guessed in a way that was inappropriate. I liked to have people who understood the environment in which I was operating.

"The important thing we do with managers, generally, is to find the .400 hitters and then not tell them how to swing. The second thing we do is allocate capital. So, with any manager, we try to make it interesting and fun for them to run their business. We try to have a compensation arrangement that's appropriate for the kind of business they're in. We have no company-wide compensation plan. We wouldn't dream of having some compensation expert or consultant come in and screw it up. Some businesses require a lot of capital, some require no capital. Some are easy businesses where good profit margins are a cinch to come by, but we're really paying for the extra beyond that. Some are very tough businesses to make money in. It would be crazy to have some huge framework that we try to place everybody in where one size would fit all. People, generally, are compensated in some manner that relates to how their business does. There's no reason to pay anybody based on how Berkshire does, because no one has responsibility for that except Charlie and me. We try to make them responsible for their own units, and compensated based on how those units do. We try to understand the businesses they're in, so we know the difference between good performance and bad performance. And that's how we work with people. We've had terrific luck over the years in retaining the managers that we wanted to retain. I think, largely, that's because—particularly if they sell us a business—to a great extent, the next day they're running it just as they were the day before. And they're having as much fun running their business as I am running Berkshire."

CM: "I believe in that concept of treating the other fellow the way you'd like to be treated if the roles were reversed—it's so simple when you stop to think about it. It's a rare evening when Ajit and Warren aren't talking on the phone. It's more than a business relationship, at least it seems that way to me. ... We like our relationships to be more than a business relationship."

WB: "Charlie and I get to work with people we like. It makes life a lot simpler."

CM: "And we tend to like people we admire."

1998 MEETING (02:27:45)

WB: "When we buy businesses, we don't have managers to put in them; we are not buying them that way. We don't have a lot of MBAs around the office."

CM: "Thank God."

WB: "So, as a practical matter, we need management with the businesses that we buy. And three times out of four, or thereabouts, the manager is the owner and is receiving tens of millions, maybe hundreds of millions of dollars for their business, so they won't have to work anymore. We have to decide when we meet them whether they love the business or love money. I'm not making a moral judgment about whether it's better to love the business or to love the money, but it's very important for me to know which of the two is the primary motivator with them.

"We have had extremely good luck in identifying people who love their business. So, all we have to do is avoid anything on our part that diminishes that love of the business or makes other conditions so intolerable that they overcome that love of the business. We have a number of people working for us that have no financial need to work at all. And they probably outwork 95% or more of the people in the world, and they do it because they just love smacking the ball. We've virtually had no mistakes in that respect.

"We have identified a number of people, in terms of proposals to us, where we've felt they really liked the money better than the business. They were kind of tired of the business. And they might promise us that they would continue on and they would do it in good faith, but something would happen six months or a year later and they'd say to themselves, 'Why am I doing this for Berkshire Hathaway?' They could be doing whatever else they wanted to do. I can't tell you exactly what filter we put them through mentally, but I can tell you that if you've been around a while, I think you can have a pretty high batting average in coming to those conclusions—as you can about other aspects of human behavior. ... When you see the extreme cases, the ones that are going to cause you nothing but trouble, or the ones that are going to bring you nothing but joy, I think you can identify those pretty well."

CM: "It's pretty simple. You've got integrity, intelligence, experience, and dedication. That's what enterprises need to run well, and we've been very lucky in getting this marvelous group of associates to work with all these years. It would be hard to do better, I think, than we've done in that respect. Look at how much gratification can come into these lives which have been mostly spent in deferring gratification. You shareholders are a very funny group of people."

BUREAUCRACY

1994 MEETING (01:29:35)

CM: "I have always preferred the system of retirement where you can't quite tell, observing from the outside, whether the man is working or retired. A problem in many businesses, particularly the more bureaucratic ones, is your employees retire, but they don't tell you."

EXECUTIVE STOCK OPTIONS

1995 MEETING (00:18:06)

CM: "There was a particular bank where one of the officers wanted stock options, and he pointed out to management that they could issue shares and it didn't cost anything. Now, imagine hiring a manager who thinks that way and paying them money to behave like Judas in your very midst."

WB: "We have had conversations with managers where they tell us how fortunate they feel because the stock is down and they can issue options cheaper. If they were issuing those to the third parties, I'm not sure whether they'd have exactly the same attitude."

CEOS AND CAPITAL ALLOCATION

1994 MEETING (03:24:10)

WB: "Capital allocation is usually a very important job for most managements. If you take a CEO in a job for ten years, and he has a business that earns 12% on equity, and he pays out a third, that means he's got 8% per year of equity. When you think of his tenure in office, how much capital he's allocated, it's an enormous factor over time. And yet, probably relatively few CEOs are either trained for, or are selected on, the basis of their ability to allocate capital. … It's a different function than other functions that exist along the routes to the CEO job at most companies.

"When many CEOs get there, they think they can solve it by either having a staff that does it, or by hiring consultants, or whatever it may be. In our view, that's a terrible mistake. If not the key function of the CEO, it's one of the two or three key functions at 80% to 90% of all companies. And if you can't do it yourself, you're going to make a lot of mistakes. … You wouldn't want anybody in any other position of that importance in the company essentially saying, 'I don't know how to do this, so I'm going to have somebody else do it,' when it's their key responsibility. But that's the way it works in business. Charlie and I take responsibility for all capital allocation decisions, other than routine expenditures at the operating businesses."

AVOIDING BAD ACTORS

1995 MEETING (03:37:50)

WB: "We basically have the attitude that you can't make a good deal with a bad person, so we just forget about it. We don't try and protect ourselves with contracts or getting into all kinds of due diligence, we just forget about it. We can do fine over time dealing with people we like, admire, and trust. The bad actor will tend to try and tantalize you in one way or another, and you won't win. It just pays to avoid them. We started out with that attitude, and maybe one or two experiences have convinced us even more so than before that that's the way to play the game."

ADDRESSING BAD NEWS

1995 MEETING (02:01:40)

WB: "Charlie and I are always more interested in bad news than good news; we figure the good news will take care of itself. We only give a couple of instructions to people when they go to work for us. One of them is to think like an owner, and the second is to just tell us the bad news immediately; we can take bad news, but we don't like bad news late."

2017 MEETING (00:16:13)

WB: "It's true that we at Berkshire certainly operate on a more decentralized plan than any company of remotely our size. We count very heavily on principles of behavior rather than loads of rules. It's one reason at every annual meeting you see that Salomon description ["Lose money for the firm, and I will be understanding; lose a shred of reputation for the firm, and I will be ruthless."] I write very few communiqués to our managers, but I send them one once every two years and it basically says that we've got all the money we need. We'd like to have more, but it's not a necessity. But we don't have one ounce of reputation more than we need, and our reputation at Berkshire is in their hands.

"Charlie and I believe that if you establish the right sort of culture, that culture, to some extent, self-selects who you obtain as directors and as managers, and you will get better results that way in terms of behavior than if you have a thousand-page guidebook ...

"At Wells Fargo, there were three very significant mistakes, but one that dwarfed all of the others. You're going to have incentive systems at almost any business. There's nothing wrong with incentive systems, but you've got to be very careful what you incentivize. You can't incentivize bad behavior. So you better have a system for recognizing it. Clearly, at Wells Fargo, there was an incentive system built around the idea of cross-selling and the number of services per customer [checking account, savings account, auto loan, etc.]. The company, in every quarterly investor presentation, highlighted how many services per customer. So, it was a major focus of the organization. And undoubtedly, people got paid and graded and promoted at least partly based on that number. Well, it turned out that that was incentivizing the wrong kind of behavior.

"We've made similar mistakes. Any company's going to make some mistakes in designing a system. And you're going to find out about it at some point. (I'll get to how we find out about it.) Obviously I don't know all the facts as to how the information got passed up the line at Wells Fargo—but at some point, if there's a major problem, the CEO will get wind of it. And at that moment, that's the key to everything, because the CEO has to act.

"That Salomon situation that you saw happened when, on April 28, 1991 the CEO of Salomon, the president of Salomon, and the general counsel of Salomon, sat in a room and had described to them, by a fellow named John Meriwether, some terrible practice that was being conducted by a fellow named Paul Mozer, who worked for them. Paul Mozer was flimflamming the United States Treasury, which is a very dumb thing to do. He was doing it partly out of spite, because he didn't like the Treasury and they didn't like him. He put in phony bids for U.S. Treasuries and all of that. And on 28 April, the CEO and all these people now knew that something had gone very wrong, and they had to report it to the Federal Reserve Bank of New York. The CEO, John Gutfreund, said he would do it, and then he didn't. He undoubtedly put it off just because it was an unpleasant thing to do. Then on 15 May, another Treasury auction was held, and Paul Mozer put in a bunch of phony bids again. At that point, it was all over, because top management had known ahead of time, and now a guy that was a pyromaniac had gone out and lit another fire. And he lit it after they'd been warned that he was a pyromaniac, essentially. It all went downhill from there. It has to stop when the CEO learns about it.

"Then Wells Fargo management made a third mistake; they totally underestimated the impact of what they had done once it was uncovered, because there was a penalty of only $185 million. In the banking business, people get fined billions and billions of dollars for mortgage practices and all kinds of things. … So, they measured the seriousness of the problem by the dimensions of the fine. They thought a $185 million fine signaled a less offensive practice than something involving $2 billion, and they were totally wrong on that. But the main problem was they didn't act when they learned about it. It was bad enough having a bad system, but they didn't act.

"At Berkshire, the main source of information for me about anything that's being done wrong at a subsidiary is the hotline. We have 4,000 or so hotline reports a year. Most of them are frivolous—the guy next to me has bad breath or something. But there are a few serious ones, and the head of our internal audit, Becki Amick, looks at all of them. ... Anything that looks serious, I will hear about, and that has led to action. We've spent real money investigating some of those. We put special investigators, sometimes, on them. And, like I say, it has uncovered certain practices that we would not at all condone at the parent company. I think it's a good system. I don't think it's perfect. I'm sure they've got an internal audit at Wells Fargo, and I'm sure they have a hotline. I don't know the facts, but I would just have to bet that a lot of communications came in on that, and I don't know what their system was for getting them to the right person. ... It was a huge, huge, huge error if they were getting some communications and they ignored them, or if they sent them back down to somebody below."

CM: "If you're in a business where you have a whole a lot of people under incentives very likely to cause a lot of misbehavior, of course you need a big compliance department. Every big wirehouse and stock brokerage firm has a huge compliance department. If we had one, we would have a big compliance department too—but doesn't mean that everybody should try and solve their problems with more and more compliance. I think we've had less trouble over the years by being more careful in whom we pick to have power, and in having a culture of trust."

WB: "Ben Franklin, who Charlie worships, said, 'An ounce of prevention is worth a pound of cure.' He understated it. An ounce of prevention is worth more than a pound of cure. I would say a pound of cure, promptly applied, is worth a ton of cure that's delayed. Problems don't go away. John Gutfreund told the troops at Salomon that it was a traffic ticket, and then it almost brought down Salomon ... You've got to act promptly. And frankly, I don't know any better system than hotlines and anonymous letters that can be sent to me. I've gotten three or four of them probably in the last six or seven years that have resulted in major changes at Berkshire. ... I will tell you, as we sit here, quite a few people are probably doing something wrong at Berkshire, and usually, it's very limited. I mean maybe stealing small amounts of money or something like that. But when it gets to some sales practice, like what was taking place at Wells Fargo, you can see the kind of damage that it can do."

2018 MEETING (00:49:19)

WB: "Wells Fargo is a company that proved the efficacy of incentives, it's just that they had the wrong incentives. That was bad. Then they committed a much greater error by ignoring the fact that they had a faulty incentive system which was incentivizing people to do things that were kind of crazy, like opening nonexistent accounts ... The important thing is to not incentivize any of that if you can avoid it, and when you find out what's going on, you have to do something about it. That is absolutely key. Wells Fargo didn't do that.

"We made a couple of our greatest investments where people had made similar errors. We bought American Express—the best investment I ever made in my partnership years—in 1964 because somebody was incentivized to do the wrong thing in something called the American Express Field Warehousing Company. We bought a very substantial amount of GEICO (what became half of GEICO as a result of share repurchases) for $40 million, because somebody was incentivized to meet Wall Street estimates of earnings and growth, and they didn't focus on having the proper reserves. That caused a lot of pain at American Express in 1964. It caused a lot of pain at GEICO in 1976. It caused a layoff of a significant portion of the workforce, all kinds of things. But they cleaned it up, and look where American Express and GEICO have moved to since that time.

"So the fact that you are going to have problems at some very large institution is not unique. In fact, all the big banks have had troubles of one sort or another. And I see no reason why Wells Fargo as a company, from both an investment standpoint and a moral standpoint going forward, is in any way inferior to the other big banks with which it competes. They made a big mistake. We have a large unrealized gain in it, but that doesn't have anything to do with our decision-making. I like it as an investment. I like Tim Sloan as a manager. He is correcting mistakes made by other people. ...

"You ought to jump on everything. Charlie has pushed me all my life to make sure that I attack unpleasant problems that surface. And that's sometimes not easy to do when everything else is going fine. And at Wells Fargo, they clearly did what people at every organization have sometimes done, but it got accentuated to an extreme point. But I see no reason to think that Wells Fargo, going forward, is anything other than a very, very large, well-run bank that had an episode in its history it wished it didn't have. GEICO came out stronger, American Express came out stronger. The question is what you do when you find the problems."

CM: "I agree with that. I think Wells Fargo is going to be better going forward than it would have been if these leaks had never been discovered. But [Hollywood producer] Harvey Weinstein has also done a lot for improving behavior, too. It was clearly an error, and they're acutely aware of it and acutely embarrassed, and they don't want to have it happen again. If I had to say which bank of all is more likely to behave the best in the future, it might be Wells Fargo."

WB: "American Express was just picking up a few dollars by having the field warehousing company in 1963. And then they were worried whether it was going to sink the company. I went to the annual meeting in 1964 of American Express after the scandal developed, and somebody asked if the auditor would step forward. The auditor from one of the big firms, which I won't mention, came up to the microphone, and somebody said, 'How much did we pay you last year?' The auditor gave his answer, and then the questioner said, 'Well, how much extra would you have charged us to go over to Bayonne, which was ten miles away, and check whether there's any oil in the tanks?' Here was a tiny little operation—some guy was calling from a bar in Bayonne and telling him this phony stuff was going on, and they didn't want to hear it. They shut their ears to it. But over time, what emerged after that near death experience for American Express, was a great company. We're going to make mistakes. I will guarantee you that we will get some unpleasant news at Berkshire. I don't know what it will be. The most important thing is that we do something about it. And there have been times when I procrastinated, and Charlie has been the one that jabs me into action. He's performed a lot of services you don't know about."

MANAGEMENT AND EMPLOYEE COMPENSATION

1995 MEETING (00:43:12)

WB: "In situations where we advance capital to a subsidiary or withdraw it, that usually ties in with the compensation plan. We want our managers to understand just how highly we value capital—and nothing creates a better understanding than to charge them for it. Sometimes it's based on the history of the company or the industry. It may be based on interest rates at the time that we draw it up. We have arrangements, depending on those variables and perhaps some others and how we felt the day we drew it up, that range between 14% and 20%, in terms of capital advanced. Sometimes we have an arrangement where, if it's a business where they have a seasonal requirement for a few months, we give it to them very cheap, at LIBOR. If they use more capital beyond that, we say, 'That's permanent capital,' and we charge them considerably more.

"Now, if we buy a business that's using a couple hundred million of capital, and we work out a bonus arrangement, and the manager figures a way to do the business with less capital, we may credit him at the same rate we would use in charging him, in terms of his bonus arrangement.

"We want our managers to know that money costs money. My experience in business is that most managers, when using their own money, understand that money costs money, but sometimes, when using other people's money, they start thinking of it a little bit like free money. And that's a habit we don't want to encourage at Berkshire. By sticking these rates on capital, we are telling them how much capital is worth to us. I think that's a useful guideline, in terms of the decisions they're making, because we don't make very many decisions about our operating business. We make very, very few. I don't see capital budgets, in most cases, from our 100%-owned subsidiaries. And if I don't see them, no one else sees them; we have no staff at headquarters looking at this kind of thing. We give them great responsibility on it, but we do want them to know how we calibrate the use of capital. So far, it's really worked quite well. Our managers don't mind being measured, and I think they enjoy seeing a batting average posted—and a batting average that does not include a cost of capital is a phony batting average."

1995 MEETING (03:28:50)

WB: "We have different bonus arrangements at different companies. It would be a big mistake, with businesses that have varying economic characteristics as they do at Berkshire, to try and pay managers in all of these different businesses based on a simple formula of one kind. ... For some businesses, capital employed is unimportant. There simply isn't a way to employ a lot of capital, so we do not even have a capital charge at those businesses. We don't believe in going through a lot of machinations if it's going to involve peanuts at the end. Some businesses have a capital charge, some don't. If they use a lot of capital, they're going to have a capital charge, is what it amounts to. Some businesses are easy businesses, some are tougher. So, we have different thresholds where things kick in based on that. We simply sit down and try and figure out, in the case of each business, what makes sense. And that usually isn't very hard to do.

"We aren't going to change the behavior of the best managers much by compensation. We may a little bit, in terms of teaching them how we think about capital employed. But in terms of their enthusiasm for the business, imagination, marketing, all that, we usually buy businesses with those people in place. It'd be wrong not to treat people fairly, and they would resent it if they weren't treated fairly—understandably. We try to have a system that rewards the things that we want to have rewarded and treats them fairly in a way such that they understand they're treated fairly.

"I don't think we have any two businesses that have the same arrangement. Incidentally, that applies in their policies, too. Very seldom, maybe once or twice, do we get involved in their different arrangements in terms of compensating their employees. Some of our businesses have budgets, some of them don't. We don't have any budgets that come up to headquarters. We let .400 hitters swing the way they want to swing. And some of them have a little different swing than others, but overall, they're extremely effective. And they feel, and we want them to feel, like they own their own business. If somebody that's independently wealthy sold us a business and we started telling them how to swing, they would tell us what we could do with it very quickly, because they don't need that in their life. What we have to do is maintain a situation where they are having more fun doing what they're doing than anything else they can do in life, and that's what's we're designing for. Then we have to treat them fairly in respect to that."

1996 MEETING (04:06:49)

WB: "We generally will be charging people something in the area of 15%, in terms of working out compensation arrangements for capital. Now, 15% pre-tax, depending on state income taxes, is only 9.0–9.5% after-tax. So, you can say that isn't even enough to charge, but we find that 15% gets their attention. And it should get their attention, but it shouldn't be such a high-hurdle rate that things that we want to do don't get done. Our managers expect to be running their businesses for a long, long time. So we don't worry about them doing something that works in the next year but doesn't work five years out. … They see themselves as part-owners of the business. We want them to be owners with a cost attached to capital.

"We think it's awful, frankly, the way businesses reward executives with absolutely no regard for cost of capital. I mean, a fixed-price option for ten years—imagine giving somebody an interest-free loan for ten years; you're not going to do it. And if a company is retaining a significant part of its earnings, and you give out a fixed-price option for ten years, they can do nothing with it but put it in a savings account and they'll make some money off it.

"Assuming you had stock options for the two of us—which we're not going to do, I want to assure you—we would say the fair way to do that would be to have an option at not less than present intrinsic value. Forget what the market price is; the idea that the more depressed your market price is, the better your option price should be, does not make any sense. So, we would have it at no less than intrinsic value. And then we would have it step up yearly based on something relating to a cost to capital. Why should we get free use of the shareholders' capital? And we could work out a fair stock option plan. That would be a perfectly appropriate way to have us compensated that involved an issuance, at an initial price of not less than intrinsic value, and involved carrying costs. Then we would be in a position, still, not totally analogous to shareholders, because we wouldn't have the downside you have, but we would at least have the carrying cost that you have of ownership. We work that into our unit compensation plans by having a cost of capital that tends to run at about

15%. And if people can give us money, we should be able to figure out a way to do something better than 15% pre-tax with it. That's part of our job, too. So, we will pay them to give us back money."

CM: "We really invented a more extreme system: Executives can buy Berkshire Hathaway stock in the market for cash. This is a very old-fashioned system. It doesn't take any lawyers or compensation consultants ... Most of them have done it, and most of them have done very well with it. I don't know why it doesn't spread more."

WB: "People say they want their management to think like shareholders. It's very easy to think like a shareholder when you are one; you'll think exactly like a shareholder. It's not a huge psychological hurdle to get over if you actually write a check to buy the stock."

1998 MEETING (02:37:41)

WB: "In my own view, the most exorbitant pay packages are not necessarily the biggest numbers. What really bothers me is when companies pay a lot for mediocrity, and that happens all too often. We have no quarrel in our subsidiaries, for example, paying a lot of money for outstanding performance. We get it back ten for one, twenty for one, or fifty for one. Similarly, in public companies we think there are managers who have taken companies to many, many, many billions of market value more than would've happened with virtually anyone else. And they sometimes take a lot of money for that.

"Sometimes, as in the case of Tom Murphy at Cap Cities, it just didn't make a difference to him. He performed in a way that would have justified huge sums, but he would tell you that he had all the money he needed and he just didn't care to take what the market might bear.

"But I am bothered by irrational pay systems, particularly when average managers take really large sums. I'm bothered when they design (or have designed for them) systems that are very costly to the company—maybe partly to make themselves look good because they want huge options themselves, so they feel if they give options widely throughout the company [it justifies it]. They design a system that is illogical company-wide because they want one that's illogical for them personally.

"But large sums, per se, don't bother me. I do not mind paying a lot for performance. It's done in athletics, it's done in entertainment, but in business the people who are the .200 hitters and the people who would not attract a crowd as an entertainer—the system has evolved in such a way that many of them take huge sums, and I think that's obscene. I can tell you, there isn't much you can do about it. The system feeds on itself. And companies do look at other companies' proxy statements, every CEO does. And they say, 'Well, if Joe Smith is worth X then I have to be worth more.' And they tell the directors, 'Certainly you wouldn't be hiring anybody that was below average, so how can you pay me below average?' And the consultants come in and ratchet up the rewards. It's not going to go away. The people who have their hands on the switch are the beneficiaries of the system. And it's very hard to change the system when the guy whose hand is on the switch is benefitting enormously, and perhaps disproportionately, from that system."

CM: "The original Vanderbilt behaved even better than the people at Berkshire Hathaway. He didn't take any salary at all. He thought it was beneath him as a significant shareholder to take a salary. That ideal, I'm afraid, died with him."

WB: "Our directors are paid $900 a year, but I tell them on an hourly basis they're making a fortune because we don't work them that hard. But what Charlie and I did not think through, when we established that $900 a year, is that they set our salaries, too. We have not followed the standard procedure, which is to load it on the directors and the directors shall load it on you."

CM: "I do think it will have pernicious effects for the country in its entirety as this thing keeps escalating, because you're getting a widespread perception that at the very top, corporate salaries in America are too high. And that is not a good thing for a civilization, when the leaders are regarded as not dealing fairly with the institutions that they head. As for the corporation consultants who advise on salaries, all I can say is that prostitution would be a step up for them."

1999 MEETING (00:44:22)

WB: "Our manager compensation arrangements vary to an extraordinary degree among the subsidiaries. We have bought existing businesses, and we have tampered with their cultures as little as possible after we buy them—and some of those cultures are very different than others. We have a number of very talented managers who have worked out the systems that they believe to be best for their companies. Now, if there's a stock option plan, we will substitute a plan that is performance-based, which ties much more clearly to the performance of the business than any option plan could. And we will design one that has an expectable cost that's equal to the expectable cost of the option plan. And we try to make it much more sensible from both the owner's standpoint and the employees' standpoint, in terms of the way it pays off based on how that business performs.

"You probably read in our annual report how we put in an across-the-board plan at GEICO that ties with our objectives. But basically, that was CEO Tony Nicely's work in terms of developing that plan. We thought alike about what counted and he developed a compensation grid that applied to everybody at GEICO based on achieving the objectives that he felt were important and that we felt were important.

"If you go to any Berkshire subsidiary, you will probably find that they have a compensation plan that's quite similar, with the exception of options, to the plan that they had before we bought them. They have successful businesses. They get there different ways. Some people bat left-handed, some people bat right-handed. Some people stand deep in the batter's box, some crowd the plate. They all have different styles. And the styles of our managers have proven successful in their own businesses. So, we don't try to superimpose any system from above, with the exception of what I've mentioned. We like paying for performance. That is kind of a fundamental tenet. Everybody says they like that, but then they design systems that pay no matter what happens, in many cases. We're reluctant to do that."

CM: "I think it's important for the shareholders to realize that we are probably more decentralized, in terms of personnel practices, than any company of our size, or bigger, in America. We don't have a headquarters culture that's forced on the operating businesses. The operating businesses have their own cultures. And in every case I can think of it's a wonderful culture. We just leave them alone. It comes naturally to me."

WB: "We have no human relations department, no legal department, no investor relations, no public relations, we don't have any of that. We've got a bunch of all-stars out there running businesses. We ask them to mail the money to Omaha. But beyond that, it would be foolish. What is interesting to me is I had a lot of preconceived ideas of what motivated people when I started out in business. But you can find certain organizations that resist paying stars on an individual basis. They like to think of themselves as a team and they'd rather have a team concept of payment. And you can see others where they're much more individually oriented."

CM: "I can't remember a case when anybody has transferred from one operating Berkshire subsidiary to another. It's very rare."

WB: "We don't try and cross-fertilize. We think we've got a good thing going in every plot of ground and we just assume they'll do best if left to their own initiative."

2000 MEETING (01:46:47)

WB: "The two operations I've recently agreed to buy, we will have rational compensation plans. ... I think it's been a huge advantage at GEICO to have a plan that is far more rational than the one that preceded it. And I think that advantage will do nothing but grow stronger over time because, in effect, compensation is our way of speaking to employees. And with a place as large as GEICO, you can't speak to them all directly. But it speaks to them all the time. It says what we think the rational measurement of productivity and performance in the business is. And over time, that gets absorbed by thousands and thousands of people. It's the best way to get them to buy into their goals. Whereas, if you use as your test what the stock market is going to do, people, I think, inherently know they have a lottery ticket. You've seen that in tech stocks in the last few months ... Those people know they're getting lottery tickets, basically, and the market's attitude toward tech stocks is what's going to determine results far more than their own individual results.

"It's silly to think that somebody working very hard at some very small job at Berkshire, with our aggregate market value of $90 billion, is going to move the stock. But their efforts may very well move the number of policyholders we gain or the satisfaction of policyholders. And if we can find ways to pay them based on that, we are far more in sync with what they can do—and they know it makes more sense. So, I hope our competitors do all kinds of crazy things on comp and everything else. The more dumb things they do, the better life is for us. We've had incredible success at keeping managers. I don't think there's any company in the U.S. of size that has had better luck on that than Berkshire. And partly, it's because we appreciate, in terms of the compensation plan and generally, managers that do a terrific job for us."

CM: "Here again, we're very much out of step with the conventions of the world. When I read annual reports, and I read a lot of them, I'm very frequently irritated by the presence of things that are totally absent from the Berkshire Hathaway annual report. ... There's a lot of insanity in conventional corporate conduct on the pay front. But if convention determined what was sane and what was insane, we're the oddballs. I mean, we're the unusual example."

WB: "I think it's very subconscious, but sometimes the desires of the top person to get an outrageous amount gets pyramided through the organization because if they're going to have some scheme that rewards them based on a lottery ticket, they feel they have to give lottery tickets to everybody else, although on a much-reduced scale. It becomes accepted, and then you hire consultants who come around and say, 'They're getting more lottery tickets someplace else, we've got some added new schemes.' It becomes very reinforcing.

"But what has happened at the top level is really unbelievable. If an executive said to his company, 'Just for working here, I want an option on $300 million worth of S&P 500 futures for the next ten years,' people would regard that as outrageous. But in effect, if they get one on their own stock and it goes up based on the fact that the S&P appreciates over ten years, they think that's perfectly acceptable to have.

"I would say there's been a lot of talk about the huge gap that exists in pay. But it seems to me the primary gap eating at American CEOs is the gap between the rich and the super-rich. That seems to be motivating the adoption of many plans. It's really got out of hand but it isn't going to change. The CEO has his hand on the switch as a practical matter. I know people on comp committees and I've been on them myself—as a practical matter, you don't stand a chance."

CM: "A lot of the corporate compensation plans of the modern era work just about the way things would work for a farmer if you put a rat colony in the granary."

2002 MEETING (02:50:37)

CM: "I think if you talk generally about stock option plans in America, you see a lot of terrible behavior ... In particular, if you have a corporation where a man has risen to be CEO, and he now has hundreds of millions of dollars in the stock of the company, he's been loyal to the company and the company's been loyal to him for decades. And then he has his directors vote him a great stock option grant annually to preserve his loyalty and his enthusiasm to the company when he's already old—I think that's demented. And I also think it's immoral. I don't think you would improve the behavior of the surgeons at the Mayo Clinic, or the partners of Cravath, Swaine & Moore, if you gave the top people stock options in their sixties. By that time, you ought to have settled loyalties, and you ought to be thinking more about the right example for the company than whether you can take another $100 million for yourself."

WB: "At Berkshire, for those that succeed me and Charlie, anybody that is in the very top position at Berkshire has got the job of allocating resources for the whole place. There could be a logically constructed option plan for that person, and it would make some sense because they are responsible for what takes place overall. But a logically constructed plan would have a cost of capital built into it for every year where we don't pay dividends. Why should we get money from you for free? We could put it in a savings account and it would grow in value without us doing anything. And a fixed-price option over ten years would accrue dramatic value to whoever was running the place, if they had a large option, for putting the money in a savings account or in government bonds.

"So, there has to be a cost of capital factor in to make options equitable, in my view. ... They should not be granted at below the intrinsic value of the company. I mean, a CEO who says, 'My stock is ridiculously low,' when somebody comes around and wants to buy the company, but then grants himself an option at a price that he's just gotten through saying it is ridiculously low, that bothers me. So, if somebody says, we don't want to sell this company for less than $30 per share this year because it's going to be worth a lot more later on, my notion is that the option should be at $30 even if the stock is $15. Otherwise you actually have a premium built in for having a low stock price in relation to value. I've never gotten too excited about that."

CM: "A lot is horribly wrong in corporate compensation in America. The system of using stock options on the theory they really don't cost anything has contributed to a lot of gross excess. And that excess is not good for the country. Aristotle said that systems work better when people look at the different outcomes and basically appraise them as fair. And when large percentages of people look at corporate compensation practices and think of them as unfair, it's not good for the country."

WB: "It will be hard to change, though … I've been on nineteen public boards and Charlie's been on a lot of them. In the end, the CEOs tend to get pretty much what they want. And what they want tends to go up every year because they see other people getting more every year. There's a ratcheting effect, and the consultants fan the flames. It's very difficult to get changed."

2003 MEETING (04:26:42)

CM: "Where a business requires practically no capital, we tend to reward the management based on the earnings. The minute the business starts requiring capital we tend to put a capital factor into this compensation system. We don't have any one standard system. They're all different based on accidents of history and circumstances. But where capital's an important factor, of course, we take it into account. To the effects on morale, as far as I've ever been able to see, the morale's pretty good in the Berkshire subsidiaries. The Berkshire managers practically never leave. My guess is that we have about as low a turnover rate as any place around."

WB: "We've never had big problems with compensation because, I think, our arrangements are rational. We don't believe in making things more complex than needed. … We have very simple systems on comp. But some of our businesses are terrific businesses, and so we have very high standards of performance before people get performance bonuses. Some of our businesses are very tough businesses, and the threshold is much lower, but the managerial talent needed to reach that threshold is just as much as with the higher threshold in other businesses. Compensation is not rocket science … In thirty-eight years, we have never had a CEO leave us to go to another business, except a few where we've made the decision ourselves, but very few. … We don't have much bureaucracy at Berkshire. … On an expectancy basis, even with all the subsidiaries we have, we may face one management succession problem, perhaps, every eighteen months or something of the sort. So, it's not a big deal at Berkshire."

2004 MEETING (00:49:14)

WB: "You could make a lot of money working for Berkshire. Not as chairman or vice chairman, but there's a chance to make a lot of money. It will relate to performance; no one is going to make lots of money at Berkshire for average performance. You mentioned [energy company] MidAmerican; I was thinking what would be appropriate for the two individuals who are key to the success of MidAmerican. I took a yellow pad and spent about three minutes sketching out a proposal. I went to Walter Scott, who is our partner in the business and now actually heads the comp committee, and said, 'This is an idea I have, what do you think of it?' He looked at it and said it looked fine. And we talked to the two managers about it; we had it so something over 50% went to the CEO, Dave Sokol, and something under 50% went to the number two man, Greg Abel. When we gave it to David, he said, 'I like it fine, but let's make it 50/50.' That's the extent of it.

"As you commented, that's wildly different to the approach at other companies. Most companies go through very elaborate procedures in working out executive compensation. I don't think Charlie and I have ever spent more than five minutes thinking about it. We have an arrangement at See's Candies with Chuck Huggins; we worked it out in 1972 and it's still in force now. John Holland took over Fruit of the Loom a couple of years ago. I met with him, suggested something that takes up a paragraph or two, and that's what we'll have with John the rest of his life. It's not highly complex. But you do have to understand the businesses.

"There is no one formula we could use at Berkshire that would fit across our businesses, that's asinine. You don't want them complicated. We don't have anything that goes on for pages and pages. It's not needed. It establishes a relationship between us and the manager that's not good. All of our stuff is very, very simple ... We do not bring in compensation consultants, we don't have a human relations department ... We don't have those things because they make life way more complicated and everybody gets a vested interest in going to conferences, calling other consultants, and it takes on a life of its own. In the typical large corporation, there's a comp committee. They don't put dobermanns on the comp committees, usually; they look for chihuahuas that have been sedated. I've been on nineteen boards. They put me on one comp committee; I was chairman and still I got outvoted ... It's difficult for directors to get a lot done. They get handed a sheet of paper that shows them comparables, and everybody thinks their CEO is in the top 25%. There's a ratcheting effect that takes place. And now stock options are coming out of favor, so restricted stock comes in."

CM: "I'd rather throw a viper down my shirtfront than hire a compensation consultant."

2004 MEETING (03:57:57)

WB: "We have a great preference for making compensation simple. We concentrate on the variables that count to us, and then we try to put that against the backdrop of the competitive nature, the true economics of the business they're in, and really reward where they're adding value, even if that value is from a very low base in a lousy business. And we make the base very high if they're in a very easy business. ... If you had a group of network television stations, all of a reasonable size, you would probably figure a chimpanzee could run the place and have 35% pre-tax margins. And you might want to pay for performance above some number like that. But it's silly to have something that starts at 10% or 15% when you do that.

"Charlie and I have seen all kinds of compensation arrangements where, basically, you get paid for showing up, but they try—by constructing some mathematics around it— to make it look like you really had to achieve something. In the end, if you get a great manager, you want to pay him very well. You want a big carrot out there for them if they achieve the results you've set out."

CM: "If you want to read one book that will demonstrate really shrewd compensation systems in a whole chain of small businesses, read *Pride in Performance: Keep It Going* by Les Schwab, who has a bunch of tire shops all over the Northwest. He made a fortune in one of the world's really difficult businesses by having shrewd systems. He can tell you a lot better than we can."

2006 MEETING (00:40:46)

WB: "If we owned a copper mining company, we would measure it more by the cost of production than by what copper was selling for per pound. Management has control—depending on the kind of ore bodies and everything—over operating conditions. They do not have control over market prices. We would have something that would tie to what we thought was under the control of the individual managing the business. That's what we try to measure. We try to understand the industry in which they operate, and we try to understand the things that the manager can have an impact on, and how well they're doing in that. ... We do not want to pay for anything that is not under their control.

"I probably have responsibility for the compensation system of forty managers; I can't think of anyone we've lost over a forty-year period because of differences in views on compensation. We've never had a compensation consultant come into Berkshire. We don't spend a lot of time on it. It is not rocket science. ...

"The SEC wants even more transparency on executive compensation, which I think is a good idea except for the fact that it becomes a shopping list for every other CEO when they see that somebody is getting their haircuts paid for by the company. They decide that they, too, need their haircuts paid for by the company."

2007 MEETING (00:27:12)

WB: "There are more problems with having the wrong manager than with having the wrong compensation system. It is enormously important who runs Procter & Gamble, Coca-Cola, or American Express; any compensation sins are generally of minor importance compared to the sin of having somebody that's mediocre running a huge company."

2016 MEETING (04:02:53)

CM: "The basic rule on incentives is you get what you reward for. So, if you have a dumb incentive system, you will get dumb outcomes. One of our really interesting incentive systems is at GEICO, because we don't have a normal profits-type incentive for the people at GEICO. Warren, tell them, because it's really interesting."

WB: "At GEICO, we have two variables, and they apply to well over 20,000 people. … These two variables determine bonus compensation. As you go up the ladder, it has a multiplier effect. It's still the same two variables, but it gets to be larger and larger, in terms of bonus compensation as a percentage of your base, but it's always significant. And those two variables are very simple. I care about growing the business, and I care about growing it with a profitable business. So, we have a grid, which consists of growth in policies in force [PIFs]—not growth in dollars, because that's reflected by average premiums, which are outside their control, but growth in policies in force. And then on the other grid, we have the profitability of seasoned business.

"It costs a lot of money to put business on the books. We spend a lot of money on advertising and all of that. The first year, any business we put on the books is going to reduce profits significantly, and I don't want people to be worried about the profit that might be impaired by growing the business fast. So, the profit of seasoned business and growth of policies in force. Very simple. We've used it since 1995 … Everybody understands it. In February, it's a big day when the two variables are announced and people figure out how they come out on it. It totally aligns the goals of the organization, in terms of comp, with the goals of the owner."

CM: "It's simple, but other people might reward something like just profits, and so the people don't take on new business they should take on because it hurts profits. You've got to think these things through, and, of course, Warren's good at that, and so is GEICO CEO Tony Nicely."

WB: "You don't want to award profits alone. It'd be the dumbest thing you could do. You just quit advertising, start shrinking the business a little. People at GEICO know that the very top person is getting paid based on those same two variables. They don't think that the guys at the top have got a cushy deal compared to them, and all of that. It's just a very logical system.

"The interesting thing is that if we brought in a compensation consultant, they would start coming up with plans that would be designed for all of Berkshire, and get us all pulling together. The idea of having a coordinated arrangement for incentive compensation across seventy or eight businesses, or whatever, is just totally nuts. And yet, I would almost guarantee you that if we brought in somebody, they would be thinking in terms of some master plan, and little subplans, and all this kind of thing, and explain it with all kinds of objectives.

"We try to figure out what makes sense in each business we're in ... We try to design plans that make sense ... We have so many different kinds of businesses. Some of them are very tough businesses. Some of them are very easy businesses. Some of them are capital intensive. Some of them don't take capital. You just go up and down the line, and to think that you'll have a simple formula that can be sort of stamped out for the whole place, and then with some overall stuff for corporate results on top of it, you'd be wasting a lot of money, and you'd be misdirecting incentives. So we think it through one at a time, and it seems to work out pretty well."

CM: "A lot of the bad examples of incentives come from banking and investment banking. If you reward somebody with some share of the profits, and the profits are being reported using accounting practices that cause profits to exist on paper that are not really happening in terms of underlying economics, then people are doing the wrong thing, and it's endangering the bank and hurting the country and everything else. And that was a major part of the cause of the Great Financial Crisis of 2007–08: The banks were reporting a lot of income they weren't making, and the investment banks were, too. The accounting allowed, for a long time, a lender to use as his bad debt provision his previous historical loss rate. So an idiot could make a lot of money by just making way-gamier loans at high interest, and accruing a lot of interest, and saying, 'I'm not going to lose any more money on these, because I didn't lose money on different loans in the past.' That was insane for the accountants to allow that. Literally insane. That's not too strong a word. Yet nobody's ashamed of it. I've never met an accountant that's ashamed of it."

WB: "... There's a lot of misbehavior. You saw it in the pricing of stock options. I would hear conversations in a boardroom where they hoped they were issuing the options at a terribly low price. Well, if you've got people interested in having options issued at a terribly low price, they may occasionally do something that might cause that. What could be dumber than a company looking for a way to issue shares at the lowest price? Compensation isn't as complicated as the world would like to make it, but if you were a consultant, you would want to make people think it's very complicated, and that only you could solve this terrible problem for them."

CM: "We want it simple and right, and we don't want it to reward what we don't want. Those of you with children, just imagine how your household would work if you constantly rewarded every child for their bad behavior. The house would be ungovernable in short order."

MANAGEMENT CONTRACTS

2009 MEETING (03:23:52)

WB: "We are not big believers in contracts. We hand people hundreds of millions or billions of dollars to sell us their business. The decision we have to make is, are they going to have the same passion for the business after they hand us the stock certificate and we hand them the money? Are they going to have the same passion that they had beforehand? And if we're wrong on that, no contract is going to save us. We don't want relationships that are based on contracts. I can't really think of a formal contract that we have … We don't try to hold people by contracts. And it wouldn't work. We basically don't like engaging in them."

CM: "Our model is a seamless web of trust that's deserved on both sides. That's what we're aiming for. The Hollywood model, where everyone has a contract, and no trust is deserved on either side, is not what we want at all."

WB: "We do not want to negotiate the size of the executive bathroom. That is not our game."

MANAGEMENT QUALITY AND BUSINESS QUALITY

1996 MEETING (02:39:50)

WB: "The really great business is one that doesn't require good management; that is a terrific business. And the poor business is one that can only succeed, or even survive, with great management. We look for people that know their businesses, love their businesses, love their shareholders, and want to treat them as partners. We still look to the underlying business, though. If we have somebody we think is extraordinary, but they're locked into one of those terrible businesses, the best thing you can do, probably, is to get out of it and get into something else.

"But there's an enormous difference, frankly, in the talent of American business managers. The CEOs of the Fortune 500 are not selected like the members of the Olympic track and field team. It is not the same process. You do not have the uniformity of top quality that you get with the American Olympic team. You get some very able, terrific people like Bill Gates, but you get a lot of mediocrity, too. In some cases, it's fairly identifiable who has done an extraordinary job—we like people that have batted .350 or .360, in terms of predicting that they're going to bat over .300 in the future. If some guy says, 'I batted .127 last year, but I've got a new bat or a new batting coach,' and some management consultant came in and told them how to do it—we're very suspicious of that. We don't like banjo hitters who suddenly proclaim that they can become power hitters.

"Then we try to figure out what their attitude is toward shareholders, and that isn't uniform either throughout corporate America. We still want them to be in a good business, I would emphasize that. I gave the illustration of Tom Murphy in the annual report: No one could top his ability or integrity, in terms of the way he ran [media company] Capital Cities for decades. And you could see it in fifty different ways. He was thinking about the shareholders. And he not only thought about them, but he also knew what to do to forward their interests. In terms of building the business, he only built it when it made sense, not when it did something for his ego or to make it larger alone. He did it when it was in his shareholders' interests. They're not all Tom Murphys out there. But when you find them, and they're in a decent business, you want to bet very heavily and not make the same mistake I made by selling out once or twice."

2001 MEETING (00:17:36)

CM: "I think almost all good businesses have occasions where their managers are willing to make today's results look a little worse than they would otherwise be to help tomorrow."

2007 MEETING (02:53:37)

CM: "There are two things: the quality of the business and the quality of the management. If the business is good enough, it will carry a lousy manager. In the other case, where a really good manager gets in a really lousy business, he'll ordinarily have a very imperfect record. In other words, it's a rare person that can take over a textile business, totally doomed, which is what Warren did in his youthful folly, and turn it into what's happened here. You should not be looking for other Warrens on the theory that they're under every bush."

WB: "If you gave me first draft pick of all the CEOs in America and said it's your job to run Ford Motor now, or pick a company in a terribly tough business, I wouldn't do it; it's just too tough. They may get it solved, if they get cooperation from unions and a whole bunch of things, but it will not be solely in the control of the CEO who has that job. He is dependent on too many good things happening outside his control to get the job, even if he's the best in the world."

2016 MEETING (04:34:58)

WB: "There have been a lot of managers who created billions and billions of dollars of value for Berkshire. Maybe you can get into the tens of billions. Having a fantastic manager that has a large potential business available to them, and who makes the most of it, is huge over time. You don't necessarily see it in a week or a month. But when you're building capital value, I mean, think of the value of Jeff Bezos to Amazon; it wouldn't have happened without him, and you're looking at huge values. The value of Tom Murphy and [his long-term business partner] Dan Burke was the difference between zero and what they ended up with. They built that thing from a bankrupt UHF station in Albany. They didn't invent the television or anything of the sort, they just managed it so well. So, really outstanding managers, they're invaluable. Charlie and I can't do it ourselves, but we want to align ourselves with them, and then have them feel about Berkshire the way we feel about it. If we do that, we have an enormous asset, as we do have in Ajit and a number of other managers."

MANAGEMENT COMPENSATION (STOCK OPTIONS)

1997 MEETING (02:14:33)

WB: "I would say that most stock options are constructed poorly, from the standpoint of the owner, but they're constructed very well from the standpoint of the person who receives them. This is not entirely unexplainable because it's a very strange form of negotiation when the beneficiary is the one that also really does all the design, and hires the experts to come in and say what is good for the company, when the expert knows that the guy who signs the check would also be quite interested in hearing what's good for him.

"There's nothing wrong with options per se; in terms of Berkshire, it would have been perfectly appropriate if a properly designed option had been given to me or to Charlie. We have responsibility for the whole enterprise, and we believe that any kind of incentive for performance should be related to the area in which you have responsibility. If you want a typist to type a hundred words a minute, you ought to pay for typing a hundred words a minute, not what the earnings per share were last year; we believe in tying incentive comp to performance for which you have responsibility. The people responsible for the entire results of the business, it's perfectly appropriate to compensate them by options that in some way reflect the performance of that entire business. The trouble is that stock prices reflect things other than the performance of the business. For one thing, over a period of time, they reflect the reinvestment of earnings. If you gave me an option to manage your savings account and you reinvested all the interest, I would take away a significant payment at the end of ten years simply because you left the interest in. With a company that pays no dividend like Berkshire, if you're going to leave all your capital in every year, for me to get a fixed-price option for ten years would mean that I was getting a royalty on money that you left with me, and I made the choice to have you leave it with me. That does not strike me as equitable.

"I think any option should have a step-up in price that reflects the fact that money is reinvested by the shareholders annually. If somebody wants to pay out 100% of the earnings every year, then you can have a fixed-price option. If you give me the money every year, and you do more with the original sum, that's fine. But if [the cumulative earnings] are left with someone for ten years, there's going to be some increase in value even if they spend every day golfing. To give a piece of that away—a royalty on the passage of time for them—is a mistake.

"I think options ought to be granted at the fair value of the business when they're granted; sometimes that's the market price, sometimes it isn't. Certainly, the management of a company would not give an option on their business to some third party at a market price they felt was way too low. I find it a little disingenuous when managements get a takeover bid and they say that the company's really worth twice that much, but they're perfectly willing to issue options to themselves at the price which they say is totally inadequate.

"But options, properly structured, for people with responsibility for the business, can make sense. And I think that if something happened to me and Charlie, in terms of the manager of the business subsequently, if it were structured properly, I would not see anything wrong with an options arrangement. We carry this philosophy down to our subsidiaries where they generally get incentive arrangements that relate to the operation of their business, but not Berkshire overall; to penalize or tie rewards to something over which a manager has no control is kind of silly.

"In terms of overall level of compensation, the real sin is having a mediocre manager; that is what costs owners very significant amounts of money over time. If a mediocre manager is paid a relatively small sum, it's still a great mistake—and if they're paid huge sums, it's a travesty. It's almost impossible to pay the outstanding manager a sum that's disproportionate to their value when you get a large enterprise. Coca-Cola had a market value of $4 billion when Roberto Goizueta took over. It had stagnated during the previous decade under an earlier management, despite having the same product. If we'd bought the entire Coca-Cola Company when Roberto came in, for $4 billion, and we now had a business worth $150 billion, Roberto would have earned more money with us than he's earned under the present arrangement.

"Having the right person in place is enormously important. How much they should take is another question, that's more philosophical. Tom Murphy, the best manager in the world, he just didn't feel like taking a lot of money out of it. And I tip my hat to him, but I don't think that necessarily makes it wrong for somebody else to take more money for doing the job ... When I ran a partnership in the 1960s, I took a quarter of the profit over 6% a year. I didn't get paid any salary, but I could make a lot of money doing that. And that thought occurred to me as I ran the place from day to day, and I think it probably helped a little. So I don't think it's a terrible thing to have somebody get paid for making money for the shareholders, but they ought to get paid for really making it, not simply because the shareholders reinvest money with them. They ought to make it based on the fair value of what they had when they took over, and they ought to make it really just for excellent performance."

CM: "We have remarked in previous meetings that we regard present mandated corporate accounting, with respect to stock options, as weak, corrupt, and contemptible. And it is ... If something is so wonderful as a standard technique of compensation, why does it have to be masked under weak, corrupt, and contemptible accounting? It is no credit to our civilization that we've drifted into this particular modality. If you overuse stock options, you can get to where the whole thing is sort of a chain letter. In Silicon Valley, there's one company that practically paid everybody in options, and as long as the chain letter galloped, it worked as far as the income account, because nothing went through as an expense. And once everybody is issuing stock options, everybody else feels they have to do it, and the practice spreads. So, I am not totally wild about the extreme prevalence of the stock option modality in American corporate life.

"Personally, I would vastly prefer different modalities, which would probably involve stock instead of stock options. I'm all for sharing with the kind of people who are doing the important work pretty well down in the organization at a place like Costco or Coca-Cola or any other such company, but I don't much like the present scheme that civilization has drifted into.

"We have some wretched excesses in American corporate compensation. I don't think the excess is necessarily the guy who got the most money. In many cases I agree with Warren, that the money has been deserved. But such is the envy effect that the practice spreads to everybody else. And then the taxi driver and everybody starts thinking the system is irrational, unfair, crazy. And I think that's what causes some people, as they rise in American corporations, to, at a certain point of power gaining and wealth gaining, start exercising extreme restraint as a sort of moral duty. And I would argue Tom Murphy's attitude is the right attitude. It goes way, way back in the history of civilization ... If you were an important citizen of Athens, it was a lot like being an important person in Jewish culture. You had duties to give back and to act as a certain example, and the civilization had social pressures that enforced those duties. I would argue that the Berkshire Hathaway compensation system, considering what the people at the top already have, it would be better if we saw a little more of it. I think Warren and I do all right."

WB: "An added problem, in terms of the accounting, is the sort of hypocrisy that it pushes people into, which then becomes accepted as a sort of a norm, particularly when leaders do it. You had a situation a few years back when there was no question that any manager would say stock options are a form of compensation, that compensation is a form of expense, and that expense belongs in the income account. But they didn't want to have stock options counted because they felt that it might restrict their use. So when the Financial Accounting Standards Board (FASB), came up with a proposal to actually have reality reflected en masse, corporate chieftains descended on Washington to pressure legislators to have Congress start enacting accounting standards. ... That sort of behavior by corporate chieftains, when they are in there arguing black is white, in order to feather their own nest and maybe create a little higher stock prices, they forfeit, to some degree, their right to be taken seriously when they claim they're operating for the good of the Republic, and march on Washington in other regards. There's a degradation that can set in through an organization whose leaders are also leaders in hypocrisy."

2003 MEETING (00:58:25)

CM: "Our system is different from most big corporations; we think it's less capricious. The stock option system will give extraordinarily liberal awards, sort of by accident, to some people. And it'll deny others any reward at all at some different time in spite of the great contributions made by the people who are getting nothing. So, except where we inherit it, we just don't use it."

WB: "We inherited some stock options, primarily in the Gen Re transaction [in 1998]. Those options turned out to be quite valuable. They would not have been valuable if Gen Re had been left alone as a standalone company; they profited from the fact that other parts of Berkshire did well, and the money went to the people with these options who delivered nothing to the performance of Berkshire for a while. That is not an indictment of anybody, in the least, at Gen Re. It's an indictment of an options system which represents a lottery ticket and a royalty on the passage of time because an option holder benefits from retained earnings and benefits not at all from dividends. And that puts his interest, maybe, quite contrary to that of the shareholders.

"We believe in paying for performance, but we believe in tying performance to what is actually under the reasonable control of the person that's being measured. And to give a lottery ticket on the overall results of Berkshire Hathaway to someone who is running a business that's 1% of the whole is really crazy. I would say you have seen more misdirected compensation throughout corporate America in the last five years than in the hundred years before that.

It's been extraordinary. There was wealth creation in the 1990s, just like in the 1980s, 1970s, 1960s, and 1950s—but there was a wealth transfer like had never been experienced before."

CM: "If we are right with our general approach, it has considerably important implications. The natural implication is that more than 99% of corporate compensation systems are more than a little crazy in America. I want to emphasize that Berkshire is not illiberal. We've got various incentive systems out where people make tens of millions, and may make hundreds of millions. We're not against rewards for people who make vast contributions. But a system that's basically capricious, and which doesn't tailor the results per person and per activity very well, we just think it's crazy."

WB: "We love to see people associated with Berkshire making money, as long as they're making money for you at the same time. It's very simple. We don't want them to get a free ride off your money ... What happens with compensation is the acid test of corporate reform. ... What you've had in the last twenty years is an enormous disparity in the rates of compensation of people at the top compared to people at the bottom, and also a disconnect between the comp of people running businesses and the results of the owners who gave them the money. So arise, shareholder."

INSTITUTIONAL SHAREHOLDERS AND COMPENSATION IN CORPORATE AMERICA

2000 MEETING (02:31:36)

CM: "Generally speaking, I think it's a mistake for corporate America to create as much hostility as it does, which is based on the way it compensates principal officers of corporations. It is simply maddening to add a little clause that the corporation will scratch the guy's back for just tiny, little bits of stuff that looks terrible. To me, that is extremely stupid. And I see it where the corporation helps him prepare his tax return for ten years after he leaves and so forth. I think that makes a terrible impression on shareholders, generally. I think corporate America's crazy to do it. They get sold this stuff by these damn consultants."

WB: "I agree ... I can't remember a case of anybody that's been with us who called in a lawyer or anything, or where we even had to reduce things to writing, basically, and it works fine. It is a little maddening to have a CEO show up with a lawyer with a twenty-page contract. It's become standard operating procedure, and once you get a big, public company with committees, consultants to the committees, consultants who are picked by the officers of the company, they look around at what everybody else is doing and say, 'Well, that's the way the other guy does it. So I'll do it.' I think the proxy statements of the last twenty years, what that's induced in the way of behavior by people at somewhat comparable companies that look at the proxy statements of their competitors and say to their lawyer, 'Joe Blow got this. Why shouldn't I have it?' It just escalates and escalates and escalates. It won't stop.

"I have never seen a compensation consultant come into a public company and suggest a plan that, net, reduces the cost of compensation ... CEO compensation is not a market system and it's not subject to market tests. And I don't know what you do about that, particularly. But it doesn't seem to bother shareholders very much."

CM: "Oh, I think it bothers them a lot, Warren. It's just that they feel powerless."

WB: "Yes, but institutional shareholders could change that. My guess is that the top thirty institutions probably control two-thirds of the big companies in the country. They don't seem to care that much. Actually, they spend their time on what I regard as peripheral issues, usually. They talk about other things. They get involved in rituals of corporate governance that, frankly, don't mean a damn in terms of how the company performs. And they seem to ignore these other issues. But we've got enough to do running Berkshire, so we can't reform the world on that. We will run Berkshire in a rational manner, and we have yet to hire a compensation consultant."

GOOD BUSINESSES AND BAD MANAGEMENT

2001 MEETING (04:37:29)

WB: "The history Charlie and I have had of persuading decent, intelligent people, who we thought were doing unintelligent things, to change their course of action, has been poor."

CM: "Worse than poor."

WB: "If you really think you're in with people that have a good business, but they're going to keep doing dumb things with your money, you'll probably do better to get out. You can get in with people who have a good business and who you think are going to do sensible things with it. You have that option. Now, you also have the option of trying to persuade them to change their mind, but it's just very, very difficult. That's been something we've faced for fifty years. And initially, we faced it from a position where nobody even knew who the hell we were, or anything of the sort. We've acquired a certain stature over time, perhaps in talking and writing on the subject—and we still don't get very far.

"When people want to do something, they want to do something. And they didn't rise to become the CEO of a company to have some shareholder tell them that their most recent idea is dumb. That is just not the type that gets to the top. So, as a matter of investment technique, and maybe as a matter of avoiding stress in your life and all of that sort of thing, and dealing with smaller quantities of stock so it's easier to sell and buy, I would say it's better to be in with a management you're simpatico with, than to be in a great business with a management that's bent on doing things that don't make much sense to you."

THE INSTITUTIONAL IMPERATIVE

2009 MEETING (00:30:03)

WB: "In terms of Moody's stock, the odds are that the rating agency business is probably still a good business ... It's a business with very few people in it that affects a large segment of the economy; the capital markets are huge. I think there will probably be rating agencies in the future. And it doesn't require capital. So, it has the fundamentals of a pretty good business.

"We have said in this meeting in the past, many times, that Charlie and I don't pay any attention to ratings. We don't believe in outsourcing investment decisions. If we buy a bond, the rating is immaterial to us, except to the extent that, if we think it's rated more poorly than it should be, it may help us buy it at an attractive price. But we do not think that the people at Moody's, or Standard & Poor's, or Fitch, or anyplace else, should be telling us the credit rating of a company. We figure that out for ourselves. And sometimes we disagree with the market in a major way. We've made some money that way."

CM: "I think the rating agencies, being good at doing mathematical calculations, eagerly sought stupid assumptions that enabled them to do clever mathematics. It's an example of being too smart for your own good. There's an old saying, 'To a man with a hammer, every problem looks pretty much like a nail.' And that's what happened in the rating agencies."

WB: "The interesting thing about all those triple-As is that the people who created them ended up owning a lot of them. So they believed their own baloney ... you had these people stirring up the Kool-Aid and then they drank it themselves. They paid a big penalty for it. I think it was stupidity and the fact that everybody else was doing it. ... The one reason you can't give for any action at Berkshire, as far as I'm concerned, is that *everybody else is doing it.* If that's the best you can come up with, something's wrong. But that happens in security markets all the time. It's very difficult to tell a huge organization that you shouldn't be doing something that well-regarded competitors are doing, particularly when there's a lot of money in it. So it's very hard to stop these things once you get sort of an industry acceptance of behavior."

THE BOARD OF DIRECTORS

2004 MEETING (00:34:08)

WB: "The real job of the board of directors is to come up with the right CEO and to prevent him or her from overreaching; if they do that job well, the rest will take care of itself. But you have to think some to determine whether that's taking place, you can't solve it by just running down a little checklist. ... If Berkshire Hathaway owns 200 million shares of Coca-Cola ($10 billion worth), it's a little silly to think that the interest that Berkshire Hathaway has in selling some hours of training at FlightSafety would cause me to do something counter to the interests of the shareholders, when we have $10 billion riding on that side of the table ... somebody doesn't understand proportionality at all when they come to that sort of conclusion. ... So, I encourage institutional shareholders and large owners to behave like owners—but I also encourage them to think logically, as owners should think, in determining what causes they take on and how they vote. ... You would hope that, in not too many years, they would actually think about what's good for the shareholders of the company."

2007 MEETING (04:06:23)

WB: "I would say most investors probably have a little bit of a distorted view of how most large corporations have operated over the years. For a long time I would say that directors, generally, were sort of potted plants. Management had its agenda and it didn't really want their input on major matters. Charlie and I can certainly testify to the fact that we have had a great lack of success, even when we were the largest shareholder of a company, in terms of talking about things that really count. I mean, if somebody spends twenty-five to thirty years rising to the position of CEO, they want to be boss, you can't blame them—and the only thing in their way is the board of directors. So, they don't really want the directors getting into the business very much.

"There's a lot more process now that's been imposed by the recent rules. But I still would say, in terms of the reality of the guts of business and the discussions that take place, I think you might be surprised at the level of that throughout corporate America. Overwhelmingly, the job of the board of directors is to have the right CEO. If you've got the right CEO, 90% of it takes care of itself. ... And if you have that CEO, you have an obligation on the board to make sure that there's not overreaching by the CEO, because the CEO can have different interests.

"I think the other thing that the board should do is really bring some independent judgment in on major acquisitions. There is a natural tendency for people who get to be CEOs—big egos, big motors—to want to do big things and to become bigger spending other people's money. And normally, when big deals come along, by the time it gets to the board, they've made the deal anyway. They have investment bankers who go through a little ritual. I've never seen one come in and make a presentation that says it's a dumb idea. They know what the answer is supposed to be, and it just becomes a little game. ... What I've seen over the years has really been pretty bad. But I can understand it because the CEO wouldn't bring in the deal unless he wants it done. And once he brings it in, he's going to stack the deck and make the presentation in such a way that it's almost impossible to exercise independent judgment."

CM: "I think big, big deals, on average, in America, are contrary to the shareholders' interest. That's the way to bet. On the acquirer's side, usually the shareholders are worse off."

WB: "Most stock deals, they think about what they're getting and they don't think about what they're giving up. I have been involved time after time where people are giving a significant percentage of the business, which they wouldn't sell at the current market price, but they hand away a piece of the business because they want to own something else. There's nothing wrong with that, you just have to be sure that you're getting as much as you're giving. I have very seldom heard a discussion—in fact, I don't think I've ever heard one—weighing what you were actually giving away on a stock deal versus what you're getting.

"I've heard a lot of discussion about dilution and when it will be overcome, all that sort of thing, but that is not the question. The real question is if more value is being created, how is it being whacked up between the two companies? And if extra value isn't being created, are you getting more than you're giving?

"When I gave away 2% of Berkshire Hathaway to acquire [shoemaker] Dexter Shoe, that was one of the dumbest deals in the history of the world. It wasn't just 2% of what we had then at Berkshire, it was 2% of the present Berkshire Hathaway company. You'd all be a full 2% richer if I hadn't done that. ... The point is that doesn't show up under conventional accounting at all. It gets brushed under the rug. At Gillette, we had ten deals in a row that never came close to meeting the business case presented to the board. Was that ever mentioned to shareholders? Did it show up in the financial report? Never—and that goes on all the time in corporate America.

"Unfortunately, to the extent shareholders get unhappy with managements, they are complaining about whether they've got diversity on the board or something like that. But when you're blowing away the value of the company, that, to me, is a whole lot more important ... At one time, we owned stock in the Third National Bank down in Nashville. They're really wonderful people, but they got the ability to acquire other banks and they went out to some very small bank, and the guy at the very small bank said, 'I want stock.' He said, 'I want you to value your stock at market and value mine at this huge premium.' And then he said, 'There's one other condition. Since I'm putting my whole net worth in your stock, I want you to promise you'll never do a deal this dumb in the future.' That fellow was a little more out in the open than is typically the case."

2016 MEETING (02:35:00)

WB: "When we select board members we are looking for people who are business savvy, shareholder oriented, and have a special interest in Berkshire. We lay it out, we've done so for years, and I think we've been much more explicit than most companies. We've found people like that, and as a result I think we've got the best board that we could have. They're clearly not in it for the money.

"I get called by consulting firms who have been told to get candidates for directors for other companies, and by the questions they ask, it's clear they've got something in mind other than what we ask in terms of directors. They really want somebody whose name will reflect credit on the institution, which means a big name.

"One organization recently, the one that did the blood samples with small pricks [Theranos], got some very big names on their board. The names were great, but we're not interested in people who want to be on the board because they want to make $200,000 or $300,000 a year for 10% of their time. And we're not interested in the ones for whom it's a prestige item and who want to go and check boxes or that sort of thing. We will continue to apply our tests: business savvy, shareholder orientation, and a strong personal interest in Berkshire. And every share of Berkshire that our [board members] own, they bought just like everybody else in this room. We want our directors to walk in the shoes of shareholders. We want them to care a lot about the business, and we want them to be smart enough so that they know enough about business that they know what they should get involved in and what they shouldn't get involved in."

CM: "Years ago, I did some work for the Roman Catholic Archbishop of Los Angeles, and my senior partner pompously said, 'You don't need to hire us to do this; there are plenty of good Catholic tax lawyers.' And the archbishop looked at him like he was an idiot and said, 'Mr. Peeler, last year I had some very serious surgery, and I did not look around for the leading Catholic surgeon.' That's the way I feel about board members."

2022 MEETING (05:03:17)

WB: "Berkshire directors don't have directors and officers (D&O) liability insurance. Virtually every company on the New York Stock Exchange has it; we don't buy it at Berkshire ... It's very interesting, people go on museum boards or college boards and they're expected to contribute money. They say it's a great honor to be on a university board or a museum board or whatever, and therefore you should raise money for us. Well, frankly, I think our board is more interesting than a university board or a hospital board or something. But people have found that they can make $300,000 a year, which is enormously important to some people.

"If somehow directors didn't get paid at all, chances are there would still be plenty of people who wanted to be directors. ... The whole idea of the independent director, frankly, just doesn't really make any sense to me."

CM: "You don't think a director who needs $300,000 a year is independent? He's independent the way a slave is independent."

WB: "I am going to read a few sentences from a letter I received many years ago, except I'm doctoring it because I don't want anybody to be identified, obviously. But these are word-for-word excerpts. It said, 'I'm writing to you with a great deal of reluctance in the sense of personal embarrassment. I have tried all of the conventional means of raising the money.' I don't know the person, but he wrote and said he needed a couple of million dollars. And then this is the item that I think you might find interesting. 'My income is composed 100% of my board fees.'

"I looked him up, and at the time, he was a director of five prestigious companies, and he'd been on others. But he was desperate for money, and he says, 'I'm getting 100% of my income from board fees.' And he was an independent director. He classifies as an independent director at every one of these companies. In 2006, we owned 9% of the Coca-Cola Company. We obviously cared about the Coca-Cola Company. And in that year, CalPERS [the California Public Employees' Retirement System] and a few others recommended that we be voted against. Two big institutional investors voted that way because they didn't think I was independent, since the people with our Dairy Queen franchises bought Coca-Cola. It's just nutty. One year, my voter approval fell from 98% to 84% because they decided I wasn't the right sort of person to be able to handle these responsibilities.

"If a board member wants to do a lot of other good things, it doesn't mean they're troubled. But if the person might go broke without those board memberships, how in the world can you call them an independent director? It's ridiculous. But it's the way the rules are."

CM: "They don't want them just independent. They want one horse, one rabbit, one cow, one whatever. Independence is not enough. You need a very diverse kind of independence."

WB: "If you desperately need the money—100% of income for this guy—and you're on five of the most prestigious boards in the country, each classifying you as independent, all you're hoping is that if a CEO of yours gets called by another CEO and asks, 'Is this guy OK?' he says, 'Of course,' which means, he doesn't cause trouble. So he gets on a sixth board. It's all a little crazy."

CORPORATE CULTURE

2015 MEETING (00:58:16)

WB: "I think culture has to come from the top. It has to be consistent, it has to be part of written communications, it has to be lived, and it has to be rewarded when followed and punished when not. And then it takes a very, very long time to really become solid. Obviously, it's much easier if you inherit a culture you like, and it's easier in smaller firms, I think … It is a grain-of-sand type of thing. … We work all the time at trying to behave with other people as if our positions were reversed. That's what Charlie's always advised in all our activities, and we've tried to follow it. We're certainly far from perfect at it, but if you keep working at it, it does get results."

CM: "I think the one thing that we did that's worked best of all is we were always dissatisfied with what we already knew and we always wanted to know more. Berkshire—if Warren and I had stayed frozen in time, particularly Warren—would have been a terrible place. It's what we kept learning that made it work, and I don't think that will ever stop."

2022 MEETING (03:00:11)

WB: "We have 1,470,000 Class A shares outstanding, fewer than we had a year ago. Those seats are filled. The shareholders are in place. We like the group we have. So, why in the world, when we have a fixed number of seats, should we go out and recruit other people to replace you? The ideal shareholder group we can have is the group we have today. If we had a church, we would want people to keep coming back week after week after week. If we had a limited number of seats, and we had wonderful parishioners, we would not go out and recruit another hundred people if we had to throw out a hundred of the ones we already had.

"Yet virtually every company I know of is wooing new people to come in, whether they're improving the group or not. It strikes us as basically crazy. We don't want anybody different than we have now. If you had a neighborhood, and the size was such that you could have ten neighbors, and they were all great neighbors, why in the world would you want to replace them? It is weird, but there's an awful lot of people who make their living by doing that and they never really question it.

"The really crazy process that has developed is people talking to analyst groups. Some companies do it more than once a month. Just imagine you go to work for that company; every month, people are repeating these things about their company, that it's important that we have a certain percentage growth or something like that. They say it month after month after month, and it becomes a catechism. How do you go out next month and say, by the way, we were really wrong. You don't say that. It's a terrible problem for a new CEO, coming in after a previous CEO, to be told 'The important thing to do is to hit your earnings targets.' In all probability they have been met by cheating from time to time. The guy handed the baton, is he going to come out and say, 'Well, we've really been cheating a little, and it's really counterproductive to the development of the companies to make earnings projections and not just to give you the results as they come rather than making up a few things in the accounting department'? They can't do that. It's not human nature … It's a totally destructive quality.

"Within GAAP accounting, I can play a lot of games with the numbers. Once you start, it's all over. You can't quit. It's like taking $5 out of the cash register. The first time you take the $5 out you'll say, 'I'm going to put it back.' But after a few times, you never stop. … If something is going to be destructive, the thing to do is not to start it—and I can't imagine anything more destructive than forecasting earnings … If you start lying, you've got a big problem. It's that simple. … If you're a human and you've said we're going to earn $3.59 per share, you can get to $3.59 per share quite often. If you have a culture of lying, the processes really just disappear."

CM: "I think Berkshire's culture is going to last a long time after we're gone. I think it will prosper pretty well. The rest of corporate America is quite different. And it gets more different, I think, with each passing decade. It's getting very peculiar. Pretty soon, they're going to hold all the shareholders' meetings online … And index funds get more and more important in the voting. It's like everything in life: It changes, and not always in ways you like."

PART FIVE:
Berkshire Hathaway

"Our goal in life is not to spend our time associating with people who are going to be disappointed with us. It's our fault if we give out the wrong advertisement. So we try to advertise what we are, and then we try to deliver on that."

"It's amazing to me that we have been as successful as we have been in buying desirable places. Human revulsion has helped us, because many of the people who sell to us are so smart that they're revolted by almost everything else."

"We care enormously about succession planning because, in addition to a lot of other reasons, we both have a very significant percentage of our net worth in Berkshire. Neither one of us has figured out how to sell it all fifteen minutes before we get hit by a truck."

"I think our chief contribution to the businesses we acquire is what we don't do."

"Warren has always planned on paying large dividends; he does it in the mode of Saint Augustine when he said, 'God, give me chastity, but not yet.'"

"We really like things that you don't have to carry out to three decimal places. If you have to carry it out to three decimal places, it's not a good idea."

INTRODUCTION

Berkshire is Buffett's painting. As it relates to many of the topics discussed in this book, it is where he implemented his own ideas on the most intelligent way to allocate capital and to run a company over six decades. In financial terms, the end result is a stock price that has risen nearly 100,000× since Buffett started buying at $7.625 per share in 1962 (as of October 2024)—not a bad outcome given that Buffett has said that the Berkshire investment was "a terrible mistake."

As we think about much of what has been discussed in prior sections—for example, the key inputs to intrinsic value and the impact of management quality on that output—Berkshire itself is a great case study. As Munger notes, the history of Berkshire offers numerous lessons on how to achieve success in investing and in business, with a key variable being the ability to survive periodic difficulties and to eventually move past earlier mistakes: "It is interesting that a wrong decision has been made to work out so well. We've done a lot of that, scrambling out of wrong decisions. I'd argue that's a big part of having a reasonable record in life. You can't avoid making wrong decisions. But if you recognize them promptly and do something about them, you can frequently turn the lemon into lemonade, which is what happened here. Warren twisted a lot of capital out of the textile business and invested it wisely, and that is why we're all here."

SUBJECTS AND MEETINGS FEATURED

BUFFETT'S ORIGINAL INVESTMENT IN BERKSHIRE

1997 MEETING (00:32:59)

WARREN BUFFETT: "We started buying Berkshire in 1962. I think the first ticket was at $7.625 per share. I've got the trading card on the wall—it was 2,000 shares and I paid a dime commission per share. I can't believe I was paying a dime commission; we pay a nickel now on much higher-priced stocks. It's a good thing I didn't have a fistfight with a broker about whether to pay it, I might not have had those 2,000 shares. As a director, Ken Chase and his family's holdings in Berkshire goes back to the 1920s. Buffett Partnership, which I ran in the 1960s, bought about 70% of the company. So that means they were roughly 300,000 shares not owned by us. Aside from the Chace family, I'm sure we've got fifty or a hundred shareholders from that earlier date still around, and I'm glad they are."

2000 MEETING (03:24:58)

WB: "The original purchase of Berkshire was a terrible mistake. I bought it because it was a cigar-butt approach to investing, where we would look around for something with a free puff left in it; it was soggy and kind of disgusting and everything, but it was free. And Berkshire was selling below working capital and had a history of repurchasing shares periodically on tender offers. … It looked to me like they were going to have a tender offer periodically. It would probably be at some figure closer to net working capital, which might have been $11 or $12 a share, and we would sell on the tender.

"Then I met Seabury Stanton, who was running Berkshire, and he told me that he was thinking of having a tender. That made me an insider, so I couldn't do anything. He wondered what price we'd tender at. As I remember, I think I said, '11 and ⅜.' He said to me, 'Well, if we have a tender at 11 and ⅜, will you tender?' And I said, 'Yes, I will.' I was then obviously frozen out of doing anything with the stock for a little while. But then he came along with the tender offer. I opened the envelope, and it was $11.25; it was ⅛ below what he had said to me and what I had agreed to. So, I found that kind of irritating and I didn't tender. Then I bought a lot of stock, we bought several blocks, and before long we controlled the company.

"At an ⅛ of a point difference, we wouldn't have bought the company. We would've been much better off if we hadn't bought it because then things like [the acquisition of insurer] National Indemnity and all of that happened, and instead of buying it into a public company with a great many other shareholders, we would've bought it privately in the partnership and our partners would've had a greater interest. So, Berkshire was exactly the wrong vehicle to use for buying a bunch of wonderful companies over time, but I sort of stumbled into it. And when I disbanded the partnership, I distributed out the Berkshire because it seemed like the easiest and best thing to do. I'm glad it all worked out this way. It did not work out the best way, economically, in all probability. It was the wrong base to use to build an enterprise around."

CHARLIE MUNGER: "It is interesting that a wrong decision has been made to work out so well. We've done a lot of that, scrambling out of wrong decisions. I'd argue that's a big part of having a reasonable record in life. You can't avoid making wrong decisions. But if you recognize them promptly and do something about them, you can frequently turn the lemon into lemonade, which is what happened here. Warren twisted a lot of capital out of the textile business and invested it wisely, and that's why we're all here."

THE RIGHT OWNERS

1999 MEETING (02:25:20)

WB: "People say, 'Do you want individual owners, do you want institutional owners?' What we want are informed owners who are in sync with our objectives, measurements, time horizons, all of that sort of thing. We want people that are going to be comfortable owning Berkshire, and we don't want people who are owning it for reasons that are different from our reasons for owning it. We don't want people who are concerned about quarterly earnings. We don't want people who are concerned about stock splits. We don't want people who need to be pumped up about the stock, periodically. It's just not of interest to us because it means we have to keep living that way in the future. And if it's not the way we want to live now, it's not the way we want to live in the future.

"What we really want are a bunch of people like we have in this audience, who sit down and read and think and understand that they're making an investment. It's not just a little ticker symbol. They're buying part of a business. They know what the business is all about. They know how we think, they know how we measure ourselves. They're comfortable with that. And they can come in individual or institutional form. When we get them, we like to keep them. So there's no change in our attitude about that. There is some limited amount of Wall Street coverage, which I guess for a company with $120 billion of market value, there should be."

2010 MEETING (04:00:45)

WB: "The interesting thing about marketable securities is that, basically, anybody can buy them. ... If you're running a public company, you can have anybody from Osama bin Laden to the Pope as your shareholder. You don't elect them, they elect you. Now, if you want a shareholder body that is going to be in sync with you, it's important, in my view, to let them know exactly what sort of institution you plan to run. And we have annual reports, television interviews, and various ways of conveying to people what kind of a place Berkshire is. To some, that says, 'Come in,' and to others it says, 'Stay out.'

"Phil Fisher described the situation this way. He said, 'You can have a restaurant that advertises French food, and if you have French food inside, you're going to get a satisfied and returning clientele. And you can have another one that advertises hamburgers. But what you can't do is have hamburgers on the marquee outside while serving French food inside.' Many companies try and promise everything to everybody. Their investor relations department tells them that any shareholder they can get interested, they want. We want people who think the way we do. And we think, on balance, we won't disappoint them too much.

"Our goal in life is not to spend our time associating with people who are going to be disappointed with us. It's our fault if we give out the wrong advertisement. So we try to advertise what we are, and then we try to deliver on that. And I do think we have the best group of shareholders in the world, among large publicly traded companies. And I think it's because we've got people that basically look into buying a business, becoming our partners over the years, and they know we'll treat them like partners. And they, in turn, give us a lot of comfort in having a stable shareholder base and a good feeling about just running the whole place."

CM: "What happened here is, to some extent, an accident. Warren and I started out investing money for our families and friends, and the people who trusted us when we were young and unknown we of course developed a strong affection for. We morphed into controlling public companies from that base, and so we tend to regard our shareholders, including the new ones, as family. That's not put on, that's the way we regard you. Other people can't do that because they morphed into their situation in a different way.

"If you were a CEO and dealt with the average institutional investor, who is interested in having his portfolio management look good the next six months, you'd find it hard to love your shareholders. They're sort of a hostile force that is putting unreasonable expectations on you. So I don't think Warren and I deserve such wonderful credit for the fact that we have better relations with our shareholders. We came up in a totally different way. Now, we did have enough sense, when we saw that it was such a good thing and so satisfying, that we stayed with it. But we got into this by accident."

WB: "We got in by accident, and we also were blessed with the fact that we did not have an investor relations department. I have seen them in operation at dozens of companies … And it is really ridiculous, the idea that you go out to try and cater to the expectations of people who are expecting you to do things you can't do by operations, but maybe you can do by accounting for a short period of time. It leads to the worst behavior. In the end, somebody's going to own all your shares … why not get a bunch of people who are in sync with you? The way they're going to be in sync is if you told them rather accurately what you expect, how you expect to do it, and tell them when you make mistakes."

BERKSHIRE'S OPERATIONAL STRUCTURE

1994 MEETING (02:36:17)

CM: "Berkshire is incredibly decentralized, in terms of power and decisions resting in the operating divisions. In terms of the marketable securities, it's incredibly centralized. And, so far, we have not had any big penalty from not being able to do the things that we did when we were young. Eventually we will reach the penalty."

RISK MANAGEMENT AT BERKSHIRE

2012 MEETING (03:21:29)

WB: "We both have the same bend of mind whereby we think about worst cases all the time, and then we add on a big margin of safety … We undoubtedly build in layers of safety that others might regard as foolish, but we've got 600,000 shareholders and I've got members of my family that have 80% or 90% of their net worth in the company. I'm just not interested in explaining to them that we went broke because there was a 0.01% chance that we would go broke and the remaining probability was filled by the chance of doubling our money, and I decided that that was a good gamble to take. We're not going to do that. We are never going to risk what we have and need for what we don't have and don't need. We'll still find things to do where we can make money, but we don't have to stretch to do it … It's always top of the mind around Berkshire. Your returns in ninety-nine years out of a hundred will probably be penalized by us being excessively conservative—and one year out of a hundred, we'll survive when some other people won't.

"In 1962, when I set up our office in Kiewit Plaza, I put seven items on the wall. Our art budget was $7, so I went down to the library, and for $1 each I made photocopies of pages from financial history. One was in May of 1901 when the Northern Pacific Corner occurred; Harriman was trying to get control of the Northern Pacific [railroad], and James J. Hill [the largest stockholder] was trying to retain control. And unbeknown to each other, they both bought more than 50% of the stock. Now, when two people buy more than 50% of the stock each, and they both really want it, they're not just going to resell—interesting things happen. And in that paper of May 1901, the whole rest of the market was totally collapsing because Northern Pacific went from $170 a share to $1,000 a share in one day, trading for cash, because the shorts needed it. And there was a little item at the top of that paper, which we still have at the office, where a brewer in Troy, New York, committed suicide by diving into a vat of hot beer because he'd received a margin call. He probably knew how impossible it was that in one day a stock could go from $170 to $1,000 to cause margin calls—but he ended up in a vat of hot beer, and I've never wanted to end up in a vat of hot beer. Life in financial markets has got no relation to sigmas. If everybody who operated in financial markets had never had any concept of standard errors and so on, they would be a lot better off."

CM: "It's created a lot of false confidence. Now it has gone away. As I said earlier, the business schools have improved. So has risk control on Wall Street. They have now taken the Gaussian curve and changed its shape; they just made a different shape than Gauss did, and it's a better curve now, even though it's less precise."

WB: "They talk about fat tails, but they still don't know how fat to make them. They have no idea."

CM: "They've learned through painful experience they weren't fat enough."

WB: "They learned the other was wrong, but they don't know what's right."

CM: "We always knew there were fat tails. Warren and I, in the Salomon meetings, would look over at one another and roll our eyes when the risk control people were talking."

BERKSHIRE'S LONG-TERM OWNERSHIP AND ACQUISITIONS

1995 MEETING (00:38:55)

WB: "If I die tonight, my stock goes to my wife, who is a member of the board of directors. She will own that stock until her death, when it will go to a foundation. So, there is a desire to have as long-term and permanent ownership structure as can really be done. ... We have invited people like [jewelry retailer] Helzberg Diamonds to join Berkshire in what we think is a particularly advantageous way for them to conduct a business and to know the future that they're joining. Part of knowing the future that they're joining involves knowing that the ownership is stable. And it will be stable for a very long period of time in Berkshire, probably about as long as anybody can plan for in this world.

"After my death, the family will not be involved in the management of the business, but they'll be involved in the ownership of the business. You will have a very large concentrated ownership position, going well on into the foundation, that will care very much about having the best management structure in place. To prepare for that over time, I think it's very advisable that family members who will not be involved in management, but who will have a key ownership role to play, become more and more familiar with the business and the philosophy behind it.

"If you've built a business since 1915 [like Helzberg Diamonds], and you care enormously about it, and you care about the people that you've developed, but you've got something else you want to do in life, it's more than advertising your car in the paper to sell it. It is a very important transaction to you—not just in terms of how much money you receive, but in terms of to whom you deliver the thousands of people who have joined you. Nothing is forever, but we have a structure that's about as good as you can do, in terms of people knowing what they're getting into when they make a deal with us and being able to count on the conditions that prevail at the time of the deal, continuing for a long period in the future."

2002 MEETING (01:29:20)

CM: "If you stop to think about it, the ordinary result when a big publicly held corporation buys another corporation is that, maybe two-thirds of the time, it's a terrible deal for the buying corporation, and yet the people have taken an enormous time doing it. We've bought all these businesses taking practically no time doing it, and on average they've worked out wonderfully. Why is that? The answer is we wait for the no-brainers. We're not trying to do the difficult things and we have the patience to wait. And then we're so peculiar that there actually are a good number of businesses in America who prefer selling to us than to other people. That's very helpful."

WB: "I just saw a review of a major company. It made ten acquisitions in a recent five-year period. Every one of those acquisitions was preceded by due diligence and all the baloney they go through. Not one lived up to, or was even close to, the expectations of the presentation that was made at the time of purchase. In aggregate, the ten earned one-quarter of what they were projected to earn in 2001. In other words, the projections were four times larger than the actual earnings. And this is a company with a strategic acquisition department, loads of people to go over the due diligence, and with investment bankers 'helping them' all along the way. And ten out of ten failed miserably. You have to ask yourself, how can you produce that result? Because the world didn't go to hell during that period, either. They were buying what was getting sold to them, and it was fulfilling some myths that the management had about itself. And managements have many myths about themselves. It isn't that complicated if you just wait for the fat pitch. And the fat pitch doesn't have to be somebody else doing something dumb or anything like that, because people don't do that.

"The people who come to us come for good reason. They usually want a transaction that is sure to close if a deal is made and they want one that will leave the people happy that are at the business. When it was announced at [insulation and roofing company] Johns Manville that Berkshire was the buyer, I understand there was a standing ovation … If you've been working at a company for twenty years and you know the owning family is getting older and has some problems to take care of, believe me, they talk in the hallways about that. What's going to happen when the family sells? People worry about that. And to have an answer for them, so that they all sleep the night that it's announced that the business has changed hands, means a lot to some owners. It doesn't mean anything to other owners. I don't think we've ever bought a business from a financial operator."

2010 MEETING (04:25:17)

WB: "The phone doesn't ring very often. When we start saying we want to buy businesses that earn $75–100 million, at a minimum, before tax, that weeds out a lot of phone calls. If we get three or four serious phone calls a year that sort of meet our criteria that look like they might be a possibility, that's a good year. I don't think there's been any major change in the frequency that something comes along that might interest us. In terms of being interested, we're as interested as ever. We wrote a big check and issued shares in connection with [freight railroad network] BNSF. But I would love it if Monday morning my phone rings with some big deal. We'll figure out a way to do it."

CM: "It's amazing to me that we have been as successful as we have been in buying desirable places. Human revulsion has helped us, because many of the people who sell to us are so smart that they're revolted by almost everything else. They don't want to sell into some fee-driven buying system that doesn't care about their employees or their business. And if they finally decide they want to join this one, they don't want to join the alternatives. Of course, that's marvelous for us. We've got a screening device out there that is protecting us, to some extent, from the wrong sort of people. We get offered things by people who would not sell to anybody else. That is really peculiar. And it's happened a lot."

WB: "It's happened, and on important ones. When I heard from [metal cutting tools company] ISCAR—and I'd never heard of ISCAR or [its founder]

Eitan Wertheimer—he basically told me that they wanted to sell to Berkshire Hathaway or they didn't want to sell to anybody. We met and we made a deal."

SUCCESSION AT BERKSHIRE

1995 MEETING (01:36:51)

WB: "We care enormously about succession planning because, in addition to a lot of other reasons, we both have a very significant percentage of our net worth in Berkshire. Neither one of us has figured out how to sell it all fifteen minutes before we get hit by a truck. So, we will not have the jump on the rest of you. And therefore, our continuing financial interest will go well beyond our deaths. In terms of foundations … it will go to organizations that we care very much about having maximum available resources. So we do have some plans. We don't name names or anything of the sort.

"It's not quite as tough as you might think because we have a collection of fabulous businesses. Some of them owned totally, some of them owned in part. I don't think razor blade sales at Gillette or Coca-Cola sales are going to fall off dramatically the day Charlie or I die. The same is true of the wholly-owned businesses. So, the question is more about allocating capital in the future. And that's a problem for Charlie and me right now, simply because of our size; it's not easy to find things to do that make sense with lots of money. Sometimes a year will go by and we don't find anything, and other times a year goes by, and we think we found something but it turns out we were wrong. But we think we will have some very smart people working on that, and we don't think it will be the end of the world if they don't find anything the first year because the businesses will run very well.

"We have a big advantage in that, as contrasted to almost every other company, we are eager to buy parts of wonderful businesses or all of them. Most investors are limited to buying parts of businesses, and most managers are psychologically geared to owning all of something that they can run themselves. It's like Woody Allen said: The advantage of being bisexual is it doubles your chances of a date on Saturday night. We can go either direction, in that respect, and our successors will also."

CM: "I think few business operations have ever been constructed to require so little continuing intelligence in corporate headquarters. An idiot who was willing just to sit here would have a very good record long after the present incumbents are dead."

WB: "I think that's true."

CM: "It would be a little better if Warren would keep alive, in terms of allocating the new capital; I don't think we'll easily replace Warren. But we don't have to keep getting rich at the same rate as we have in the past."

1999 MEETING (01:56:26)

WB: "We have, today, the people to take over Berkshire. There's no problem about that at all. They have been named in letters that the directors have. Exactly who it will be will depend on when Charlie and I are out of the picture. If we'd written the letter ten years ago, it might have been different than today. It might be different fifteen years from now. The timing of our death or incapacity will determine exactly who will be the persons in that letter. But we have those people in place, and they don't need to be groomed from this point forward. They'd be ready to run Berkshire tomorrow morning. I think you'd be quite pleased with the job they did. I've got 99.75% of my net worth in Berkshire; if I knew I was going to die next week, I wouldn't want it sold, and I don't want it sold after I die. I feel comfortable with the businesses, the managers, and the successor top management that we have—I just don't want them to take over too early."

CM: "I actually think that the prospects for continuity of corporate culture, to the extent that we have one at Berkshire, is higher than the prospect for continuity of corporate culture at most other large public companies. I don't see Berkshire changing its way of operating, even if Warren were to expire tonight. I think the capital, the fresh cash, would be allocated less well. But as I've said at past shareholder meetings, that's too damn bad. I don't think the job would be ill done; I just don't think it would be done quite as well as Warren does it."

2001 MEETING (04:21:06)

WB: "About every two years, I send our managers a letter and say, 'If you die tonight, what will I wish you had told me tomorrow morning?' I want them to put in writing to me, once every couple of years, what they think about succession; who they think should succeed them, or whether there are several candidates, or what their strengths and weaknesses are. I have that information available, and you're entitled to the same sort of answer about succession at Berkshire; it's a part of buying into this business. I can tell you no one has more of an interest in it than I do. Charlie has a similar interest, because we have a very high percentage of our net worth in the business. Plus, we've got a lifetime of effort in the business. And we want it to succeed for, at least in my case, the ultimate reward, the foundation I have. But also because we like what's happened so far and we want to prove that it's not dependent upon a couple of guys like us, but that it can be institutionalized, in effect.

"We know who will succeed me in what are likely to be two jobs, one in marketable securities and one in business operations. We want to be very sure that the culture is maintained. And I think it's so strong that I think it'd be very hard to change it. But, in addition, the stock ownership situation with me is such that if there were any inclination to change it, it can be prevented from happening ... In terms of who succeeds me, that depends when I die. There's no sense telling you today; twenty years ago, it would've been Charlie, obviously, but it won't be Charlie now because of his age. It'll be somebody else. But we feel very good about succession. We feel very good about the stability of the organization, in terms of the stock ownership situation, because that is insured for a very, very long time to come. We couldn't feel better about the managers we have in place and the culture we have in place."

CM: "The main defense is to have assets that will do well, more or less, automatically. And we have a lot of those. To the extent that you improve that further by having very good managers in place, and very good individualized systems for bringing new managers in, there's a lot of momentum here that would go on very nicely with the present management gone. ..."

WB: "The managers don't need me. We have to make sure they're treated fairly. But we are not making decisions around the place except in the allocation of capital. And that will be important. But some of that is semiautomatic. Others, it does require some imagination ... We are far, far, far stronger now than we were ten years ago. So I'm very comfortable with 99% of my estate being in Berkshire. I think it's an intelligent holding for the foundation knowing that I won't be around at some point before the foundation gets it."

2007 MEETING (01:16:11)

CM: "What on earth has caused Berkshire's extreme record to go on for such a very long time? I would argue Warren, who was reading everything he could when he was ten years old, became a learning machine, and then he had a very long run when he kept learning. If Warren had not been learning all the while, I'm telling you, having watched the process closely, the record would be a pale shadow of what it is. And Warren has improved since he passed the retirement age of man. In other words, in this field, at least, you can improve when you're old. Now, most companies don't even try to create that kind of a record. They pass power from one sixty-five-year-old to one fifty-nine-year-old and then do it over and over again. But you get an enormous advantage from practice in this field ... Our system ought to be more copied than it is. This idea of passing power from one old codger to another, in a settled way, is not necessarily the right system at all."

2009 MEETING (00:52:43)

WB: "If we had a good way to inject somebody into some role that would make them a better CEO of Berkshire, we would try it. But the truth is that the candidates we have are running businesses. They're making capital allocation decisions. They're doing things every day of an operating nature. And these are major businesses. To sit around at headquarters while I'm sitting in there reading and on the phone and who knows what else, there wouldn't be anything to do … It'd be a waste of talent. … These are people who know how to run big businesses. They are 100% ready for the job now. They know how to allocate capital. The biggest job they'll have is the fact that they will have to develop relationships with potential sellers of businesses, with the world generally, with you, the shareholders, and with other managers. That takes some time.

"Probably the biggest challenge is that all these operating managers at Berkshire have different styles and different needs to some degree. They have different ways of operating. Some bat left-handed and some bat right-handed, some stand deep in the box and some crowd the plate. They all have a little bit of variation [in how they manage their businesses]. The CEO of Berkshire does require some knowledge of individual personalities. Which ones like to run by themselves totally and which ones like to check in occasionally and all that. But that is no reason to take a talent that's now running a business very successfully and building value and to have them sit in an office next to me and have us chew over the day's events. Charlie and I have worked together now for decades. I've learned a lot from Charlie—but I haven't done it by having him sit next door and have hourly meetings or anything of the sort."

CM: "Averaged out, you're more likely to be qualified to be CEO by running a subsidiary with an enormous amount of discretion than by being around headquarters watching somebody else do it his way. A lot of the models that have worked well in the world are quite Berkshire-like, in that they're decentralized and they let people pop up from the subsidiaries. They don't try and just create CEOs in a hothouse in headquarters.

WB: "We have an unusual situation at Berkshire in that most of the people at the top are doing what they want to do. They like running their businesses. That's what they came in expecting to do. And that's what they're doing, and we're letting them do it the way they like to do it. So, we don't have fifty people who all think they're on some pyramid to get to the top. If we named who it could be, that might change in the future; it could create some problems. We saw that at General Electric: When Jeff Immelt got appointed CEO from among three internal candidates, the other two left. I don't really see any advantage in having some crowned prince around."

2013 MEETING (00:23:32)

WB: "The culture is all important ... and the key is preserving the culture and having a successor as CEO who will have more brains, more energy, and more passion for it, than even I have. It's the number one subject that our board considers at every meeting, and we're solidly in agreement as to who that individual should be. I think the culture has just become intensified year after year after year ... That took time, and I think it's really one of a kind now, and I think that it will remain one of a kind. Any foreign-type behavior that came in would be cast out because people have self-selected into this company, and it would be rejected like a foreign tissue if we got the wrong sort of person in there. We have a board that is especially devoted to Berkshire ... It will be the same. You can count on that."

CM: "My thoughts are very simple. I want to say to the many Mungers in the audience: Don't be so stupid as to sell these shares."

WB: "That goes for the Buffetts too."

2023 MEETING (01:17:47)

WB: "Greg Abel [Vice Chairman of Berkshire's non-insurance operations], absent some extraordinary circumstance, is going to succeed me. He will be sitting in a position where he needs something close to his equivalent ... he will need that substitute. We know Ajit Jain's [Vice Chairman of Berkshire's insurance operations] opinion on that, but Greg will probably be the one that will make the final decision. It's his responsibility. Ajit will give him his best advice, and I think the odds are very, very high that Greg will follow it. But those are not easy questions.

"Everybody talks about the executive bench and all of that sort of thing, which is baloney. You don't have many people that can run the largest GAAP net worth company in the country, and all kinds of diverse businesses—but you don't need five people either. You need a lot of good operating managers, and you need somebody at the top who allocates capital well and who makes sure you've got the right operating managers. We've designed something where we separate the insurance and the rest of the operating businesses, and I think it's a very good design. But we wouldn't be smart to name that decision now about the two different areas of the business because a lot can change between now and then. And the most likely change is that this job changes."

CM: "We have a lot of good people who have risen in the Berkshire subsidiaries. There's a reason our operations have, by and large, done better than other big conglomerate companies. One of them is that we change managers way less frequently than other people do. That has helped us."

WB: "We had one of our managers die not long ago, Seymour Lichtenstein of [apparel manufacturer] Garan. I wrote Seymour a letter when he was eighty, and I said, 'I'm glad you're eighty, and I'll write you again when you're ninety.' And I wrote him again when he was ninety. He didn't make it to a hundred. But he had a terrific fellow following him, and they really managed it jointly to some extent as the years went by. But it's a case-by-case decision. The main thing to do is to have the right person running the place."

BERKSHIRE'S STRATEGIC VISION

1998 MEETING (00:30:02)

WB: "We do know our main business is insurance; it will be accidental, to some extent, over the next ten years, which business ends up being the second or third or fourth largest. That'll be determined by opportunity … We have no predetermined course of action whatsoever at Berkshire. We have no strategic planning department. We don't have any strategic plan. We react to what we think are opportunities. And if it's a business we can understand, and particularly if it's big, we would love to make it number two."

CM: "I also want to proudly say that we have no mission statement."

WB: "We've never had a consultant. And we try to keep things pretty simple. We still have twelve people at headquarters … We hope to grow a lot, but we don't hope to grow at headquarters."

2001 MEETING (01:07:24)

WB: "At least twenty years ago, we did say that we thought insurance would be our most significant business over time. We had no idea that it would get to be as significant as it is now. But we've always felt that insurance was likely to be our largest business. It's our largest business in terms of revenue, and we hope it gets a lot bigger over time.

"But we don't have a master plan. Charlie and I do not sit around and strategize or talk about the future of various industries or anything of that sort. It just doesn't happen … We try to survey the whole financial field. We try to look at what comes in and look for things we understand, where we think they have a durable, competitive advantage, where we like the management, and where the price is sensible. We had no idea three years ago that we would be the 87% owner of the largest broadloom carpet company in the world [Shaw Industries]. We don't plan these things.

"Twenty or so years from now, we will own a lot more businesses. I think it's certain that insurance will be a bigger business for us in twenty years than it is now, probably much bigger. And I think it's also likely it will still be our biggest business. But that could change. We could get a deal offered to us tomorrow that was a $20 billion deal, and then we've got a lot of money in that industry at that point. So we have no more master plan now than we had back in 1965 when we bought the textile mill. We had a lousy business. I didn't realize it was as lousy as it was when I got into it. We just had to start trying to deploy capital in an intelligent way ... That's our business and we enjoy it. And we get opportunities to do it. But the bigger you are, the fewer the opportunities you're likely to get."

CM: "I think it's almost a sure thing that twenty years from now there will be way more strength and value behind each Berkshire share. I also think it is an absolutely sure thing that the annual percentage rate of progress will go way down from what it has been in the past."

2012 MEETING (02:42:35)

WB: "Cash-consuming businesses, by their nature, are unattractive unless the cash they consume gets to earn a reasonable return. In the electric utility business, we can expect cash retained to perhaps earn an average of 12% or something like that, which we regard as quite satisfactory. It's not as exciting as having some business that's going to grow 20% a year and not require any capital. There are a few wonderful businesses like that, but it's perfectly satisfactory. Same way with the railroad business; we are going to invest a lot of capital over the next ten years in railroads. Every year we will spend way more than depreciation charges. I think the prospect of earning reasonable returns on that are pretty darn good.

"But if I had to put a lot of money into some capital-intensive business where all we were doing was staying alive with that money, we would be in a terrible situation. We don't have, in any meaningful way, capital-consuming businesses where I see that as a prospect. If you go back to a world where we thought we could earn 20% on equity or something, then there's very few capital-consuming businesses where huge amounts of incremental capital can earn at a 20% rate. So that would be disadvantageous. We don't know how to make 20% on equity going forth in the future with the kind of sums we're now working with. We will be very happy if we can earn 12% or something like that on equity, particularly when some of that capital being consumed is generated by float, which doesn't cost us anything. We've got some small advantage there."

2016 MEETING (00:14:59)

WB: "The ideal business is one that takes no capital, but yet grows; there are a few businesses like that, and we own some. We'd love to find one that we could buy for $10, $20, or $30 billion, that was not capital intensive, and we may, but it's harder.

"If you have a business that grows and gives you a lot of money every year and it isn't required in its growth, you get a double-barreled effect from the earnings growth that occurs internally without the use of capital, and then you get the capital it produces to go and buy other businesses. See's Candies is a good example of that. Back when the newspaper business was good, our Buffalo newspaper was making, at one time, $40 million a year and had no capital requirement, so we could take that whole $40 million and go buy something else with it.

"But increasing capital acts as an anchor on returns in many ways. One way is that it drives us—just in terms of availability—into businesses that are much more capital intensive. At Berkshire Hathaway Energy, we just announced a $3.6 billion investment in wind generation. And we pledged overall $30 billion in renewables. Anything BH Energy does, anything that BNSF does, takes lots of money. We get decent returns on capital, but we don't get the extraordinary returns on capital that we've been able to get in some of the businesses we acquire that are not capital intensive. As I mentioned in the annual report, we have a few businesses that actually earn 100% a year on true invested capital. Clearly, that's a different sort of operation than something like Berkshire Hathaway Energy, which may earn 11% or 12% on capital; that's a very decent return, but it's a different sort of animal than the business that's very low capital intensity."

CM: "When our circumstances changed, we changed our minds."

WB: "Slowly and reluctantly."

CM: "In the early days, quite a few times we bought a business that was soon producing 100% per annum on what we paid for it and didn't require much reinvestment. If we'd been able to continue doing that, we would have loved to—but when we couldn't, we went to plan B. And plan B is working pretty well. In many ways, I've gotten so I sort of prefer it."

WB: "When something's forced on you, you might as well prefer it. But we knew that was going to happen. It leads you from what looks like a sensational result to a satisfactory result. We're quite happy with a satisfactory result. The alternative would be to go back to working with very tiny sums of money, and that really hasn't gotten a lot of serious discussion between us."

2022 MEETING (00:00:37)

WB: "The idea of permanently losing the money of people who trust us is a future I just don't want to have. As Charlie says, 'All I want to know is where I'll die, so I'll never go there.' It has worked so far. We would die psychologically if we lost other people's money ... I can't predict what our earnings will be and I can't predict what the stock will do. We don't know what the economy will do and all of that. But we do know, when we wake up every morning, we want to be safer in terms of your investment … Anything could change at Berkshire, but the one thing that won't change is that we will always have a lot of cash on hand. And when I say cash, I don't mean commercial paper; in 2008 and 2009, when the financial panic came along, we didn't own anybody's commercial paper. We didn't have money market funds. We had Treasury bills. We believe in having cash. There have been a few times in history, and there will be more times in history, where if you don't have it, you don't get to play the next day. It's like oxygen. It's there all the time—but if it disappears for a few minutes, it's all over."

2022 MEETING (02:16:54)

WB: "I would say that Berkshire's future, for a long time, is about as assured as you can have in this world. We have a culture that has worked; the shares and the shareholders will carry it a long way. You've got a board of directors that understands that our culture is 99.9% of running the business … Berkshire is just plain different. We are a business that exists for people that trust us. All we have to do to is fulfill that trust. We've got the people to do it. We've got unbelievable resources to do it. It isn't that difficult as long as you've got the freedom to do it.

"We would hope that maybe the superiority of this culture might be somewhat better understood by the world. If we have the same culture, we'll be here a hundred years from now. Berkshire is being built for forever. There is no finish line. Nobody is waiting to retire or have their options vested. We don't have anybody who's thinking about taking another job … I don't know whether we could build it again, but we've got it. We didn't know we were building it exactly when we had a lousy textile mill. It isn't like Charlie and I sat down and work out some plan—we'll run the dumb textile business for twenty years and then we'll finally have to fold it, then we'll do this and that and everything. We just kept putting one foot in front of the other.

"We did know how we felt about running a public company. One thing we wanted to do, always, was to have people who were in sync with us. We wanted people who trusted us. Our partnerships were the same thing … We sat down with people, and in my case I handed them a little sheet of paper, it said the ground rules. I wanted to be sure we were on the same page. You don't have to read the partnership agreement. There's no way in the world I would take advantage of you. You shouldn't be here if you think I would. But I do want you to be on the same page and be measuring me by the same yardsticks I measure myself. Those people stayed with me; their children, and their children's children, are shareholders of Berkshire. They're partners. It'd be hard to do that again. But if I were going to be in the field, I would try and do the same thing. I would try to find people who trust me. I don't want to be with people who are asking how

I did versus the S&P 500 last month. I sold securities for three years, and I just didn't want to be in that position where essentially they thought maybe I could do things that I couldn't do.

"I finally found a way to get a few people. I stumbled into it. But a few people trusted me, and they gave me their money, and we've lived happily ever after. The new management at Berkshire [after Warren and Charlie], and the managements after them, they'll just be custodians of a culture that's embedded. The owners believe in it. People who work here believe in it. We have the directors. We've got the share ownership and the size that essentially can ward off any attempts to change the culture ... We run it for a group of people who trust us, and we appreciate that trust."

CM: "I remember when you had a textile mill, and textiles are really just congealed electricity the way modern technology works. And electricity rates elsewhere were 60% lower than the rates of New England. It was an absolutely hopeless hand, and you had the sense to fold it."

WB: "Twenty-five years later."

CM: "Well, you didn't pour more money into it. Recognizing reality when it's really awful and taking appropriate action just involves often the most elementary good sense. How in the hell can you run a textile mill in New England when competitors are paying way lower power rates?"

WB: "Another problem was the fellow that I put in to run it was a really good guy. He was 100% honest with me in every way. He was a decent human being and he knew textiles. If he'd been a jerk, it would have been a lot easier. I probably would have thought differently about it. But we stumbled along for a while, and we got lucky that Jack Ringwalt decided to sell us his insurance company [National Indemnity]. But I even bought a second textile company in New Hampshire, seven or eight years later. It is incredible how many dumb decisions we made. Charlie and I and [early Berkshire investor] Sandy Gottesman bought the department store in 1966 ... The whole idea was crazy. We figured it out finally ..."

CM: "We reversed course."

WB: "Yes—but why the hell were we doing it in the first place?"

CM: "Because we were stupid."

WB: "That is important to realize. We paid $6 a share for that stock. If the department store had succeeded, it might be worth $30 a share now. But we did other things and we merged into Berkshire ... it is up to $150,000 a share now from $6 a share. So, if it succeeded, we would have maybe made a few dollars.

Because it failed, we made hundreds of thousands of dollars per share. But that's the way life is. You just keep going."

CM: "Keep learning. That's the secret. Keep learning."

2023 MEETING (01:29:02)

WB: "The important thing is that Berkshire be regarded as a national asset rather than a national liability. We've got to be a plus to the country with our form of operation … I think we will win if we deserve to win. And I think the odds of that happening are very, very, very high …

"We do plan. I've got a model in my mind of what Berkshire has been. Of course, that model has been modified plenty of times over fifty-eight years. Very importantly, one thing I knew was that it shouldn't be a textile company. That was an important decision. Then we've just played the hand as it came along. We made a few really good decisions, and we'll never make a decision that kills us.

"We keep ourselves in better shape than anybody else; we just aren't going to have big maturities of debt that come along. We aren't going to have insurance policies that can be cashed in en masse. And we will sit with what looks like a huge amount of capital. Well, it *is* a huge amount of capital, but there's also a huge amount of earning power, and there's a huge amount of diversity—everything. So, I think we're handing something very secure over to the future managers. And I think we've got a shareholder base like nobody has. That is the product of fifty-eight years of regarding the shareholder as the owner. What does that mean? It means having happy customers. It means being welcomed by your community rather than having them turn you away. It means that the government feels better with you if there's a financial crisis, because you can provide something that actually the country can't, under some circumstances, and you'll be there, and at the same time, it will be good for the business. We will have crises of one sort or another. But we'll be a plus to the United States. And if we're a plus to the United States, we'll survive."

BERKSHIRE'S BEST INVESTMENTS

2005 MEETING (02:59:17)

WB: "Probably the best investment was getting Charlie as a partner—and he works cheap, too … See's was enormously important; it doesn't contribute a huge percentage of our net income now, but it provided income that let us buy other things in the past and it taught us a lot of lessons about business. … In terms of what it's done already and where it's going to go over time, the single best investment was probably the first 50% of GEICO, which we purchased for $40 million. The second half cost us $2 billion; I'm glad I didn't buy it in thirds."

CM: "The search expenses that brought us Ajit Jain, there was an investment that really paid a dividend. I can think of no higher return investment that we've ever made than that one. And I think that's a good life lesson; in other words, getting the right people into your system can frequently be more important than anything else."

SELLING TO BERKSHIRE

2008 MEETING (01:35:35)

WB: "I always tell the owner, the best thing to do with a wonderful business is to just keep it. It's going to be worth more next year and the year after. There's no reason to sell a wonderful business except for extraneous factors. … We never urge people to sell good businesses. We urge them to keep them. But there come times when they do want to sell for one reason or another; if they have a business they're enormously proud of—if it's a really fine business—they can keep more of the attributes that they love in that business by selling to Berkshire than they can by selling to anyone else, by far. We are the logical buyer."

CM: "I watched a man in southern California who built a wonderful business, one he devoted his whole life to creating. Then, when the time came to sell, he sold it to a known crook who was obviously going to ruin the business, just because he could get a slightly higher price. I think that's an insane way to live your life if you own a prosperous business. I think the better course is to sell it to somebody who you know is going to be a good steward of what you've created."

UNWILLINGNESS TO SELL WHOLLY-OWNED BUSINESSES

1995 MEETING (02:09:35)

WB: "Our unwillingness to sell businesses goes back a long way. If that hurts performance, it's peanuts. That's simply a function of the attitude Charlie and I have, how we want to live our lives.

"We find it a rarity when we find people in a business we want to associate with, and when we do find it we enjoy it. We don't see any reason to sell businesses to make an extra 0.5% a year or an extra 1% a year—don't try us on higher numbers. But we don't see any reason to go around ending friendships, contacts, and relationships with people, it just doesn't make any sense to us. We don't want to get committed to that sort of activity. We know we wouldn't do it if we were a private company. In Berkshire, we feel we've enunciated that position and we want to get that across to everybody who might join with us because we don't want them to expect us to do it. We want them to expect us to work hard to get a decent result, to make sure the shareholders get the same result we get, and all of that sort of thing. But we don't want to enter into any implicit contract with fellow shareholders that will cause us to have to behave in a way that we really don't want to behave. If that's the price of making more money, it's a price we don't want to pay. There's other things we forgoe also, but that is the one that people might disagree with us on. So, we want to be very sure that everybody understands that going in. I don't think it'll hurt performance that much anyway. But to the extent that it does, it's a limitation you get with us."

CM: "I don't think there's any way to measure it exactly, but my guess is if you could appraise something that you might call the character of the people running the operating businesses in Berkshire, many of whom helped create the businesses in the first place and who are leading citizens in their community like the Helzbergs, I don't think there's any other corporation in America that has done as well as we have if you measure the human quality of the people in it. You can say we've collected high-grade people because we sure as hell couldn't create them, but one way or another, this is a remarkable system. Why would we tinker with it?"

WB: "If you want to attract high-grade people, you probably ought to try and behave pretty well yourself. Besides, it wouldn't be any fun doing the other. I was in that position a little when I ran the partnership back in the 1960s. People were coming into partnership with me, and my job was to turn out the best return I could. And I found that if I got into a business, that presented certain alternatives I didn't like. So, Berkshire's much more satisfactory in that respect."

2000 MEETING (01:40:08)

WB: "In terms of businesses that we own, we have this quirk that we want our shareholders to understand, that even if we get offered a price that is far above its economic value, we have no interest in selling. We don't break off the relationships that we develop simply because we get offered a fancy price for something. And we've had a chance to do that sometimes.

"That may help us, actually, in acquiring businesses; both of the companies that I've committed to buy in the last few weeks are very concerned about whether they have found a permanent home. People who build their businesses lovingly over thirty, forty, or fifty years, frequently care about that. A lot of people *don't* care about that, and that's one of the things we evaluate when buying a business. We look at the owner and we ask ourselves, 'Does he love the business or does he love the money?' Nothing wrong with liking the money; in fact, we'd be a little disappointed if most of them didn't like the money. But in terms of whether the primacy is loving the money or loving the business, that's very important to us. When we find somebody who likes the money but loves their business, we are a very, very desirable home, because we're just about the only people that they can deal with, of size, where we can commit that they are going to be part of this operation, really, forever, and be able to deliver on that promise.

"I tell sellers that the only person that can double-cross them is me. There's never going to be a takeover of Berkshire. There's never going to be a management consultant who comes in and says, 'I think you'd better do this.' There's never going to be a response to Wall Street. None of that's going to happen. We can tell them, with 100% assuredness, that for a very long time, if they decide to come with Berkshire, that decision will be the final decision as to where their company resides ... We will not sell operating businesses, even though someone might offer us far more than, logically, they're worth. On stocks, we're not quite with Phil Fisher on that, but we're very close. We love buying stocks where we think the businesses are so solid, and have such economic advantage, that we can essentially ride with them forever.

"Twenty or twenty-five years ago we would've thought that a daily newspaper in a single newspaper town, or a network TV-affiliated station, was about the solidest investment you could find. And they *were* very solid—but events over the last two decades have certainly changed that to some degree, maybe to a very big degree. So we will occasionally re-evaluate the economic characteristics that we see ten years out from the ones that we saw ten years ago, and maybe come to a somewhat different conclusion.

"In my first twenty-plus years of investing, my decision to sell was almost always based on the fact that I found something else I was dying to buy. I sold stocks at three times earnings to buy stocks at two times earnings because I was always running out of money. Now, I run out of ideas. I've got a lot of money but fewer ideas."

CM: "We almost never sell an operating business. When it does happen, it's usually because we've got some trouble we can't fix."

BERKSHIRE'S INTRINSIC VALUE

1995 MEETING (03:15:02)

WB: "There's more to intrinsic value than just adding up what you think you can sell the pieces for at any given time, because it is a prospective figure. It is the future cash discounted back to the present. And capital allocation is a good part of that.

"What you expect the insurance float to do over time, for example, would lead to a large swing in possible numbers relative to value. When we bought National Indemnity in 1967, it had $15 or $20 million in float; we didn't see it then, but if we could have foreseen the eventual development of insurance float over time, it might have turned out that the intrinsic value of National Indemnity was many multiples of what most people might have thought at the time, and probably what we thought at the time."

1996 MEETING (01:19:34)

WB: "To the extent that people have made a mistake in the past in valuing Berkshire—and they have made this mistake over time, including many commentators and some institutions—the error is to look at it simply as the breakup value of our businesses. You could do the same with General Electric, a magnificently run operation by Jack Welch. But I don't think the way you should look at a business like General Electric is to think about what would happen if they sold each division today, paid the taxes, and then distributed the proceeds. That has tended to be the case with many people looking at Berkshire, they look at it on a static basis. That is not the way that Charlie and I have looked at it over time.

"Berkshire is a collection of businesses, some of which we own in their entirety, some of which we own part of. And some of those businesses have very interesting dynamics to them. The value of our insurance business, for example. Twenty-nine years ago we paid Jack Ringwalt $8.7 million for two companies that Jack controlled [National Indemnity and National Fire and Marine]. If you had the foresight at that time—and I didn't—to see what would develop out of that insurance business, you would've come to the conclusion that their value to us was going to be far, far greater than the value at which they were then carried on our balance sheet. They were part of a business which had enormous potential. That's probably been the most significant asset that's developed at Berkshire … It would've been a big mistake to think in terms of the book value of that business being representative of its actual value to us over time if it was run properly. And that situation probably prevails today.

"Berkshire is a group of, on balance, very fine businesses to which we hope to add. The intrinsic value will be affected by the job we do in allocating capital. It'll be affected by the job our managers do in running their businesses. It'll be affected by some items we don't foresee and, perhaps, have no control over. But it is not measured, essentially, by what we could sell each separate business for and pay the tax on now. We haven't run it that way. We've run it so that we get the use of a lot of capital at very low cost; between deferred taxes and our insurance float, we have $12 billion or so on the liability side that we think will be a very low cost. And that doesn't show as an asset, but it can be quite valuable."

2001 MEETING (04:44:39)

WB: "We don't know the exact intrinsic value of Berkshire, obviously. If we had written down secret figures ever since 1965, some of them would look silly now, in terms of what has actually transpired … The biggest judgment you have to make is how well capital will be deployed in the future. It's relatively easy to figure out the present value of most of our businesses, but the question becomes, 'What do we do with the money as it comes in?' That will have a huge impact on the value ten years from now. And it will depend a lot on the environment in which we operate over the next ten years. There will be a lot of luck in it. I think there's a reasonable chance of good luck, but who knows?"

2009 MEETING (01:10:18)

WB: "I think it's perfectly reasonable to look at Berkshire as the sum of two parts: a lot of marketable securities—at least fairly priced, maybe even undervalued—and a lot of earning power. If you look at it that way, you would come to the conclusion that Berkshire was cheaper in relation to its intrinsic value at the end of 2008 than it was at the end of 2007, but you would also come to the conclusion that that was true of most securities.

"Every stock is affected by what every other stock sells for. If the value of ABC stock goes down, then XYZ, absent any other variables, is worth less. If you can buy good companies at 8× earnings, it reduces the value of Berkshire, as opposed to when stocks were selling at 18× earnings. Everything is affected by everything else in the financial world. When you say a bird in the hand is worth two in the bush, you've got to compare that to every other bush that's available. So, you're correct that Berkshire was cheaper in relation to intrinsic value at the end of 2008 than at the end of 2007 … Over time, we particularly hope the operating business earnings increase, because that's our major focus. We'd like to move money into good operating businesses over time and build that number a lot."

CM: "I would argue that last year was a bad year for a float business. It was naturally going to make the owner of the float appear, briefly, to be at a disadvantage. But long term, having a large float, which you're getting at a cost of less than zero, is a big advantage. And I wouldn't get too excited about the fact that the stock goes down. I happen to know one buyer who rather inartistically bought about 10,000 shares when Berkshire was driven to its absolute peak. How much significance does that have in the big scheme of things over the long term?

"What matters are things like this: Our casualty insurance business is probably the best big casualty business in the world. Our utility subsidiary—if there's a better one, I don't know of it. And if I had to bet on one carbide cutting tool business in the world, I'd bet on ISCAR against any other. I could go down the list a long way. I think those things are going to matter greatly over the long term. And if you think it's easy to get in that kind of a position—the kind of position that Berkshire occupies—you are living in a different world from the one I inhabit."

WB: "Our insurance business is a remarkable business—and it has some remarkable managers."

TURNOVER IN BERKSHIRE STOCK

2006 MEETING (02:17:36)

WB: "I think Berkshire has the lowest turnover, by some margin, of any major company in the United States. ... This is a reflection of the fact that we've got a really unusual shareholder body in that they think of themselves as owners, and not just people who are moving around little pieces of paper every week or month. In my view, we have the most honest-to-God ownership attitude among our 400,000 or so shareholders of any big traded company in the United States.

"People buy Berkshire to own it, and hold it, and that's reflected in our turnover. That does mean if, for some reason, our stock gets real cheap that we would not be able to buy a lot of stock. But we are not looking to buy out our partners at a discount. If it sells there and we tell shareholders we're going to buy it, we'll buy it. But that's not the way that we're trying to make money."

ADVANTAGES WITHIN BERKSHIRE HATHAWAY

1995 MEETING (03:48:11)

WB: "In a business that earns a high rate on capital—that doesn't have natural ways to employ that money within the business—we may contribute significantly to the long-term results of that business by taking the capital out. ... We have the whole universe to spread that money over [to invest elsewhere]. We can use money earned in an operating business to buy shares of Coca-Cola, or to buy into another wonderful business, whereas very few managements probably would do that. There's an advantage there.

"On the other hand, Helzberg Diamonds, for example, will probably grow very substantially. They'll probably use all the capital they generate. Maybe they'll use even more. They don't really need us for that; they would've done that under any circumstances. We may actually give them the ability to grow a little faster because if a company is earning 20% on equity but can grow 25% a year, they're going to feel equity strains at some point. And obviously we would love the idea of supplying extra capital to earn 20% on equity. So, there can be some advantage to having us as a parent, in terms of sending capital to the business, as well as taking capital from the business.

"I think we can also be helpful in some situations. Once we are there, a lot of the rituals at public companies—a lot of the things that people waste time doing in business—don't have to be done with us. There's an awful lot of time spent in some businesses preparing for committee meetings, directors' meetings, and all kinds of things like that: show-and-tell stuff. None of that's needed with us. We won't go near them. We really free them up to spend a 100% of the time thinking about what is good for the business over time. If they have extra money, they don't have to worry about what to do with it. If they need extra money for a good business, it'll be supplied. There are some advantages that way."

CM: "I think our chief contribution to the businesses we acquire is what we don't do."

2001 MEETING (00:51:10)

WB: "We have some significant advantages in buying businesses over time. We would be the preferred purchaser, I think, for a reasonable number of private companies, and public companies as well. Our checks clear. We will always have the money. People know that when we make a deal, it will get done, and it will get done as fast as anybody can do it. It won't be subject to any kind of second thoughts or financing difficulties. We bought Johns Manville because the other group had financing difficulties. People know they will get to run their businesses as they've run them before, if they care about that, and a lot of people do. Others don't. We have an ownership structure that is probably more stable than any company anywhere near our size in the country. That's attractive to people. And we are under no pressure to do anything dumb … Those are significant advantages.

"The biggest disadvantage we have is size. It is harder to double the market value of a $100 billion company than a $1 billion company, using what we have in our arsenal. … I hope, in fact, we have the agony of becoming a much larger company."

CM: "This is not a hog heaven period for Berkshire. The investment game is getting more and more competitive. And I see no sign that that is going to change."

WB: "But people will do stupid things in the future. I will guarantee you that sometime in the next twenty years people will do some exceptionally stupid things in equity markets. Then the question is, are we in a position to do something about that when that happens?"

2009 MEETING (01:47:57)

WB: "Our sustainable competitive advantage is we have a culture and a business model, which people are going to find very, very difficult to copy, or even semi-copy.

"We have an unusual group of shareholders. We have a business that's owned by people where the turnover on our stock may be 20% a year, when virtually every stock in the S&P 500 turns over 100% a year. We have a different shareholder base. We have people who understand their business differently. And we have a business that can offer, to people who own private businesses, the chance to keep running their businesses as they have in the past, and to get rid of the problems of lawyers, bankers, and all kinds of things like that. I don't see any other company in the United States that has the ability to do that now, or probably the ability to adopt that model in any big way.

"It's not peculiar to me and Charlie. We may have helped create it, but it is a deeply embedded culture which any CEOs that follow us are going to be well versed in when they come into the job. ... I think anybody wanting to copy Berkshire is going to have a very hard time. And I think the advantages we have are going to be very, very long lasting. They're not peculiar to the fact that Charlie and are I sitting up here anymore. They may have been originally, but no longer. Our managers join that culture, our shareholders join that culture. It gets reinforced all the time. They see that it works ... There will be businesses, as with ISCAR a while back, just as with GEICO management back in the mid-1990s, where people want to join us. And they really won't have a good second choice. They'll be plenty that don't too, but that's OK. We just need to have some of the right ones join us. It can go on a long, long time."

CM: "A lot of corporations in America are run stupidly from headquarters, as they try and force divisions to come up with profits for every quarter that are better than the profits from the same quarter in the previous year. A lot of terrible decisions and terrible practices creep into those businesses. In the Berkshire Hathaway model, that doesn't happen. So, while Warren and I will soon be gone—not too soon in my case, but I'm a little worried about Warren—the stupidity of management practice in the rest of the corporate world will likely remain ample enough to give this company some comparative advantage way into the future."

2014 MEETING (02:22:48)

WB: "Owning a group of good businesses is not a terrible business plan. A good many of the earlier conglomerates were put together to perform financial magic of one sort or another. They were based upon the idea of serial issuances of stock, where you issued stock that was selling at 20× earnings to buy businesses that were at 10× earnings. If you go back to the Litton Industries and the Gulf and Westerns, you could name them by the hundreds. The concept was that somehow you could fool people into continuously riding along on a chain-letter scheme, without the primary thought being given to what you were actually building in the management.

"I think our business plan makes nothing but great sense: to own a group of great businesses, diversified, with outstanding managers, and conservatively capitalized. And with one enormous advantage, which people don't really understand. In an important way, capitalism is about the allocation of capital. And we have a system at Berkshire where we can allocate capital without tax consequences. We can move it from See's Candies, as we generate surplus capital, to other areas. It doesn't hurt See's in the process, and we can move it, as the textbooks say, to places where capital can be usefully employed, like wind farms or whatever it may be. There's nobody else really better situated to do that than Berkshire Hathaway, and it makes perfectly good sense.

"But it has to be applied with business-like principles, rather than with stock promotion principles. I would say a great many of the conglomerates have had, as their underlying premise, stock promotion. You saw what happened with Tyco; the serial acquirers were usually interested in issuing a lot of stock. One of the primary indicators of what sort of species you're viewing is whether they're issuing stock continuously; if they are, one way or another they've probably got a chain-letter game going on. And that does come to a bad end. I think our method of acquiring for cash, and acquiring good businesses, and building many, many sources of growing earning power, is a terrific model."

2016 MEETING (02:30:17)

WB: "By far the main factor in keeping Berkshire's culture is that you have a board and you'll have successor board members, you have managers and you'll have successor managers, and you have shareholders, who all clearly recognize the special nature of the culture, who embrace the culture. When they sold their businesses to us, they wanted to join that culture. It thrusts out people that really aren't in tune with it, and there are very few of them. And it embraces those who enjoy and appreciate it. To some extent, we don't have a lot of competition on that. So it becomes very identifiable, and it works. I think the chances of us going off the rails in terms of culture are very, very, very slight. ... I don't see any evidence that there'd be anything that could in any way really move us away from what we have done now for many, many decades."

CM: "I'm even more optimistic than you are."

WB: "I've never noticed it."

CM: "I really think the culture is going to surprise everybody—how well it lasts, and how well they do. They're going to wonder why they ever made any fuss over us in the first place. It's going to work very well."

WB: "We've got so many good ingredients in place just in terms of the businesses and people already here, at the companies."

CM: "That's what I'm saying. There's just so much power in place."

WB: "Another thing that's interesting is how little turnover we have. The number of managers that have been needed, that we've had to replace in the last ten years, are very few. We don't have a retirement age—I tend to bring that up at every meeting to reinforce the idea. Without a retirement age, and with people working because they love their jobs, we get long tenure out of our managers. They like the money as well, but their primary motive is that they really like accomplishing what they do in their jobs. The directors are also not here for the money, and we have great tenure among the directors as well. I would argue that's a huge plus."

MCLANE

2017 MEETING (04:47:11)

WB: "McLane [wholesale distributor of groceries and non-food items to convenience stores, quick service restaurants, etc.] is a company that has an extraordinary amount of sales in relation to intrinsic value or net income. Basically, it's a distributor; it's a huge customer, for example, of the food companies, the candy companies, the cigarette companies, up and down the line of anything sold in convenience stores. We bought it from Walmart, and Walmart is our biggest customer. If you get Walmart and Sam's together, you're getting up to 20%-plus of McLane's volumes. It operates on about 6% gross margins and 5% operating expenses, so it has 1% pre-tax margin. And, obviously, a 1% margin only works in terms of return on capital if you turn your inventory extraordinarily fast. That's what McLane does; it's moving things in and out very fast and very efficiently … We've got thousands and thousands of trucks, big distribution centers all over the country. If you're Mars Inc., or something of the sort, we'll be the biggest customer. It's a business that earns good returns in relation to invested capital and in relation to our purchase price. Every tenth of a cent is important in the business …

"It was an interesting deal. Walmart wanted to sell it. The CFO came to see us, and we made a deal. We talked for a while. He went into the other room, called the CEO, and came back and said, 'You have a deal.' Walmart has told me subsequently that they never had a deal that closed as fast as the McLane deal with Berkshire. We said what we would pay, and we got it done very promptly. They were terrific on their side."

CM: "By the way, that reputation for being quick and simple, and doing what we promised and so on, has helped at Berkshire time after time."

WB: "We wouldn't have made that deal without having that reputation."

CM: "You bought the Northern Natural Gas Company in one weekend. They wanted the money on Monday. Before the lawyers could complete the legal papers, we managed to do it."

WB: "They not only wanted the money on Monday, they needed the money on Monday. Not only that, but I think it took some clearance in Washington. I think I wrote a letter and said that if they decided, after looking at it, that they didn't want to clear it, we'd undo the deal. But these guys needed the money so bad, we were going to give them the money, essentially, based on the deal clearing. There wasn't any reason why it wouldn't clear, but it was just a procedural problem. But most companies can't do that. We can. We've got a flexibility that, really, in most large companies just plain doesn't exist. Too many people have to sign off on it or something. The Northern Natural deal would not have been made if we had to follow the normal timetable."

2018 MEETING (03:49:14)

WB: "I think Berkshire's culture is very, very strong. And frankly, I think it gets reinforced by the shareholders we have. I mean, we have a different body of shareholders and we look at those shareholders, I think, in a somewhat different way than a good many companies do. I think there are a fair number of public companies that wish they didn't have public shareholders. We're happy to have public shareholders. And we like having individual shareholders. We don't favor institutions. And we're not going to give guidance and talk especially to them on investor calls and all that sort of thing. We want shareholders who are partners, basically. And it begins with that. It goes to the directors. I've been on nineteen boards, and I've never seen another board like ours. I think it's terrific that we've got the people who represent, in many cases, lots of shares themselves. They didn't get special deals. It's a group of owner-oriented, Berkshire-conscious, business-savvy owners. We don't have anybody on the board because they're a leading educator or whatever it may be.

"We want people who basically think about how to run a business well for themselves and for their partners. And we've got managers who fit into that culture, who have chosen that culture by coming in with us. Sometimes we have the second or the third or fourth generation that share that, like at the Nebraska Furniture Mart. Is it perfect? No, it's far from perfect. You don't get everybody thinking the same way. We have people who are very independently minded running a lot of businesses. And they see through different lenses than we do, to some degree. But in terms of having a common, strong, positive culture, I don't think there's any big public company that has it any better than Berkshire. And I think that will continue because people opt into it a great deal. Cultures get passed along.

"You do things that are consistent with the culture; what you talk about is what you do. You don't find people saying, 'We're a wonderful partnership,' and then voting themselves huge options. Then a whole bunch of other people will say options are beneath them because they can't look like they're taking it all for themselves. But we've got as good a culture as you can get. And I would say, net, it grows stronger. We have a few people who don't buy into it entirely. It is not 100%, but it's close to it. And I think it gets closer all the time as we go along. And we will try to keep behaving in a way that reinforces it and doesn't dilute it. I think that will not only work for Charlie and me, but it will work for our successors well. It won't be perfect."

CM: "Every time I come to one of these meetings and sit with the managers, I feel more strongly at the end that the culture and values of Berkshire Hathaway will go on and on for a long time after the present management is gone. In fact, I think it'll go on after all of the present managers are gone. I think we've started something here that will work well enough that it will last. And one of the reasons it will last is that it's not that damned easy to duplicate. So, the one that is present is likely to just keep going and going. Think of how little direct copying of the Berkshire system there's been. I think it's going to last a long time for a very simple reason: it deserves to last a long time. It's going to work."

2018 MEETING (01:15:01)

WB: "There is no question McLane's margins have been squeezed. They were very, very narrow, at about one cent on the dollar pre-tax, and they have been squeezed from that. It's a very, very tight margin business. The situation is actually even worse than you portray because within McLane we have a liquor distribution business in a few states and that business has actually increased its earnings moderately. We've added to that business, so within McLane's figures there is about $70 million pre-tax from the liquor part that has nothing to do with the massive parts you're talking about in terms of food distribution. The decline is even greater there. That's just become very much more competitive.

"If you look at our competitors, they're not making much money either. That's capitalism. There comes a point where the customer says, 'I'll only pay X,' and you have to walk away. There's a great temptation, particularly when you're employing thousands of people and have built distribution facilities and all of that sort of thing, to meet what you'd like to term irrational competition, but that is capitalism. ...

"The earnings went up quite a bit from the time we bought it. We're still earning more than then, and we've earned a lot of money over time. But, as I say, a fair amount of that is actually coming from liquor distribution, activities in about four states that we purchased and which are very well run. We will do our best to get the margins up. But your guess is almost as good as mine as to what margins will be in that distribution business five years from now. It's a very essential service. We do ~$40 billion. And we move more of the product of all kinds of companies whose names you know than anybody else. But when you get Kraft Heinz, Philip Morris, or whoever it may be, on one side of the deal, and you get Walmart and 7-Eleven on the other side of the deal, sometimes they don't leave you very much room in between."

BERKSHIRE VALUE ADD TO SUBSIDIARIES

1999 MEETING (05:04:51)

WB: "The biggest thing we bring to the party on a generalized basis is we enable terrific managers to spend, in many cases, a greater percentage of their time and energies on what they do best, and what they like to do best, and what is the most productive for owners, than would be the case without our ownership. In other words, we give them a very rational owner who expects them to spend all of their time focused on what counts for the business and eliminates the distractions that often come with running a business, particularly a publicly-owned business.

"I would guess the CEOs of most public companies waste a third of their time, at least, on all kinds of things that really don't add a thing to the business—and in many cases, subtract from the business, because they're trying to please various constituencies and waste their time with them. We eliminate all of that. We think we can create the best ownership environment, frankly, that can exist—other than maybe owning it 100% yourself—for any business.

"That happens to also go along with how we like to lead our lives, because we don't want to run around and attend a lot of meetings and do all of these things that people do. That can be a significant plus. I think GEICO has probably grown a fair amount faster as a subsidiary of Berkshire than it would have if it had remained an independent company, although it was a hell of an independent company and would have continued to be one. But I think billions and billions of dollars will be added to the value of GEICO, over and above what would have happened if it had remained a public company. We haven't taught the management one thing about the classification of insurance risk or how to run better ads. We've just let them spend 100% of their time focused on what counts. And that is a rare occurrence in American business."

CM: "The kind of subsidiaries we buy, they are not looking for a lot of people looking over their shoulder from headquarters, and a lot of unnecessary flights back and forth, and so on. I would say a great part of what we do is to just not interfere in a counterproductive way. That non-interference has enormous value, at least with the kind of managers and the kind of businesses that have joined us."

WB: "In a great many corporate operations, the importance of a large group of people is tied to how much they meddle in the affairs of other people who are out there doing the work. We stay out of the way. We're appreciative owners and we're knowledgeable owners. We know when somebody has done a good job, particularly when industry conditions are terribly tough. We can look at our shoe operations, for example. They are in tough industry conditions now. We've got some absolutely terrific people. And we are knowledgeable enough about that, so that we don't go simply by a bunch of figures and make a determination whether people are doing the right thing.

"We have no one whose job at headquarters is to tell our managers how to run their HR departments, their legal departments, or a dozen other things. And not only do people have more time to work on the productive things, but I think they probably actually appreciate the fact that they're left alone. So, I think you get even more than the proportional amount of effort out of them than would be indicated simply by the amount of time you free up, because I think you get an added enthusiasm for the job. I think having people in a large organization that truly are enthusiastic about what they're doing, that doesn't happen all the time. But I think it does happen to a pretty good degree at Berkshire."

BERKSHIRE'S VALUATION (CLASS B SHARE CREATION)

1996 MEETING (03:48:11)

WB: "At present prices, Charlie and I do not think Berkshire stock is undervalued. That is not what has been reported; sometimes people have said we thought it was overvalued. If you look at the prospectus, you will see we said that we do not think it's undervalued. I find it somewhat entertaining that people regard that as kind of an amazing statement by somebody making a public offering.

"If you think about it, can you imagine a management that goes out and says to the world, 'We are selling you something and it's way undervalued.' What do you say to your present shareholders if you go out and say, 'We're selling something that's worth $1, and we're going to sell it for $0.80?' That would leave me very unhappy. So, I feel that any management that is talking about selling their stock and they say it's very undervalued, either doesn't know what's good for their present shareholders or they may have their tongue in cheek.

"We would not sell a part of your interest in Berkshire at a price which we did not feel was adequate for the present shareholders. It's that simple. If we sell 1% of the company, we're selling 1% of your ownership in See's Candies, 1% of your ownership in GEICO, 1% of your ownership in The Buffalo News—those are all valuable assets. We have no intention of selling 1% or 10% or 100% of any of those entities at a price that is not fair to present shareholders ... We would not be selling the stock if we thought it was undervalued."

BERKSHIRE'S STOCK PRICE

1996 MEETING (01:50:21)

WB: "On the price of their shares, most managements feel the higher, the better. That's an understandable feeling—but the trouble is, the game isn't over at any time. We really feel the fairer, the better.

"Our goal is that every shareholder participates in the progress that Berkshire makes as a business during their holding period. In other words, we don't want one party getting wealthy off the other. We want them to share based on the gain in value of the business. And to the extent that the stock got way overvalued or way undervalued, that may make one party—in the first case, the seller, and in the second case, the buyer—very happy. But there's somebody on the other side of the transaction.

"In economics, whenever somebody tells you something, the first question to ask yourself is, 'And then what?' The stock going up is not an end in itself, because the next question is, 'And then what?' And to the extent that the stock goes up because the intrinsic value goes up, everyone is getting their fair share of the pie as they go along. To the extent it exceeds that in some way, the selling shareholder gets a benefit but the entering shareholder is at a disadvantage. We really like the idea of the price tracking intrinsic value over time. And we think that, by having the right kind of shareholders and by communicating with them properly and following the right kind of policies, we can come as close to that as is attainable in a world where markets are fairly volatile.

"One thing to remember: In the end, the owners of businesses, in aggregate, cannot come out any better than the businesses comes out. And not just our businesses, I'm talking about all American business; the profitability of American business determines the profitability of what the owners of American business have, and you can forget all about the ticker symbols and everything else. The owners suffer to the extent they have some extra costs imposed in brokers' commissions, fees, all kinds of things; that diminishes the return from the business.

"No one has yet figured out how to perpetually have owners do better than their businesses. Our idea is to have them do it as they go along in proportion to the gain that occurs during their tenure as a shareholder. That isn't easy to do, and it's not attained perfectly—but that's the goal as we go along."

CAPITAL ALLOCATION AT SUBSIDIARIES

1997 MEETING (02:57:49)

CM: "There's a huge class of businesses in America which are very strong and will throw out large amounts of cash in relation to their size, but which can't rationally be expanded very much. And if you try and expand certain kinds of businesses, you're throwing money down the rat hole. The beauty of the Berkshire Hathaway system is that such businesses are very welcome here because the cash comes into headquarters and is allocated there. If there's anything sensible to do at the subsidiary level, we always want it done. But there are lots of businesses where there isn't much of a way to redeploy the cash."

BERKSHIRE'S OPPORTUNITIES

1998 MEETING (04:12:30)

WB: "We are probably about as well prepared as any company can be for adversity because Berkshire has been built to last. Net, we would benefit over a twenty-year period by having some periods of terrible markets. That doesn't mean we're wishing for them and it doesn't mean they're going to happen. We make our money by allocating capital well, and the lower the general stock market, the better we can allocate capital."

CM: "We're never going to sell everything and go to cash and wait for a crash so we can go back in. On the other hand, we are structured so that a lot of turmoil in the next twenty years will help us, not hurt us. I don't mean it'll be pleasant to go through the downcycle, but it's part of the game."

BERKSHIRE'S LIMITATIONS (SIZE)

2010 MEETING (01:19:24)

WB: "We are putting big money into good businesses, from an economic standpoint, but they are not as good as some of what we could buy when we were dealing with smaller amounts. If you take See's Candies, it has $40 million or so of required capital in the business, and it earns something well above that. Now, if we could put another $40 million in it at anything like the returns we receive on the first $40 million, we'd be down there this afternoon with the money. Unfortunately, the wonderful businesses don't soak up capital; that's one of the reasons they're wonderful.

"At our size—operating earnings were $2.2 billion in the first quarter—our job is to put that out as intelligently as we can. We can't find the See's Candies that will sop up that kind of money. When we find them, we'll buy them, but they will not sop up the kind of money we'll generate.

"Then the question is, can we put it to work intelligently, if not brilliantly? So far, we think the answer has been yes. We think it makes sense to go into the capital-intensive businesses that we have. So far, it has made sense, it's worked quite well. But it can't work brilliantly. The world is not set up so that you can reinvest tens of billions of dollars, and many, many tens of billions over time, and get huge returns. It just doesn't happen. And we try to spell that out as carefully as we can so that the shareholders will understand our limitations. Now, you could say, 'Well then, aren't you better off paying it out?' We're not better off paying it out as long as we can translate it into a little something more than a dollar of present value, and we'll keep looking for ways to do that. In our judgment, we did that with BNSF, but the scorecard will be written in ten or twenty years. We did it with MidAmerican Energy. We went into a very capital-intensive business, and so far we've done very well in terms of compounding equity. But it can't be a Coca-Cola, in terms of a basic business where you really don't need very much capital, if any, and you can keep growing if you're lucky. See's is not a growing business. It's a wonderful business, but it doesn't translate itself around the world like Coca-Cola would. … I hope we don't disappoint you, in terms of putting money out to work at decent returns. But if anybody expects brilliant returns from this base, we don't know how to do it."

CM: "I'm just as good at not knowing as you are."

BUSINESS ETHICS

2008 MEETING (00:29:29)

WB: "We let our managers run their businesses. And we've got some terrific managers, not only in terms of ability; what we have seen of the ethical standards of our managers has been extraordinary over the years. That doesn't mean there aren't slip-ups here or there. But taken as a group, over decades, I'm very happy turning over the keys, not only to the financial performance of the business, but in terms of how they behave.

"I also tell them we've got all the money we need. It's nice to have more money, but we're not going to lack for money at Berkshire. We don't have a shred of reputation more than we need, and we never want to trade away reputation for money. So we give them the consistent message, which is that not only should they behave in a way that conforms with the laws, but they should behave in a way where, if a story were written by an unfriendly but intelligent reporter and published the next morning in their local paper, they would have no problem with their neighbors and family reading it.

"There is no pressure from Berkshire's corporate office to report X dollars of earnings in any given quarter. They don't give me budgets, that way there's no feeling that they have to come through with a given number or I'll be embarrassed in public in terms of publishing earnings or anything of the sort. We have no incentives to cause people to do anything that would go against their conscience, to play games or to cut corners, anything of the sort. And, overall, I think it's worked well. It isn't perfect. You can't have 250,000 people like we do at Berkshire without having something going on at some point. But I'm not unhappy with our batting average."

BERKSHIRE'S STRUCTURE AND TAXATION

1998 MEETING (05:17:51)

WB: "We are structured very poorly. If you were going to start all over again and do most of the things we've done, you would probably not do it in corporate form, or precisely like we do it ... If we own Coca-Cola with a cost of $1.2 billion and a market value of $15 billion, if we sold it, we would incur a capital gains tax on the order of $5 billion. That means $15 billion becomes $10 billion. Now, if that $10 billion is reflected in Berkshire's value and you bought your stock when we bought Coke, you pay a second tax, in turn, in reflection of the Coca-Cola appreciation that has taken place after-tax. So, it's a very disadvantageous way of owning securities, to have a corporation between you and the securities themselves. If we ran as a partnership that would not be the case.

"I ran Buffett Partnership for many years and we only had one tax at the individual level. To the extent we own marketable securities—and we own a lot of them—and to the extent we have a lot of profits in those, we own those securities in a disadvantageous way. Now, we also have float, which helps us own them, which is a big plus. But corporate ownership of securities is disadvantageous if you have the option of owning them directly or through a partnership.

"We're stuck with it, and we've got no plans to do anything about it. We probably couldn't do anything if we wanted to. So that is a drag on our performance, compared to what would be the situation if we operated as a partnership. Some insurance companies that operate in Bermuda may not have that problem to the same extent. Certainly, partnerships don't have that problem, to the extent they own securities. But it's a fact of life with us and we're going to pay a lot of taxes."

CM: "We have no cure for the corporate income tax, and it is a big disadvantage for the indirect owner of securities. So far we've surmounted it well enough but we're carrying a load there."

WB: "It's become a bigger disadvantage since the individual rate went to 20% with our corporate rate being 35%. If we make $1 on a stock, it becomes $0.65, and to the extent that you've owned Berkshire, that $0.65, now 20% off that, becomes $0.52. Whereas if you'd owned the stock directly, you'd have had $0.80. Now, when we owned GEICO and it wasn't consolidated with us, you carried that one more extreme; GEICO had capital gains and we had a capital gain proportionately in GEICO, and so on. How you're structured does make a real difference. But usually once you get into a given structure you're kind of stuck with it."

CM: "To the extent we have very long holding periods at the corporate level, the real mathematical disadvantage shrinks."

WB: "And we might not have been able to get the float that we have if we hadn't been operating it in a corporate structure, so that is a mitigating factor too. But we like to have the mitigating factors without anything to mitigate if we get our choice."

DUE DILIGENCE IN M&A

1998 MEETING (05:22:12)

WB: "We've been burned [in M&A] only in the sense that we've made mistakes on judging the future economics of a business, which had nothing to do with due diligence. We regard what people normally refer to due diligence as really sort of boilerplate in most cases. It's a process that big companies go through, and they feel they have to go through it. Oftentimes they're ignoring, in our view, what really counts, which is evaluating the people they're getting in with and evaluating the economics of the business. That's 99% of the deal.

"You may run into an environmental liability problem, one time in a hundred, or you may find a bad lease. I ask, 'Do you have any bad leases?' That's the easiest way to do it. I could read them all and try and look for every clause or something, but that is not the problem. We've made lots of bad deals. For example, we made a bad deal when we bought the department store operation Hochschild Kohn back in 1966. It had fine people but we were wrong on the economics of the business. The leases didn't make any difference; that sort of thing just was not important.

"I can't recall any time when what other people refer to as due diligence would've avoided a bad deal for us. That's thirty-some years. I've been on nineteen public company boards. Their idea of due diligence is to send the lawyers out and have a bunch of investment bankers come in and make presentations and all that. I regard that as terribly diversionary, because the board sits there, entranced by all of that, and everybody reporting how wonderful this thing is and how they checked out patents and all that sort of thing. And nobody is really focusing on where the business is going to be in five to ten years.

"Ninety-nine per cent of deal making is business judgment about economics and, to some extent, people. People may do the rest for their protection. I think they too often do it as a crutch just to go through with a deal that they want to do anyway. Of course, all the professionals know that—so, believe me, they come back with the diligence, whether due or not. We are not big fans of that. I don't know how many deals we've made over the years, but I cannot think of anything that traditional due diligence has had a thing to do with. The kind of people that we've generally dealt with have usually told us the bad things first and good things after we made the deal."

BUYING BUSINESSES VS BUYING STOCKS

1999 MEETING (01:29:06)

WB: "We've always wanted to acquire entire businesses. People never seemed to really believe that back when we were buying See's Candies or The Buffalo News or National Indemnity. But that's been our number one preference right along. It's just that we've found, much of the time, we could get far more for our money, in terms of wonderful businesses, by buying pieces in the stock market, than we could by negotiated purchase …

"It's almost impossible to make a wonderful buy in a negotiated purchase. You will never make the kind of buy in a negotiated purchase that you can in a weak stock market. It just isn't going to happen. The person on the other side cares too much. Whereas, in the stock market in a 1973 or 1974, you're dealing with the marginal seller, and whatever price they establish for the business, you could buy it. I couldn't have bought the entire Washington Post Company for $80 million in 1974—but I could buy 10% of it from a bunch of people who were calculating betas or doing something of the sort. They were in a terrible market. And it was possible to buy a piece of it on that valuation. You never get that kind of buy in a negotiated purchase.

"We are always more interested in large, negotiated deals than we are in stock purchases. But we are probably not going to find a way to use all the money that way. Occasionally we may get chances to put big chunks of money into attractive businesses through the stock market to buy 5% or 10% of a company."

BERKSHIRE'S LONG-TERM SUCCESS

1999 MEETING (04:12:34)

WB: "The record of Berkshire Hathaway, to the extent it's been good, has not been because we've done brilliant things, but because we've done fewer dumb things than most. Why smart people do things that are against their self-interest is really puzzling."

2012 MEETING (02:17:24)

CM: "We have a very peculiar model, and it works very well for us. I think it's very hard for other people to get the same result."

WB: "I think it's almost impossible to copy Berkshire. It has taken a long, long time to get here. It's also taken a great amount of consistency, and that consistency has been allowed because, basically, we've had a controlling shareholder during that time. We have not had to bow to any of the urgings of

Wall Street or the fad of the day. We have had a culture where we could write out thirteen or fourteen principles more than thirty years ago, and we've been able to stick with them. That's very hard to do for most American corporations, and I think it's very hard to do when managers come and go and have small shareholdings. I think it takes a very unusual structure to be able to do it.

"It took a long time to get to the point where people with large private businesses in this country really cared about where those businesses were lodged after they gave up their stewardship. It took a long time to have it get so that a great many of those people would think of Berkshire first. And the nice thing about it is, if they think of Berkshire first, they don't think of anybody second, so we get the call ... The big private acquisitions are going to come to Berkshire because they want to come to Berkshire. And that's a significant competitive edge, and I don't see how anybody really challenges us on that."

CM: "Not only do I think other people will have a hard time copying it effectively, I think if Warren went back to being thirty years of age with a modest amount of capital and not much else, he'd have a hell of a time doing it again, too."

2015 MEETING (00:39:39)

WB: "I had three extraordinary pieces of luck, in terms of the insurance business. One was, at twenty years old, when I spent a Saturday afternoon in 1951 with a fellow named Lorimer Davidson [CEO at GEICO]. He spent four hours with some twenty-year-old kid he had never heard of before, and he explained the insurance business to me. I received an education at age twenty that I couldn't have gotten at any business school in the United States. That was just pure luck ... Then, in 1967, I got lucky again. Jack Ringwalt, for about five minutes every year, wanted to sell his company because he would get mad about something, some claim would come in that he didn't like. And I told my friend Charlie Heider, 'Next time Jack is in the mood, be sure to get him to my office.' Charlie got him up there one day, and we bought National Indemnity ... And then I really got lucky in the mid-1980s when, on a Saturday, some guy came in the office and he said, 'I've never worked in the insurance business, but maybe I can do you some good.' And that was Ajit Jain. How lucky can you get? So, if you ask me whether we can pull off a trifecta like that again in the future, I'd say the odds are very much against it.

"The whole thing in business is being open to ideas as they come along, and insurance happened to be something I could understand. That was in my sweet spot ... There's an awful lot of accident in life, but if you keep yourself open to having good accidents happen, and get past the bad accidents, some good things will happen."

CM: "Mostly we bought wonderful businesses and nourished them. But the reinsurance division was just created out of whole cloth right here in Omaha … Insurance has been different for us."

BERKSHIRE HATHAWAY ENERGY (MIDAMERICAN ENERGY)

2003 MEETING (02:11:58)

WB: "MidAmerican is a big part of Berkshire, and I would say it's likely to become much bigger. It will be easier if the Public Utility Holding Company Act were repealed.[1] Melodiously called PUHCA, it was enacted in 1935 in a reaction to what Sam Insull and people like that had done in the 1920s. It was very understandable. But I really think it is quite outdated now. And I think we bring something to the utility field. In fact, we brought it in the last year; there might be a couple companies that would be in bankruptcy now if we hadn't been in a position to act very quickly on certain things. But with or without the repeal—and I think there's a reasonable chance it'll be repealed—MidAmerican, which is big now, will become quite a bit bigger, and it could become a whole lot bigger.

"Now, in terms of what kind of assets we'll buy, we don't have any clear-cut preference as to whether it would be, for example, a natural gas pipeline, a domestic utility, or conceivably, a utility in some country. We will look at things as they come along. We're always ready to act … The nature of the energy field is you're talking big money; these are not lemonade stands. We're talking in the billions, frequently, on the kind of assets involved. We've got two people in Dave Sokol and Greg Abel who are terrific businesspeople. And incidentally, they have done things that have made Berkshire significant money that had nothing to do with MidAmerican. They spent their time and energy putting together a couple of things that MidAmerican itself could not do, but Berkshire could. And MidAmerican didn't get paid a dime for that. So, they've contributed to Berkshire's welfare beyond what they've contributed simply as managers of MidAmerican. So it's a terrific asset. We love the idea of pouring money behind them, and you'll see something happen."

CM: "The really interesting thing is that the field is so big; it's enormous. One thing a modern civilization needs is energy. So, we'll be very disappointed if there aren't more activities."

---

1 PUHCA was repealed in 2005.

2009 MEETING (03:08:06)

WB: "I believe we're the largest utility in the country, in terms of owned capacity in wind. And Iowa has the greatest percentage of its electricity generated by wind. But, of course, the wind only blows about 35% of the time in Iowa, so you can't count on it for your base load or anything. But Iowa has been very, very receptive and, I would argue, progressive, in encouraging us to bring in a lot of wind capacity—and we've encouraged them in return. We are a net exporter of electricity in Iowa. Iowa's far more than self-sufficient in our service area in terms of electric generation. And I think that works to the benefit of the people of Iowa. As you may know, we have not increased our rates at all for more than a decade. That's been achieved by efficiencies. It's been achieved with wind generation. We have a return that's built in on that that's fair to us and that's fair to the people of Iowa. Part of that return comes in the form of a tax credit—I think it's 1.8 cents per kilowatt hour—that is given to anybody in the U.S. that develops wind-power generation. We love the idea of putting in more wind. We're doing it, and I think we'll continue to be a leader in it.

"One advantage we have, perhaps, over some people is that we are a big taxpayer, so that we don't have to worry about whether the tax credits are useful. I guess the tax credit could be sold, also, but we don't need to do that in our particular situation. So you'll see more and more wind generation by the MidAmerican companies. When we went into PacifiCorp out on the West Coast, to six states out there, they had virtually nothing at all in wind generation. We've developed a lot, and we've got more coming."

CM: "I think in practically anything that makes sense in utilities, the Berkshire subsidiaries will be leaders. I think we can all be very proud of MidAmerican and its two leaders."

WB: "We're enormously proud of MidAmerican, and we will do a lot more in utilities over time. Constellation Energy didn't work out. I wish it had. We learned of their troubles on a Tuesday at noon; Dave Sokol and Greg Abel were in Baltimore that evening with a firm, all-cash bid to solve Constellation's problems. Constellation was likely to get downgraded within 24–48 hours, and they would've had posting requirements in connection with various derivative transactions that they probably would not have met. They were facing bankruptcy. We literally went from a phone call Dave made to me at noon to handing them a firm bid that evening. That's one of the advantages of Berkshire, and I think that's a durable competitive advantage. There are very few organizations that will act in that manner, where you have talent that you feel you can back up as the CEO with that kind of money without worrying about it. So, that is a plus for Berkshire, even though it didn't work in that case. We'll do more in the utility business."

CM: "Well, you bought a pipeline, didn't you, in about two hours?"

WB: "We did, and it's turned out very well. In that particular case, the company, Dynegy—back in 2002—needed the money enormously. They had gotten the pipeline from Enron. It was a very complicated transaction. They needed the money, and we needed the Federal Trade Commission (FTC) approval on the deal, as would anybody that was buying it. I wrote a letter to the commission saying, 'These guys need the money. They need it before the thirty-day period is up. Let us go through with this early, and we'll do any damn thing you tell us, subsequently.'

"Berkshire can make that kind of a transaction. We don't ask the lawyers before we do it or anything, we just do it. And that is an advantage. And it was an advantage to Dynegy. It got them through a period [in July 2002] that I'm not sure they would've gotten through otherwise. So, we can move fast when the time comes. There's a couple of reasons we move fast. For one, we've always got the money; we've got a mental attitude toward that. But we also know we've got the managers that can deliver on the properties, once we own them. That's a huge, huge advantage."

2011 MEETING (04:33:17)

WB: "Wind power is terrific, but only when the wind blows. You can never count on wind power for your base load, which is a real limitation. On the other hand, wind power is basically the cleanest energy you can come up with ... The economics only make sense with an incentive credit—a tax credit provided by the federal government, which they've been doing for a considerable period of time. ... [Y]our government has made a decision that it wants to subsidize, in effect, wind power ... And it's kind of interesting: One of the assets of Berkshire is that it pays a lot of taxes. That doesn't sound like much of an asset, but a lot of utilities ... really don't have the tax-paying capacity to be able to use tax credits. They are in a different position than Berkshire, which pays a lot of taxes.

"We've probably paid something like 2% of all the corporate taxes in the United States over the last five years. We have a lot of tax-paying capacity. We can build more wind projects. I think it's very likely we continue to do it. It helps our Iowa customers. Because these projects are successful it's enabled us to keep rates absolutely unchanged for more than a decade, which is very unusual among electric utilities in the United States."

2012 MEETING (01:02:53)

WB: "We've been doing wind for quite a while, and I think the subsidy is 2.2 cents for ten years per kilowatt hour, and that's a federal subsidy ... The government, by putting in that 2.2 cents subsidy, has encouraged a lot of wind development. If there had been no subsidy, my guess is there would have been no wind development. I don't think any of our projects would make sense without that subsidy."

CM: "Eventually we're going to have to take a lot of power from these renewable sources and, of course, we're going to have to help the process along with subsidies. I think it's very wise that that's what the various governments are doing."

WB: "... I would guess that perhaps 80% of the utilities in the United States cannot reap the full, or maybe any, tax benefits, from doing the things we just talked about because they don't pay any federal income taxes. They've used bonus depreciation, which was enacted last year, where you get to write-off 100% in the first year. They wipe out their taxable income. And if they've wiped out their taxable income, they cannot have any appetite for wind projects where they get a tax credit, or in the solar arrangement. So, by being part of Berkshire Hathaway, which is a huge taxpayer, MidAmerican has extra abilities to go out and do a lot of projects without worrying about whether they have exhausted their tax capacity."

2015 MEETING (01:08:16)

WB: "BH Energy's safety record is extraordinary in terms of utilities. Every new utility we purchase at BH Energy, the safety statistics become far better after Greg Abel takes over."

2015 MEETING (01:27:30)

CM: "Obviously, we're going to use a lot more renewable energy because the fossil fuels aren't going to last forever. And, obviously, Berkshire is very aggressive and very well located, in terms of this development ... To have [>50% of] the power of Berkshire's utilities in Iowa coming from the wind, I regard as a huge stunt. And it's, of course, very desirable, in a windy place like Iowa where the farmers like the extra income, to be getting a lot of power out of the wind.

"We're going to have a lot better storage, and the technology has been improving. It's not a threat, it's a huge benefit to humanity. I think it will be a huge benefit to Berkshire. Everything is working for us. I love owning MidAmerican in an era where we're going to have more storage, more wind, more solar, more grid. And I think we're so lucky. What the hell would we do if the fossil fuels run down, if we didn't have the sun to use indirectly in these forms? It's going to be a lot more storage. And, of course, there will be some disruption in the utility industry, but there will be more opportunity, I think, than disruption."

2016 MEETING (00:55:42)

WB: "Any decision we make about new generation or changes in generation has to go through what's usually called a public utility commission; they may have different names in a few states. The utility industry is overwhelmingly regulated at the state level, and we cannot make changes that are not approved by the public utility commission. We've had more problems, for example, in bringing in renewables in our western utility, Pacific Corp, because it's, in effect, regulated by six states and they don't necessarily agree on how the cost and benefits should be divided if we put in a bunch of renewables, and we have to follow their instructions.

"Iowa has just been marvelous about encouraging it at every level—consumer groups, the governor, you name it—they've seen the benefits. In Iowa, we have one major competitor, called Alliant, and I don't know the reasons why, but they have not pursued renewables the way we have, so our rates are considerably lower than theirs. If you look at their budget projections, although they already have substantially higher rates than we have now, they may need a rate increase within a year or so. With our latest expansion, we have said we will not need a rate increase until 2029—thirteen years off—at the earliest. So, there have been great benefits if you have a regulation that works, but it is a determination that is made at the state level.

"The federal government has encouraged, in a major way, the development of renewables by this production tax credit ... We would not have the renewable generation we have if it hadn't been for the fact that building those projects is subsidized by the federal government. The benefits of reducing carbon emissions are worldwide, and therefore it's deemed proper that the citizenry as a whole should participate in subsidizing the cost of reducing those emissions. And that has encouraged—in fact, it's allowed—things like have happened in Iowa. It will depend on governmental policy. I think, so far, it's been quite sensible in having the cost borne by society as a whole, in terms of reduced tax revenues. The benefit, which is less carbon dioxide into the atmosphere, is not just limited to the people of Iowa when we build that. That's a benefit that accrues to the world. ..."One thing you might find kind of interesting: Nebraska has not done much with wind power. Two miles from here, right across the river, people are buying their electricity cheaper in Council Bluffs, Iowa, than they are in Omaha. And yet Nebraska is entirely a public power state, so there's no stockholders who have to have any earnings, the bonds are issued on a tax-exempt basis, and yet electricity is considerably cheaper right across the river ... The real irony is that because electricity is so much cheaper in Iowa, you have these massive server farms from people like Google. It's become a tech haven for these operations that just gobble up electricity. Iowa has gotten plant after plant after plant and job after job, and gotten more property tax revenues. Google is in Iowa because we have cheap wind-generated electricity ... Nebraska has prided itself on public power. It originated, I believe, back in the 1930s, when George Norris was a very powerful senator. It's been a source of pride, but lately, it's been a source of cost, too."

2017 MEETING (04:41:46)

WB: "I'd be surprised if ten years from now, we don't have significantly more money in not only wind and solar, but we'll probably own more utility systems than we own now. We're a buyer of choice with many utility commissions. Greg Abel and his group have done an extraordinary job. They've done it in safety, reliability, price, and in renewables. It's hard to imagine a better run operation than exists at MidAmerican Energy. And with that record, people want us to come to their state in many cases."

CM: "Our utilities are not normal. The way Greg Abel has run those things, they're so much better run in every way than normal utilities. They're better regarded by the paying customers. They're better regarded by the regulators. They have better safety records. Everything about it is way better. It's a pleasure to be associated with people like that and to have assets of that quality."

WB: "We have public power here in Nebraska. It's been sort of the pride of Nebraska for many decades. There are no privately-held utility systems, it's totally public power. And, those utilities have no requirements for earning a return on equity. They can borrow at tax-exempt rates. We have to borrow at taxable rates. The wind in Nebraska is not that much different than Iowa. And we're selling electricity across the river, a few miles from here, at lower prices than exist in Nebraska. So, it's an extraordinary utility. I thank Walter Scott, our director, for introducing me to it almost eighteen years ago or so. But I don't think the utility business—I mean, if I were putting together a portfolio of stocks, I don't think there would be any utilities in that group now. But I love the fact that we own Berkshire Hathaway Energy."

CM: "But it's different, radically different. And better."

WB: "A lot better."

2019 MEETING (03:27:13)

WB: "We have three owners of Berkshire Hathaway Energy. We are the 91% owner. And there are no three owners that are more interested in pouring money into sensible deals within the utility industry or that are better situated in terms of the people we have to maximize any opportunities. Other utility companies pay high dividends; we have never had a penny of dividends in close to twenty years of owning MidAmerican Energy. They really just don't have the capital appetite, essentially, that we do. So, it's just a question of finding sensible projects. I would say that there's no group that is as smart about it and as motivated about it as our group."

CM: "In short, we're about as good as you can get, and you should worry about something else."

WB: "We will put a lot of money into energy."

CM: " We're really in marvelous shape in this department."

WB: "Incidentally, Walter Scott [CEO of Kiewit Corporation] gets excited looking at all these projects, and goes out and visits them. He's forgotten more about it than I'll ever know. But we've got a great partnership. We've got unlimited capital and there's a need for huge capital in the industry. So, I think in ten or twenty years, our record will be looked at and there'll be nothing like it in the energy business."

CM: "Greg, is there anybody ahead of where we are in Iowa in terms of energy?"

GREG ABEL: "Charlie, there's realistically no one ahead of us in the U.S., let alone in Iowa. When you look at the amount of energy we produce relative to what our customers consume, we really do lead the nation and Iowa."

CM: "And aren't our rates about half that of our leading competitor in Iowa to boot?"

GA: "Exactly. We're right in that range."

CM: "If this isn't good enough for you, we can't help you."

NEBRASKA FURNITURE MART

2014 MEETING (00:56:18)

WB: "We paid probably 11× or 12× after-tax earnings for the Nebraska Furniture Mart. We bought 80% of the company. It was bought on the basis, as I remember, of a $60 million purchase price. There was a second transaction involved in it. But $60 million was 100% of the value; we ended up with 80%. The $60 million would've been more than book value at the time. Not way more, but more than book value. The sales were about $100 million and pre-tax margins were in the 7% range, it was about $7 million pre-tax, and probably $4.5 or $5 million after-tax—in that ballpark. It was not a bargain purchase. It was a great business. It was a wonderful opportunity to join, and as fine a family as I've ever met.

"Incidentally, there was another company, I believe from Germany, that was trying to buy it at the time. Believe it or not, my friend Erskine Bowles, of Simpson-Bowles, was representing them—I didn't know that at the time. I went out on my birthday, August 30, 1983. I had that contract, which is in the annual report, and I gave it to Mrs. B. She didn't read, but her son Louie told her what was in it. I never asked her for an audit. I just asked her if she owed any money. I asked her if she owned the building; she said yes. And we made the deal. But it was not a bargain purchase."

NETJETS

2003 MEETING (00:38:10)

WB: "[Fractional jet ownership company] NetJets had a significant loss in the first quarter. A large portion of that was caused by the write-down of planes ... In the trade, they call them pre-owned planes; I call them used planes. In any event, putting aside euphemisms, the entire business aircraft market is very soft. The used plane market has far more planes for sale than four or five years ago. That's affecting the production of new planes. And it affects pricing in used planes; we have bought back planes from people leaving the programs, which we do and will continue to do. But we have bought during a declining market and we have had write-downs in connection with those planes ... It's a popular product, it's a growing business, and it's going to be a very big business in my opinion over the years.

"There are three main competitors. I think it's fair to say they're losing significant money, forgetting about any markdowns they might have on their own inventories. Our market share—we get figures from the FAA on registrations and people that are selling their planes—has gone up dramatically in the last couple of years. It's up to roughly 75%, in terms of value of planes. We're talking 75% of a four-company market ... But the pricing we are receiving in the U.S. would be very, very modestly profitable.

"In Europe, we have lost and are losing significant amounts of money. The total number of business jets in Europe is roughly one tenth the number of the United States, even though the population is similar. So, we have grown from a small base quite rapidly over there. Nobody else will be taking us on.

"It will be part of a very big business worldwide, in my view, over the years. I don't think anybody else can come in after us. So, I think it's integral to our operation. Roughly half the miles flown in Europe arise from American owners. And that will get bigger over the years, because every month our number of owners goes up significantly. We have people here from Marquis, who have essentially become a customer of ours, and then they resell cards for twenty-five hours; they have added forty to fifty customers a month in recent months. So, it's a popular service. It will be a much bigger business.

"I think there will be a shakeout at some point, and maybe fairly soon. I don't know the answer as to when the shakeout will occur, but I can assure you that we will not be one of the competitors who gets shook ... The long-term business model is basically that we believe that perhaps ten times the number of people who are now flying with us will be flying with us some years in the future. Having the best service, the best record, and the best policies for safety and security, will leave us very dominant in the field, and people will pay an appropriate price for the service. And we see all kinds of evidence of that. But we do not see a profit this year, in my view, at NetJets."

2010 MEETING (01:56:30)

WB: "We'll make mistakes from time to time, and some of our managers may make mistakes. And sometimes you run into conditions that are really extraordinary. The biggest mistake made with NetJets is essentially we were buying planes at prices that were fictitious, in terms of the prices at which we would later be able to sell them. And there's a certain time lapse involved in buying fractional shares. There's a lot of explanations for it, but in the end, we didn't properly prepare for what was obviously happening. And we lost a lot of money, a good bit of which was attributable to the write-down of planes, our inventory, where we bought them at X and we couldn't sell them at X or 90% of X. Some of those were new planes that we should not have taken on, and many of them were planes coming back from owners.

"We also let our operating costs get out of line with recurring revenues. But I've made plenty of mistakes. I stayed in the textile business for twenty years. I knew it was a lousy business. Charlie was telling me it was a lousy business; twenty years later, I woke up. I was like Rip Van Winkle ... The one thing we will guarantee: We'll make some mistakes. It was a big mistake at NetJets, $711 million is the figure. We are now operating at NetJets at a very decent profit, a pre-tax profit of well over $50 million in the first quarter, and that's not with any big boom in plane sales or anything else. It's just with a business plan that involves not an iota of diminution of safety or service, but just got things in line that needed to be in line. And I give Dave Sokol enormous credit. He turned that place around like nobody could have, and all the shareholders owe him a big vote of thanks for that."

CM: "I believe that the episode ought to be reviewed in context. If we buy thirty big businesses and generally let the people who run them successfully before run them with very little interference from headquarters, and it works out 95% of the time very well, and we have one episode when the basic franchise was protected but we lost profit opportunities for a while, it's not a big failure record. Nor does it indicate that we should stop being pretty easy with the remarkable people who join us with their companies."

WB: "No, it does not change our management approach at all. I think that we have gotten performance, overall, from managers that are beyond the dreams I would have had when I was first putting this company together. We let managers do their stuff, and it's worked very well for us, net. We're going to keep doing it."

BERKSHIRE HATHAWAY HOME SERVICES (REAL ESTATE BROKERAGE)

2005 MEETING (04:32:58)

WB: "We are hoping to build a powerhouse on the model of today; in other words, we do not envision big changes in residential real estate brokerage … We are the second largest residential real estate brokerage firm in the country. We expect that business to be conducted quite similarly in the future to how it has been in the past. Now, there are people that disagree with that who think way more will happen via the internet. But the purchase of a home is the single most important transaction for most people in their lives. It can be partly emotional, something that they appreciate people guiding them through. It's something where I think one-on-one will be very important in the future as it has been so far.

"In this country, there are going to be millions and millions of homes that get sold every year; real estate brokerage business is going to be a very, very big business. And I think it will tend to be a very local business. We have bought leading local firms in a number of markets, which have retained their individual identity. We have not gone for a Century 21 approach where we put them all under the umbrella of a single brand. Rather we have these individual brands in given communities, and they're usually very strong brands. But we've only scratched the surface … We would like to be very big in that business.

"We already are big, but I think it's almost certain we will be a lot bigger five to ten years from now. It's a question of acquiring these firms. Generally, they're proprietorships; they're owned by a single individual or a family. And they come up periodically because of the family circumstances or individual circumstances. There's a lot of them out there, and we're a logical buyer. We've been found to be a good owner. So, it's going to be a good-sized field for us."

BERKSHIRE DIVIDEND POLICY

2008 MEETING (04:04:57)

WB: "I do believe in dividends in a great many situations, including many of the companies in which we own stock. The test about whether to pay dividends is whether you can continue to create more than $1 of value for every $1 you retain. Take See's Candies, which we own. See's has paid virtually everything out to us that they've earned because they do not have the ability within to use the large sums they earn intelligently in their business. So it would be an enormous mistake for See's Candies to retain the money. They distribute to Berkshire, and we hope that we move it in some other area where that $1 becomes worth $1.10 or $1.20, in present-value terms.

"If we do that, the shareholders are better off if we retain the money, because if they were going to get $1 in dividends versus it being worth $1.10 in market value immediately on a present-value basis, they're better off selling a small percentage of their stock and realizing the required amount that way; they will have more money when they get through doing that than if we paid it in dividends. But if the time comes—and it will someday—when we don't think we can use the money effectively to create more than $1 of market value per $1 retained, then it should be paid out. And, like I say, we do that individually within Berkshire. But because we have this ability to redistribute money in a tax-efficient way within the company, we have more reason to retain all of our earnings. If See's were a standalone company, we would pay out practically all of the earnings in dividends—just like we do now, except it goes to Berkshire.

"We like companies in which we have investments to pay to us the money they can't use efficiently in their own business. In some cases that's 100% of what they earn; in some cases it's 0%. We own some stocks that don't pay any dividends. Did Costco pay any dividend for a while, Charlie?"

CM: "While they were growing very rapidly, they paid no dividend. Now they're paying one. Berkshire's policy is much the same. Warren has always planned on paying large dividends; he does it in the mode of Saint Augustine when he said, 'God, give me chastity, but not yet.'"

WB: "I've always admired that."

2011 MEETING (01:32:40)

WB: "Who knows how soon, because the numbers are getting big, but there will come a time when we do not think we can lay out $15–20 billion a year and get something that's immediately worth more than that for our shareholders. When the time comes, where a dollar is only buying us 90 cents of value, we'll quit spending the dollar. We'll give it to shareholders. But I predict the day that Berkshire declares a dividend the stock will go down—and it should go down, because it's an admission, essentially, that a compounding machine has lost its ability to continue on that course."

BORSHEIMS (JEWELRY BUSINESS)

1998 MEETING (04:50:40)

WB: "Borsheims operates at very considerably lower gross margins than does a Tiffany or publicly-held jewelry operations. We are giving customers considerably more for their money. We've got way lower operating costs than the public companies. Our operating costs are fifteen to twenty percentage points, and even more in some cases, less than publicly-owned competitors. So, we've got a lot to offer.

"Now, the big question people always have with jewelers is, 'How do you know who to trust?' It is an item (jewelry) that most people feel very uncomfortable buying. And I think that the Berkshire Hathaway identification can help people feel comfortable on it. I think that the experience of customers around the country as they see it can help. It's a high-ticket item, so saving money gets to be really important, just like in auto insurance. So, I think that the internet could be of significant assistance to Borsheims in terms of spreading and facilitating its nationwide reputation. Borsheims could have a lot of growth and the internet could be a big part of it.

"Our job is to get the message to people around the country that they can have us send half a dozen items to them, that they can look at with no high-pressure salesmanship at all or anything of the sort, and look at the prices, decide what they want in their own homes, and they will do very well with us. We have a lot of people taking advantage of that now, but we could have ten, twenty or fifty times that number as the years go by. I think we should work very hard on that ... Anything where you're offering a terrific deal to the consumer, but one of the problems has been how do you talk to that consumer, the internet offers possibilities. The thing is that everybody in the world is going to be there, and why should they click on you instead of somebody else?"

OCCIDENTAL PETROLEUM

2020 MEETING (03:22:10)

WB: "Essentially, when you buy into a huge oil production company, how it works out is going to depend to a great extent on the price of oil. It's not only based on your geological home runs or super mistakes or anything like that. It is an investment that depends on the price of oil. And when oil goes to minus $37 as happened the other day for the May contract, that's off the chart.

"If you own oil, you should only own oil if you expect these prices to go up significantly. I don't know whether they'll go up significantly or not. We're in the transaction. Our commitment was made on a Sunday when the management of Anadarko favored Chevron, and Chevron had a breakup fee of $1 billion. The Occidental people had been working on it for several years, and it was attractive at oil prices that then prevailed. And it doesn't work obviously. It certainly doesn't work at minus $37 a barrel, but it doesn't work at $20 a barrel either. And everything the oil companies have been doing—Exxon, Occidental, or anybody else—it doesn't work at these oil prices. That's why oil production is going to go down a lot in the next few years because it does not pay to drill now. That's happened at other times in the past. But the situation is, you don't know where you're going to store the incremental barrel of oil, and oil demand is down dramatically.

"For a while, the Russians and the Saudis were trying to outdo each other in how much oil they could produce. And when you've got too much in storage, it doesn't work its way off that fast. Now you will have production of oil go down in the United States significantly. It does not pay to drill in all kinds of formations that paid before and it doesn't pay to have paid the price that oil was trading at in the ground a year or two ago. To that extent, if you're an Occidental shareholder or any shareholder in any oil-producing company, you'll join me in having made a mistake so far in terms of where oil prices went. Who knows where they go in the future."

PRECISION CASTPARTS

2021 MEETING (00:28:35)

WB: "Berkshire didn't make a mistake on Precision Castparts [industrial goods and metal fabrication]; I made the mistake. Any time we look at buying a business, we're evaluating the competitive strengths, the price, the management, everything. We didn't make a mistake on the management, but I did make a mistake in terms of their average earnings power. All kinds of things can happen, like when Boeing had troubles with the MAX. We have seen some of those things happen. But I paid too much in relation to average earning. It's a terrific company and I'm happy with management, but GE doesn't need as many engines as we thought they would need ... Other businesses we bought, sometimes they end up doing better than we think. I'll continue making mistakes.

"But we've also had some wonderful deals. And when we're disappointed in a business, it usually becomes a smaller and smaller percentage of our business, just by the nature of things, because it isn't going any place. And when we have a successful business like GEICO, it's now doing 15× as much business as when we bought control in 1990. They become a much more important part of our mix. So, through natural forces, you get more money in the things that have developed more favorably than you thought. You actually end up getting a greater concentration in the ones that work out. Charlie would say it's not like having children, where the bad ones cause you more problems."

DEXTER SHOE

2002 MEETING (04:34:38)

WB: "We lost a very significant amount of money on Dexter Shoe, thanks to a dumb decision I made, and maybe several dumb decisions. That is a business that went offshore in a huge way. There are close to 1.2 billion pairs of shoes used in this country, four for every man, woman, and child. And I don't know whether it's 5% now, but something in that area are made in this country, and hundreds of thousands of jobs have gone offshore with that. The textile business, as you know, has been almost destroyed in this country ... In the end, if you're paying 10× as much per hour for labor as somebody else, it's awfully hard to be that good.

"Dexter is now part of H.H. Brown, and it's selling products which, overwhelmingly, are produced abroad. And H.H. Brown sells a very significant amount of product that's produced outside the United States, although they still produce a lot of products in the United States. But Dexter will have a significant shoe business ... I think our shoe business will be OK. It won't be a bonanza over time, but we've got very good management in there ... I would expect we would have a substantial and a reasonably profitable shoe business in the future, but we will not be able to do it with 100% or 90% or 80% domestic-produced shoes. And in that respect, I was very wrong in paying what I did, and paying it in the manner I did, which was stock in the case of Dexter, for a domestic shoe manufacturer."

CM: "That shows ... that no matter how hard you work at having systems for avoiding error and practices of trying to stay within your circle of competency, etc., you still make mistakes. And I think I can confidently promise that it won't be our last mistake."

2003 MEETING (02:50:56)

WB: "I have never seen an investment banker's book—I hope to see one someday, and I hope I can survive the shock when I see it—where the earnings of the business being offered go down. But a lot of businesses' earnings go down ... They project it out for ten years and it always goes up. It just isn't the real world. Some businesses will be subjected to enormous competitive pressures that aren't extant today. I made that mistake, for example, at Dexter Shoe. We bought a business earning $40 million pre-tax and we assumed that the future would be as good as the past, and I couldn't have been more wrong. That's part of business. Probably 20% of the Fortune 500 are going to be earning significantly less money five years from now than they are today—but I don't know which 20%. That's what the game is all about."

LUBRIZOL

2011 MEETING (01:03:13)

WB: "Petroleum additives initially struck me as a business that I didn't know anything about. I'd never understand the chemistry of it, but that's not necessarily vital. What is important is to understand the economic dynamics of the industry. Are there competitive moats? Is there ease of entry? All of that sort of thing ... What Dave Sokol passed along to me after having dinner with James Hambrick [CEO of Lubrizol], and which I later confirmed in a lunch when James came out here on February 8, gave me a good understanding of industry dynamics and how the business had developed over time, what the role of oil companies was and would be in relation to a chemical additive. The oil companies are the biggest customers. They sell base oil to Lubrizol, but they are the big customers; they have gotten out of the business to quite a degree, although there's two of them left in it. So this industry had consolidated over time.

"Every time I look at a business, I look at the question of ease of entry. When we bought See's Candies in 1972, I said to myself, if I had $100 million and I wanted to go in and take on See's Candies, could I do it? And I came to the conclusion, no, so we bought See's Candies ... Subject to a second conversation with James, I concluded it's not impossible at all for people to enter this business. But in terms of the service and the relatively low cost of what Lubrizol brings to the party, and in terms of people trying to break into what isn't a huge market (probably only about a $10 billion market overall), I decided that there was a pretty good-sized moat around this. They've got lots of patents, but more than that, they have a connection with customers. They work with customers when new engines come along to develop the right kind of additive.

"So I didn't understand one thing more about chemistry than when I started, but I felt that I had an understanding of the economics of the business, the same way I felt when the ISCAR people talked to me ... That's the conclusion Charlie and I came to, that Lubrizol is the number one company in terms of market share in that business, and it's a sustainable position and likely to be a very good business over time. They are helping engines run longer and smoother; when metal is acting on metal, the lubricants are important, and they're always going to be around. I think Lubrizol will be the leading company for a very long time ... It will be a very good addition to Berkshire. Despite the turmoil around this, they are very enthused about becoming part of Berkshire; they regard it as the ideal home."

CM: "ISCAR and Lubrizol, to some extent, are sisters under the skin. You've got very small markets that aren't really too attractive to anybody with any sense to enter, and fanaticism in service. If you have any more like that, why, please give Warren a call."

PETROCHINA

2004 MEETING (03:20:32)

WB: "PetroChina is very similar to other big oil companies around the world. It was the fourth most profitable oil company in the world last year. They produce 80–85% as much crude daily as Exxon does. It's a big, big company and it's not complicated. It's fairly easy to get your mind around the economic characteristics that will exist in the business. And in terms of being opaque, their annual report may well tell you more about that business than you will find from reading the annual reports of other oil giants. They do one thing I particularly like: They tell you they will pay out 45% of their earnings, absent some change in policy. I like the idea, in a big enterprise like that, of knowing that 45% of what they earn is going to come to Berkshire, with the remainder plowed back in. It was bought simply because it was very, very cheap in relation to earnings, reserves, daily oil production, refining capacity—whatever metric you want to use. It was far cheaper than Exxon, BP, or Shell. Now, you can say it should be cheaper because 90% is owned by the government in China, and that's obviously a factor you stick in your valuation. But I did not think that was a factor that accounted for the huge differential in the price at which it could be bought ... We aren't there because it's China, but we're not avoiding it because it's China, either. If you read the annual report, you will have as good an understanding of the company as you would if you read the annual report of any of the other big oil majors."

CM: "If a thing is cheap enough, you can afford a little more country risk or regulatory risk."

2005 MEETING (00:46:47)

WB: "We bought PetroChina a few years ago after reading the annual report. Fortunately it was in English. It was the first Chinese stock that we've owned. We put about $400 million into it. Last year it earned $12 billion. If you look at the Fortune 500, my guess is you won't find more than about five companies in the U.S. that earn $12 billion. So, it's a major company. At the time we bought it, the total market value was $35 billion. So, we paid about three times what it earned last year. It does not have unusual amounts of leverage. In the annual report, they say they will pay out about 45% of the amount they earn. So, if you can buy it at what turned out to be three times earnings, and you get 45% of 33%, you're getting a 15% cash yield on your investment ... It's a very major business at what was a very attractive price.

"We had to reveal our ownership; we would have bought more but the price jumped up ... We never had any contact with management before we bought the stock. We'd never attended an investor presentation or anything of the sort. I mean, it's right there in black and white, in a report that anybody can get. We just sit in the office and read those things, and we were able to put $400 million out that's now worth $1.2 billion ... The discount at which PetroChina was selling at that time, compared to other international oil companies, was ridiculous in my view; so, that's why we bought it."

2008 MEETING (02:41:38)

WB: "The PetroChina annual report came out and I read it. That's the only thing I ever did. I never contacted management, read a brokerage report, or asked for anybody's opinion ... I came to the conclusion it was worth $100 billion and it was selling for $35 billion. What's the sense of talking to management? If you talk to management of almost any company, they'll say they think their stock is a wonderful buy—it doesn't make any difference. Now, if I thought the company was worth $40 billion, then at that point you have to try to refine your analysis more. But I didn't need to know whether it was worth $95 billion or $105 billion if I was buying it at $35 billion.

"Any further refining of analysis would be a waste of time when what I should be doing is buying the stock. We really like things that you don't have to carry out to three decimal places. If you have to carry it out to three decimal places, it's not a good idea. It's like if somebody walked in the door and they weighed somewhere between 300 and 350 pounds; I might not know how much they weigh, but I would know they were fat. That's all I'm looking for, something that's financially fat. ... It should hit you between the eyes."

CM: "I would argue that we have lower due diligence expenses than anybody else in America, and that we have had less trouble because we had less expense ... I think our operation is safer because we think like engineers. We want these margins of reliability. Others are trying to do something really difficult, which is to have fine-grain judgments in very complex areas, and rely on other people to do it who are getting paid fees ... I think it's much safer to do it our way."

WB: "If you think the auditors know more about making an acquisition than you do, you ought to take up auditing and let them run the business, as far as we're concerned. When we get a call on something like [candy and chewing gum company] Mars/Wrigley ... if the value of Wrigley depends on a specific lease or a given environmental problem, forget it. There are these overriding considerations that are enormously important, and then there's a whole lot of trivia that doesn't mean anything.

"I've made plenty of big investment mistakes. I've never made one, in my view, that would have been avoided by conventional due diligence. And we would have spent a lot of money, and we would have wasted a lot of time and, in some cases, missed deals, simply because we wouldn't have committed fast enough. We have a significant advantage, and it gets bigger as we get bigger, because, in terms of big deals, people rely more and more often on process; when people want to get a deal done … they will come to us.

"The Mars people—in terms of this financing aspect of the Wrigley situation—only wanted to deal with Berkshire because they knew we didn't have any lawyers involved. We didn't even have any directors involved. We got a call, it made sense, and we said yes. And when we say yes, we don't say yes with a material adverse change clause. We don't say yes if financing is available. We just say yes. So when we make a deal I can tell people that, if we're going to have $6.5 billion available, it's going to be available if a nuclear bomb goes off in New York City, if there's a flu epidemic, or if Ben Bernanke runs off to South America with Paris Hilton. The check is going to clear. For the guy who wants $6.5 billion, that assurance is worth something—and you really can't get it anyplace. It's a real advantage to us."

RAILROADS AND BNSF

2007 MEETING (03:50:15)

WB: "The relative competitive position of the rails has improved somewhat from really not a very good competitive position twenty or twenty-five years ago. There's been a lot of progress on the labor front. They benefit in their competitive position vis-a-vis trucking as oil prices go up. Higher diesel fuel, obviously, raises costs for the rails, but it raises costs for their competitors, the truckers, by probably a factor of close to four. And there isn't a whole lot of new capacity being created in the rail industry. So, what was a terrible business twenty to twenty-five years ago operating under regulation—and it still operates under the threat of reregulation, which has a tempering effect on their pricing power—is a better business now. It will never be a sensational business. It's very capital intensive. And when you put tons of capital out every year, it's very hard to earn really extraordinary returns on capital. But if they earn a decent return on capital, it can be a good business over time—a lot better than it was in the past."

2010 MEETING (02:14:04)

WB: "I think the Service Transportation Board (STB) has adopted something like 10.5% or thereabouts on invested capital. And if you had a major enough change in interest rates or something, you could argue that there should be some adjustment in one direction or another.

"Usually, in the case of regulated utilities, they talk about return on equity; some states may be 11%, some may be 12%, usually in that range. With the railroads, they've gone toward return on invested capital, which includes debt as an adjusted figure. I don't think that's a crazy standard. In the electric utility, you get an allowed return in the utility that you're almost certain of earning if you behave yourself; your demand is never going to fall off that much, probably, that you'll go way below your return.

"The railroad's got more downside in it if you run into a terrific industrial recession, so you're not as protected on the downside. But there should be some figure, and I would argue 10.5% or whatever it may be, on invested capital that's been achieved by the four big railroads in recent years. Something around that figure makes sense. You want the railroads investing a whole lot more than depreciation, and it's certainly an inducement to me to invest money in improving the transportation system. On the other hand, if that return were far lower, it would be crazy to put money in, because you can't change that railroad system and do something else with it. So I think the country and the railroad systems have a very common interest in not earning exorbitant profits or anything like that, but getting a decent return on what is sure to be much-needed investment over the next ten, twenty, thirty years. If the STB says 10.5% or some number like that, I don't think that's a crazy number."

CM: "The railroads have been a hugely successful system, in terms of a regulated business. If you stop to think about it, the railroads of America have essentially been totally rebuilt in the last thirty to forty years. They've improved the tracks, changed the size of the tunnels, and improved the bridges. The average train can be more than twice as long and twice as heavy. You can hardly imagine a business that's done a better job in adapting to the needs of the rest of us than the railroad industry. That's by and large been a system of wise regulation accompanied by wise management. That was not always the case. If you go back a long time, neither the management nor the regulation was all that wise. It has worked very well for all of us."

2012 MEETING (03:06:35)

WB: "There's no question that railroads, utilities, and insurance companies are all affected by the political process. Fortunately, in the railroad industry, we've got economics on our side, and economics usually win out. We can move a ton of product 500 miles on one gallon of diesel, and that may be three times or so as efficient as trucking. And that may be why the railroads currently move about 42% of all intercity traffic. I don't think the percentage is going to go down for the railroad industry as a whole, no matter what the politics may be. It's just too compelling to move heavy traffic long distances over steel rail. So, we've got a wonderful product, and there will always be struggles in the political arena between competitors and railroads, and customers and railroads. It's the nature of the game, and there will be some of that in utilities, too. But overall, I like our position in it."

CM: "It's in the nature of things that there are waves of good breaks and bad breaks. BNSF was enormously helped when you could double the container carriage by making the tunnels a little higher and the bridges a little stronger. And they were enormously helped when they found all this oil in North Dakota and there weren't any pipelines. But they will get some bad breaks, too, occasionally. Averaged out, it's a terrific business with terrific management. I don't think our main problems are political at all."

WB: "Right after World War II, I think the U.S. railroad industry had as many as 1,700,000 employees. Today, it's fewer than 200,000. Railroads have become much more efficient, by a huge factor. It's fundamentally a very good way to move heavy stuff a long distance."

2019 MEETING (00:22:03)

WB: "Precision scheduled railroading (PSR), as it's labeled, was invented by a fellow named E. Hunter Harrison. I think he was at the Illinois Central Railroad at the time. There's a book that came out about Hunter, called *Railroader,* and it describes his procedure toward railroading. It's an interesting read if you're interested in railroading. There are six big railroads in North America, and he took that to Canadian National, CN, and he was very successful. Bill Gates is probably the largest holder of CN, and I think he's done very well with that stock.

"Then later Canadian Pacific was the subject of activist pressure. As they proceeded, they got Hunter to join them, and they brought in an associate, Keith Creel, and they instituted a somewhat similar program. Now the same thing has happened at CSX. All of those companies dramatically improved their profit margins, and they had varying degrees of difficulty with customer service in the implementation. Union Pacific is doing a somewhat modified version.

"At BNSF, we are not above copying anything that is successful. And I think a good deal has been learned by watching these four railroads, and if we think we can serve our customers well and get more efficient in the process, we will adopt whatever we observe. But we don't have to do it today or tomorrow. We do have to find something that gets at least equal, and hopefully better, customer satisfaction and that makes our railroad more efficient. And there's been growing evidence from the actions of these other four railroads that we can learn something from what they do."

CM: "I doubt anybody is very interested in un-precision in railroading."

PART SIX:
The Insurance Business

"If you are willing to do dumb things in insurance, the world will find you. You can be in a rowboat in the middle of the Atlantic and just whisper out, 'I'm willing to write this,' and then name a dumb price, and you will have brokers swimming to you with their fins showing."

"You can do enormous damage in the insurance business with a pen. You have to be very careful about who you give your pen to."

"If you have a lot of capital in this business, or if you have attracted a lot of capital, you will do something; you might like to do something smart, but if need be, you'll do something dumb."

"It is a very wonderful thing to generate millions and millions, and then billions and billions, of dollars of float at a cost way below the Treasury rate. There are people who would kill for such opportunities."

"The nature of insurance is that the surprises are on the unpleasant side."

INTRODUCTION

IN EARLY 1967, WARREN BUFFETT MADE A DEAL TO ACQUIRE INSURANCE company National Indemnity for $8.6 million. That first domino led to the creation of a very large and highly profitable insurance operation at Berkshire. As Buffett and Munger discuss in this section, that long-term success has been hard earned. The nature of the insurance business—receive money today in exchange for a piece of paper, a promise to pay against claims in the future—is an attractive arrangement that invites a lot of competition. That delay between receiving funds and paying claims can also lead to very expensive mistakes. For example, Buffett has discussed a notable example from GEICO in the early 1980s: "They took in about $70,000 of premiums for a few policies, and they thought they were just picking cherries at the time ... So far, we've lost $93 million from those policies."

The avoidance of those mistakes isn't just a question of intelligence or the ability to make sound underwriting decisions. As you'll read in the section on incentives in insurance underwriting, National Indemnity's experience in the 1980s and 1990s—where annual written premiums increased from $53m in 1982 to $366m in 1986, before making a long retreat back to $55m in 1999—is a textbook case study on how to deal with the uncomfortable challenges of managing an insurance entity for the long-term (through hard and soft markets). As Munger concludes, there's a notable takeaway here: "The main thing is practically nobody else does it [acts like National Indemnity did from 1982 to 1999]. And yet, to me, it's obvious it's the way to go. There's a lot in Berkshire like that. It's a little different from the way other people do it; it's partly the luxury of having a controlling shareholder of strong opinions. It would be hard for a committee, including a lot of employees, to come up with these decisions." (If interested in more on National Indemnity, I wrote about this topic at TSOH Investment Research—see "The Right Way To Run An Insurance Company", which is reprinted in the appendix.)

SUBJECTS AND MEETINGS FEATURED

THE ROLE OF INSURANCE AND REINSURANCE

1995 MEETING (00:48:05)

WB: "As a general matter, there are only two reasons for buying insurance. One is to protect yourself against a loss that you are unable or unwilling to bear yourself. That is partly objective and partly subjective. For example, a manager who's terribly worried that his board of directors may second-guess him if he has an uninsured loss is probably going to buy a lot more protection than the company really needs ... He may do something very unintelligent from the company's standpoint merely to protect his own position. But the reason for buying insurance is to protect against losses that you're unwilling or unable to bear yourself.

"The second reason, which occasionally comes up, is if you think the insurance company is actually selling you a policy that's too cheap, so that you really expect over a period of time to have a mathematical advantage by buying insurance.

"We try to avoid selling the second kind and to concentrate on selling the first kind. And much of the insurance we sell is to other insurance companies; we are selling them insurance against a loss that they are either unable or unwilling to sustain. A typical case might be a company that had a lot of homeowners' policies in California. If those include earthquake coverage, they may not be able to sustain the kind of loss that is possible, even though they want to keep a distribution system in place that merchandises en masse to homeowners in California. So, we will write a policy. They may take the first $5 million or $50 million of loss depending on their own capabilities, but then they come to us. And we are really uniquely situated to take care of problems that those companies can't bear themselves and that they can't find anybody else to insure.

"But we really don't want to insure someone for a loss that they can afford it themselves; it may be because they're dumb, but it may also be because they have a loss expectancy that's higher than the premium we're charging, which is not what we're trying to do. As compared to thirty years ago, I think risk managers at corporations are probably more intelligent about the way they buy insurance. They're more sophisticated. But there's a fair amount of insurance bought that doesn't make sense. And there's a fair amount of insurance that isn't bought that should be bought. There are certain companies exposing themselves in this country to losses which would wipe them out. They prefer not to buy reinsurance because it's 'expensive.' But what they're really doing is betting on something that won't happen very often to not happen at all. If you take a huge hurricane on Long Island or a major earthquake in California, there are a number of companies that have not positioned themselves to withstand those losses. If you're a sixty-three-year-old CEO and you figure, 'I'm going to retire in a couple of years,' the odds are pretty good that it won't happen on your watch. But it will happen on somebody's watch."

INTELLIGENT UNDERWRITING

2003 MEETING (01:28:10)

WB: "In the insurance business, people hand you a lot of money for writing out a little piece of paper—and what you put on that piece of paper is enormously important. But the money that's coming in seems so easy that it can tempt you into doing very, very foolish things.

"We had a situation here in Omaha in the mid-1980s where Mutual of Omaha—the largest health and accident association in the world at one point—decided to go into the property-casualty reinsurance business. And in a very short time they wrote not that many contracts—yet they resulted in wiping out half of the net worth of everything that had built up over many decades.

"If you are willing to do dumb things in insurance, the world will find you. You can be in a rowboat in the middle of the Atlantic and just whisper out, 'I'm willing to write this,' and then name a dumb price, and you will have brokers swimming to you with their fins showing. It is brutal. You will see a lot of cash upfront and you won't see any losses, and you'll keep doing it because you won't see any losses for a little while. You'll keep taking on more and more, and then the roof will eventually fall in.

"In the early 1980s GEICO took in about $70,000 of premiums for a few policies, and they thought they were just picking cherries at the time, and they reinsured a lot of it; and so far, we have lost $93 million from those policies … When you're playing in a game like that, you can't afford to make a mistake … You will make a few cents on the dollar when you're right, and you will lose incredible sums when you're wrong."

SUPER-CAT PRICING

1994 MEETING (01:11:46)

WB: "I think that the insurance industry has vastly underestimated the full potential of what a super cat [extreme catastrophic event] could do—maybe not now, but up until a few years ago. Hurricane Andrew and the LA quake may have been something of a wake-up call. They were far from a worst-case situation. A really big Category Five hurricane on Long Island would end up leaving a lot of very major insurance companies in significant trouble. We define our losses … There are limits on our policies. That is not true of people who are just writing the basic homeowners' business. Those losses could go off the chart.

"There were certain companies in the LA quake that thought they had a 'probable maximum loss' for California quakes. And the LA quake, which was far from the worst case you can imagine, turned out to far exceed those probable maximum losses. So, I think the industry has had, and may still have, its head in the sand a little bit in terms of what can happen—either in terms of a quake in California or, more probably, a hurricane along the East Coast ... It's a business we like at the right rates because there are very few people who can afford to write it at the level that the underlying company (the reinsured companies) need. We're in a position, if the rates are right, to do significant business."

1998 MEETING (01:25:34)

WB: "The super-cat business, you can price wrong. You can be pricing it at half what it should be priced at. I used an illustration in the report of how you could misprice a policy where you should be getting, say, $1.5 million for a $50 million policy on something that had 1-in-36 chance of happening. I said that if you price it instead at $1 million a year, about 70% of the time you will think you are making money after ten years. The interesting thing is that if you priced it for $1 a year, you would make money 70% of the time. When you are selling insurance against very infrequent events, you can totally misprice them but not know about it for a long time.

"Super-cat bonds open that field wide open. You've always had the problem of dumb competitors, but you have a bigger chance of having dumb competitors when you have ... hedge funds (which have bought some of these) where the manager gets 20% of the profits in a year when there are profits and no hurricane, and doesn't take the loss when there happens to be a hurricane or an earthquake. Instead his limited partners do. It's very likely to be a competitive factor that brings our volume down a lot, but it won't change our prices.

"The thing to remember is that the earthquake does not know the premium you received. The earthquake happens regardless. You don't have somebody out on the San Andreas Fault that says, 'He only charged a 1% premium so we're only going to do this once every hundred years.' It doesn't work that way.

"So, we will probably do a whole lot less new business volume in the next few years in the super-cat business. GEICO is by far the most important part of our insurance business. That will be the big part of our insurance business. But we may be in the insurance business in some other ways, too, as time goes along. It's a business where if you exercise discipline you should find some ways to make money, but it won't always be the same way."

REINSURANCE BUSINESS

1994 MEETING (02:07:16)

WB: "It's no plus for us any time new capacity enters a business we're in, and that certainly goes for the reinsurance business. The reinsurance business, by its nature, will be a business in which some very stupid things are done, en masse, periodically. You can do dumb things and not know it in reinsurance, and then all of a sudden wake up and find out the money is gone. It's what people who were speculating on bonds with low margins recently found out; you don't find out who's been swimming naked until the tide goes out. Essentially that's what happens in reinsurance. You don't find out who's been swimming naked until the wind blows at them."

1994 MEETING (02:24:30)

WB: "The difference in our reinsurance business from many others is essentially the difference that may exist in our operations in securities versus others: We will offer reinsurance at any time in very large quantities at prices that we think make sense. But we won't do business if we don't think it makes sense. Just like we will buy securities, to the extent we have cash available, if they make sense; but we have no interest in being in the stock market just to be in it. We want to own securities that make sense to us.

"I think for most managers, if the only thing they're in is the reinsurance business, they may like it better when prices make sense, but they will be prone to do quite a bit of business when prices don't make sense as well, because there's no alternative, except to give the money back to the owners—and that is not something that most managements do somersaults over. So, I think we are in a favored position, having the flexibility of capital allocation that lets us take the lack of business with a certain equanimity that most managements probably can't, because of their sole focus on the reinsurance business.

"Insurance rates will get silly, in all likelihood, after a period when nothing much happens, when you've had a couple years of good experience. We price to what we think our exposure is, we don't price to experience. The fact that there was no big hurricane last year has nothing to do with the rates next year ... We are pricing to exposure. Everyone says that, but the market tends to price and respond to experience, and generally to recent experience ... We will never knowingly do that. We may get influenced subconsciously in some way to do that, but we will not do that any more than we will accept stock market norms as being the proper way for us to invest money in equities. When you lay out money or accept insurance risks, you really have to think for yourself. You cannot let the market think for you."

CM: "I think Berkshire is basically a very old-fashioned kind of a place, and it tries to exert discipline to stay old-fashioned. And I don't mean old-fashioned stupid, I mean the eternal verities, so to speak: basic mathematics, basic horse sense, basic fear, basic discriminations regarding human nature; all very old-fashioned. If you just do that with a certain amount of discipline, I think it's likely to work out quite well."

1999 MEETING (01:49:50)

WB: "Our reputation is stronger than ever. Berkshire's preeminent position as the reinsurer most certain to pay after any conceivable natural disaster is stronger today than it's ever been, and Gen Re's reputation is right along with it. The commercial advantage inherent in that reputation is very important. I can't tell you exactly how it rates compared to 1994 but I can tell you that it's important. It tends to be more important when we're reinsuring other very large entities, either primary insurers or large reinsurers, than it is with a smaller company. The smaller company probably focuses on that less. But we are probably writing a very large cover for a very important reinsurer this week. I don't think they'd want to buy that from almost anyone else. A couple people maybe, but I don't think they would have a list of ten people from whom they'd buy it. They're too smart for that because it's a very high-level cover, and if that is called upon, there will be a number of people whose checks will not clear. Berkshire's check, undoubtedly, will clear. The reputation has never been better.

"The commercial advantage is significant. How much it translates into can vary from year to year. But I think it's a permanent advantage Berkshire will have. I think five to ten years from now, and particularly after there has been a huge super-cat, it will be a great asset to Berkshire to be thought of as, essentially, Fort Knox. We will pay under any circumstances. There aren't many people in the business that can truly say that. When the very big cover comes along, we should have very few competitors."

2000 MEETING (04:43:43)

WB: "We have been in the reinsurance business at Berkshire Hathaway for thirty years. We've gotten some scars from it at times, but overall we've done extremely well. The reason why is because we've had an absolutely sensational manager in Ajit Jain. He is a good example of what somebody with brains, energy, discipline, the right temperament, and some capital behind him can do in a business.

"It's not the world's most efficient business, and it never will be the most efficient business, because it's not strictly actuarial. All excess returns will not be competed away. There will be people who will earn very subnormal returns in the business, and there will be people who get killed in the business. And that means there will be quite a deviation from the mean in terms of the results of individual insurers. We think that both National Indemnity under Ajit and Gen Re have advantages, so that our returns will be significantly better than average.

"There's always dumb competitors and there's always a lot of capital in the reinsurance business. In 1985 and 1986, people felt very poor; but it wasn't really a lack of financial capital, it was psychological capital that disappeared. People were just plain scared. And that was the best of times to be writing business, obviously. But there are always people who misevaluate risk. And when they do so, it's our job to let them have the business. That's easier to do with National Indemnity than it is with Gen Re because Gen Re has long-term relationships with many accounts. The question of what you do when your competitor offers a price that's a little too low, with somebody you've been doing business with for fifty years, is very tough. Sometimes, they probably do business that might be labeled as 'a necessarily evil.' Charlie always says he doesn't mind an occasional transaction like that, as long as you underline *evil* and not *necessary* … Gen Re has done a terrific job, over the years, of balancing the necessity of continuing a relationship with the discipline of making sure they get paid enough … At Ajit's operation and at Gen Re, we have two businesses that will do very well, in terms of what we get out of them and compared to their competition, but occasionally we'll have a very bad year … That's what we're getting paid for. If we price with discipline, our twenty-year results can't be bad, no matter what any one year produces. And if we don't price with discipline, we'll get killed over time."

CM: "I don't think the reinsurance business is quite as much of a commodity business as it might first appear. It's not like an execution transaction when you sell government bonds or something, where one broker is roughly just as good as another. There's such a huge time lag between when the premium is paid and the time the performance is given that the customer is making a big prediction about the insurer's willingness and ability to pay what it really owes. I think we have a huge edge in reputation and actuality, with reference to both those two factors."

WB: "I can't think of a case where there's been any problem with having Berkshire or Gen Re write a check very promptly for anything it owed. We have never been subject to people suing us and getting money later or anything like that after fighting it out in courts. It's not the nature or the attitude we bring toward the reinsurance transaction. So we have a reputational advantage. But like I said, I don't think it's quite as wide as it should be in some cases, even.

"Then we have a huge attitudinal advantage in that we have no need—none—to write more business, the same amount of business, or even something close to the amount of business that we wrote this year. There are no insurance volume goals at Berkshire Hathaway at all. That is not true at most insurance organizations. We report the results as they come in, which also, I think, gives us an advantage in being realistic about all aspects of our business. We have huge amounts of capital behind us, so we can take large pieces of attractive business and keep them all for our own accounts.

"So we have a lot of advantages in the business and they will translate into something better than the rest of the world gets. I don't know how much better. And I don't know how much the rest of the world will get. But it's not insignificant, the advantages we have in the business."

2009 MEETING (01:05:49)

WB: "It would be impossible to replace Ajit Jain; we wouldn't try. We wouldn't give the next guy the latitude, in terms of size of risk or that sort of thing, that we give to Ajit. We've got a unique talent there, in my view. When you get somebody like that, you give enormous authority to them after you firmly establish in your mind that's who you're dealing with. But that doesn't mean the authority goes with the position. The authority goes with the individual. Giving your pen away in insurance, as they say, is extraordinary dangerous.

"In this town we have Mutual of Omaha, which had been built up carefully over seventy-five years by the 1980s and become the largest health and accident association in the world, I believe. And they got the idea that they should write property-casualty reinsurance. They gave a pen to somebody within the place, and in just a few contracts they lost half their net worth in a very short period of time; they were worried they might have lost more than that. You can do enormous damage in the insurance business with a pen. You have to be very careful about who you give your pen to. And we've given our pen to Ajit in a way that we wouldn't give it to anyone else … We won't find a substitute for him."

CM: "Stated differently, sometimes you say if it won't stand a little mismanagement, it's not much of a business. Of course, you prefer a business that will prosper pretty well even if it's not managed very well. But that doesn't mean you don't like it even better when you get such a business that's managed magnificently. Both factors are quite important. We're not looking for mismanagement. We like the capacity to stand it if we stumble into it, but we're not looking for it."

WB: "We will not assign tasks to people that we think are beyond their capabilities. It just so happens that Ajit has enormous capabilities. So he gets assigned some very unusual things. But you don't see that prevailing throughout our insurance operation. And our managers don't expect to operate that way. That's a one-off situation with Ajit and he's in good health."

2011 MEETING (04:45:03)

CM: "Insurance, and particularly reinsurance, is not that easy. It's taken us a long time to do it as well as we do. If it weren't for Ajit, we'd be a lot smaller in the insurance business."

WB: "We really didn't succeed at all in the reinsurance business in the first fifteen years. We started in reinsurance around 1970, and we had a fellow that I thought the world of running it, George Young—but, net, counting the value of float, it was not a good business for us for fifteen years until Ajit came along. It is not an easy business, but it looks easy most of the time."

CM: "That's the trouble with it. It looks easier than it is."

WB: "It looks way easier than it is. It's like having a pair of dice, and accepting bets on boxcars [rolling a pair of sixes]. It's going to come up once in thirty-six times, so you can win a lot of bets by giving the wrong odds, but if you do it long enough, you will lose a lot of money. These infrequent events, you better have factored them into your pricing, and not fool yourself by whether you make money in a given year, or two years, or even four years. Most people have a little trouble with that, and we had a little trouble with it for about fifteen years."

2016 MEETING (00:28:15)

WB: "I said in the annual report that I thought it was very likely that the reinsurance business would not be as good in the next ten years as it has been in the last ten years; that's a judgment based on seeing the competitive dynamics now versus ten to twenty years ago. We sold our entire holdings, which were substantial, of Munich Re and Swiss Re. We owned about 3% of Swiss Re and more than 10% of Munich Re. They're fine, well-managed companies, and I like the people that run them. But I think the business of the reinsurance companies generally is less attractive for the next ten years than it has been for the last ten years. In part, that's because what's happened to interest rates.

"A significant portion of what you earn in insurance comes from investment of the float. Both of those companies, and for that matter almost all of the reinsurance industry, is somewhat more restricted in what they can do with their float, because they don't have this huge capital cushion that Berkshire has, and also because they don't have this great amount of unrelated earnings power. We have more leeway in what we can do simply because we do have capital that's many times what our competitors have, and we also have earnings power coming from a whole variety of areas unrelated to insurance. It was not a negative judgment on their managements—but it was at least a mildly negative judgment on the reinsurance business.

"At Berkshire, we are certainly affected by industry factors—but we have the ability to rearrange, to a degree. We have more flexibility in modifying business models, in insurance generally, and particularly in reinsurance. All the major reinsurance companies, except for us, are pretty well tied to a given type of business model. They don't really have as many options, in terms of where capital gets deployed. They have to continue down the present path … I don't think if we played the same game as we were playing the last ten, we would do as well—but we have considerably more flexibility in terms of how we conduct all of our insurance operations, particularly in reinsurance. We have an extra string to our bow that the rest of the industry doesn't have."

CM: "There's a lot of new capacity in reinsurance and there's a lot of very heavy competition. A lot of people from finance have come into reinsurance, and all the old competitors remained, too. That's different from Precision Castparts, where most of the customers would be totally crazy to hire some other supplier, because Precision Castparts is so much more reliable and so much better. Of course, we like the place with more competitive advantage. We're learning."

WB: "In reinsurance, supply has gone up and demand has not gone up. Some of the supply is driven by investment managers who would like to establish something offshore where they don't have to pay taxes, and reinsurance is sort of the easiest beard behind which to actually engage in money management in a friendly tax jurisdiction. And you can set up a reinsurance operation with very few people, by taking large chunks of what brokers may offer. It's not the greatest reinsurance in the world, and a couple of the operations that have done that have proven that statement to be right. But nevertheless, it is a very, very easy way to have a disguised investment operation in a friendly tax jurisdiction. But that becomes supply in the reinsurance field, and supply has gone up relative to demand, and it looks to me like that will continue to be the case. Couple that with the poor returns on float, and it's not as good a business as it was."

RETROACTIVE INSURANCE

2002 MEETING (00:48:05)

WB: "Insurance is our main business. It's always going to be our main business. It's a very, very big business, and it's going to get bigger … Our goal is to obtain more and more float at minimal or no cost. And there have been a number of years in the past when we've run an underwriting profit, which means that the use of that money is essentially free, or even better than free.

"We have written a good bit of retroactive insurance. In retroactive insurance, a company may come to us that's merging with another company, and they want to put a cap on their liabilities from past incidents, or define them better. So they may come to us and say, we want you to pick up all the losses that are going to be paid from things that happened prior to, say, 1990, and we think we owe $1 billion that has yet to be paid in losses from that period, but we want to protect ourselves up to $2 billion. This is called retroactive reinsurance; they write us a check and we take over their losses from the past for a specific period and for a specific amount. When we do that, the accounting creates a charge which will occur over time in the future ... So, if a company comes in and says, we want you to protect us up to $1.5 billion for losses that occurred in the past, and we'll give you $1 billion for it, we will credit cash for $1 billion and we'll debit this deferred charge for $1.5 billion, we'll set up a liability for $1.5 billion. That $500 million we set up as a deferred charge; we amortize it over a period of time as we expect to pay the claims. There's a lot of room for judgment in terms of how fast we amortize that; we try to be conservative. We make an estimate of when we will pay claims and how much we will pay ... I should emphasize that in all of these contracts we cap our liability."

COMPETITION IN INSURANCE

1995 MEETING (00:53:51)

WB: "There is an ease of entry into the catastrophe business. It's particularly attractive for promoters, because if you start an insurance company to write earthquake insurance in California and you raise a few hundred million dollars, you'll either have essentially no losses or you'll go broke ... If your intention is to sell your stock publicly in a year or two, the odds are very good that you will have a beautiful record for a couple of years and you can sell. Maybe one time out of ten, you'll go broke, and nine times out of ten you'll sell to somebody else who will eventually go broke. There's a real ease of entry. The only thing that may restrict that is if the buyer is sophisticated enough to question the viability of that company under really extreme conditions, which is the only conditions that count when you're buying catastrophe insurance.

"None of the people who have started up can offer anywhere near the amount of coverage Berkshire has. Berkshire is really one of a kind in terms of its capital strength in the business. I don't think anybody in Bermuda, that I can remember, has $1 billion of net worth. At present, we have $13 billion of net worth and considerably more of value. So we can sustain shocks, and we will sustain shocks that others can't. And we try to get paid appropriately for that. We can take a $1 billion loss, and we will have a $1 billion loss at some point; anyone buying it knows we can take it, or something greater. And they should know that very few of our competitors can.

"We do an unusual proportion of our business with the ten largest reinsurance and insurance companies in the world. With the people who understand the real risks of the business, they come to Berkshire a lot more often than they stop in Bermuda, because they know we'll pay, and they've been around long enough to know that, in the end, that's what really counts. If there were enough capacity at really ridiculous rates, we wouldn't be writing business at that time. I don't think that will happen. And if it happens, so be it; we'll all play golf until the loss occurs."

1996 MEETING (02:58:03)

WB: "There has been capital coming into the reinsurance business, and that is negative for our business because any capital that's brought in, basically, will get employed. At Berkshire, we're willing—and we do it—to sit on the sidelines in the reinsurance business. We'll offer quotes, but somebody will cut those prices substantially if they've got a lot of capital and want to keep busy. If you have a lot of capital in this business, or if you have attracted a lot of capital, you will do something; you might like to do something smart, but if need be, you'll do something dumb. You'll rationalize it so you think it's smart. You won't just sit there and write the shareholders at the end of the year and say, 'We asked you for $300 million last year. We'd like to report that it's all safely in a bank account.' It just doesn't work that way. So, they will go out and do something. People don't like to sit around all day and do nothing. And that means prices will get cut under certain circumstances, and that's happening now.

"At Berkshire, we have a rule about downsizing. We have promised people at all of our insurance operations that we will never have layoffs because of a drop in volume. We do not want the people who run our insurance business to feel they have to write X dollars in order to keep everybody there. We can afford some overhead costing us a little money for lack of using it at full capacity, because it isn't that much relative to the size of our insurance operation. What we can't afford are people feeling some internal compulsion to keep writing business in order to keep their job. So, we have a strong policy on that. And if the business falls away, in terms of price, we won't do it—but we will be around to do business in a big way when the circumstances reverse.

"They reversed in the casualty business for a while in 1985 or thereabouts, and we did a terrific amount of business [at National Indemnity]. They reversed in catastrophe reinsurance four or five years ago, and we became very active in that.

"We will have times that are very good for us in insurance. It's a lot like investments. If you feel you have to invest every day, you're going to make a lot of mistakes. It isn't that kind of a business; you have to wait until you get the fat pitch. And in insurance, it's similar. If we had a budget for premium volume for our insurance companies, it would be the dumbest thing we could do; they could meet any budget I set out. I could tell some operation that wrote $100 million last year to write $500 million this year, they would meet it—and I would be paying the bills for decades to come. It's a very illogical way to try and run the business.

"Now, GEICO is a different story; it's a low-cost operator and can attract business from a huge pool at a very good rate of growth simply by letting people know what's available out there. So, that is a business I see growing under almost any circumstances. But our reinsurance business will swing around enormously, in terms of volume, based on what competitors do. And what competitors will do depends, to a great extent, on how much money they've got burning a hole in their pocket. Right now, it's going one direction. But it will change, just like markets change. I've been through at least a half a dozen periods where people thought they're never going to get a chance to buy securities at intelligent prices, and it always changes. In the insurance business, people that misprice policies will pay the price for it. The world will still need insurance, and we'll be there."

2010 MEETING (02:17:48)

CM: "I would say that the main difference between our practice and that of most other people in the insurance business is that we are deliberately seeking a method of operation which will give us occasional big losses in a single year—big overall losses. And everybody else is trying to avoid that. We just want to be rich enough so a big loss in a single year is a blip. And that's a big competitive advantage, that willingness to endure fluctuating annual results."

WB: "It's a huge advantage. And it's one that no one else is going to pick up on. They know what we do; they just don't want to do it, or they're unable to do it in terms of financial resources. So, I would say that comes very close to a permanent and substantial advantage at Berkshire. Just the financial consequences of a Hurricane Katrina, when we lost $3 billion, I didn't feel any different the next day financially. It just doesn't make any difference, because we are in that particular game. As long as we make the right decisions over time, in terms of the premiums we get, and as long as we never expose ourselves to a loss that would really shake up our capital structure, that is a game in which we have a huge competitive edge. And it gets wider every year. In insurance, we are in the business of taking the other guys' desire to smooth their earnings, and, in exchange, get what we think are larger, lumpy earnings over time."

CM: "I was going to say Warren has a different position than a lot of other people in the insurance business. After a year in which Berkshire has a big loss, he can look into his mirror and say, 'Your shareholder still loves you.' Other people are not in that position."

INSURANCE FLOAT

1996 MEETING (01:54:47)

WB: "The insurance business provides us with float, which is money we hold that doesn't belong to us. It's like a bank having deposits. The money doesn't belong to the bank, but it holds the money. Now, when a bank holds deposits, on everything except demand deposits, there's an explicit cost, an interest rate attached to it. And then there are the costs of running the system and gathering the money which also must be attributed both to demand and time deposit. So there's a cost to getting what they would call deposits and what we could call float.

"In the insurance business, a similar phenomenon takes place in that policyholders give us their money at the start of the policy period—therefore, we get the money paid in advance for the product. And secondly, it takes time to settle losses, particularly in the liability area. If you bang up the fender on your car, it's going to get settled very quickly. But if there's a complicated injury or something, it may take some years to settle. And during that period, we hold the money. So, we have, in effect, something that is tantamount to the deposits of a bank. But with the deposits of a bank, it's quite easy to calculate the approximate cost. In the case of the float that an insurance company has, you don't really know the cost of that float until all your policies have expired and your losses have all been settled. You're only making an estimate, as you go along, of what that float is costing.

"To date with Berkshire, in the twenty-nine years we've been in the business, our float has not cost us anything on average. There's been years when we've had an underwriting loss when there's a cost. There's been years when we had an underwriting profit. So we have obtained that float on very advantageous terms over the years. The other important thing is that we've grown it dramatically. And so, we've gotten more and more money without having any cost attached to it. If we still had our $17 million of float that we had in 1967 and it was no cost, it would be very nice—$17 million of free money is worth something, but it's not worth a ton. Having $7 billion, if we can achieve that as free money, it's worth a lot. And that growth has not, probably, been appreciated fully in connection with Berkshire, nor has the interplay of having zero-cost money, in terms of affecting our gain in value over time. Charlie and I pay a lot of attention to that, and it's not entirely an accident that the business has developed in this manner. And we have intentions of trying to make it continue to develop in that manner in the future.

"Float, per se, is not a blessing. We can show you many insurance companies that thought it was wonderful to generate float, but they have lost so much money in underwriting that they'd be better off if they'd never heard of the insurance business. The job is to get it in increasing quantities, but above all, to get it cheap. You do it by having some kind of competitive advantages. You won't do it just by having an ordinary insurance company. The ordinary insurance company is not a good business. We have it in certain respects because of our attitude toward the business. We have it because our financial strength gives us certain competitive advantages. And we have it, in the case of GEICO, because of a very low-cost operation. And it's up to us to try and figure out ways to maximize each one of those competitive advantages over time. We've built those advantages; in 1967, we were not looked at that way in the insurance business. We've built a position of competitive strengths. At GEICO, they had it without us, but we have bought into it over time. It's a very important asset. And you ought to pay a lot of attention over the years as to what is happening with that asset as to both growth and costs. That will aid you in calculating Berkshire's intrinsic value."

1996 MEETING (04:45:39)

WB: "We're not interested in the typical insurance business because we think the float will end up costing us too much. We'd rather borrow money with an explicit cost attached to it rather than have the implicit costs of an underwriting loss."

2000 MEETING (03:37:00)

WB: "We consciously add float sometimes at a given cost ... We have different layers of float, if you will, that we've entered into. We've entered into some transactions recently where we will take on some float which will not have zero cost, but it's acceptable to us. We would be willing to take on float at costs only modestly below the Treasury rate, if that was the only way we could get that float and if it didn't impede our ability to get other float at zero cost ... It's the cost of float and it's the amount of growth of float. If you told me I could add $50 billion of float and have a 3% cost to that, I would take that any day over adding $10 billion at zero cost."

CM: "I've been amazed how well we've done with the float. It is a very wonderful thing to generate millions and millions, and then billions and billions, of dollars of float at a cost way below the Treasury rate. There are people who would kill for such opportunities."

WB: "There are plenty of other people who think about it in a similar vein. Like everything else in capitalism, it's competitive. We think we've got an edge in several very important respects, and we think that edge is sustainable. We intend to push it as hard as we can. We'll see where it leads. I would've had no idea, ten or twenty years ago, that we would have the present situation.

"Every now and then, you see something that makes sense to do. And we do find them occasionally. The hard part is finding them where they are material relative to our present size. If we were running a very small business, we would find plenty of things that would make good sense. We find a few things that make good sense now, relative to our size. And there's really no answer for that except to shrink dramatically, which is not an action we're contemplating."

2010 MEETING (01:31:43)

WB: "Ajit Jain's operation has competitive advantages that go beyond him, but they were developed by Ajit, he has maximized them, and he knows how to use them in a way that's far better, in my view, than anyone else in the world could. But they won't all go away. He has a cadre of about thirty people who are schooled in it, in a way that would make the Jesuits look quite liberal, in terms of what they let their membership do. You can't imagine a more disciplined operation than what Ajit has.

"But Ajit cannot be replaced. I'll state that absolutely, categorically: It would be a huge loss to Berkshire if anything happened to Ajit. But it would not mean that Berkshire's reinsurance operation would not continue to be an extremely special place that would do large deals that nobody else would do, that could think and act quickly in ways that virtually no other insurance organization can. We've got something very special in that unit, and then we've got the most special of leaders in Ajit.

"As to our float, every year I think it has peaked. I never see how we can add to it. It's $60 billion now, and we have things like the Equitas deal that are runoffs. Every day, some of the float runs off, it's just that we add more. I was ready to quit at $20 billion, thinking we had reached the apex. Berkshire has become, in my view, the premier insurance organization of the world, and a lot of good things come from that. I don't see, with $60 billion of float, how we can increase it significantly unless we make some very significant acquisition. We will not organically grow the float of Berkshire at a fast clip from here. It can't be done. And we may fight to stay even. But we may come up with something out of the blue. I mean, who would have known that Equitas was going to come along three years ago? There are various things that could happen of a positive nature. But when I tell you about the value that Ajit Jain has added to Berkshire, if anything, I've understated it."

2012 MEETING (02:45:20)

WB: "Berkshire's float could shrink because we have lots of retroactive contracts, that by their nature run off, although not at a really rapid rate. The float at GEICO is going to grow. The float at our smaller insurance companies will probably, net, grow over time a little bit, but it's not a lot of money. In Ajit's operation, where we have a lot of the retroactive stuff, it's very, very tough.

You've always got a melting ice cube that you've got to add a little more water to. I felt when the float was $40 billion it probably wasn't going to grow very much, and now we're at $70 billion. So, we are looking for ways to intelligently grow the float all the time. That's been true ever since I got in the insurance business in 1967. The desire is always there.

"We've been reasonably imaginative in figuring out ways to do it and still have the float cost us less than nothing. We've got the smartest guys in the business working on it. But the numbers are huge now, and you do have a natural runoff from the retroactive contracts. So I just thought that it was fair to tell the shareholders that, while they look at that history of float growth, they really can't extrapolate that. If we get lucky, we could add a fair amount more, but it's possible that it will actually dwindle down a little bit—not at a fast rate—and it certainly is more than possible that it won't grow very much from here on.

"Ajit told me that when I put that in the annual report it became a challenge to him, so I'm glad I stuck it in there. He wants to make me look like an idiot, which isn't too hard sometimes, and I may have to stick some things in the annual report next year to get the attention of the other managers. If I had to bet on whether float will be higher or lower five years from now, I probably would bet just slightly higher, but I also wanted the shareholders to know there's a possibility it will decline a bit. But every day we're working on things to try to figure out how to increase it."

CM: "The casualty insurance business, by its nature, is not a terribly good business. You have to be in the top 10%, really, to do at all well in it. We're very lucky: We probably have the best large-scale casualty insurance business in the world. If you have something that is very good and it doesn't grow wildly, that's not the end of the world."

2023 MEETING (00:00:04)

WB: "... Our float is now $165 billion. Ajit Jain is responsible for moving that number up from a pittance in 1986 to this incredible figure, which in practically all years, hasn't cost us anything. It's like having a bank with no employees, no interest, and no ability to withdraw the money that we have working for us in a hurry. And it's a very valuable asset that shows up as a liability.

"That float, just think of a balance sheet; you've got liabilities here and you've got assets over there. The liability side finances the asset side. It's very simple. Stockholders' equity finances it, long-term debt finances it, and so on. But stockholders' equity is very expensive in a real sense. Long-term debt has been cheap for a while, but it can get expensive; it also becomes due eventually and it may not be available. But float is another item which shows as a liability but hasn't cost us anything, and it can't disappear in a hurry. It finances the asset side in the same way as stockholders' equity. And nobody else thinks of it much that way. But we have always thought of it that way, and it's built up over time."

INVESTING INSURANCE FLOAT

1995 MEETING (01:47:38)

WB: "We have a lot of flexibility when investing insurance float. We are not disadvantaged by that money being in float, as opposed to equity, in any significant way. If we had a very limited amount of equity and a very large amount of float, we would impose a lot of restrictions on ourselves as to how we did it, because we'd want to be very sure we were in a position to distribute that float, in effect, to policyholders, claimants, whatever it may be at the time that was appropriate. But we have so much net worth that, in effect, that float is just about as useful to us as equity money, and that means it is quite useful. It's a big asset for Berkshire."

2000 MEETING (04:02:53)

WB: "The float is in no way limited to fixed-income securities. It is really available for anything we feel is the most intelligent use at any given time. The reason we can say that and other insurance companies can't say is because we have an incredible abundance of capital, plus other streams of earning power which are unrelated to the insurance business. We could have the float entirely in equities—and we have had that in the past, or tantamount to that. We can have it any place where it makes the most sense. But the only reason we can do that is because we have extraordinary capital and we don't have much debt.

"We think about the business differently than probably 90% of managements do. We look at the assets on a consolidated basis with a few little exceptions. We look at the asset and the liability side completely absent any linkage to specific assets and liabilities. Our job at Berkshire is to get the liabilities as cheaply as possible. We want all the liabilities we can get as cheap as we can. And then we want all the assets to be employed as intelligently as possible. We don't match up $1 billion of assets against $1 billion of specific liabilities on the right-hand side. When Charlie and I think about Berkshire, we're thinking about, 'How do we get as much money as we can as cheap as we can without in any way endangering our ability, ever, to pay anybody, under any circumstances? And then, how do we put it out in a way that we feel the most comfortable on the asset side, at the best returns?' Frequently, that will be equities. Sometimes it won't be. But that's the goal. And float is available in virtually all cases just like common equity; we don't distinguish those in our mind. That flexibility gives us some edge and, perhaps, quite an edge, at times, over our competitors."

CM: "You can see that in the results to date. We have used that edge in the past, and we hope to use it in the future."

2003 MEETING (00:44:37)

WB: "Our float is $42.5 billion; I think the entire float of the American property-casualty industry is in the area of $500 billion, so we have 8–9%, somewhere in that range ... We love the idea of growing, but what we really want is cost-free float. That is the goal. I hold our managers responsible not for delivering more float; I hold them responsible for delivering profitable float. That is key in our mind at all times. If the $42.5 billion can be obtained at no cost, or even better yet at a profit, its utility to us is like equity.

"Now, you wouldn't realize it upon liquidation and you couldn't necessarily realize it on sale, so I'm not telling you how to count it in terms of intrinsic value. You have to make that decision. But it has the utility to us of $42.5 billion of funds derived from equity without issuing common shares. And that's one of the reasons we've always been so enthused about it; it's a great business for us ... We have some exceptional companies and some exceptional managers, and I truly believe that we will obtain our float at considerably less cost than the industry ... If we get insurance float at zero or less cost, it has the utility of equity in a very big way."

LLOYD'S OF LONDON

1995 MEETING (02:53:45)

WB: "Lloyd's is not an insurance company. Originally it was a coffee house, a place where a large number of syndicates operated and congregated in a given physical location. And it's had a history for larger, more exotic risks. Lloyd's has lost its relative position to a fairly significant degree in the last ten or so years, in significant part because of bad results, which had the other effects of causing capital to withdraw and people who backed the syndicates to become unhappy.

"Lloyd's is still an important competitive factor in the reinsurance business, and in certain specialized kinds of primary insurance it's a very important factor—but it's not the factor it was ten or fifteen years ago. I'm not sure how Berkshire's capital compares with the capital of all those syndicates at Lloyd's, but it's certainly changed in its relative importance in the last ten years. And the ability of Lloyd's to attract capital with the problems they had has diminished, although they're working on that. We regard Lloyd's as a competitor just like any number of reinsurance companies. But we also do business with a number of syndicates at Lloyd's, and we'll probably do a lot of business over the next ten years with various syndicates."

CM: "Lloyd's is a very interesting institution because it had this reputation for integrity, what they paid off in the San Francisco fire and so on. But I would argue that, ten or fifteen years ago, a lot of slop and folly got into Lloyd's, in certain syndicates particularly. And too many commissions coming off the top as the same risks circulated around the system. Too much fine tailoring and three-hour lunches with fine wines. It wasn't right, and they got in a lot of trouble."

WB: "In the history of Berkshire, the most significant insurance problem we ever had was in connection with certain syndicates of Lloyd's almost twenty years ago. And as Charlie said, they had this terrific behavioral reputation over centuries, and I think they coasted on that for a while. We had a behavioral problem in one situation, and it was very expensive to us. So, we may have gotten an early lesson in what was coming.

"There are a lot of different syndicates at Lloyd's, and there are different people running them, and they have had different standards of behavior to some extent. And people who assumed that, because they were dealing with Lloyd's, that they would have no problems of any kind, have found out otherwise. But they will continue to be a major force in insurance, and they will get by their present troubles, and they'll probably come out of it better structured than they went in."

1996 MEETING (04:00:49)

WB: "It's fair to say that the problems at Lloyd's have helped us because Lloyd's had a terrific reputation. Twenty years ago, it was the first and, usually, last stop for all kinds of unusual and large risks. And the fact that they have lost some of their luster in that period has helped us. It obviously benefits us as a competitor when questions develop about an organization which has been a premier player in the industry.

"Berkshire probably possesses more capital than all of Lloyd's put together, and it has established a reputation for being willing to quote on very large risks, very quickly, and to do exactly what it says. And it might very well be that, in many cases, we would get a call before they would now. So we've been a beneficiary … from their problems. And it's more difficult for them to make inroads on us now than it would've been ten years ago. I don't like to lay it on too strong, but we have a preeminent position in a certain area of really large-scale reinsurance that will be difficult for anyone else to replicate. Now, they may not like our prices. There may not be demand for some of the things we can do. But if there is demand, we are very likely to get some very significant business out of that position. We've seen it some in recent years, and we'll see it more in the future."

VALUING BERKSHIRE'S INSURANCE BUSINESSES

1996 MEETING (03:16:14)

WB: "I will tell you this. We have $7 billion of float. That's money we're holding that belongs to someone else but that we have use of. If I were asked, would I trade that for $7 billion and not have to pay any tax on the gain, but I would have to stay out of the insurance business forever, would I accept that? The answer is no. That is not because I would rather have $7 billion of float than $7 billion of net proceeds; it's because I expect the $7 billion to grow. If I had been offered that trade twenty-years ago—'Will you take $17 million for the float you have, no tax to be paid, but you have to get out of the insurance business,'—I might've said yes in those days."

CM: "Oh, you would've?"

WB: "Yeah."

CM: "He keeps learning. That's one of his tricks."

WB: "It would've been a terrible mistake. It would've been a mistake to do it ten years ago with $300 million. It is not worth $7 billion to us to forego being in the insurance business forever at Berkshire Hathaway. Even though it would all be pure addition to equity, we would not take it. We wouldn't even think about it very long. That is not the answer I would've given some time back. It's a very valuable business. It has to be run right … it's not automatic. But they have the people, distribution structure, reputation, capital strength, and competitive advantages. They have those in place. And if nurtured, they can become more valuable as time goes by."

ADVANTAGES OF BERKSHIRE'S INSURANCE BUSINESSES

1996 MEETING (04:20:20)

WB: "We know that we had to be the biggest in terms of premium volume last year. We simply take on so much more than anyone else will; we were getting the calls on the big risks. We had a quote we put out on $1 billion on the New Madrid fault a little while ago. Nobody else will be doing that. We got market share by our willingness to do large volume, by the fact that people knew we would pay subsequently.

"We also know our market share is slipping now, but that makes no difference to us; we'd only be interested if we were slipping in profitable markets … We are willing to think about a whole variety of things to do in insurance. We'll do other things in insurance over the next ten or fifteen years, it's just bound to happen, but I can't tell you what they will specifically be. We have expanded some in the structured settlement business, we are the preferred provider of structured settlements. Those are annuities, essentially, that are payable to people who are usually the victims of a very bad accident. They're very severely injured with injuries that will probably last for life. So we will be making payments to people who are incapable of earning a living, and who may incur substantial medical bills for many decades. Those annuities are provided, usually, with the approval of the injured person's attorney. And when the advisors to the injured person think, 'Who is going to be around in fifty years to pay money to this person who's been incapacitated?' they frequently, and in our view logically, think of Berkshire.

"It's not a big business and it won't be a big business, but it's a perfectly decent business. And it's one where we have a competitive advantage over time. We don't obtain that competitive advantage by price. We obtain the competitive advantage from the peace of mind that the injured party obtains from knowing that that check will be in the mail fifty years from now. That's the kind of business where we have some edge. And we'll find other things to do over time. We're aware, generally, of what's going on in the insurance business. We're very ready to move when the time comes so we can do something intelligent."

2017 MEETING (02:09:59)

WB: "Nobody could possibly replace Ajit Jain ... But we have a terrific operation in insurance. We really do terrific outside of Ajit, and it's terrific-squared with Ajit. There are things only he can do. But there are a lot of things that are institutionalized, a lot of things in our insurance business where we have extraordinarily able management too. For example, Ajit bought a company called Guard Insurance a few years ago, a firm in workers' comp primarily. It's based, improbably, in Wilkes-Barre, Pennsylvania, and it's expanding like crazy. It's been a gem. Ajit oversees it, but we've got a terrific person running it. We bought Medical Protective some years ago. Ajit oversees it, but Tim Kenesey can run a terrific insurance company, with or without Ajit. But he's smart enough to realize that, if you've got somebody like Ajit who's willing to oversee it to a degree, that's great. But Tim is a great insurance manager all by himself, and Medical Protective has been a wonderful business for us. Most people don't know we own it.

"Ajit has made more money for Berkshire than I have, probably. But we've still got what I would consider the world's best property-casualty insurance operation even without him. With him, I don't think anybody comes close."

CM: "A few years ago, California made a little change in its workers' compensation law, and Ajit saw instantly that it would cause the underwriting results to change drastically. He went from a tiny percentage of the market to 10% of the market, which is big, and he just grasped at least a couple billion dollars out of the air, like he was snapping his fingers. And when it got tough, he pulled back. We don't have a lot of people like Ajit; it's hard to just snap your fingers and grab a couple billion dollars out of the air."

WB: "We have a lot of terrific insurance managers. I don't know of a better collection any place. Ajit has found some of those. I've gotten lucky a few times. Tom Nerney at U.S. Liability, that goes back, what, sixteen years. He has a terrific operation. It's not huge, but it is so well managed. Now we've added Peter Eastwood with Berkshire Hathaway Specialty. When you can produce underwriting profits, and on top of that just hand more float—those are great businesses. We have $104 billion that we get to earn on, while at the same time on balance we're likely to make some additional money for holding it [from insurance underwriting]. If you can get somebody to hand you $104 billion and pay you to hold it while you invest and get the proceeds, it's a good business.

"Most people don't do well at it. The problem is that what I just described tempts lots of people to get into it. Recently, people have gotten into it just for the investment management. It's a way to earn money offshore. So there's a lot of competition in it. But we have some fundamental advantages in certain areas, and we also have absolutely terrific managers to maximize those advantages. We're going to make the most of it."

2019 MEETING (01:34:33)

WB: "Our insurance business gives us float that's other people's money, which we temporarily hold, but which gets regenerated all the time, so as a practical matter, it has a very, very long life, and it's probably a little more likely to grow than shrink. We have $124 billion now. It's like having a bank that just consists of one guy; he comes in, deposits $124 billion, and promises not to withdraw it forever.

"And we've got a very good insurance business. It's taken a very long time to develop it, a very long time. In fact, I think we probably have the best property-casualty operation, all things considered, in the world, of any size. So, it's worth a lot of money. We think it's worth more to us, and we particularly think it's worth more inside Berkshire. We'd have a very, very high value on that. I don't know the exact number; any number I would have given you in the past would've turned out to be wrong, on the low side.

"We have managed to earn money on float—given to us for nothing—and to also have earnings from underwriting, alongside these large earnings from investing. It's an integral part of Berkshire. There's a certain irony to insurance that most people don't think about. If you really are prepared as a diversified property-casualty insurance business to pay your claims under any circumstances that come along in the next hundred years, you have to have so much capital in the business that it's not a very good business. And if you really think about a worst-case situation, the reinsurance—the insurance you buy from other people to protect you against the extreme losses, among other things—could likely be not good at all. So, even though you'd think you're laying off part of the risk, if you really take the worst-case examples, you may well not be laying off the risk. And if you keep the capital required to protect against that worst-case example, you'll have so much capital in the business that it isn't worthwhile.

"Berkshire is really the ideal form for writing insurance. We have this massive amount of assets that, in many cases, are largely uncorrelated with natural disasters. And we don't need to buy reinsurance from anybody else. And we can use the money in a more efficient way than most insurance companies. It's interesting: In the last thirty years, the three largest reinsurance companies—I'm counting Lloyd's as one company, although it's a group of underwriters assembled at a given location—all three came close to extinction. And, during that period, we didn't really have any truly extraordinary natural catastrophes. The worst was Katrina in 2005. But we didn't have any worst-case situation. And of those companies, which everybody looks at as totally good on the asset side, two of the three actually made some deals with us to help them in some way. They're all in fine shape now—but it's really not a good business, as a standalone insurer, if you keep enough capital to really be sure you can pay anything that comes along, under any kind of conditions. But Berkshire can do that. And it can use the money in ways that it likes to use it. So it's a very valuable asset. We certainly wouldn't want to sell it for its float value, which is shown on the balance sheet as a liability. It's extraordinary. I don't think anyone could build anything like it. It just takes so long, and we continue to plow new ground."

CM: "Warren, is there anybody in the world who has a big casualty insurance business that you'd trade our business for theirs?"

WB: "Oh no, it has taken a long time, and it's taken some tremendous people. At GEICO, Tony Nicely has created with his associates—he's got 39,000 of them, and probably more now, because he's growing this year—more than $50 billion of value for Berkshire Hathaway."

CM: "It's such an easy business—taking in money now in cash, just keeping the books, and giving a little of it back—that a lot of stupidity gets into it. And if you're not way better than average at it, you're going to lose money in the end; it's a mediocre business for most people. It's only good at Berkshire because we're a lot better at it. And if we ever stop being a lot better, it wouldn't be safe for us, either."

WB: "Somebody would have to give me more than $50 billion to undo everything Ajit Jain has produced for Berkshire. He walked into my office on a Saturday in the mid-1980s and he had never been in the insurance business before. I don't think there's anybody in the insurance world that doesn't wish he'd walked into their office instead of Berkshire's that Saturday.

"We had two tiny insurance operations many, many years ago, and they both went broke; the underwriting was bad, but we paid all the claims. We did not walk away. We paid every dime of claims. Nobody worries about doing any kind of financial transaction with Berkshire. On a Saturday, at about 9 a.m., I got a phone call, and we made a deal the next day committing to pay out $10 billion, come hell or high water, no outs for material adverse change or anything like that. The people know we'll be there with the $10 billion. They know when we write a policy that may be payable during the worst catastrophe in history, or may be payable fifty years from now, Berkshire will pay—and that's why we have $124 billion of float."

2023 MEETING (00:49:33)

WB: "Ajit was the key to this, he put the AIG deal together. We got handed $10 billion, but we weren't restricted to putting that into bonds. It goes into a general pool of assets ... it is not set aside in some little compartment as people like to think. No other insurance company could do that. They can't think that way because they don't have our balance sheet. They aren't even used to thinking that way. We account for about 26% of the net worth of all property and casualty companies in the United States ... The amount we have had to pay on the AIG deal has run slightly below the amount we anticipated, in terms of our share of the losses. But it served AIG's purposes. They came to us and we were in a unique position. There was nobody else that was able to write that, just like when we took on Lloyd's. Lloyd's said there was no choice other than Berkshire Hathaway when they essentially resuscitated their market by laying off a lot of liabilities on Berkshire Hathaway. We won't see those deals very often. If they're for $500 million, somebody else will go in and offer more money. But if they start talking about a deal like the AIG deal, there isn't any other stop."

AJIT JAIN: "One way to look at how the deal is performing since we did it is at the point in time when we did the deal, we had made certain projections of how much we will pay out each year. And what we do is monitor what the actual payments are since the inception of the deal and how that compares with what we expect it to be at. Specifically, the actual payouts are 96% of what we had projected to pay out at this point in time, which is good but not great. We are still ahead of the curve. If we do end up paying out less than we projected, not only would we have borrowed money at a very attractive rate, meaning significantly less than 4%, but in addition to that, we would have made a fee, which in 2015 dollars would be $1 billion. So net-net, we're very happy with the deal. We are happy we did it. But the game is not over. Their liabilities are coming down the pike every day. So I'm cautiously optimistic that the deal will work out better than what we expected it to work out."

CM: "The really interesting thing is that Berkshire's casualty insurance companies have 4× as much stockholder capital behind each $1 of premium volume, 4× what's normal. And of course we see big deals; who would you trust if you had a big liability to dump on somebody?"

WB: "We have $25 billion or more coming in from things other than insurance, uncorrelated to insurance, every year. We don't pay dividends. If you pay dividends and you cut your dividend, try going around trying to write insurance the next day. It's a business where people are counting on you to pay. And when we take that $10 billion, we don't agree to put it in five-year or ten-year bonds. We don't even think that way.

"The people who do business with us know that they have somebody like nobody else, who's going to be able to pay $10 billion no matter what happens to the economy. It's not only the presence of enormous strength in the insurance companies, it's the fact we've got all these earnings. We don't have a lot of debt. We have debt at the railroad and the energy level, and we don't guarantee that debt. There just isn't another Berkshire. Ajit recognizes that when he's negotiating, and so does the other party if the sums are big enough."

UNPLEASANT SURPRISES IN INSURANCE

1999 MEETING (03:56:19)

WB: "It's the nature of insurance that you get unpleasant surprises from time to time. Loews bought CNA in the early 1970s. And just in the last few years, there was a fiberboard settlement on a policy written in the late 1950s. There was, as I remember, a $1.5 billion loss on something where the premiums were a few thousand dollars. GEICO has lost, as I remember, $60 million on a book of business that was written in the early 1980s, where the total premium was less than $200,000.

"The nature of insurance is that the surprises are on the unpleasant side … I think we have a claim at a small workers' comp company that we have, where the policy goes back twenty-five years or so, and it just popped up to life in the last year. And it costs real money. So it's a business where the surprises can come big and they can come late. And that will happen even with good management."

INCENTIVES IN INSURANCE UNDERWRITING

2004 MEETING (03:10:56)

WB: "Having the wrong incentives in insurance underwriting could be very harmful ... At National Indemnity, premium volumes in 1980 were $79 million; in the 'hard market' of the mid-1980s, we got up to $366 million. And then we took it down—not intentionally, but just because the business became less attractive—from $366 million to $55 million.

"The market has become more attractive in the last few years, and it soared back up again to almost $600 million. I don't think there's a public company in America that would feel they could survive a record of volume going down like that, year after year after year after year [from 1986 to 2000]. But that was the culture of National Indemnity.

"... When our premium volumes went all the way down, we never had a layoff during that period. Other people would have, but we didn't ... Our expense ratio went up dramatically, as high as 41% in 1999 ... When we were writing a lot of business, our expense ratio was as low as 26%. Some companies would feel that was intolerable—but what we feel is intolerable is writing bad business. We can take an expense ratio that's out of line, but we can't afford to write bad business. For one thing, if you get a culture of writing bad business, it's almost impossible to get rid of. We would rather suffer too much overhead than teach our employees that to retain their jobs they need to write any damn thing that came along, because that's a very hard habit to get rid of once you get hooked

"With a high expense ratio, we made money underwriting in virtually every year. You'll see in 1986, we had this incredible year, a 30% underwriting margin—and the nice thing about it is, we did it with the most volume we ever had to that point, $366 million. We coined money when we wrote huge amounts of business, and we made a little money when we wrote small amounts of business. I think we're almost the only insurance company in the world ... that sends the absolutely unequivocal message to the people associated with us that they will never be laid off because of a lack of volume, and therefore, we don't want them to write one bit of bad business.

"We'll make mistakes, and we'll have a high expense ratio when business is slow, but we'll win the game. That's what National Indemnity has done over time. National Indemnity was a no-name company thirty years ago, operating through a general agency system which everybody said was obsolete; it had no patents, no real estate, no copyrights, no nothing, that distinguished it, essentially, from dozens of other insurance companies. But they have a record almost like no one else's because they had discipline. They really knew what they were about.

And they've intensified that over time. Their record has left other people in the dust ... You put your finger on having the right incentives in place to write the right kind of business ... We try to think those things through. You can't run an auto company without having layoffs; you can't run a steel company this way. But this is the right way to run an insurance company. And that's why these cookie-cutter approaches to employment practices or bonuses are nonsense. You have to think through the situation in a given industry, with its given competitive conditions and its own economic characteristics."

CM: "The main thing is practically nobody else does it. And yet, to me, it's obvious it's the way to go. There's a lot in Berkshire like that. It's a little different from the way other people do it; it's partly the luxury of having a controlling shareholder of strong opinions that accounts for this. It would be hard for a committee, including a lot of employees, to come up with these decisions."

2013 MEETING (02:14:45)

WB: "One of the problems some insurers have had is that they have a pressure for increasing premium volume every year, brought upon by Wall Street. We actually contracted the business written by National Indemnity ... by 80% or something of the sort when it became less attractive. I'm not sure any manager of a public company answering to quarterly earnings calls and that sort of thing could've really stood up to the kind of pressure that they would receive if they followed a similar policy. If we do something stupid, it's because we did something stupid. No external factors are pressing on us ... Most people, if you own a half of 1% of the company or less, and other people are doing things that Wall Street is applauding and you're not doing them, it could be very hard to resist ... You get offered a lot of opportunities to do things that are stupid. We were major writers of natural catastrophe insurance in the United States some years ago when the prices were right. We don't think the prices are right now, so we don't write it. We haven't left the market, the market left us; we are not about to do something where we get paid 90 cents for running a probabilistic loss of a dollar. It just doesn't make any sense and we won't do it—and we don't put any pressure on anybody to do it, and their incomes are not dependent on doing it."

CM: "It is very hard to shrink an insurance operation by 80% when the people who come in every day don't have enough to do, and it's a counter-intuitive thing to do. But it's absolutely required that you do it in a place where people go as crazy as they do in insurance."

GEN RE ACQUISITION (POSTMORTEM)

2009 MEETING (03:18:40)

WB: "We strongly believe in postmortems. We think they're conducted at far too few companies. It's easy to propose a deal, but it's much harder to account for it later on. Charlie is a big fan of rubbing anybody's nose in their own problems ... Gen Re has worked out well after a terrible, terrible start. I was dead wrong, when I bought it in 1998, in thinking that it was the Gen Re of fifteen years earlier, which had absolutely the premier reputation in the insurance world. Certain practices, in terms of reserving and underwriting, had changed somewhat. But thanks to the combined work of Tad Montross and Joe Brandon, when they took over in September 2001, right about the time of the World Trade Center terrorist attacks, they went right after all of the problems—reserving, underwriting, whatever it might be.

"And Gen Re is now the company that I thought it was when I purchased it in 1998 ... It was a very tough job. It wasn't one that was going to get done by itself. When you tighten up on an organization that has fallen into some lax ways, that is not an easy job. Each of them could've left for some other place and made just as much money, maybe more, and not had to face the problems that they faced at Gen Re. But they hung in there. Now we have an organization that we feel terrific about, which has a great future."

CM: "I think that's right. But it's very important that you have an ability to turn your lemons into lemonade. And we were very, very lucky to have Joe and Tad to help us in the process. It wasn't pleasant and it wasn't pretty, but it was very successful. It wasn't something ordinary managers would've been at all likely to do. You had to be very tough minded to fix Gen Re, and they really did fix it ... The really brilliant decision in the Gen Re transaction was made by Joe Brandon. He was the one who decided that Berkshire should buy Gen Re ... It wouldn't have happened, I don't think, if he hadn't been there. Would you agree with that?"

WB: "Yeah, that's true."

CM: "And Joe was the steward for the Gen Re shareholders. We got a decent result, and they got a fabulous result. So, if capitalism has any heroes in that transaction, why, Joe's the hero."

2012 MEETING (02:34:18)

WB: "Gen Re got off the track. It was probably off the track when we bought it, and I didn't spot it. They had become more concerned about growth and satisfying certain personnel, in terms of their activities, than they were about emphasizing profitability, and it took us awhile to figure that out. When Joe

Brandon came in, he focused on underwriting profit instead of premium volume, and Tad Montross has followed through on that, with terrific results. But it did mean getting rid of a lot of business that didn't make any sense. They did an awful lot of what I would call 'accommodation business.'

"So, it's true the premium volumes dropped very significantly during that period, but it's not volume that we miss. The life business kept growing consistently during that period; that strikes me as very, very good. They've got a little long-term care mixed in there that we wish we didn't have. But I think Gen Re is right-sized, in terms of people. It's got an underwriting discipline to it. And I wouldn't be surprised if it grows at a reasonable rate in the future. But there was a major change that had to be made in the culture at Gen Re. And you don't make that change overnight, and you don't keep some of the business that you got through a wrong culture when you do straighten it out. It's a terrific asset to us now ... That's one we feel enormously better about than we did some years back."

CM: "It was a major fix-up operation, but we finally got it done."

WB: "We don't go looking for those, though."

PART SEVEN:
Accounting

"It's bad enough that people want to cheat on their accounting, and they do cheat on their accounting. But to want it to be endorsed as the system is really kind of disgusting."

"When the accounting confuses you, I would just tend to forget about that company."

"I don't know why we ever got into this business of trying to get the accounting result as close to the chalk as we could possibly get it. What is wrong with a world where everything is a little bit under-reported?"

"Much of what we don't like in modern corporate capitalism comes from an unreasonable expectation, communicated from headquarters, that corporate earnings have to go up with no volatility and great regularity. That kind of an expectation from headquarters is not just the kissing cousin of evil. It's the blood brother of evil."

INTRODUCTION

In commenting on the behavior of others, Buffett likes to say that one should praise by name, but criticize by category. On the topic of accounting, most notably the issue in the late 1990s and early 2000s about expensing stock-based compensation, Buffett and Munger were not shy in voicing their views. As Munger said at the 2001 meeting, "We don't like the accounting, which we've called corrupt, or at least I have—and I don't think that's too strong a word. It's corrupt to have false accounting because you like a certain outcome better than another."

Stock option accounting is one example of the rise in non-GAAP results and earnings management at public companies. As Buffett and Munger highlight, there are numerous ways to play with the numbers—for example, by slightly tweaking loss assumptions on long-tail insurance contracts. The problem is when earnings targets, along with internal pressures—explicit or implied—lead companies down a dangerous path. As Buffett puts it, "[Earnings management] is a quick fix, but it's like heroin. You get on it and it's not easy to get off. We've seen that time and time again … It catches up with you. You might as well face reality immediately, and take whatever steps are necessary to solve problems … Whatever you do, playing with the numbers never works."

SUBJECTS AND MEETINGS FEATURED

STOCK OPTION ACCOUNTING

1995 MEETING (01:28:33)

WB: "I would argue that the most intelligent form of capital formation follows from the most accurate form of accounting ... I don't think bad accounting is an aid to capital formation. In fact, over time it probably distorts capital formation ... I've talked privately to a number of managers about this, and they understand it, but they prefer the present situation and they used a lot of muscle in Washington ... FASB [The Financial Accounting Standards Board] caved on the accounting for stock options, and they hated it; they knew they were right. Most of the big six auditing firms, many years ago, sided with their position. In my opinion, the auditing firms [ultimately] caved to their clients in that respect ... Many years ago, in the Indiana legislature, a legislator introduced a bill to change the value of the mathematical symbol pi to three because he said that it was too difficult for schoolchildren to work with this complicated 3.14159. He was right, it was difficult. Congress, in connection with the stock option question, received all kinds of pressure to, in turn, pressure FASB and the SEC to not count stock option costs as part of compensation. I've never met anybody who felt, if he received his present salary plus an option, that he was not getting compensated more than if he just received a salary. So, he thought it was compensation.

"I really think that it makes you a bit of a cynic about American business when you see the extent to which a group has—even talking about withdrawing financial support from FASB—pressured people to make sure the value of pi stays at three instead of 3.14159, simply because it was their own ox that was being gored a bit. In any event, it looks like it's all over; in fact, now they're pressuring them to weaken further the standards that have been set. So, self-interest is alive and well in corporate America."

CM: "I think dishonor won. And I think it is quite important for a civilization to have sound engineering and good accounting. It is a very regrettable episode for leading politicians and leading venture capitalists. I think, to some extent, it's an indictment of the educational system, that this thing could be so widely looked at and so wrongly."

WB: "It's bad enough that people want to cheat on their accounting, and they do cheat on their accounting. But to want it to be endorsed as the system is really kind of disgusting."

CM: "Corruption won."

2001 MEETING (02:03:58)

CM: "We don't like the accounting, which we've called corrupt, or at least I have—and I don't think that's too strong a word. It's corrupt to have false accounting because you like a certain outcome better than another. All that said, I don't think we spend a lot of time fighting FASB or trying to create a better one. It's like splitting your lance against stone; you can get a lot of back pressure from the butt of the lance. We can't be expected to cure all the ills of the world."

WB: "The pressure was incredible that American business brought on Congress. They tried to put pressure on FASB and they weren't getting a result, so they just said, 'Well, we're not going to let FASB set the accounting rules, we'll have Congress set the accounting rules.' I thought that was a bad idea, but they got a huge number of supporters. ... One of the arguments was that it makes it very tough for start-up companies if they have to expense this; well, it makes it tough if they have to pay their electricity bill, too. But those were the kind of arguments you got ... Every client would put pressure on them; they don't want to report expenses. They particularly don't want to report expenses that are paid to them, which could be huge and might prove obnoxious if recorded by conventional accounting. But if it's sort of lost in a table in the proxy statement, people don't pay much attention.

"The only way it will get changed—and this is the only way corporate governance problems generally will get changed—is if fifteen or twenty large institutional investors band together in some way. But some of them have the same problem because they're getting paid extraordinary sums for doing something that is really not adding that much value. So, they're not really inclined to call attention to what Charlie would refer to as obscenities in other people's compensation. I think it's going to go on.

"The institutional investors seem to focus very much on matters of form and not substance. They cluck a lot about little things that don't have anything to do with their economic return over time, whereas stock options are terribly important. They're the ones paying the costs, and the costs are there whether they get recorded or not. But American management will not change its position voluntarily. Consultants will never change their position; they're getting paid to encourage people to look at other companies, and as a result it just keeps ratcheting up. So, I don't think you'll see change unless institutional investors do it."

CONFUSING ACCOUNTING

1995 MEETING (02:50:30)

WB: "There are people out there who will try to paint pictures with accounting that are something far from the economic reality. When the accounting confuses you, I would just tend to forget about that company. It may well be intentional; in any event, you don't want to go near it. We have never had any great investment results from companies whose accounting we regarded as suspect. It's a very bad sign.

"Accounting can offer you a lot of insight into the character of management ... Some companies have been able to push their auditors pretty far, and I would be very skeptical of anything that looks suspicious to you ...

"We frequently see weak accounting in life insurance. When you don't have a product where revenues and expenses are being matched up on something close to cash in the short term, you have the opportunity for people playing games with numbers. Some people have learned how to do that very well, and they've sometimes created long-lasting stock manipulation or promotion schemes that have enriched themselves, or they've enriched the managers or the creators of it, at the expense of the public over time. If you ever get suspicious about accounting, just go on to the next company."

RATIONAL, HONEST ACCOUNTING

1999 MEETING (00:56:05)

CM: "I go so far as to say it's fundamentally wrong not to have rational, honest accounting in big American corporations. And it's very important not to let little corruptions start because they become big corruptions. Then you have vested interests that fight to perpetuate them. There are a lot of wonderful companies that issue stock options, and those stock options go to a lot of wonderful employees that are really earning them. But that said, the accounting in America is corrupt. And it is not a good idea to have corrupt accounting."

WB: "You can see the problems creep in once it starts. It's much like campaign finance reform. If you let it go for a long time, the system becomes so embedded and the participants become so dependent upon it, that there becomes a huge constituency that will fight like the very devil to prevent any change, regardless of the logic of the situation. Once you get a significant number of important players benefiting from any kind of corruption in any kind of system, you're going to have a terrible time changing it. That's why it should be changed early. It would've been easier to change the accounting for stock options some decades back when it was first proposed than now, because basically corporate America's hooked on it.

"This does not mean that we are against options, per se. If Charlie and I die tonight and you had two new faces up here who didn't have the benefit of having bought a lot of Berkshire a long time ago, and they had responsibility for the whole enterprise, it would not be inappropriate to pay them in some way that was reflective of the prosperity of the whole enterprise ... A properly designed option system—which would be much different to the ones you see, because it'd be much more rational—could well make sense for people who have responsibility for this whole place ...

"Any option system should involve not giving an option at less than the price it could be sold for today, regardless of the market price; it should reflect the cost of capital, and very, very few systems reflect the cost of capital. If we're going to plow all the money back every year into the business and, in effect, use your earnings, interest-free, to increase our own earnings in the future, there has to be a cost of capital to have a properly designed option system. Option consultants aren't interested because that isn't what their clientele want."

2003 MEETING (03:39:30)

CM: "We are so horrified by the terrible business decisions that we see made by people relying on over-optimistic accounting, that we tend to almost reach for opportunities to make our accounting very conservative—way more so than other people. We think it protects our business decision-making, as well as our financial integrity. I don't know why we ever got into this business of trying to get the accounting result as close to the chalk as we could possibly get it. What is wrong with a world where everything is a little bit under-reported?"

WB: "Generally, people think reporting and transparency has improved over the years. I felt much better working with the financial statements in 1960 than I feel working with financial statements in 2000. In many ways I thought they taught me more about what the company was really about than the current ones do, even though there was far less detail.

"What we really deplore is solving operating problems by accounting maneuvers. Gen Re had some problems in the 1980s, when everybody did, and they went to discounting their workers' comp reserves. It was a quick fix, but it's like heroin. You get on it and it's not easy to get off. We've seen that time and time again ... It catches up with you. You might as well face reality immediately, and take whatever operating steps are necessary to solve problems. Or, if you can't solve them, just give up on them. Whatever you do, playing with the numbers never works—although, I guess if you're sixty-four-and-a-half years old and you're going to retire at sixty-five, it might get kind of tempting."

EARNINGS MANAGEMENT

2005 MEETING (01:52:08)

WB: "You should not have a system that causes people to, for example, worry about quarterly earnings. I have no idea what we're going to earn next quarter. And I have no implicit body language out there, or anything of the sort, to our managers that I'm hoping to earn X dollars per share next quarter. In the insurance business, you can report any number, basically, that you want to, if you write long-tail business for a short period of time. We've got $45 billion of loss reserves. Who knows whether the right figure is $45 billion, $46 billion, or $44 billion? And if the desire is to report some given number in a quarter, instead of saying $45 billion, you could say $44.75 billion ... We try to avoid that sort of thing."

CM: "Much of what we don't like in modern corporate capitalism comes from an unreasonable expectation, communicated from headquarters, that corporate earnings have to go up with no volatility and great regularity. That kind of an expectation from headquarters is not just the kissing cousin of evil. It's the blood brother of evil. We don't need that in our headquarters."

WB: "Businesses do not meet expectations quarter after quarter and year after year. It just isn't in the nature of running businesses. And, in our view, people that predict precisely what the future will be are either kidding investors, themselves, or both ... Setting up a system that either exerts financial or psychological pressure on the people around you to do things they probably really don't even want to do, in order to avoid disappointing you, that's a terrible mistake."

GOODWILL: INVESTMENT ANALYSIS AND BUSINESS QUALITY

2011 MEETING (03:21:29)

WB: "Goodwill should not be used in evaluating the fundamental attractiveness of a business. You should look at the return on tangible assets, and even then there are some other adjustments you may want to make. But basically, in evaluating the businesses we own—in terms of what the management are doing and what the underlying economics are—forget about goodwill. In terms of evaluating the job we're doing in allocating capital, you have to include goodwill, because we paid for it.

"If you were to buy the whole Coca-Cola Company, you'd be putting in a goodwill figure of $100 billion or something like that. You shouldn't amortize that, and in judging the economics of the business, you shouldn't look at that.

But in terms of judging the economics of the business that purchased it—in terms of their investment decision—you have to allow for the goodwill, because you are allocating capital and paying a lot for it. I don't think amortization of goodwill makes any sense. I think write-offs of goodwill make sense when you find out you've made the wrong purchase and the business doesn't earn commensurate with the tangible assets employed plus the goodwill. But when looking at businesses as to whether they're good, mediocre, or poor businesses, you should look at the return on net tangible assets."

CM: "I think that's right. When we buy a whole business, we never get a huge bargain; we may get down toward 10% pre-tax earnings yield (10×) on what we pay. That isn't so awful as you think when a lot of the money comes from insurance float that costs you nothing. In other words, if you have $60 billion of float and God gives you $6 billion a year of earnings, it's not all bad."

WB: "On Lubrizol we're paying close to $9 billion for the equity, and current earnings are probably $1 billion pre-tax. Lubrizol itself is employing $2.5 billion of equity to earn that $1 billion pre-tax, so it's a very good business in terms of the assets employed. But when we pay the premium to buy it, it becomes $1 billion pre-tax on $9 billion. You have to judge us based on close to a $9 billion investment. You have to judge Lubrizol CEO James Hambrick on running the business based on the much lower capital that he has employed. It can turn out to be a very good business, and we could turn out to have made at least a minor mistake if it isn't as good a business as we think, but still is a very satisfactory business based on the tangible capital employed."

STOCK SPLITS

1994 MEETING (00:24:17)

CM: "I think the idea of carving ownerships in an enterprise into tiny $20 pieces is almost insane. It's quite inefficient to service a $20 account and I don't see why there shouldn't be a minimum as a condition of joining some enterprise. Certainly, we'd all feel that way if we were organizing a private enterprise."

WB: "Yeah, we would not carve it up in $20 units. It's interesting because every company finds a way to fill up its common shareholder list. Every company in the NYSE, one way or another, has attracted some constituency of shareholders. And frankly, we can't imagine a better constituency than is in this room. We don't think we can improve on this group, and we followed certain policies that we think attracted certain types of shareholders and actually pushed away others. And that is part of our eugenics program here at Berkshire."

CM: "Just look around this room as you mingle with one another. This is a very outstanding group of people. Why would anybody want a different kind of a group?"

WB: "If we follow some policies that cause a whole bunch of people to buy Berkshire for the wrong reason, the only way they can buy it is to replace somebody in this room, or in this larger metaphorical room, of shareholders that we have. So, someone in one of these seats gets up and somebody else walks in. The question is, would we have a better audience? I don't think so."

1994 MEETING (00:47:48)

WB: "Most people think that the stock would sell for more money [after a stock split]. We wouldn't necessarily think that was advisable in the first place, but in the second place, we don't think it would necessarily be true over a period of time. We think our stock is more likely to be rationally priced over time following the present policies than if we were to split it, and we don't think the average price would necessarily be higher; we think the volatility would probably be somewhat greater, and we see no way that volatility helps our shareholders as a group."

1995 MEETING (04:34:44)

WB: "We want to attract shareholders who are as investment-oriented as we can possibly obtain, with long-term investment time horizons. If we had something that was a lot easier for anybody with $500 to buy, we would get an awful lot of people buying it who didn't have the faintest idea what they were doing, but heard the name bandied around in some way. And secondly, to the extent that [action] ever created a market that was stronger [the split alone pushed the stock price higher], you would then have people buying simply because it was going up … We don't know the degree to which it would happen, but we are almost certain we would get a shareholder base that would not have the level of sophistication and synchronization of objectives that we have now. That is almost a cinch.

"Ideally, we would have the stock price exactly parallel to changes in intrinsic value over time because then everybody would be treated fairly among our shareholders. They would gain or lose, just as the company gained or lost, over their ownership period. Anything that artificially stimulated the price in one period would simply mean that some other period's shareholders are going to be disappointed. We don't want the stock to sell at twice intrinsic value or 50% above intrinsic value. We want the intrinsic value to grow a lot. And I don't think there's any question that we would get a worse result in that aspect if we introduced splits.

"They had a tabulation in *Businessweek* a couple of months ago on turnover on the exchange. We were at 3%, and I don't think anybody else on the list was under double digits. Those are shareholders leaving frequently, and new shareholders coming in with shorter-term anticipations. We have wanted this to be as much like a private partnership as we can have, with everybody having the ability to buy it. We don't think the minimum investment is too high in this investment world. There are all kinds of investment opportunities that are limited to $25,000 or $50,000, that sort of thing … I do think once you get a shareholder base that has different objectives or expectations, you can't get rid of it. You can keep a shareholder base like Berkshire, but you can't reconstruct it if you destroy it in some way. And it's important to us who we're in with. I think it helps us in our operation. In some cases, it may even help us in acquisitions, in terms of who we attract."

2004 MEETING (02:59:00)

WB: "We have no religious view against stock splits. We don't think companies that do them are evil or anything of the sort. We do think we've got the best group of shareholders in the world, and I think that a meeting like this, to some extent, is evidence of it. We've got people that are more in sync, I think, with the policies of the company. We certainly have people who are more long term in their intentions regarding Berkshire … There's this self-selection process of who comes in … And I would say that people who say they aren't interested in a stock that sells in the thousands of dollars a share simply because it sells in the thousands of dollars a share, would not, as a group, be as intelligent, as informed, as long term in their outlook, and as in sync with the policies of management, as the current group of shareholders … We like the group we've got. We're not looking for people who think it would be more attractive if, instead of selling at $90,000 a share, it sold at $9 a share. Nothing wrong with those people, but if choosing partners, we would choose the group we have over the people who think a $9 stock is a wonderful thing."

CM: "I think the notion, taught in so much of modern academia, that liquidity of tradable common stock is a great contributor to capitalism, is mostly twaddle. The GNP of the United States grew at very good rates long before we had highly liquid markets for common stock. I don't know where people got that silly notion. The liquidity gives us these crazy booms, which have many problems as well as virtues. England, after the South Sea Bubble, banned tradable common stocks for decades. It was absolutely illegal to have a company so widely held you got a liquid market in the shares, and England did fine during that period. So, if you think that liquidity is a great contributor to civilization, then you probably believe all the real estate in America, which is relatively illiquid, hasn't been developed properly."

ACQUISITIONS AND ACCOUNTING TREATMENT

1995 MEETING (00:27:35)

WB: "Some companies care about the consideration they give in a deal, whether it's cash, preferred stock, or so on, because they care about the accounting treatment ... That is of absolutely no consequence to us. We care not a whit about the accounting treatment we receive. We feel we have a shareholder body that's intelligent enough to understand the economic reality of a transaction. Playing various games, in terms of how we structure it, and maybe flowing part of the purchase price back through the income statement, that's not something we care about at all. We would rather do whatever makes the most sense for us and for the seller, and then explain to you whatever accounting peculiarities may arise out of the transaction. That probably differentiates us from most companies. And it probably helps us to make a deal, occasionally."

PART EIGHT:
Circle of Competence

"It's a very useful thing to know the edge of your competency. And I always say it's not a competency if you don't know the edge of it."

"We're trying to find a business with a wide and long-lasting moat around it, protecting a terrific economic castle with an honest lord in charge of the castle."

"We try not to get into things that we don't understand. If we're going to lose your money, we want to be able to come before you and tell you we lost your money because we thought this and it turned out to be that. We don't want to say, somebody wrote us a report in some field we don't understand, and therefore we lost your money."

"Charlie and I try to distinguish between businesses where you have to be smart once and businesses where you have to stay smart."

"We are perfectly willing to trade away a big payoff for a certain payoff. That's the way we're put together."

"I think a great strategy, for the great mass of humanity, is to specialize. Nobody wants to go to a doctor who's half-proctologist and half-dentist."

INTRODUCTION

During the late 1990s, there was somewhat different tone to certain questions at the annual meetings. Specifically, a growing group of shareholders asked (in some cases forcefully) why Buffett and Munger kept avoiding tech companies despite their continued strong showing in the stock market, especially during the final few years of the 20th Century.

As you'll see in this section, that provided a useful opportunity for Buffett and Munger to reiterate their views on security selection, along with certain filters that determine which companies fall within their circle of competence. As was often the case, Munger's response (from the 1999 meeting) to shareholders who kept pressing for tech investments was concise and clear: "It's not an easy investment decision for us—and that's what we're looking for."

As the details of this topic are explored, we glean key insights about how Buffett and Munger think about this in practice—not only its impact on security selection, but also on position sizing (the willingness to take sizable long-term positions that are held for decades, as Berkshire has done with companies like American Express and Coca-Cola). Along those lines, this comment from Buffett is key: "we are perfectly willing to trade away a *big* payoff for a *certain* payoff".

SUBJECTS AND MEETINGS FEATURED

DETERMINING YOUR CIRCLE OF COMPETENCE

2002 MEETING (03:36:13)

WARREN BUFFETT: "If you have doubts about something being in your circle of competence, it isn't. I would bet you can understand a Coke bottler, Coca-Cola, McDonald's, Walmart, and Costco, in a general way, even if you are not able to value them. But there are all kinds of businesses ... If you get to something your friend is buying, or that everybody says a lot of money is going to be made in, and you're not sure whether you understand it or not, you don't. It's better to be well within the circle than to be trying to tiptoe along the line. And you'll find plenty of things within the circle. It's not terrible to have a small circle of competence. I'd say my circle of competence is pretty small, but it's big enough. I can find a few things."

CHARLIE MUNGER: "I think that if you have competence, you almost automatically have a feeling of where the edge of the competence is. Because, after all, it wouldn't be much of a competence if you didn't know its boundary ... My guess is you do know what you're perfectly competent to do in all kinds of areas. And you have all kinds of other areas where you know you would be out of your depth. You're not trying to play chess against Bobby Fischer or do stunts on the high trapeze if you've had no training for it. My guess is you know pretty well where the boundaries of your competence lies, and also where you want to stretch the boundary. You stretch the boundary by working at it, including practice."

2019 MEETING (03:13:35)

WB: "It's much more competitive now than when I started. When I started, I literally could take the Moody's industrial manual and the Moody's banks and financial manual and I could go through page by page, or at least run my eyes over every company, and think about which ones I might think more about. I would just do a whole lot of reading. I'd try and learn as much as I could about as many businesses as possible, and I would try to figure out which ones I really had some important knowledge and understanding of that was probably different than most of my competitors. And I would also try and figure out which ones I didn't understand. I would focus on having as big a circle of competence as I could have, and also focus on being as realistic as I could be about where the perimeters of my circle were.

"I knew when I met Lorimer Davidson in January of 1951, I could get insurance. What he said made so much sense to me in the three or four hours I spent with him. I dug into it and I could understand it. My mind worked well in that respect. I didn't think I could understand retailing. All I'd done was work for the same grocery store that Charlie had, and neither one of us learned that much about retailing, except it was harder work than we liked. You've got to do the same thing, and you've got way more competition now. But if you get to know more about even a relatively small area than other people, and you don't feel the compulsion to act too often—you just wait until the odds are strongly in your favor—it's still a very interesting game. It's harder than it used to be."

CM: "I think a great strategy, for the great mass of humanity, is to specialize. Nobody wants to go to a doctor who's half-proctologist and half-dentist. The ordinary way to succeed is to narrowly specialize. Warren and I really didn't do that. And we didn't because we prefer the other type of activity. But I don't think we could recommend it to other people."

WB: "Yeah, a little more treasure hunting in our day, and it was easy to spot the treasures."

CM: "We made it work, but it was kind of a lucky thing. It's not the standard way to go."

WB: "The business I best understood was insurance, and I had very little competition. One time, I drove to the insurance department in Harrisburg, Pennsylvania, to check on some Pennsylvania company. This was when you couldn't get all this information on the internet. I went in and asked about the company, and the guy said, 'You're the first one that's ever asked about that company.' And there weren't a lot of companies. I would go over to the Standard and Poor's library and ask for all this obscure information. There wasn't anybody around. They had a whole bunch of tables that you could set and examine things through. So, there was less competition. Even knowing one thing very well will give you an edge at some point. It's what Thomas J. Watson Sr. [chairman and CEO] said at IBM: 'I'm no genius, but I'm smart in spots and I stay around those spots.' That's basically what Charlie and I try and do, and I think that's probably what you can do."

CM: "We did it in several fields. That's hard."

WB: "And we got our heads handed to us a few times, too."

PREDICTING CHANGE

1996 MEETING (03:27:03)

CM: "If you have something you think you understand that looks very attractive, we think it's smart to do what you understand. If we'd been unable to find companies that fit our slender talents, we might have been in Pfizer and Microsoft, but we've never had to revert to it. We don't sneer at it. Other people with more talent have found that a wonderful course of action."

WB: "We feel change is likely to work against us. We do not think we have great ability to predict where change is going to lead. We think we have some ability to find businesses where we don't think change is going to be very important. At Gillette, the product is going to be better ten and twenty years from now; the shaving technology gets better and better. But you know that Gillette—although they had that little experience with Wilkinson in the early 1960s—is basically going to be spending many multiples more money on developing better shaving systems compared to anyone else. They've got the distribution system, they've got the believability. If they bring out a product and say, 'This is something that men ought to look at,' men look at it. And they found out here a few years ago that the same thing happened when they said to women to look at the shaving field. They wouldn't have that same credibility someplace else. But in the shaving field, they have it. Those are assets that can't be built. And they're very hard to destroy.

"We think we know, in a general way, what the soft drink industry, shaving industry, and candy business is going to look like ten to twenty years from now. We think Microsoft is a sensational company run by the best of managers, but we don't have any idea what that world is going to look like in ten or twenty years. Now, if you're going to bet on somebody who is going to see out and do what we can't do ourselves, I'd rather bet on Bill Gates than anybody else. But I don't want to bet on anybody else. In the end, we want to understand, ourselves, where we think a business is going. On Wall Street, if somebody tells you the business is going to change a lot, they see that as a great opportunity. They don't think it's a great opportunity when Wall Street itself is going to change a lot, incidentally. We don't think it's an opportunity at all; it scares the hell out of us because we don't know how things are going to change.

"When people are chewing gum, we have a pretty good idea how they chewed it twenty years ago and how they'll chew it twenty years from now. We don't really see a lot of technology going into the art of the chew. And as long as we don't have to make those other decisions, why in the world should we? Why go around trying to bet on things we don't know when we can bet on the simple things?"

1999 MEETING (04:44:41)

WB: "In terms of picking out the businesses that are going to do wonderfully as businesses—not as stocks for a while, but as businesses—I don't think it's so easy in the internet world. If you were to ask some very top names in the field to name the next five to ten companies out of the chute, and predict which one of them will earn, say, $200 million six or seven years from now, I'm not so sure they could accurately name a single one. That doesn't mean they won't make a lot of money being early investors, because they can sell out to the next group and so on. But in the end, they have to succeed as businesses. A few will succeed and the internet will have a huge impact on the world—but I'm not so sure that makes it an easy investment decision."

CM: "It's not an easy investment decision for us—and that's what we're looking for."

2019 MEETING (02:58:21)

WB: "We used to be able to identify moats in a newspaper that was the only newspaper in town, or in TV stations where we felt they had a dominant position and where we felt the product was underpriced in terms of advertising. We saw it in brands sometimes. And it is true that in the tech world, if you can build a moat, it can be incredibly valuable. I've not felt confident that I was the best one to judge that in many cases.

"It wasn't hard to figure out who was winning at any given time or what their business was about, but there were a huge number of people who knew more about the game than I did. And we don't want to try and win at a game we don't understand. We may hire people, such as Ted [Weschler] and Todd [Combs], who are better at understanding certain areas of investing than Charlie or me. But the principles haven't changed. Some old companies have lost their moats and there are going to be companies in the future that have them that will be enormously valuable. We hope we can identify one every now and then. But we'll still stay within where we think we know what we're doing.

"Obviously, we'll make mistakes even within that area. But we won't go into something because somebody else tells us it's a good thing to do. We are not going to subcontract your money to somebody else's judgment. You can take your money and follow somebody else's judgment directly; we're not in the business of thinking that if we hire ten people with specialties in this area or that, that it will lead to superior investment results. We do worry that we could blow a lot of money that way.

"So, we'll do our best to enlarge the circle of competence of the people at Berkshire so that we don't miss so many. But we'll miss a lot in the future, just like we missed a lot in the past. The main thing to do is to find things where our batting average is going to be high. And if we miss the biggest ones, that really doesn't bother us, as long as the things we do work out OK."

CM: "I think we've still got an awful lot of companies with big moats; some are industrial brands that are just incredibly strong in the niches we're in. Berkshire shareholders don't need to worry that we're just one big morass of unprofitability or anything like that. But we have not covered ourselves with glory in the new tech fields … We're trying to improve."

IMPACT OF TECHNOLOGICAL CHANGE

1999 MEETING (00:34:15)

CM: "It is tricky predicting whether technological change will or won't destroy some business. When I was young, the department stores had a bunch of sort of monopolistic advantages. They were downtown where the streetcar lines met. They had a sort of monopoly on extending revolving credit. And they had one-stop shopping in all kinds of weather. Nobody else did. And they lost all three of those advantages. Yet, they've done well, a lot of them, for many decades since. Other times, you get a change and you get destroyed. Our trading stamp business was destroyed by changes in the economic world. Our World Book business has been seriously hurt by the PC, the CD-ROM, and so forth. We agree it's a big risk—but it's not easy to make predictions in which you have great confidence."

WB: "If you go down to 16th and Farnam in Omaha, where the streetcar tracks used to cross, that was the best real estate in town. People signed fifty-year and a hundred-year leases on it. It looked like there was nothing safer because they weren't going to move the streetcar lines; the only thing was they moved the streetcars. They took them and converted them into junk. And it had seemed very permanent.

"The advantage of the big department store—the Marshall Field's in Chicago, or the Macy's in New York—was this incredible breadth of merchandise. You could go and find 300 different types of spools of thread, you could see 500 different wedding dresses, or whatever. And you had these million square-foot, even two million square-foot, downtown stores, these huge emporiums. Then the shopping center came along, which created, in effect, a store of many stores. So you had millions of square feet now, but you still had this incredible variety being offered.

"The internet becomes a store on your computer, and it has an incredible variety of offerings, too. Some of them don't lend themselves very well, it seems to me, to retailing. Others do. But Charlie's right—it's hard to predict exactly how it will turn out. I would expect automobile retailing to change in some important ways, and in very significant part, influenced by the internet. I don't think it'll look the same ten or fifteen years from now, but I can't predict exactly how that'll happen."

1999 MEETING (02:44:26)

WB: "We think all of that activity [in the technological field] is very beneficial from a societal standpoint. Our own emphasis from an investment perspective is trying to find businesses that are predicable in a general way, as to where they'll be in ten, fifteen or twenty years. That means we're looking for businesses that, in general, are not going to be susceptible to very much change. We view change as more of a threat in the investment process than an opportunity. That's quite contrary to the way most people are looking at equities now. But we do not get enthused—with a few exceptions—about change as a way to make a lot of money. We're looking for the absence of change to protect ways that are already making a lot of money and allow them to make even more in the future. So, we look at change as a threat.

"Whenever we look at a business and we see lots of change coming, nine times out of ten, we're going to pass. And when we see something we think is very likely to look the same ten or twenty years from now, we feel much more confident about predicting it. Coca-Cola is still selling a product that is very, very similar to one it sold 110-plus years ago. And the fundamentals of distribution and talking to the consumer, and all of that sort of thing, really haven't changed at all. Your analysis of Coca-Cola fifty years ago can pretty well serve as an analysis now. We're more comfortable in those kind of business. It means we miss a lot of very big winners, but we would not have picked those out anyway. It does mean also that we have very few big losers and that's quite helpful over time."

2000 MEETING (00:27:23)

WB: "We should be thinking all the time about whether developments in tech threaten the businesses we're in now, how we might counter those threats, how we might capitalize on opportunities because of it. It's a very, very important part of business now and will become more important in the years to come.

"We own a newspaper called *The Buffalo News* in New York; believe me, Stan Lipsey, who runs that paper, and I have talked many hours about what we are doing on the internet, what we should be doing, what others are doing, how it threatens us, how we can counter those threats, all of that sort of thing. Newspapers are a category that, in my view, are very threatened by the internet.

"The internet is terrific for delivering information. We have a product, World Book, that's terrific for delivering information. And fifteen years ago, print encyclopedias were the best tool for educating not only young children, but for educating me or Charlie when we wanted to look up something on a subject. And the World Book is a marvelous product. But it requires chopping down trees, operating paper mills, binding and printing, and delivery of a seventy-pound UPS package. It was put together in a way that for 400 or 500 years was the best technique for taking that information and moving it from those who assembled it to those who wanted to use it. Then the internet changed that in a very major way. So, we have seen firsthand the business consequences of the improvement offered by the internet and the delivery of information. And newspapers, although not as immediately susceptible to that problem, still face that overpowering factor.

"We pay a significant percentage of our circulation revenue at *The Buffalo News* to our carriers, and we pay additional money to the district managers, and we pay for the trucks to deliver the product out, and we pay for huge printing presses, and all of that sort of thing. And people chop down trees in order to give us the raw material to transmit information in Buffalo, about what the Bills did on Sunday. Now you have the internet that has virtually no incremental unit cost and can deliver the information instantaneously. So, it's a big factor for newspapers. The newspaper world in my view will look very, very, very different in not that many years ... It's going to change how the world gets entertainment, it's going to change how the world gets information. And it is incredibly low cost compared to most of the methods of conveying entertainment and information now."

CM: "[We were] asked if we're afraid the internet would hurt some of our business; the answer is yes."

2009 MEETING (02:06:25)

WB: "The current economic environment has accentuated the problems in newspapers, but it is not the basic cause ... For most newspapers, we would not buy them at any price. They have the possibility—in certain places, they've already hit it—of just going to unending losses. They were absolutely essential to a very high percentage of the American public twenty, thirty, forty years ago. They were the ultimate business. It was a business where one person won, basically, in almost every town in the country. There were 1,700 papers in the United States; about fifty of those, twenty years ago, existed in a city where there were multiple papers. So, they were a product that had pricing power, that was essential to the customer and to the advertiser. They've lost that essential nature. They were primary thirty to forty years ago if you wanted to learn sports scores or stock prices or news about international affairs. And then that nature, what Walter Annenberg used to call 'essentiality,' started eroding. The erosion has accelerated dramatically. And they were only essential to the advertiser as long as they were essential to the reader. Nobody liked buying ads in the paper, it was just that they worked. That is changing every day. And I do not see anything on the horizon that causes that erosion to end.

"At *The Buffalo News*, Stan Lipsey would greet me ten years ago, and he would say, 'Warren, on an economic basis, you should sell this paper.' And I said, 'I agree 100%, but we're not going to do it.' We could have sold *The Buffalo News* for many hundreds of millions of dollars; we couldn't sell it for remotely anything like that now. That's one of our policies at Berkshire for wholly-owned businesses. We have a bunch of unions that have been quite cooperative with us in recent months in trying to have an economic model that will at least keep us making a little money. As long as we don't think we face unending losses or have major union problems, we will stick with the businesses, even though it would be a mistake if you were acting as a trustee for a bunch of crippled children or something of the sort. That's just our policy at Berkshire ... We all keep looking around for somebody that will find the model; I think there are about 1,400 daily papers now in the United States, and nobody has found it yet. We are as well-positioned in Buffalo, believe it or not, I think, to play out the game as anyone else. But whether we find something before the lines get so that we're inexorably in the red, or whether the situation gets so we're inexorably in the red, I don't know. But we will play it out as long as we can. It's not what they teach you in business school. But it's the way we run Berkshire."

CM: "I think that's 100% right. And it's really a national tragedy. These monopoly daily newspapers have been an important sinew of our civilization. By and large, they were impregnable from advertiser pressure. By and large, they were desirable editorial influences. And by and large, they kept government more honest than it would otherwise be. So as they disappear, I think what replaces it will not be as desirable as what we're losing. But this is life."

COMPETITIVE IMPACT FROM THE INTERNET

2000 MEETING (03:03:34)

CM: "Will the internet, by making competition much more efficient, make business generally harder for American corporations, meaning more competitive, lower returns on capital? My guess would be yes."

WB: "My guess would be yes, too. I would say that, on balance, for society, the internet is a wonderful thing. For capitalists, it's probably a net negative."

CM: "So, all of you can be happy that the progress of the species will affect your economic futures for the worse."

WB: "The internet, if you analyze it, you have to think it's much more likely that it will reduce the profitability of American business than improve it. It will improve the efficiency of American business, but all kinds of things improve the efficiency of American business without making it more profitable. And I think that the internet is likely to fall into that category. So far, it's improved the monetized value of American business. But that will eventually follow the underlying economics of what the internet does. And I think it's way more likely to make American business, in aggregate, worth less than compared to what it would've been otherwise."

CM: "By the way, that's perfectly obvious and very little understood."

INVESTING IN TECH COMPANIES

1995 MEETING (00:57:42)

WB: "We try not to get into things that we don't understand. If we're going to lose your money, we want to be able to come before you and tell you we lost your money because we thought this and it turned out to be that. We don't want to say, somebody wrote us a report in some field we don't understand, and therefore we lost your money. So, we won't do it ourselves, but I think Ben Graham's principles are perfectly valid when applied to high-tech companies. We don't know how to do it, but that doesn't mean somebody else doesn't know how to do it.

"My guess is if Bill Gates were thinking about some company in an arena that he understood and that I didn't understand, he would apply much the same way of thinking about the investment decision as I would; he would just understand the business. He may have the ability to understand a lot of other businesses that seem as clear to him as Coke or Gillette seem to me. Once he identified those, I think he would apply pretty much the same yardsticks in deciding how to act. He would have a margin of safety principle that might be a little different because there's essentially more risk in a high-tech company, but he would still have the margin of safety principle, adjusted for the mathematical risk of loss in his mind. He would look at it as a business, not as a stock. He would not buy it on borrowed money. A bunch of principles would be carried through. But our circle of things we understand is really unlikely to enlarge; maybe a tiny bit here or there. If the capital doesn't get too large, the circle we have is okay. If we have trouble finding things within our circle, we will not enlarge the circle. We will wait. That's our approach."

CM: "Having flunked when we were young and strong at understanding some complex businesses, we're not looking to master what we earlier failed at in our latter years."

WB: "It's a question of being able to identify businesses that you understand and feel very certain about. If you understand Microsoft and Intel, you have the opportunity to evaluate them. And if you decide they're fairly priced and they have marvelous prospects, you're going to do very well. But there's a whole group of companies, a very large group, that Charlie and I just don't know how to value—and that doesn't bother us ... There's all kinds of financial instruments that we just don't feel we have the knowledge to evaluate. And it might be a little too much to expect that somebody would understand every business in the world.

"When I say *understand,* my idea of understanding a business is that you've got a pretty good idea where it's going to be in ten years. I just can't get that conviction with a lot of businesses, whereas I can get it with relatively few—but I only need a few. You only need six or eight or something like that.

"It certainly would have been better for you if we had the insights about what we regard as the somewhat more complicated businesses, because there was and may still be a chance to make a whole lot more money if those growth rates are maintained. I don't think you'll find better managers than Andy Grove at Intel and Bill Gates at Microsoft, and they certainly seem to have fantastic positions in the businesses they're in. But I don't know enough about those businesses to be as sure that those positions are fantastic as I am with Gillette and Coca-Cola. You may understand those businesses better than you understand Coke and Gillette because of your background or the way your mind is wired, but I don't. Therefore, I have to stick with what I really think I can understand—and if there's more money to be made elsewhere, I think the people who make it are entitled to it.

"Bob Noyce, one of the two primary founders of Intel, grew up in Grinnell, Iowa … He was chairman of the board of trustees of Grinnell College when I went on the board back in the late 1960s. And when he left Fairchild [transistors and circuits] to form Intel with Gordon Moore, Grinnell bought 10% of the private placement that was the initial funding for Intel. And Bob was a terrific guy; he was a very down to earth Iowa boy who could tell you the risks and tell you the upside, enormously likeable, 100% honest, every way. We did buy 10% of the original issue at Grinnell. The genius who ran the investment committee managed to sell it a few years later, I won't give you his name [it was Warren], and there's no prize for anybody who calculates the value of those shares now … Intel had a total transformation in the mid 1980s when the product on which they relied also ran out of gas.

"Andy Grove has written a terrific book, *Only the Paranoid Survive,* which describes strategic inflection points at Intel. I recommend every one of you read that book because it is terrific. But they had an Andy Grove there who made that transformation, along with some other people. That doesn't happen every time; companies get left behind. We don't want to be in businesses where we feel companies can be left behind. Intel could have gone off the tracks and almost did. IBM owned a big piece of Intel, and they sold it in the mid 1980s. So, here are a bunch of people who should know a lot about that business but they couldn't see the future either. I think it's very tough to make money that way, but I think some people can make a lot of money understanding those kinds of businesses.

"That doesn't bother me at all. What would bother me is if I think I understand a business and I don't."

1998 MEETING (01:57:51)

WB: "I've been an admirer of Andy Grove and Bill Gates, and I wish I had translated that admiration into backing it up with money. But the truth is, I don't know what that world will look like in ten years. And I don't want to play in a game where I think the other guys have an advantage over me. I could spend all my time thinking about technology for the next year and I wouldn't be the 100th, 1,000th, or the 10,000th smartest guy in the country in looking at those businesses. That is a seven- or eight-foot bar I can't clear—and no matter how I train, I can't clear it. The fact that there will be a lot of money made by somebody doesn't bother me. There may be a lot of money made by somebody in cocoa beans, but I don't know anything about them. There are a whole lot of areas I don't know anything about. I think it would be a very valid criticism if it were possible that Charlie and I, by spending a year working on it, could become well enough informed so that our judgment would be better than other people's, but that wouldn't happen. It would be a waste of time. It's much better for us to swing at the easy pitches."

CM: "Whatever you think you know about technology, I think I know less."

1999 MEETING (03:12:34)

WB: "I think it's much easier to predict the relative strength that Coke will enjoy in the soft drink world than the amount of strength that Microsoft will possess in the software world. That's not to knock Microsoft at all. If I had to bet on anybody, I'd certainly bet on Microsoft—but I don't have to bet. And I don't see that world as clearly as I see the soft drink world.

"Now, somebody who has a lot of familiarity with software may very well see it that way, and if it's true they have superior knowledge and they act on it, they're entitled to make money from that superior knowledge. There's nothing wrong with that. I know I don't have that kind of knowledge. I do think that if you have a general knowledge of business over decades that you would regard the industry they're in as less predictable than the soft drink industry.

"It may also be that, even though it's less predictable, there's a whole lot more money to be made, so that if you're right the payoff is much larger. But we are perfectly willing to trade away a big payoff for a certain payoff. That's the way we're put together. It does not knock the ability of other people to make those decisions ... Different people understand different businesses. The important thing is to know which ones you do understand and when you're operating within your circle of competence. And the software business is not within my circle of competence."

CM: "I think there are interesting questions, too, about how far the whole field can go. Take jet airplane travel below the speed of sound. It's been pretty static in terms of the technology for a long, long time; the big Boeing airliner is much the same as it was twenty or thirty years ago. And I think a lot of these businesses are quite dependent on the technology continuing to gallop and to do more and more for people ... I don't know what happens once you get unlimited bandwidth into the house and way more options, etc. Beyond a certain point, it strikes me that there might be a surfeit of anybody's interest in the field. I don't know where that point is, whether it's twenty or thirty years out, but it would affect me a little."

WB: "In the United States, by far the most prosperous country in the world, there are probably 400 companies that are earning $200 million a year, after-tax. Of those 400, you can probably name 350. Five years from now, instead of 400 being on that list, there will probably be 450 or 475. A lot of those will be companies that are earning $150 to $200 million now. So there'll probably be some number like twenty that come from nowhere. Now, if you look at the number of companies that are selling today at a price which implies $200 million or more of earnings, you will find dozens and dozens in the high-tech arena. And a very large percentage of those companies are not going to fulfill people's expectations. I can't tell you which ones, but I know there won't be dozens and dozens of those companies making a couple hundred million dollars a year. And I know they are now selling at prices that require them to be making that much money or more. It just doesn't happen that often.

"Biotech was all the rage some years back. How many of those companies are making a couple hundred million dollars a year? It just doesn't happen. It's not that easy to make lots of money in a business in a capitalistic society. People are looking at what you're doing every day and trying to figure out a way to do it better and to underprice you or bring out a better product or whatever it may be. And a few companies make it. Here in the United States, after decades and decades of wonderful economic development, we've got about 400 companies that have hit the profit level that would be required of a company that has a market cap of $3 billion. And some companies are getting $3 billion of market cap virtually the day they come out. You want to think about the math on all of this."

2006 MEETING (01:03:38)

WB: "I know enough to know that I don't know enough to make an investment decision on the tech companies. Charlie and I have circles of competence that extend to evaluating a number of types of businesses, and there are a whole lot of businesses that we won't be able to evaluate. Some of them, I think very few people can evaluate. You just get into businesses where the future is so likely to be different than the present that maybe there's a few people who have great insights on it, but we sure don't. We are best at the businesses where we can come to a judgment that they're going to look a good bit like they do today five to ten years from now.

"I can name a number of businesses that are bound to change dramatically. When you think of how much the telecom business, for example, has changed over the last fifteen or twenty years, it's startling. Even with hindsight, it's a little hard to figure out who was going to make all the money and so on. There are just games that are too tough. Charlie says, 'We've got three boxes at the company: in, out, and too hard.' And a lot of things end up in the 'too hard' pile, and it doesn't bother us; we don't have to be able to do everything well ..."

CM: "One of the foreign correspondents last year, after looking at us carefully, said, in effect, 'You guys don't seem smart enough to do so much better than other people as you're doing. Have you got an explanation?' And we said, 'We know the edge of our competency better than most people do.' It's a very useful thing to know the edge of your competency. And I always say it's not a competency if you don't know the edge of it."

2011 MEETING (01:00:07)

WB: "This isn't going to happen, but if I could really become expert in the tech field, knowing more than almost anybody else about the subject, I think that would be terrific. It's going to be a huge field. There are likely to be a few enormous winners and a lot of disappointments. So the ability to pick the winners there is far disproportionate to the ability to pick the winners, say, among integrated major oil companies where they're all equated in price. You're not going to have a big edge in trying to pick Chevron against Exxon against Continental and Occidental, you name it. But the degree of disparity in results among larger tech companies in the future is likely to be very, very dramatic. And if I had the skills where I could pick the winners there I would do a lot better than if I had the skills to pick the winners in the major integrated oil field."

CM: "I think if we were going to do it, it would have already happened. I do think we might identify someone else who has abilities that we lack. That's been very hard for us, but we've done a little better lately."

2012 MEETING (03:03:43)

WB: "Google and Apple are extraordinary companies, obviously, and they're both huge companies. They make lots of money. They earn fantastic returns on capital. They look very tough to dislodge, where they have their strengths. I would not be at all surprised to see them be worth a lot more money ten years from now, but I wouldn't want to buy either one of them. I do not get to the level of conviction that would cause me to buy them. But I sure as hell wouldn't short them, either."

CM: "I think we can fairly say that other people will always understand those two companies better than we do. We have the reverse of an edge. And we're not looking for that. I think IBM is easier to understand."

WB: "The chances of being way wrong in IBM are probably less, at least for us, than being way wrong with Google or Apple. But that doesn't mean the latter two companies aren't going to do far better than IBM. But we wouldn't have predicted what would happen with Apple ten years ago. And it's very hard for me to predict what will happen in the next ten years. They've come up with these brilliant products. There are other people trying to come up with brilliant products. I just don't know how to evaluate the people that are out there working, either in big companies or in garages, who are trying to think of something that will change the world the way they have changed it in recent years."

2013 MEETING (02:45:23)

CM: "We think BNSF will have a competitive advantage fifteen years from now, with a high degree of confidence. We would never have that degree of confidence about Apple, no matter what their financial statement showed. It's too hard."

2017 MEETING (00:50:49)

WB: "I view IBM and Apple differently. Obviously, when I started buying IBM six years ago, I thought it would do better in the years that have elapsed than it has. I regard Apple as being in quite different businesses. Apple is much more of a consumer products business, in terms of analyzing the moats around it, consumer behavior, that sort of thing. It's obviously a product with all kinds of tech built into it. But in terms of laying out what their prospective customers will do in the future, as opposed to, say, IBM's customers, it's a different sort of analysis. That doesn't mean it's correct. We'll find out over time. But IBM and Apple are two different types of decisions. I was wrong on the first one, and we'll find out whether I'm right or wrong on the second. But I do not regard them as apples and apples, and I don't quite regard them as apples and oranges; it's somewhat in between."

CM: "We avoided the tech stocks because we felt we had no advantage there. And I think it's a good idea not to play where other people are better. But, if you ask me, in retrospect, what was our worst mistake in the tech field, I think we were smart enough to figure out Google. Those ads worked so much better in the early days than anything else. So I would say that we failed you there. We were smart enough to do it and didn't do it. We do that all the time, too."

WB: "We were their customer very early on with GEICO, for example. As I remember, we were paying them $10 or $11 a click or something like that. Any time you're paying somebody $10 or $11 every time somebody just punches a little thing where you've got no cost at all, that's a good business, unless somebody's going to take it away from you. We were close up, seeing the impact of that ... And I knew the founders; they actually designed their prospectus, when they went public, a little bit after Berkshire. So I had plenty of ways to ask questions or anything of the sort, educate myself—but I blew it."

CM: "We blew Walmart, too. It was a total cinch, we were smart enough to figure that out, and we didn't."

WB: "It's harder to predict, in my view, the winners in various items, or how much price competition will enter into something like cloud services and all of that. It's really remarkable, one person who built an extraordinary economic machine in two really pretty different industries, almost simultaneously, from a standing start at zero, while facing competitors with lots of capital and everything else. To do it in retailing and to do it with the cloud, like Jeff Bezos has done at Amazon ... Andy Grove at Intel used to say, 'If you had a silver bullet and you could get rid of one of your competitors, who would it be?' Well, I think there are a lot of people that would aim that silver bullet at Bezos ... It's a remarkable business achievement, where he's been involved in the execution—not just the bankrolling—of two businesses that are as feared by competitors as any you can find ... We missed it entirely, incidentally. We have never owned a share of Amazon."

2017 MEETING (03:51:02)

WB: "I made a large investment in IBM, which has not turned out that well. We haven't lost money, but in terms of the bull market we've been in, it's been a significant laggard. And, then, recently, we took a large position in Apple, which I regard as more a consumer goods company, in terms of certain economic characteristics. It has a huge tech component in terms of what that product can do, or what other people might come along to do, to leapfrog it in some way. No guarantees, but I think I'll end up being one for two instead of zero for two. We'll find out.

"I make no pretense whatsoever of being on the intellectual level of a fifteen-year-old with an interest in tech. I think I have some insights into consumer behavior. I can get a lot of information on consumer behavior and try to draw inferences about what that means about what consumer behavior is likely to be in the future. But the other thing I'll guarantee is I'll make some mistakes on marketable securities, and I've made them in other areas than tech ... You don't bat a thousand. But I have gained no real knowledge about tech ... since I was born."

CM: "I think it's a very good sign that you bought Apple. It shows one of two things: Either you've gone crazy or you're learning. I prefer the learning explanation."

WB: "Well, so do I, actually."

2018 MEETING (04:49:13)

WB: "We don't think of whether we should be in tech companies or not, that sort of thing. We are looking for … durability of competitive advantage, and whether our opinion might be better than other people's opinion in assessing the probability of that durability. The truth is that I watched Amazon from the start, and I think what Jeff Bezos has done is something close to a miracle. The problem is, if I think something requires a miracle, I tend not to bet on it. It would have been far better, obviously, if I had some insights into certain businesses. In fact, Bill Gates told me early on about Google. But the trouble is I saw that Google was skipping past [defunct search engine] AltaVista, and then I wondered if anybody could skip past Google. I saw at GEICO that we were paying a lot of money to Google for something [ads] that cost them nothing incrementally. … I made a mistake in not being able to come to a conclusion where I really felt that, at present prices, the prospects were far better than the prices indicated.

"I didn't go into Apple because it was a tech stock. I went into Apple because I came to certain conclusions about both the intelligence with which the capital would be employed, but more important, about the value of an ecosystem and how permanent that ecosystem could be, and what the threats were to it, and a whole bunch of things. I don't think that required me to take apart an iPhone or something and figure out what all the components were. It's much more the nature of consumer behavior.

"Some things strike me as having a lot more permanence than others. But I'll miss a lot of things that I don't feel I understand well enough. And there is no penalty in investing if you don't swing at a ball that's in the strike zone; as long as you swing at something at some point, eventually you find the pitches you like. That's the way we'll continue to do it. We'll try to stay within our circle of competence. And Charlie and I generally agree on sort of where that circle ends, and what kind of situations where we might have some kind of an edge in our reasoning or our experience or something, where we might evaluate something differently than other people. But the answer is, we're going to miss a lot of things."

CM: "We have a wonderful system. If one of us is stupid in some area, so is the other. And of course, we were not ideally located to be high-tech wizards. How many people of our age quickly mastered Google? I've been to Google headquarters, it looked like a kindergarten."

WB: "A very rich kindergarten. It's extraordinarily impressive what they've done. And like I say, at GEICO, we were paying them a lot of money at the time they went public. And all three of the main characters—Eric Schmidt, Larry Page, and Sergey Brin—came and saw me. They were interested in talking about going public and the mechanics of it and various things along that line. It wasn't like what they were doing was a mystery to me. The mystery was how much competition would come along, and how effective they would be, and whether it would be a game where four or five people were slugging it out without making as much money as they could if one company dominated. Those are tough decisions to make.

"You can have industries where there's only two people in it, and they still don't make out very good because they beat each other's brains out. That's one of the questions in the airline business. It's a better business now than it used to be, but it used to be suicide. The competitive factors are extraordinary in airlines, and how much better business is it with four people operating at 85% capacity than with seven or eight operating at 75% and with more planes run? Those are tough decisions. But I made the wrong decision on Google. Amazon, I really consider that a miracle, that you could be doing web services and changing retail at the same time, without enormous amounts of capital, and with the speed and effectiveness of what Amazon has done. I had a very, very, very high opinion of Jeff's ability when I first met him—and I underestimated him."

CM: "My comment would be that the shareholders have one thing to be thankful for. Some of the age-related stupidity at headquarters has been ameliorated by Todd and Ted joining us. We are looking at the world with the aid of some younger eyes now. And they've made a contribution beyond their own investments. You're very lucky to have them, because there's a lot of ignorance in the older generation that needs removal."

2021 MEETING (00:43:04)

WB: "We've always known that the dream business is the one that takes very little capital and that grows a lot. Apple, Google, Microsoft, and Facebook are terrific examples of that. Apple has $37 billion in property, plant, and equipment, while Berkshire has $170 billion—and they're going to make a lot more money than we do. It's a much better business than we have, and the same is true for Microsoft and Google. We found this out with See's Candies in 1972. See's just doesn't require that much capital. It has a couple of manufacturing plants, but it doesn't have big inventories, except seasonally, or a lot of receivables. Those are the best kind of businesses, but they command the best prices too. And there aren't that many of them, and they don't always stay that way. So, we're looking for them all the time.

"We've got a few that are pretty darn good, but we don't have anything as large as the big tech guys. But that's what everybody is looking for, that's what capitalism is about: getting a return on capital. And the way you get it is having something that doesn't take too much capital. If you have to really put out tons of capital, like in the utility business, it's not a super high-return business. You get a return on that capital, but you don't get a fabulous return. You don't get Google-like returns or anything remotely close to it."

INVESTING IN TELECOM COMPANIES

2003 MEETING (03:22:07)

WB: "I don't have the faintest idea how to evaluate telecommunications companies. That doesn't mean I don't understand what they do at all. I probably understand a little bit of what they do. But in terms of figuring out the future economics, what this player or that player is going to look like five to ten years down the road, I simply don't know. It looks like the people who thought they knew three or four years ago didn't know either, I might add. Charlie, what do you know?"

CM: "A little less than you do."

WB: "Pull out a name, BellSouth, Verizon—I have no idea how that all comes together five to ten years from now. I know people are going to be chewing Wrigley's chewing gum or eating Hershey bars five, ten, fifteen or twenty years from now. They're going to be using Gillette blades, they'll be drinking Coca-Cola. And I have some idea what the profitability of each one of those will be over time and all of that. I don't have any idea how telecommunications shakes out, and I wouldn't believe anybody in the business who told me they knew because what would they have been telling me five years ago?

"It's just a game I don't understand. There are all kinds of things I don't understand. I don't know what cocoa beans are going to do next year; it'd be a lot easier if I did, I could just make all my money on cocoa beans and it would be much simpler than trying to run a whole bunch of businesses out of Berkshire. But I don't worry about what I don't know. I worry about being sure about what I do know. And telecommunications doesn't fall in that group."

DIFFICULT PREDICTIONS

1998 MEETING (00:08:29)

CM: "I would say that if our predictions have been a little better than other people's, it's because we've tried to make fewer of them."

WB: "This is not like Olympic diving where they have a degree of difficulty factor, where if you can do some very difficult dive, the payoff is greater than some very simple dive. That's not true in investments. You get paid just as well for the simplest dive, as long as you execute it all right ... We look for one-foot bars to step over rather than seven-foot or eight-foot bars to try and set some record by jumping over. You get paid just as well for the one-foot bars."

MOATS AND SUSTAINABLE COMPETITIVE ADVANTAGES

1995 MEETING (01:51:03)

WB: "We're trying to find a business with a wide and long-lasting moat around it, protecting a terrific economic castle with an honest lord in charge of the castle. In essence, that's what business is all about ... We're trying to find a business that, for one reason or another, has this moat around it—it can be because it's the low-cost producer in some area, it can be because it has a natural franchise because of surface capabilities, it can be because of its position in the consumers' mind, it can be because of a technological advantage, or any kind of reason at all.

"All moats are subject to attack in a capitalistic system; if you've got a big castle in there, people are going to be trying to figure out how to get to it. And most moats aren't worth a damn in capitalism, that's the nature of it, and that's a constructive thing. We are trying to figure out why is that castle still standing, and what's going to keep it standing or cause it not to be standing five, ten, twenty years from now? What are the key factors? How permanent are they? How much do they depend on the genius of the lord in the castle? And then if we feel good about the moat, we try to figure out whether the lord is going to try to take it all for himself, whether he's likely to do something stupid with the proceeds, and so on. That's the way we look at businesses."

CM: "He wants it translated into the ordinary terms of economics. The honest lord is low agency cost. And the microeconomic business advantages are, by and large, advantages of scale—scale of market dominance, which can be a retailer that just has huge advantages in terms of buying cheaper and enjoying higher sales per square foot. By and large, you're talking economies of scale. You can have scale of intelligence, you can have a lord with enough extra intelligence that he has a big advantage. By and large, you're talking scale advantages and low agency costs."

WB: "Charlie and I try to distinguish between businesses where you have to be smart once and businesses where you have to stay smart. Retailing is a business where you have to stay smart. You're under attack all of the time. If you're doing something successful, people are in your store the next day trying to figure out what it is about your success that they can transplant and maybe add a little something to in their own situation. You can't coast in retailing.

"There are other businesses where you only have to be smart once, at least for a very long time. There was once a southern publisher who was doing very well with his newspaper and someone asked him the secret of his success; he said monopoly and nepotism. He wasn't so dumb, he didn't have any illusions about himself. If you had a big network of television affiliate stations thirty years ago—although there's still a major difference between good and bad management—you could've been a terrible manager and made a fortune, basically. The one decision, to own the network TV affiliate, overcame almost any deficiency that existed from that point forward. That would not be true if you were the first one to come up with some concept in retailing. You would have to be out there defending it every day. Ideally, you want terrific management at a terrific business. That's what we look for. If you have to choose between the two, get the terrific business."

1999 MEETING (04:12:34)

WB: "There's no formula for precisely assessing the moat, that says its twenty-eight feet wide and sixteen feet deep, or anything of the sort. You have to understand the businesses. And that's what drives academics crazy, because they know how to calculate standard deviations and all kinds of things, but that doesn't tell them anything. What really tells you something is if you know how to figure out how wide the moat is and whether it's likely to widen further or shrink on you over time."

2000 MEETING (00:40:23)

WB: "We think of business risk in terms of what can happen five, ten, fifteen years from now that will destroy, modify, or reduce the economic strengths that we perceive currently exist in a business. In some businesses, that's impossible to figure—or at least it's impossible for us to figure—and we don't even think about it then. We are enormously risk averse. We are not risk adverse in terms of losing $1 billion if there were an earthquake in California today. That doesn't bother us as long as the math is in our favor. But in terms of doing a group of transactions like that, we are very risk averse. In other words, we want to think that we've got a mathematical edge in every transaction. And we'll do enough transactions over a lifetime so that, no matter what the result of any single one, the group expectancy gets almost to certainty.

"When we look at businesses, we try to think of what can go wrong with them. We look for businesses that are good businesses now, and we think about what can go wrong with them. If we can think of a lot that can go wrong, we just forget it. We are not in the business of assuming a lot of risk in businesses. That doesn't mean we don't do it inadvertently and make mistakes, because we do. But we don't intentionally, willingly, or voluntarily go into situations where we perceive really significant risk that the business is going to change in a major way.

"Every business that we look at we think of as an economic castle, and castles are subject to marauders. In capitalism, any castle you have—in razor blades, soft drinks, whatever—millions of people are out there with capital thinking about ways to take your castle away from you, and appropriate it for their own use. And then the question is, what kind of a moat do you have around the castle that protects it? See's Candies has a wonderful moat around its castle. Chuck Huggins has taken that moat, which he took charge of in 1972, and has widened it every year. He throws crocodiles, sharks, and piranhas in the moat, and it gets harder and harder for people to swim across and attack the castle, so they don't do it. ... Forrest Mars Sr. tried with [chocolatier] Ethel M about twenty years ago; I hate to think of how much money it cost him to try that, and he was a very experienced businessman.

"We think in terms of that moat and the ability to keep its width and its impossibility of being crossed as the primary criterion of a great business. And to our managers, we say we want the moat widened every year. That does not necessarily mean the profit is more this year than last year, because it won't be sometimes. But if the moat is widened every year, the business will do very well. When we see a moat that's tenuous in any way, it's just too risky. We don't know how to evaluate that, and therefore we leave it alone. We think virtually all of our businesses have pretty darn good moats, and we think our managers are widening them."

BETTING ON INDUSTRY GROWTH

1999 MEETING (01:12:39)

WB: "There's a lot of difference between making money and spotting a wonderful industry. The two most important industries in the first half of the 20th century in the U.S. and in the world, probably, were the auto industry and the airplane industry. You had these two discoveries essentially in the first decade of the century. And if you'd foreseen, in 1905 or thereabouts, what the auto and the airplane would do to the world, you might have thought that it was a great way to get rich. But very, very few people got rich by riding the back of the auto industry. And probably even fewer got rich by participating in the airline industry over that time. Millions of people are flying around every day, but the number of people who've made money carrying them around is very limited. The capital that has been lost in that business, the bankruptcies—it's been a terrible business but a marvelous industry. So you do not necessarily want to equate the prospects of growth for an industry with the prospects for growth in your net worth by participating in it."

PART NINE:
Mr. Market

"We don't think of stocks as little items that wiggle around in the newspaper and that have charts attached to them; we think of them as parts of businesses."

"Investment is about valuing businesses. That is all there is to it; you sit around and you try to figure out what a business is worth, and if it's selling below that figure, you buy it."

"If you're going to live a long time, you have to keep learning. What you formerly knew is never enough. If you don't learn to constantly revise your earlier conclusions and get better, you're like a one-legged man in an ass-kicking contest."

INTRODUCTION

ONE OF THE ADVANTAGES OF INVESTING IN PUBLICLY TRADED companies is liquidity and low trading costs. Unfortunately, those same features (which have been taken up to new levels in recent decades with the rise of online brokerage accounts) enable market participants to disregard Benjamin Graham's maxim: "Investment is most intelligent when it is most businesslike".

Maintaining a long-term perspective in the face of daily market trading can be difficult. It requires an ability to react calmly in response to the vagaries presented by Mr. Market. To do so, one must have a clarity of purpose (a well-defined investment philosophy and opportunity set), as well as an underlying rationale for their decisions (investment thesis). Otherwise, trouble looms. To quote Munger, "The fretful disposition is an enemy of long-term performance."

In this section, Buffett and Munger highlight why temperament is critical to long-term investment success, not just IQ points. As Buffett explains, if an investor can learn to live with Mr. Market's mood swings, to recognize that he is there to serve you and not to advise you, that investor is well on his or her way to a more effective investment approach: "All you have to do is occasionally oblige him when he offers to buy or sell from you at the same price on any given day and on any given security."

SUBJECTS AND MEETINGS FEATURED

MR. MARKET

2012 MEETING (01:27:03)

WARREN BUFFETT: "We've run Berkshire now for forty-seven years. There have been four or five times when we've thought it was significantly undervalued. We saw the price get cut roughly in half at least four times, and in fairly short periods of time. I would say this: If you run any business for a long period of time, there are going to be times when it's overvalued and times when it's undervalued.

"Tom Murphy ran one of the most successful companies the world has ever seen in Capital Cities, and in the early 1970s his stock was selling for about a third of what you could have sold the properties for. Berkshire, back in 2000 or 2001—when I wrote in the annual report that we were also going to repurchase shares—was selling at what I thought was a very low price. The beauty of stocks is they do sell at silly prices from time to time. That's how Charlie and I have gotten rich. Ben Graham writes about it in chapter eight of *The Intelligent Investor*, it says that in the market, you're going to have a partner named 'Mr. Market', and the beauty of him as your partner is that he's kind of a psychotic drunk; he will do very weird things over time, and your job is to remember that he's there to serve you and not to advise you. And if you can keep that mental state, then on all those thousands of prices that Mr. Market is offering you every day on every major business in the world practically, he is making lots of mistakes and he makes them for all kinds of weird reasons. All you have to do is occasionally oblige him when he offers to either buy or sell from you at the same price on any given day and on any given security.

"It's built into the system that stocks get mispriced, and Berkshire has been no exception to that ... The important thing is that you make your decisions based on what you think the business is worth. If you make your buy and sell decisions based on what you think a business is worth, and you stick with businesses that you've got good reason to think you can value, you simply have to do well in stocks. The stock market is the most obliging, money-making place in the world because you don't have to do anything. You sit there with thousands of businesses being priced at the same price for the buyer and the seller, it changes every day, and you've got lots of information about most of those businesses, and you don't have to do anything. Compare that to any other investment alternative. You can't do that with farms; if you own a farm and the guy has the farm next to you and you'd like to buy it, he's not going to name a price every day at which he'll buy your farm or sell you his farm. But you can do that with Berkshire Hathaway or IBM. It's a marvelous game. The rules are stacked in your favor if you don't turn those rules upside down and start behaving like the drunken psychotic instead of the guy that's there to take advantage of it."

CHARLIE MUNGER: "What's interesting about this place is I think we've had a lot more fun and we got rich enough so we could buy businesses and stocks to hold instead of to resell. It's an enormously more constructive life. So, as fast as you can work yourself into our position, the better off you'll be."

WB: "You should be very encouraged by the fact he's only eighty-eight and I'm only eighty-one. Just think, it may take you a little while."

THE MARKET

1999 MEETING (00:11:03)

WB: "Charlie and I don't think about the market ... We look at individual businesses. We don't think of stocks as little items that wiggle around in the newspaper and that have charts attached to them; we think of them as parts of businesses. And it is true that, currently, we have great trouble finding businesses that we both like and where we like the management and find them at an attractive price. We do not find bargains in this market among the larger companies that are in our universe. That is not a stock market forecast in any way, shape, or form. We have no idea whether the market is going to go up today, next week, next month, or next year. We do know that we will only buy things that we think make sense, in terms of the value that we receive for Berkshire. And when we can't find things, the money piles up. When we do find things, we pile it in. But I know of no one who has been successful and really made a lot of money predicting the actions of the market itself. I know a lot of people who have done well picking businesses and buying them at sensible prices. And that's what we're hoping to do."

2020 MEETING (02:11:20)

WB: "I'm not recommending that people buy stocks today, tomorrow, next week, or next month. It all depends on your circumstances. You shouldn't buy stocks unless you expect, in my view, to hold them for a very extended period, and you are prepared financially and psychologically to hold them the same way you would hold a farm and never look at a quote—you don't need to pay attention to it. You're not going to pick the bottom and nobody else can pick it for you. You've got to be prepared when you buy a stock to have it be down 50% or more and be okay with it, as long as you're comfortable with the business.

"There have been three times in Berkshire's history when the price of Berkshire stock went down 50%. If you held it on borrowed money, you could have been cleaned out. There wasn't anything wrong with Berkshire when those three times occurred. But if you're going to look at the price of the stock and think that you have to act because it's doing this or that or somebody else asks you, 'How can you stay with that when something else is going up?' … You've got to be in the right psychological position. And frankly some people are more subject to fear than others. It's like the virus [Covid-19]. It strikes some people with much greater ferocity than others.

"Fear is something I really never felt financially, and I don't think Charlie's felt it either. Some people can handle it. If you can't handle it psychologically, then you really shouldn't own stocks because you're going to buy and sell at the wrong time. And you should not count on somebody else telling you. You should do something you understand yourself. If you don't understand it yourself, you're going to be affected by the next person you talk to. You should be in a position to hold. I don't know whether today is a great day to buy stocks. I know it will work out over twenty to thirty years. I don't know if it will work over two years."

MARKET EFFICIENCY

1999 MEETING (00:52:14)

CM: "What we did forty years ago was in some respects simpler than what you're going to have to do. We had it very easy compared to you … It's harder now, you have to know more. Just sifting through the manuals until you find something at two times earnings, that won't work for you."

WB: "It'll work—but you won't find any."

1999 MEETING (03:27:01)

WB: "To me, it's almost self-evident if you've been around markets for any length of time, that the market is generally fairly efficient. It's fairly efficient at pricing between asset classes and it's fairly efficient in terms of evaluating specific businesses. But being fairly efficient does not suffice to support an efficient market theory approach to investing or to all of the offshoots that have come off that in the academic world. If you'd believed in efficient market theory, and been taught that and adopted it for your own twenty years ago—it probably hit its peak then—it would have been a terrible, terrible mistake; it would have been like learning the earth is flat … It became terribly popular in the academic world. It almost became a required belief in order to hold a position. It was what was taught in all the advanced courses. And a mathematical theory that involved other investment questions was built around it, so if you went to the center of it and destroyed that part of it, it really meant that people who'd spent years and years and years getting PhDs found their whole world crashing around them.

"It's been discredited in a fairly significant way over the last decade or two. You don't hear people talking the same way about it as you did fifteen or twenty years ago. But the market generally is fairly efficient in most ways. It is hard to find securities that are inefficiently priced ... I think the high priests of efficient market theory are probably not in the same demand for speaking engagements and seminars as they were twenty years ago. It's hard to dislodge a belief that becomes the dogma of a finance department. It's challenging, at age thirty or forty, to go back and say, 'What I've learned up to this point, and what I've been teaching students and all of that, is silly.' That doesn't come easy to people."

CM: "Max Planck, the great physicist, said in physics, the old guard really didn't accept new ideas. The new ideas prevail in due course because the old guard fades away, clinging to the asininities of the past. And that's what's happened to the hard-form efficient market theorists. They're an embarrassment to the scene and they will soon be gone. People who think the market is roughly efficient, of course, are absolutely correct and that will stay with us for the long pull."

WB: "Thinking it's roughly efficient, though, does nothing for academia. You can't build anything around it. What people want are elegant theories ... Investment is about valuing businesses. That is all there is to it; you sit around and you try to figure out what a business is worth, and if it's selling below that figure, you buy it. You can't find a course virtually anywhere in the country on how to value businesses. You can find all kinds of courses on how to compute beta or whatever it may be because that's something the instructor knows how to do, but he doesn't know how to value a business. So, the important subject doesn't get taught. It's tough to teach.

"I think Ben Graham did a good job of teaching it at Columbia, and I was very fortunate to run into him many decades ago. But the average PhD in finance, if you ask him to value a business, he's got a problem. And if he can't value it, I don't know how he can invest in it, so therefore, it's much easier to take up efficient market theory and say it doesn't make any difference because everybody knows everything about it, anyway. And there's no sense in trying to think about valuing businesses; if the market's efficient, it's valued them all perfectly. I never knew what you'd talk about on the second day in that course. You walk in and say, 'Everything's valued perfectly, class dismissed.' It puzzles me. But I encourage you to look for the inefficiently priced. Berkshire, incidentally, was inefficiently priced for a long time. If you asked an academic how to value it, they wouldn't have known what to look at exactly."

2018 MEETING (04:24:52)

WB: "We're not anti-business school at all. We do think that the priesthood, say, thirty or forty years ago, in terms of efficient market theory and everything, strayed pretty far from the reality of investing ... What we do is not a complicated business. It's got to be a disciplined business, but it does not require a super IQ. There are a few fundamentals that are incredibly important, and you do have to understand accounting. And it helps to get out and talk to consumers, start thinking like a consumer in many ways, all of that. But it just doesn't require advanced learning.

"I don't know whether I would have done better or worse if I'd just quit after high school, and read the books I read and all of that. I think that if you run into a few great teachers, and they really change the way you see the world to some degree, you're lucky. You can find them in academia and in ordinary life. I've been extraordinarily lucky in having great teachers, including Charlie. He's been a wonderful teacher. Any place you can find somebody who gives you insights into things you didn't understand before, maybe makes you a better person than you would have been before, that's very lucky, and you want to make the most of it. Whether in academia or the rest of your life, make the most of it."

CM: "When you found Ben Graham he was unconventional, and he was very smart. And, of course, that was very attractive to you. And then when you found out it worked and you could make a lot of money while you're sitting on your ass, of course you were an instant convert. But the world changed.

"Before he died, Ben Graham recognized that the exact way he sought undervalued companies wouldn't necessarily work for all times under all conditions. And that's certainly the way it worked for us. We gradually morphed into trying to buy the better companies when they were underpriced, instead of the lousy companies when they were underpriced. And, of course, that worked pretty well for us. Ben Graham outlived the game that he personally played most of the time. He lived to see most of it fade away. Just to find some company that's selling for one third of its working capital, and figure out it could easily be liquidated and distribute $3 for every $1 of market price—lots of luck if you can find those in the present market. And if you can find them, they're so small that Berkshire wouldn't find them of any use anyway. So we've had to learn a different game. And that's a lesson for all the young people in the room. If you're going to live a long time, you have to keep learning. What you formerly knew is never enough. If you don't learn to constantly revise your earlier conclusions and get better, you're like a one-legged man in an ass-kicking contest."

WB: "If anybody has suggestions for another metaphor, send them to me. Graham, incidentally, was not scalable. You could not do it with really big money. When I worked for Graham-Newman [investment partnership], Graham was the dean of all analysts. He was an intellect above all others around that time. But the investment fund was $6 million, and the partnership that worked in tandem with the investment company also had about $6 million, so we had $12 million that we were working with. You can make adjustments for inflation and everything, but it was just a tiny amount. It wasn't really scalable. And the truth is that Graham didn't care, because he really wasn't interested in making a lot of money for himself. He had no reason to want to find something that could go on and on, become larger and larger. So the utility of chapter eight in *The Intelligent Investor*, in terms of looking at stocks as a business, is of enormous value. The utility of chapter twenty, about the margin of safety, is of enormous value. But it's not complicated stuff."

CM: "I finally figured out why the teachers of corporate finance often teach a lot of stuff that's wrong. When I had some eye troubles early in life, I consulted a very famous eye doctor. And I realized his place of business was doing a totally obsolete cataract operation. They were still cutting with a knife after better procedures had been invented. I said, 'Why are you in a great medical school performing absolute obsolete operations?' And he said, 'Charlie, it's such a wonderful operation to teach.' That's what happens in corporate finance. They get these formulas, and it's a fine teaching experience. You give them a formula, you present the problem, they use the formula. You get a real feeling of worthwhile activity. There's only one trouble: It's all balderdash."

WB: "Whenever you hear a theory described as elegant, watch out."

THE NATURE OF MARKETS

2000 MEETING (01:58:07)

WB: "It's just extraordinary what happens in markets over time. It gets sorted out eventually, but we have seen companies sell for tens of billions of dollars that are worthless. And at times, we have seen companies—not hard to find and with perfectly decent people running them—that sold for literally 20–25% of what they were worth. We have seen and will continue to see everything. It's just the nature of markets. They produce wild, wild things over time.

"The trick is, occasionally, to take advantage of one of those wild things and not to get carried away when other wild things happen, because the wild things create their own truth for a while. That's the reason they're happening, and people are getting pleasant experiences and all that. You'll see everything if you're around markets for a reasonable period of time ... We do find a lot of cases today where we think valuations on the high side are just unbelievable. We have been in periods in the past where we felt almost everything was being given away, too. You'll get those extremes. Most of the time the market's in a position where there's a little of both, but every now and then it gets into a position where there's a lot of one or the other."

CM: "I do think that the present time is a very unusual period. It's hard to think of a time when residential real estate, common stocks, and so on, rose so rapidly in price and there was so much easy money floating around. This is a very unusual period."

WB: "What's fascinating is you can have a business selling for $10 billion where the business itself could not have borrowed $100 million [if it was private] ... But the owners of that business, because it's public, can borrow many billions of dollars on their little pieces of paper, because they have this market valuation. If it's a private business, the company itself couldn't borrow one-twentieth or so of what individuals could borrow. That's happened, to a degree, before. But this has probably been as extreme as anything that's happened probably, including the 1920s. That doesn't mean there's a parallel to it, but it's been pretty extreme."

CM: "I think it's probably the most extreme thing that has happened in modern capitalism. In my lifetime, I would say the 1930s created the worst recession in the English-speaking world in 600 years. And it was very extreme. You could buy an 'all-you-can-eat' meal in Omaha through the 1930s for a quarter from Henderson's Cafeteria. And now we're seeing the other face of what capitalism can do. This is almost as extreme as the 1930s were but in a different direction."

WB: "That does not make it easy to predict the outcome. It says to us there are certain things we want to stay away from. Basically, it's precautionary to us. It does not spell opportunity. In the last year, the ability to monetize shareholder ignorance has never been exceeded, I think."

2007 MEETING (01:33:40)

WB: "Markets will do crazy things over time. When Charlie and I were at Salomon, they'd always talk about five- or six-sigma events—and that's fine if you're talking about flipping coins, but it doesn't mean anything when human behavior is involved. Very intelligent people do things that are totally irrational, and they do them en masse. You saw it in 1998, you saw it in 2002, and you'll see it again. And it's more likely to happen when you have people trying to beat markets day by day. I think it's a fool's game, but it may be what's required to attract money."

CM: "When people talk about sigmas, in terms of disaster potentialities in markets, they're all crazy. They got the idea that bad results in markets would be predicted by Gaussian distributions. And the way they decided on that outcome was it made everything so easy to compute. They don't follow Gaussian distributions. You have to believe in the tooth fairy to believe that."

PART TEN:
Economics and Investing

"It's man's nature to take the progress as a right; not something to be earned or strived for, but something that should automatically just flow in over the transom. That attitude is poison. It doesn't do anybody any good."

"Anytime we get a chance to do something that makes sense, we do it. And if it makes even more sense the next day, and if we've got money, we may do more."

"I don't know what the next big thing will be. I do know there will be a next big thing."

"We're not predicting the currents that will come, just how some things will swim in the currents, whatever they are."

"Interest rates basically are to the value of assets what gravity is to matter."

"In a world where you sometimes have to amputate a limb to stay alive, you can't expect that every business can stay exactly as it is."

INTRODUCTION

This section of the book effectively consists of two parts: the first is Buffett and Munger explaining why they do not put much weight on macroeconomic forecasts or market timing in their investment decisions; the second is Buffett and Munger explaining why these topics, particularly macroeconomic factors like inflation and interest rates, are still relevant to intelligently thinking about the long-term ownership of businesses. That apparent inconsistency reflects a nuanced view on weighing various factors/predictions when making investment decision. As Munger put it, "We're not predicting the currents that will come, just how some things will swim in the currents, whatever they are." (I discussed this topic in more detail at TSOH Investment Research—see "Always Looking For Context".)

SUBJECTS AND MEETINGS FEATURED

CAPITALISM

2020 MEETING (04:21:35)

WARREN BUFFETT: "The market system works wonders, but it's also brutal if left entirely to itself. We wouldn't be the country we are if the market system hadn't been allowed to function. And, to some extent, you can say that other countries around the world that have improved their way of life dramatically have copied us.

"The market system is marvelous in many respects, but it needs government. It is creative destruction—but for the ones who are destroyed, it can be a very brutal game; I do not want to come up with anything different than capitalism, but I certainly do not want unfettered capitalism. We capitalists ... should give a lot of thought to what would happen if we all drew straws again for particular market-based skills. Somewhere way back, somebody invented television. And then they invented cable, then they invented pay systems and all of that. So a baseball player who could bat .406 in 1941 was worth $20,000 a year. Now a marginal big leaguer will make vastly greater sums because, in effect, the stadium size was increased from 40,000 or 50,000 people to the whole country, and the market system capitalism took over. It's very uneven. Similarly, I think that [baseball player] Ted Williams was worth a whole lot more money than I ever should make. But the market system can work toward a winner-takes-all type situation.

"We don't want to discourage people from working hard and thinking—but that alone doesn't do it. There's a lot of randomness in the capital system, including inherited wealth. I think we can keep the best parts of a market system and capitalism while doing a better job of making sure that everybody participates in the prosperity that it produces."

2023 MEETING (04:57:15)

WB: "Society benefits and some people get killed [as a result of manufacturing moving overseas]. One way or another, a rich society should take care [of the people who are negatively impacted]. When we took over our textile operation in 1964, half of our workers only spoke Portuguese. They weren't getting great wages at all, but now you could do it in the South, and we were going to go out of business. It wasn't the fault of the worker in any way, shape, or form, and it wasn't our fault. We kept trying to compete ... But then it moved offshore. Net, the country is better off because of it, but at these places a lot of people really can't do something else. You can't talk about retraining somebody who's fifty-five and only speaks Portuguese, to really tell them they're going to have a great future in New Bedford, Massachusetts. You don't want to be glib about it, and we can afford to take care of those people. We've got some systems that work reasonably well, but ... these are not easy problems to solve.

"I would say, by and large, we want the whole world to prosper. We don't want the United States to be a country of extraordinary prosperity and the rest of the world starving. It isn't going to work, and it particularly is not going to work in a nuclear world. ... And, of course, the work week in the United States in my lifetime has dropped dramatically. And people still feel busy.

"The world just keeps looking at everything moving up as becoming a base that leaves them somewhat dissatisfied. With our prosperity, we can do a lot of things that we couldn't do in 1930, including taking care of people who got displaced by the fact that somebody else can do that work and improve their lot in life. We need to be sure we have the best system, which takes care of the people who get displaced by that. We will make a lot of mistakes along the way, but we have got to keep moving in that direction."

CHARLIE MUNGER: "Adam Smith was right: Free market capitalism, with private property and free trade and all that, automatically creates GDP growth that helps everybody, including the people at the bottom. It helps everybody a lot. But inherent in that process, there's a lot of pain ... Nobody has figured out how to take all the pain out of it. We do have government safety nets that take some of the pain out of it, and we make those safety nets a little bigger as time goes by. But apart from that, if you try and take all the pain out of it, you will also take all of the gains out of it. You won't have growing GDP per capita. You'll have an economy like Russia's, characterized by the saying, 'They pretend to pay us, and we pretend to work.'"

WB: "The other systems haven't worked better, but capitalism also produces more and more disparities in wealth ... It is the job of government to keep the best aspects of capitalism, while not causing people that only speak Portuguese to suffer in the process. The two aren't compatible politically over time. We stumbled along making progress on things like social security and all that, and we are a lot better off now than when I was born."

CM: "Net, the United States has done a very good job on this tension between capitalistic growth and growing the social safety net. We can be pretty proud of our country looking backwards."

WB: "We have 25% of the world's GDP, despite starting with 0.5% of the global population, in a few centuries. It's a miracle. It wasn't because we were smarter. There must be something to the system ... There's been progress, but it's mankind's nature to see the things wrong with it."

CM: "It's man's nature to take the progress as a right; not something to be earned or strived for, but something that should automatically just flow in over the transom. That attitude is poison. It doesn't do anybody any good."

GLOBAL DIVERSIFICATION

1994 MEETING (01:34:59)

WB: "All we want to be in is businesses we understand, run by people we like, and priced attractively compared to future prospects. There is no specific desire to be in the rest of the world or to avoid it. It's not a big factor. There may be more chances for growth in some countries; roughly 80% of Coca-Cola and Guinness's earnings will come from outside the U.S., but Guinness is domiciled outside the U.S., whereas Coca-Cola is domiciled here.

"Certainly, in many cases, there are markets outside the U.S. that have way better prospects for growth than the U.S. would have, but they probably have some other risks to them that the U.S. may not have. We like the international prospects, obviously, of a company like Coke ... On a look-through basis, we might get something like $150 million of earnings, indirectly, for Berkshire's interest from the rest of the world just through Coca-Cola this year. But we don't think in terms of, 'I like this region so I want to be there' ... Coke is expanding in China; I forget what they showed last year, maybe 38% growth in case volumes. It's nice to have markets like that which are relatively untapped."

MARKET TIMING

1994 MEETING (01:40:20)

WB: "You may have trouble believing this, but Charlie and I never have an opinion about the market, because it wouldn't be any good and it might interfere with the opinions we have that are good. If we're right about a business, and we think it's attractive, it would be very foolish for us to not take action because we thought something about what the market was going to do or anything of that sort. Because we just don't know. And to give up something that you do know and that is profitable for something that you don't know and won't know, it just doesn't make any sense to us. It doesn't really make any difference to us.

"I bought my first stock in April of 1942 when I was eleven. The prospects for World War II didn't look so good at that time; the U.S. was not doing well in the Pacific. I'm not sure I calculated that into my purchase of my three shares, but just think of all the things that have happened since then. Atomic weapons, major wars, presidents resigning, massive inflation at certain times, all kinds of things. To give up what you can do well at because of guesses about what's going to happen in some macro way just doesn't make any sense to us.

"The best thing that can happen from Berkshire's standpoint—we don't wish this on anybody—is, over time, to have markets that go down a tremendous amount. We are going to be buyers of things over time. And if you're going to be buyers of groceries over time, you like grocery prices to go down. If you're going to be buying cars over time, you like car prices to go down. We buy businesses. We buy pieces of businesses, stocks. And we're going to be much better off if we can buy those things at an attractive price than if we can't. So, we don't have any fear at all. What we fear is an irrational bull market that's sustained for some long period of time.

"You, as shareholders of Berkshire, unless you own your shares on borrowed money or are going to sell them in a very short period of time, are better off if stocks get cheaper, because it means that we can do more intelligent things on your behalf than would be the case otherwise. But we wouldn't care what anybody thought about it, most of all ourselves."

CM: "If you're agnostic about those macro factors and therefore devote all your time to thinking about the individual businesses and the individual opportunities, it's just a way more efficient way to behave, at least with our particular talents and lack thereof."

WB: "If you're right about the businesses, you'll end up doing fine. We don't think about when something will happen; we think about what will happen. It's not so difficult to figure out what will happen. It's impossible, in our view, to figure out when it will happen. So, we focus on what will happen. In 1890 or thereabouts, the whole Coca-Cola Company sold for $2,000. It's got a market value now of about $50 billion. Somebody could've said to the fellow who was buying this in 1890, 'You're going to have a couple of great world wars, you'll have the panic of 1907, all these things will happen—wouldn't it be a better idea to wait?' We can't afford that mistake."

2004 MEETING (04:10:46)

WB: "At any given point in history, including when stocks were their cheapest, you could find an impressive number of negative factors. You could've sat down in 1974 when stocks were screaming bargains, and you could've written down all kinds of things that would've caused you to say the future is going to be terrible … We really don't pay any attention to that sort of thing. You might say our underlying premise—and I think it's a pretty sound underlying premise—is that this country will do very well, and in particular, it will do well for business. Business has done very well; the Dow went from 66 to 10,000-plus in the one hundred years of the 20th century. We had two world wars, nuclear bombs, flu epidemics, you name it. There are always problems in the future, there are always opportunities in the future, and in this country the opportunities have won out over the problems over time. I think they will continue to do so.

"I can't remember any discussions Charlie and I have ever had, going back to 1959, where we ... passed on buying a business because of external conditions. It won't be the American economy, in my view, that does in investors over a five, ten or twenty-year period, it will be the investors themselves ... American business, really, has never let investors down as a group, but investors have done themselves in quite frequently."

2009 MEETING (04:19:48)

WB: "Stocks got much cheaper in 1974 than they are now. But you were also facing a different interest rate scenario, so you could say they really weren't that much cheaper. You could buy very good companies at four times earnings or thereabouts with good prospects, but interest rates were far higher then. That was the best period I've ever seen for buying common equities.

"The cheaper things get, the better I like buying them. If I was buying hamburgers at McDonald's for X, and they reduced the price to 90% of X tomorrow, I'm happy. I don't think about what I paid yesterday; I think I'm going to be buying hamburgers the rest of my life. The cheaper they get, the better I like it. I'm going to be buying investments the rest of my life. And I would much rather pay half of X than X. The fact that I paid X yesterday doesn't bother me, as long as I know the values in the business. I like lower prices.

"I realize that that is not the way all of you feel when you wake up in the morning and look at quotes. But it just makes sense that, when things are on sale, you should be more excited about buying them than otherwise. When I wrote that article in *The New York Times* ['Buy American. I Am.', October 16, 2008], I did not predict what stocks were going to do [in the short term], because I never know what they're going to do. But I do know when you're starting to get a lot for your money, and that's when I believe in buying."

CM: "Well, if stocks go off 40% on average, they're obviously closer to an attractive price than they were before. And, of course, short-term interest rates have gone down a lot recently. It's nothing like 1973–1974. I knew when that happened that that was my time and my only time. I knew I was never going to get another trip to the buy counter like that one. Unfortunately, I had practically no money available at that time—and that's why those times occur. If I were you, I wouldn't wait for 1973–1974."

WB: "No, we don't try to pick bottoms. We don't have an opinion about where the stock market's going to go tomorrow, next week, or next month. To sit around and not do something that's sensible because you think there will be something even more attractive tomorrow, that's just not our approach. Anytime we get a chance to do something that makes sense, we do it. And if it makes even more sense the next day, and if we've got money, we may do more. Picking bottoms is basically not our game; pricing is our game, and that's not so difficult. Picking bottoms is probably impossible, but when you start getting a lot for your money, you buy. And as I say, after I wrote that *New York Times* op-ed, stocks did get cheaper. The corporate bond market got very, very, very disorganized. And we bought some fairly good-sized pieces of bonds for Berkshire. And I also bought a few little things for myself."

CM: "Warren, by now, don't we have our small life insurance companies pretty well full of desirable debt instruments at 10%?"

WB: "We certainly have got a lot more than we had. We bought some corporate bonds very, very cheaply—at least in my view—a few months back. We had money in life companies that can't be used in certain other areas and for which this was an ideal time to barrel in. Anytime we like to do something, we really like to do it. Our idea is not to tiptoe into anything. We buy them as fast as we can when prices are right."

CM: "Yeah, that bond thing didn't last very long; there were perfectly safe bonds that yielded 9% or more with very fancy call protections. And some of those bonds are up 20% or 25%."

2022 MEETING (01:36:07)

WB: "The interesting thing is, obviously, we haven't the faintest idea what the stock market is going to do when it opens on Monday. We never have. In all our time working together, I don't think Charlie and I have ever made a decision where either one of us said or was thinking we should buy or sell based on what the market is going to do. Or for that matter, on what the economy is going to do. We don't know.

"Sometimes I get some credit for how wonderful it was that we were optimistic in 2008 when everybody was down on stocks. The reality is that I spent a big percentage of our net worth at a very dumb time. We spent about $16 billion, which was a lot more to us then than it is now, in a period of three or four weeks between Wrigley and Goldman Sachs, at a terrible time as it turned out [September/October 2008]. I didn't know whether it was going to be a good time or a bad time, but it was really bad timing in hindsight. If I had any sense of timing I would've waited six months until the lows in March 2009. I totally missed that opportunity. I totally missed March 2020 as well.

"We have not been good at timing, but we've been reasonably good in figuring out when we were getting enough for our money. When we bought anything, we always hoped it would go down for a while so we could buy more. And we also hoped, even after we were done buying, that if it was cheap, then the company would keep buying, taking our interest up. We haven't ever timed anything. We've never figured out insights into the economy. When I was eleven years old, I bought stock; that day, the Dow closed at 99. Now it's 34,000.

"It's amazing how hard a game people make of what is a simple game. But of course, if they told everybody what a simple game it was, 90% of the income of the [financial professionals] would disappear. It's a little too much to expect of human nature that people will explain why they really aren't adding any value to what you can do yourself."

CM: "In the wealth advisory business, it used to be you went to your investment advisor and you would say, 'What should I do to protect myself for the future?' And he would say, 'Why don't you give me $50,000 of your net worth now? That's my contribution to your first year.'

"It's a peculiar business … I would argue that with a lot of the wealth advisory business, people are charging for skill while delivering closet indexation. In other words, nobody can stand being that different from the crowded results there, because they're afraid they'll lose their fees. So, everybody does the same thing. It's mildly ridiculous. The world is mildly ridiculous."

INTEREST RATES

1994 MEETING (00:48:37)

WB: "It's part of the job of the Fed, as Mr. Bill Martin [chairman of the Federal Reserve, 1951–1970] said many years ago, to take away the punchbowl at the party occasionally. That's a very difficult policy to quantify working with markets day by day. And, of course, it's always been the job of the Fed, basically, to lean against the wind. Which, of course, means if the wind changes, you fall flat on your face. But that's another question. I think what [Alan Greenspan] has done has probably been somewhat appropriate. I think he's probably been surprised, a little bit, as to what has happened with long-term rates as he's nudged up short-term rates. I think he was hoping that action, sort of early in the cycle on the short-term rate front, might make people feel more confident about the longer-term rates and therefore that the yield curve would flatten some. I don't know that. And, he may have been a little surprised on that. But it's not an easy job he has. So, I would not second guess him myself. Charlie, how do you feel about him?"

CM: "Fine."

GOLD AND INFLATION

2005 MEETING (01:48:58)

WB: "We're not enthused about gold. People, historically, have felt that gold was a refuge from a currency that was going to decline in value. But so is a barrel of oil, an acre of land, or ownership in Coca-Cola or See's Candies; if the dollar goes down 50%, we will sell See's Candies for double the present price. We'll be getting the same real price for See's Candies. People will work the same number of hours per week in order to buy a two-pound box of the candy. So, we would much prefer some asset that is going to be useful whether the currency is worth what it is today, 10% of what it is today, or whether people are using seashells to transact. Their preferences will translate, in real dollars, into more or less the same economics for us. And we would not trade the ownership of those kind of assets for us for a hunk of yellow metal, which has very little real utility except for people who are looking to flee from the dollar and, in our view, really haven't thought through the consequences of where they should flee."

CM: "If you have the opportunities of Berkshire, averaged out, gold is a dumb investment."

2005 MEETING (03:29:53)

WB: "Gold would be way down on my list as a store of value. I would much prefer owning a hundred acres of land here in Nebraska, or an apartment house, or an index fund. If you go back to 1900, you were talking $20 gold; it went from $20 to $400 over 100 years. The Dow went from 66 to 12,000 in that same period, and paid you dividends during the time you owned it ... In the meantime, if you owned the gold, you paid insurance and perhaps some storage cost. It really isn't a store of value. I'm not arguing for paper money, but if you're worried about paper money—and I think it makes a lot of sense to worry about paper money over long periods of time—gold is just about the last thing I'd want to own under those circumstances. A farm has utility, an apartment has utility, a business will produce earnings. Some businesses will produce them in real terms as they go along. I would rather have the ability to sell people a pound of candy twenty years from now. And if they're dealing in seashells, I'll get an appropriate number of seashells instead of paper money for it. But I don't see gold as a store of value. The truth is it hasn't worked very well; I see no reason why it should work well in the future."

2011 MEETING (01:44:08)

WB: "When we started with Berkshire, a share was worth about 3/4 of an ounce of gold—gold was $20 an ounce, and Berkshire was at $15. So gold, even at $1,500, has a way to go. [At the time, Berkshire Hathaway Class A traded at

~$125,000 per share.] If you take all of the gold in the world and put it into a cube, it would be about sixty-seven feet on each side. That would be about 170,000 metric tons. So, if you owned all the gold in the world, you could get a ladder and climb on top of it, and you could think you're king of the world. You could fondle it, polish it, stare at it—but it isn't going to do anything. All you are doing when you buy that is you're hoping that somebody else, at some point in the future, will pay you more to own something that, again, can't do anything ... Any time you buy an asset that can't produce anything, you're simply betting on whether somebody else will pay more for it in the future ... That's different from assets that you can value based on what they will produce, what they will deliver. You buy a farm because you expect a certain amount of corn, soybeans, cotton, whatever it may be, to come your way every year. And you decide how much you will pay based on how much you think the asset itself will deliver over time. Those are the assets that appeal to me and Charlie."

CM: "I certainly agree with that. Besides, it's somewhat peculiar to buy an asset which will only really go up if the world really goes to hell. It doesn't strike me as an entirely rational thing to do ... There's another class of people who think they can protect themselves by buying paintings of soup cans. I don't recommend that, either."

WB: "In addition to that sixty-seven-foot cube, more gold is produced every year. So you need buyers not only to offset sellers in the natural course of events, but you have to absorb something like $100 billion worth of added items of no utility. It's really interesting. They dig it up out of the ground in South Africa, then they ship it to the Federal Reserve in New York, and they put it back in the ground. If you were watching this from Mars, you might think it was a little peculiar."

2012 MEETING (01:47:57)

WB: "One thing I would bet my life on is that over a fifty-year period, not only will Berkshire do considerably better than gold, but common stocks as a group will do better than gold, and probably farmland will do better than gold. If you own an ounce of gold now and you caress it for the next hundred years, you'll have an ounce of gold a hundred years from now. If you own a hundred acres of farmland, you'll also have a hundred acres of farmland a hundred years from now and you'll have taken the crops for a hundred years and sold them and presumably bought more farmland in the process. It's very hard for an unproductive investment to beat productive investments over any long period of time.

"It's interesting: I can say bonds are no good and Ben Bernanke still smiles at me. But if you say anything negative about gold, it arouses passions with people, which is kind of fascinating, because usually if you thought through something intellectually, it shouldn't really make much difference what people say. The question is whether your facts are right and your reasoning is right. But you run into people who are really excited about gold ... My dad loved gold. But he was tolerant, he could take a discussion of it. I find many people have trouble with it."

CM: "I have never had the slightest interest in owning gold. It's a much better life to work with businesses and people engaged in business. I can't imagine a worse crowd to deal with than a bunch of gold bugs."

FORTUNE 500 RETURN ON EQUITY (ROE)

1994 MEETING (03:45:04)

WB: "The average return on equity in the Fortune 500 has been higher in the last few years ... It's tended to stick between 12% and 13% over time. The return in certain businesses has gotten a big kick because they finally put the health liabilities on the balance sheet, and therefore reduced equity. ... It's leveraged American business, in effect ... I think competitive factors tend to keep pushing that number down somewhat over time. And 12% or 13%, when you think about it, is not bad at all. It's a level, with 7% interest rates, that allows stocks and equity to be worth much more when employed in equity than elsewhere in the world. But if I had to pick a figure for the next ten years, I would pick between 12% and 13%. That doesn't mean I'd be right on it."

CM: "I think all of those published averages overstate what's earned anyway. They're the biggest companies, the winners, the ones whose stock sells at high multiples, so they can issue it to other people for high-earning assets. And many of the low-return people are constantly being dropped out of the figures. Now, you can say that was true in the past, too. But it would be remarkable to me if, on average, American business earned 13% on capital after taxes."

BUSINESS PRODUCTIVITY AND EFFICIENCY

1996 MEETING (02:50:55)

WB: "Every industry is interested in downsizing or becoming more efficient at all times. If the industry is growing, you can achieve efficiency by doing more work, by turning out more output, with the same people. But if you go back 150 years and look at the percentage of people in farming, for example, it has downsized from being a very appreciable percentage of the American workforce to a very small percentage. And that's released people to do other things. So, it's in the interest of society to get as much output as it can per unit of labor input.

"It's very difficult on the individuals involved; it's no fun being a horse when the tractor comes along, or a blacksmith when the car comes along. I don't quarrel with downsizing or efficiencies. I quarrel, sometimes, with how it's done; in certain cases, I do think there's been a lack of empathy or sensitivity …

"You should try to make your businesses more efficient. We hope we're not in businesses that will require us to lay off people over time; we hope that physical output grows and that we become more productive and can keep the same number of people to get greater output … But sometimes industry trends change. At World Book, we have fewer people than we had a year or two ago. We don't have any answer to that. Over time, we got out of the textile business. I wish we didn't have to, but we did not know how to run a textile company in New England and compete effectively. I love avoiding those businesses, and to the extent we can, we will … But it is in the interest of society to do jobs more effectively.

"It's also in the interest of society, it seems to me, to take care in some way of the people who are affected by [creative destruction]. In some cases, it may be retraining. But that doesn't work so well if you're fifty-five years old and you've been working in a textile mill all your life, and all of a sudden the guy who runs the place can't make any money out of selling your output; it's not the fault of the fellow who's been working at the textile mill for thirty years.

"I don't think there is more displacement going on now, as a percentage of the labor force, annually, than there was ten years ago … But it's gotten a lot of attention lately. There could be a backlash to that, in terms of corporate tax rates or a number of things. At Berkshire, we want to do everything as efficiently as we can. A big part of that is not taking on a lot of people that we don't need. A lot of the mistakes that are being corrected now are because businesses got very fat and took on all kinds of people they didn't need. As long as they're very prosperous, no one does much about it. Then, when the time comes, they all of a sudden find out they can get way more output.

"The oil companies are a classic example. The people actually needed to produce, refine, and market oil probably hasn't changed that much. But if you look at employment relative to barrels produced, refined, and marketed, it's gone down dramatically over twenty years. That just means they weren't being run that well twenty years ago; it never should've occurred in the first place. We don't want to take on more people than we need in any business, because we don't want to lay people off, either."

CM: "If you put it in reverse, you'd say, name a business that has been ruined because it was over-downsized. I cannot think of a single one. But if you asked me to name businesses that were half-ruined, or ruined, by bloat, I could rattle off name after name after name. It's gotten fashionable to assume downsizing is wrong. Well, it may have been wrong to let the business get so fat that it eventually had to downsize. If you've got way more people than are needed in a business, I see no social benefit in having people sit around half employed or unemployed."

2004 MEETING (02:12:17)

WB: "As the economic machine of the United States works better and better over time, the main beneficiaries are going to be consumers. If you took the best business manager in the U.S. and you put a clone of that person in charge of each one of the Fortune 500 companies, the profits of the Fortune 500 would not necessarily go up, because there's this competitive nature to capitalism where the improvement you get one day, your competitor gets the next day. And it very much tends to work to the benefit of consumers, but not to increase overall profitability.

"We were in the textile business for a long time, and various new machinery would come along and it would promise to deliver a 40% internal rate of return and get rid of forty-three employees or something. We just did one after another of those, and when we got all through we didn't make any money, because the other guy was doing the same thing. I liken it to everybody at a parade, a huge crowd watching it and somebody stands up on tiptoes and, ten seconds later, everybody in the crowd is up on tiptoes and they're not seeing any better and their legs hurt. Well, that was the textile business. There's an awful lot of self-neutralizing things in capitalism."

2017 MEETING (03:04:52)

WB: "3G Capital [the investment firm that Berkshire partnered with on the Kraft Heinz deal] believe in having a company as productive as possible. The gains in this world, and for the people throughout America, have come through gains in productivity. If there had been no change in productivity, we would be living the same life as people lived in 1776. Now, the 3G people do it very fast. And they're very good at making a business productive with fewer people than operated it before. But we've been doing that in every industry—steel, cars, you name it. And that's why we live as well as we do.

"At Berkshire we prefer to buy companies that are already run efficiently because, frankly, we don't at all enjoy the process of getting more productive. It isn't pleasant. But it is what has enabled the country to progress, and nobody has figured out a way to double people's consumption per capita without, in some way, improving productivity per capita. Whether it's smart overall, if you think you're going to suffer politically because political consequences do hit businesses, I can't answer the question categorically. But I can tell you that they not only focus on productivity and do it in a very intelligent way, but they also focus, to a terrific degree, on product improvement, innovation, all of the other things you want management to focus on. Product improvement and innovation is just as much a part of the 3G playbook as productivity.

"Personally, we bought into a textile business that employed a couple thousand people and went out of business over a period of time, and a department store business that was headed for oblivion. It is not as much fun to be in a business that cuts jobs rather than one that adds jobs. So, Charlie and I would probably forego having Berkshire directly buy businesses where the main benefits would come from increasing productivity by having fewer workers. But I think it's pro-social to think in terms of improving productivity. And I think 3G does a very good job at that."

CM: "I agree. I don't see anything wrong with increasing productivity. On the other hand, there's a lot of counterproductive publicity to doing it. Just because you're right doesn't mean you should always do it."

WB: "I'd agree with that."

2017 MEETING (03:30:30)

WB: "Over time, we fired 2,000 people—some retired and left and all of that—at the textile operation. It didn't work. At Hochschild Kohn's, they eventually closed the department stores because that particular one, and a good many of our competitors in Baltimore, could not make it work. Walmart came along with something, and now Amazon's coming along with something.

"We mentioned CTB, which designs and makes a lot of different farm equipment. The idea behind the farm equipment that CTB develops is that it's more productive than what already is out there, which means fewer people are employed on farms. We had 80% of the American working population on farms a couple of hundred years ago. If nobody had come up with things to make farming more productive, we'd have 80% of people working on farms now to feed our populace. We would be living in a far, far more primitive way. If you look at any industry, they're trying to get more productive. That will continue in America. And it better continue or our kids won't live any better than we do. Our kids will live better than we do, because America does get more productive as it goes along. People do come up with better ways of doing things.

"When Kraft Heinz finds that they can do $27 billion worth of business, and they can do it with fewer people, they're doing what American business has done for a couple hundred years, and it's why we live so well. But they do it very fast. They're more than fair, in terms of severance pay and all of that sort of thing. But they don't want to have two people doing the job that one can do. Frankly, I don't like going through that … I faced that down at Dempster Mill [farm equipment manufacturer] in Beatrice, Nebraska. It really needed change. But change is painful for a lot of people. I would rather spend my days not doing that sort of thing, having had one or two experiences. But I think that it's absolutely essential to America that we become more productive, because the only way we have more consumption per capita is to have more productivity per capita."

CM: "You're absolutely right. We don't want to go back to subsistence farming. I had a week of that when I was young on a western Nebraska farm. I hated it. And I don't miss the elevator operators who used to sit there all day, running the little crank. On the other hand, as you say, it's terribly unpleasant for the people who have to go through it. Why would we want to get into the business of doing that over and over ourselves? We did it in the past when we had to, when the businesses were dying. I don't see any moral fault in 3G at all, but I do see that there's some political reaction that doesn't do anybody any good."

WB: "I think Milton Friedman, probably apocryphally, would talk about a huge construction project in some communist country. They had thousands and thousands of workers with shovels digging away at this major project. Meanwhile they had a few of those big, earth-moving machines behind them that were idle, but could've done the work in one-twentieth of the time of the workers. So, the economists suggested to the local party worker, 'Why not use these machines to get the job done in one-twentieth of the time instead of having all these workers out there with shovels?' And the guy replied, 'Well, yes, but that would put the workers out of work.' And Friedman said, 'Well, then, why don't you give them spoons to do it instead of shovels?'"

2019 MEETING (03:18:39)

WB: "I think in reality we measure up well [on environmental impact], but we don't participate in preparing reports for anybody that asks about it. And we have this idea that even though all shareholders are equal, we sort of prefer individual shareholders. We actually prefer people we know as co-owners. And we don't want to be preparing a lot of reports and asking sixty subsidiaries each to do something, where they'll set up a team, and they'll mail things to headquarters, and then we'll supply them to somebody who, if our stock goes up some, is probably going to sell it anyway.

"We want our managers to do the right things. We give them enormous latitude to do that. And I think that our batting average really is quite good. We talked about having 100% of the electricity we sell in Iowa coming from, essentially, wind generation. Now that doesn't mean that we get to do it twenty-four hours a day. But essentially, we will be creating as much wind energy as all of our customers use in electricity. There's one other electric utility that's roughly our size in Iowa, and they have practically no wind resources. And the wind blows where they exist, too. Partly because we do so well on wind generation, a number of the high-tech companies want to locate in Iowa and get clean energy from us at very low prices. But we're not going to spend the time of the people at Berkshire Hathaway Energy responding to questionnaires or trying to score better with somebody who is working on [environmental impact scores].

"We trust our managers and I think the performance is at least decent. And we keep expenses and needless reporting to a minimum at Berkshire. I can't imagine another company like it: With $500 billion of market capitalization, we do not have a consolidated monthly P&L. We don't need it. We're not going to tie up people and resources doing things we don't need to do just because it's the standard procedure in corporate America. In corporate America, in general, they're very worried about whether somebody's going to upset their apple cart, with activists and everything. So, they want to be very sure that every shareholder is happy on issues like that. And in the end, fortunately, we don't have to worry about that. We don't have to run up a lot of expenses doing things that don't actually let us run the business better."

CM: "I think at Berkshire the environmental stuff is done one level down from us. And I think Greg Abel is just terrific at it. I think we score very well. When it gets to so-called best corporate practices, I think the people who talk about them don't really know what the best practices are. They just know what they think are the best practices. And they determine that based on what will sell, not what will work. So, I like our way of doing things better than theirs, and I hope to God we never follow their best practices."

2019 MEETING (03:44:49)

WB: "If somebody asked that question 200 years ago [about the impact of automation on U.S. employment], and said, 'With the outlook for development of farm machinery, tractors, and combines, meaning 90% of the people on farms were going to lose their job,' it would look terrible, wouldn't it? But our economy, our people, and our system, has been remarkably ingenious in achieving whatever we have now—about 160 million jobs—when throughout the period since 1776, we've been figuring out ways to get rid of jobs. That's what capitalism does. It produces more and more goods per person. We never know exactly where they're going to come from, but we find ways, in this economy, to employ more and more people. And we now have more people employed than ever in the history of the country, even though company after company, in heavy industry and that sort of thing, has naturally been trying to figure out how to get more productive all the time, which means turning out the same number of goods with fewer people, or more goods with the same number. That is capitalism.

"I don't think you need to worry about American ingenuity running out. If you look at all kinds of businesses, people like to make money, but they really like to be inventive. They like to do things. This economy works. It will continue to work. It's very tough in certain industries, and there will be dislocations. We didn't make as many horseshoes when cars come along. But we found ways to employ 160 million people, supporting a population of 330 million, when we started with four million people, with 80% of labor being employed on farms. So, the system works and it will continue to work. I don't know what the next big thing will be. I do know there will be a next big thing."

CM: "We want to shift the scut work to the robots to the extent we can. That's what we've been doing for 200 years. Nobody wants to go back to being a blacksmith, scooping along the street, picking up horse manure, or whatever the hell people used to do. We're glad to have that work eliminated. A lot of this worry about the future comes from leftists who worry terribly that the people at the bottom of the economic pyramid have had a little stretch when the people at the top got ahead faster. That happened by accident because we were in so much trouble that we had to flood the world with money and drive interest rates down to zero. And, of course, that drove asset prices up and helped the rich. Nobody did that because they suddenly loved the rich, it was just an accident, and it will soon pass. We want to have all this productivity improvement, and we shouldn't worry a little about the fact that one class or another is a little ahead at one stretch."

WB: "Charlie and I worked in a grocery store. When people ordered a can of peas, we had ladders that we climbed up to reach the peas, and then we placed it in a folding box, and then we put it on a truck. If you looked at the amount of food actually transferred between the producer and the person who consumed it, and the number of people involved in the transaction, I don't know whether it was one-third or one-quarter or one-fifth as efficient as the best way now to get food delivered to you. And my grandfather was distressed about the fact that this particular credit and delivery kind of store would be eliminated. And it was eliminated."

CM: "It's coming back."

WB: "It's coming back, but more efficiently. Anyway, we've seen a little creative destruction. And frankly, we're glad it freed us up to go into investments. It worked out better for us."

IMPORTANT AND KNOWABLE

1998 MEETING (00:54:40)

WB: "We are just looking for decent businesses. We try to think about two things: things that are important and things that are knowable. Now, there are things that are important that are not knowable. In our view, the questions that you raised [about macroeconomic developments] fall in that. There are things that are knowable but not important. We don't want to clutter our minds up with those. So, we say, 'What is important and what is knowable? And what among the things that fall within those two categories can we translate into some kind of an action that is useful for Berkshire?'

"We do think we know something about what Coca-Cola, Gillette, Disney, and our operating subsidiaries are going to look like in ten years. We care a lot about that; we think a lot about that and we want to be right about that. If we're right about that, other things are less important. And if we started focusing on those other things, we would miss a lot of big things.

"Coca-Cola went public in 1919. A share cost $40. And the first year it went down a little over 50%, to $19 per share. There were some problems with bottler contracts, various kinds of problems. If you'd had perfect foresight, you would have seen the world's greatest depression staring you in the face, when the social order even got questioned. You would have seen World War II; you would have seen atomic bombs and hydrogen bombs. You would have seen all kinds of things. And you could always find a reason to postpone why you should buy that share of Coca-Cola. But the important thing was to see they were going to be selling one billion eight-ounce servings of beverages a day this year, or some large number. And that the person who could make people happy a billion times a day around the globe ought to make a few bucks off doing it. And so that $40, which went down to $19, has to be worth well over $5 million now with dividends reinvested. If you developed a view on other subjects that in any way forestalled you acting on this more important, specific narrow view about the future of the company, you would have missed a great ride. So that's the kind of thing we focus on."

CM: "We're not predicting the currents that will come, just how some things will swim in the currents, whatever they are."

1998 MEETING (03:27:26)

WB: "I don't think the end of the Cold War is something that I would factor into my evaluation of businesses. There are all kinds of events that happen, and their impact, in terms of being quantified, are very difficult to figure over time. It is very difficult to isolate any single variable in a complex economic equation.

In terms of how the world is going to work ten years from now, or the returns on equity in business, I don't know what all the variables will be that impact that. I would not rely on making such a projection on the fact that the Cold War has ended, or on really any political or economic development around the world ... When I look at all of the great historic events of the past, nothing there gives me much in the way of a clue as to which ones would signal major changes in the profitability of American business."

CM: "[An interesting question is], if the rest of the world becomes very much more prosperous, as it will if it adopts the free enterprise system, which investments are likely to do best? I'd argue Coke, Gillette, and so on are likely to be helped by a great increase in prosperity in what is now the Third World. I'm not so sure that's true of a lot of other businesses."

WB: "It's very hard to evaluate how the ball is going to bounce, generally, around the world. But it is a plus to have products like Gillette and Coke have, which have demonstrated that they travel extraordinarily well around the world and that people crave those products. No one is going to find a way to do it better than those two companies in their respective fields—and they sell an inexpensive product, so all of that's going for us. But in terms of how stocks generally sell or the profitability of American business generally in the future, it doesn't help me much."

MACROECONOMIC FACTORS IN INVESTMENT DECISIONS

1999 MEETING (02:20:04)

WB: "We don't really get too concerned about the things that come and go. Take See's Candies, which we bought in 1972. Look what happened in 1973 and 1974, the oil shocks and what this country was going through, inflation, all that sort of thing. And let's say in 1972 somebody laid out a roadmap from 1972 to 1982, with the prime rate going to 21.5%, long-term rates going to 15%, the Dow going to 560. That wasn't important. The important thing was that this peanut brittle tastes like it does, which is terrific. And over time, we could get a little more money for it. See's made $4 million, pre-tax, when we bought it in 1972. It made $62 million last year. We don't want to be thinking about the wrong things when we're buying businesses. And that applies to marketable securities just as much as it does when buying 100% of the business. If we're right about the business, the macro factors aren't going to make any difference. And if we're wrong about the business, macro factors are not going to bail us out."

2000 MEETING (02:40:26)

WB: "I'm no good on the macro questions … I've not earned any stars for my past economic predictions. The good thing about my economic predictions, even if I do make them, is that I pay no attention to them myself. The way we pick our investments is we just don't get into the macro factors … We don't talk about anything remotely macro, and that's the way it'll stay.

"I've seen a lot of bank mergers recently. And one of the things they do, because they want to cut costs and justify a merger, is to cut costs they wouldn't have cut if they weren't dying to do the merger in the first place. Frequently they'll cut out the economics department. I always wondered why the hell they had it in the first place. Because what do they do? I mean, the guy comes in and says, 'I think GDP will be 4.6% this year instead of 4.3%.' So what? You're still trying to make every good loan you can make. You're still trying to take in deposits as cheap as you can. And you should be trying to cut costs wherever you can. It's got nothing to do with running the business, but it's fashionable … It has always struck me as just a lot of nonsense. So, if we ever get an economics department at Berkshire, sell the stock short."

2012 MEETING (01:32:40)

WB: "To my memory, in fifty-three years, I don't think Charlie and I have ever had a discussion about buying a stock or a business, or selling a stock or a business, where we've talked about macro affairs. If we find a business that we think we understand and we like the price at which it's being offered, we buy it. It doesn't make any difference what the headlines are—what the Federal Reserve is doing, what's going on in Europe—we buy it. There's always going to be good and bad news out there, and what gets emphasized the most depends on the moods of people, newspaper editors, whomever. … We look to value, and we don't look to headlines at all. Everybody thinks we sit around and talk about macro factors. We don't have any discussions about macro factors."

CM: "We did keep liquid reserves at the bottom of the [2008] panic that, if we'd known it was not going to get any worse, we would have spent, but we didn't know that."

WB: "We know we don't want to go broke, so we start with that. And we know you can't go broke if you've got a fair amount of liquid reserves around and you don't have any near-term debts and so on. So our first rule is always to play it tomorrow, no matter what happens. But if we've got that covered, and we can find things that are attractive, we buy. Charlie has a company called the Daily Journal. He sat there with a whole lot of cash, and when 2008 came along, he went out and bought a few stocks. That was the time to use the money, not to sit on it."

2015 MEETING (01:38:07)

WB: "I think Berkshire, in almost any kind of environment, will do better than most big companies. We are, and always will be, prepared for anything. If we see really unusual opportunities, we're prepared to act. That gives us a real advantage over most big companies. We don't count on anybody else. We're sitting with over $60 billion right now. I'd rather be sitting with $20 billion, having made a great $40 billion acquisition. But we will be very willing to act if economic turbulence of any kind occurs; we'll be prepared when most people won't be."

CM: "We have made very little progress in life by trying to outguess these macroeconomic factors. We basically have abdicated. We're just swimming all the time, and we let the tide take care of itself."

WB: "And we've not seen great successes by others who have been all involved in macro predictions. They get a lot of air time, but that's about all that happens."

MACROECONOMIC/EXTERNAL FACTORS

2000 MEETING (01:23:02)

WB: "If we thought we knew what the dollar or interest rates were going to do, we would just engage in transactions involving those commodities, or directly in futures. In other words, if we thought that the dollar was going to weaken dramatically, we would buy other currencies. It might benefit Coca-Cola in dollar terms if that happened, but it would be much more efficient to directly pursue a currency or an interest rate play than pursue it indirectly through companies that have big international exposure. But we don't really think much about that … In the end, we're really more interested in whether more people around the world are going to drink Coca-Cola, and, over time, we're better at predicting that than we are at predicting what the yen will do. If Coca-Cola satisfies liquid needs for more and more people, we will probably get a reasonable percentage of the purchasing power of those people around the world for their right to drink Coca-Cola.

"If the world's standard of living improves, bit by bit over time in an irregular fashion, and we supply something the world wants, we will get our share in dollars eventually. Quarter to quarter or year to year, how that moves around because of currency really doesn't make any difference to us. In terms of where Coca- Cola's going to be ten or twenty years from now, it would be a big mistake to focus on currency moves as opposed to focusing on the product itself … We don't understand what currencies are going to do week to week, month to month, or year to year. We always try to focus on what's knowable and what's important. Currency might be important, but we don't think it's knowable. Other things are unimportant, but knowable. What's knowable and important about Coca-Cola is the fact that more and more people are going to consume soft drinks around the world and have been doing so year after year after year, and that Coca-Cola's going to gain market share, and the product is extraordinarily inexpensive relative to the pleasure it brings to people.

"In the 1930s, when I was kid, I bought six for a quarter and sold them for a nickel. That was a six-and-a-half-ounce bottle for a nickel. And you can buy a twelve-ounce can at a supermarket sale for not much more than twice per ounce what it was selling for in the 1930s. You won't find many products where that kind of value proposition has developed over the years. That's the kind of thing we focus on. Interest rates and foreign exchange rates, important as they may be in the short term, really are not going to determine whether we get rich over time."

CM: "We have a willful agnosticism on all kinds of things. And that makes us concentrate on certain other things. This is a very good way to think if you're as lazy as we are."

ECONOMIC CORRELATIONS

2002 MEETING (03:07:04)

WB: "I'm very leery of economic correlations. I spent years fooling around with that sort of thing; I correlated stock prices with everything in the world, and the problem was when I found a correlation. You've seen these things on which NFL conference wins the Super Bowl and all of that sort of thing. You can find something that correlates with something else. But in the end a business, or any economic asset, is going to be worth what it produces in the way of cash over its lifetime ... All investment is laying out some money now to get more money back in the future. There are two ways of looking at getting the money back. One is from what the asset itself will produce. That's investment. One is from what somebody else will pay you for it later on, irrespective of what the asset produces, and I call that speculation. So, if you are looking to the asset itself, you don't care about the quote because the asset is going to produce the money for you either way. That's what society, as a whole, is going to get from investing in that asset."

CM: "What makes common stock prices so hard to predict is that from time to time a generally liquid market creates, either in sectors or in the whole market, a Ponzi scheme. In other words, you have an automatic process where people get sucked in and other people come in because it worked last month or last year. And it can build to perfectly ridiculous levels, and the levels can last for considerable periods … By definition that's going to be very, very hard to predict. But that's why it's so dangerous to short stocks, even when they're grossly overvalued. It's hard to know just how overvalued they can become … and I don't think you're going to predict Ponzi scheme effects in markets by looking at the price of gold or any other correlation."

WB: "Charlie and I have probably agreed on at least a hundred companies, maybe more, that we felt were frauds, bubble-type things. And if we had acted on shorting those over the years, we might be broke now. But we were right on probably just about a hundred out of a hundred. It's very hard to predict how far what Charlie calls the Ponzi scheme will go. It's not exactly a scheme in the sense that it isn't concocted, in most cases, by one person. It's sort of a natural phenomenon, nursed along by promoters and investment bankers and venture capitalists and so on. It just plays on human nature in certain ways and it creates its own momentum, and eventually it pops. And nobody knows when it's going to pop, and that's why you can't short; at least, we don't find it makes good sense to short those things. You don't know how high they will go or when it will end."

ZERO INTEREST RATES

2021 MEETING (01:35:02)

WB: "Interest rates basically are to the value of assets what gravity is to matter … On Thursday, the U.S. Treasury sold some four-week notes, Treasury bills. They accepted bids for $43 billion worth and an average price of $100.000000—six zeros. Essentially, people were giving $43 billion to the Treasury … and the Treasury received the money at zero … For twenty-five or more years, Paul Samuelson's book [*Economics*] was the definitive book on economics. It was taught in every school … He was a wonderful writer, the definitive writer … I looked for negative interest rates, there's nothing there. I finally found zero interest rates. And Paul Samuelson, a brilliant man … says that you can technically perhaps conceive of negative interest rates, but it can't ever really happen. And that was written in the 1970s. This wasn't back in the Dark Ages … Here we are in a world where we had zero interest rates this week on the four-week note … In economics, you can never do one thing. You always have to say, 'And then what?' We will see where it all leads. Charlie and I consider it the most interesting movie by far we've ever seen in terms of economics."

CM: "Yes. And the professional economists, of course, have been very surprised by what's happened. It reminds me of what Churchill said about [political rival] Clement Attlee; he said he was a very modest man, and he had a great deal to be modest about. That's exactly what's happened with the professional economists.

They were so confident about everything, and it turns out the world is more complicated than they thought."

INFLATION AND EQUITY RETURNS

2003 MEETING (01:08:07)

WB: "There's no question that a lack of inflation is a plus for owners. The real return from owning American business, if purchased at similar prices, will be higher if we have long periods of low/no inflation than if we have long periods of high inflation. Low inflation over any long period is better for investors … There's nothing wrong at all, in a low-inflation environment, in earning 6% or 7%. That's as good as will happen, because in a low inflation environment, how much is GDP going to grow? If you have a 2% inflation and even 3% real growth, you're talking about 5% GDP growth in nominal terms. If GDP grows at that rate, over time corporate profits will grow, more or less, at that rate. And if corporate profits grow 5% a year, the capitalized value of those corporate profits will probably grow at something like that over the long term with a normal starting point. Add dividends and you get 6–7% before frictional costs …

"So, the math isn't bad, it's just bad for those people who expected very high returns based on looking in the rearview mirror in 1998 or 1999 … If the people who own American business get 5–6% of the pie—a $10 trillion economy now, someday a $20 trillion economy— those of us who put our capital out to produce goods and services, it doesn't strike me as crazy in either direction. It provides what I would regard as a pretty decent real return if you have low inflation. If you get into high inflation, you could easily have the real return to investors get to a very, very low number, and perhaps negative. Inflation can swindle the equity investor, as I wrote back in 1977, and I used 7,000 words to explain why … Inflation is the one thing that, over a long period of time, can turn investors' results, in aggregate, into a negative figure. It's the investors' enemy."

2003 MEETING (03:08:21)

WB: "I personally don't really worry about the American dollar getting worth far less, relative to other currencies. But I think there's a probability that sometime in the next twenty to thirty years you could have rampant inflation in this country again. You'll probably have it around the world, and it's probably more likely in a good many other countries than in the United States. But inflation is always a latent danger to an economy. I think of inflation as being in remission at all times because it's something that has a cause that will recur, in terms of human behavior, from time to time, in terms of how legislatures behave and how governments behave. So, I think that the probability of high inflation at some point during the next, say, twenty or thirty years, is not a low probability. I hope it doesn't happen."

CM: "In the long term, practically all currencies go to hell ... If you want to go out 200 years and ask will some politicians in the United States have ruined the currency? I think the answer is yes. But I wouldn't anticipate some horrible event in the near future. When things really went to hell in Argentina, the government started confiscating the property of shareholders. If that starts happening and the government is doing it, we probably won't be able to protect you."

INFLATION AND PURCHASING POWER

2004 MEETING (00:39:58)

WB: "The best thing to do to preserve purchasing power is to have a lot of earning power of your own. If you're the best brain surgeon or lawyer in town, you will retain purchasing power, in terms of your income, no matter what happens as time goes by. In the investment world, it's tougher. Charlie and I think the best answer is to own fine businesses that will be able to price in inflationary terms and will not require huge capital investment to handle the larger dollar volume of sales. See's Candies is the kind of business that, more or less, can handle an inflationary world and maintain investment and value, no matter what happens to the currency.

"Unfortunately, most businesses will not come out well in real terms during inflation. Their earnings may go up a fair amount over time, but they're compelled to put more and more dollars into the business just to stay in the same place. The worst kind of business is one that makes you put more money on the table all the time and doesn't give you greater earnings. So, you really want a business that can have pricing that reflects inflation and does not have very much capital investment that reflects inflation. Inflation is the enemy of the investor, in terms of real returns."

CM: "Most people are going to get a very small real return from investment after considering inflation and taxes. I think that's an iron law of the world and if, for a brief period, some of us do better than that, we ought to be very thankful. One of the great defenses to being worried about inflation is not having a lot of silly needs in your life. In other words, if you haven't created a lot of artificial demand to drown in consumer goods, you have a considerable defense against the vicissitudes of life."

2007 MEETING (03:47:49)

WB: "Your own earning power is the best hedge against inflation. The second-best hedge is to own a wonderful business ... If you own Coca-Cola, Hershey, anything that people are going to want to give a portion of their current income to keep getting, which also has relatively low incremental capital investment attached to it so that you don't have to keep plowing tremendous amounts of money in just to meet inflationary demands, that's the best investment you can probably have in an inflationary world. But inflation is bad news for investors under almost any circumstances ... I don't think Berkshire would do as well during high rates of inflation—in real terms—as it does in periods of low inflation, but I think we would do better than many companies."

2009 MEETING (02:00:57)

WB: "It's certain we will have inflation over time ... We are following policies in this country now which are bound to have some inflationary consequences. And to the extent that we borrow money from the rest of the world, it would be very human on the part of politicians in the future to decide that they would rather pay the rest of the world back in dollars that are worth far less than the dollars they borrowed; it's the classic way of reducing the impact and cost of external debt. We're building up a lot of external debt ... and we're taking less money from taxpayers.

"The people who are really paying for the things we're doing now will probably be the people who are buying fixed-dollar investments, much of it from the U.S. government, and who will find the purchasing power when they go to redeem those investments to be far less.

"So you might say that the AIG bonuses, the Chinese are the people that are ultimately paying the most in terms of the loss of purchasing power they will have with their holdings of U.S. government bonds, many years down the road. But it sounds better to say the taxpayers are paying for it than to say the Chinese are paying for it. It's an interesting situation. I read that comment everyday about how the taxpayers are doing this and that. I haven't had my taxes raised. You haven't had your taxes raised. The taxpayers haven't paid anything so far. And my guess is that the ultimate price of much of this will be paid by a shrinkage in the real value of fixed-dollar investments down the road. That will be the easiest thing to do—and if it's the easiest thing to do, it's the most likely thing to have happen. So, you will see plenty of inflation.

"Now, the best protection against inflation is your own earning power. If you're the best teacher, surgeon, lawyer, whatever it may be, you will command a given part of other people's production of goods and services no matter what the currency is, whether it's seashells, reichsmarks, or dollars. Your own earning power is the best; you will get your share of the national economic pie, regardless of whatever the currency may be, as measured against some earlier standard.

"The second-best protection is a wonderful business. If you own Coca-Cola, you will get a given portion of people's labor twenty years from now and fifty years from now for your product. It doesn't make any difference what's happened to the price level, generally, because people will be willing to give up three minutes of labor, or whatever it may be, to enjoy 12 ounces of a product they like. Those are great assets: your own earning power first, and then the earning power of a wonderful business that does not require heavy capital investment. If it requires heavy capital investment, you get killed in inflation. With those guidelines, I would tell you the best thing to do is invest in yourself."

CM: "The young man who asked the question should become a brain surgeon, and he should invest in Coca-Cola instead of government bonds."

WB: "I get paid by the word, Charlie doesn't."

2010 MEETING (01:40:55)

WB: "I may be a little biased on this because I've always worried a lot about inflation, and there's been a lot of inflation. Charlie has pointed out that since I was born in 1930, the dollar has depreciated by well over 90%. But, as he also points out, we've done OK. So it isn't the end of the world, necessarily. I think that the prospects for significant inflation have increased—not only here, but around the world—with the situation that governments have either been forced into or elected to embrace. And they may well have been the correct responses, but we may find that weaning ourselves from the medicine—massive dosages of debt—was harder than solving the original illness. I don't see any way that countries running very high deficits, relative to GDP, don't have a significant diminution in the value of their currency over time ... I do think that if you had to bet your life on higher or lower inflation, I'd bet on higher, and maybe a lot higher."

INFLATION AND BUSINESS QUALITY

2005 MEETING (02:29:54)

WB: "Inflation destroys value, but unequally. The best business to have during inflation is one that retains its earning power in real dollars without commensurate investment to, in effect, fund the inflation-produced nominal growth. The worst kind of business is one where you have to keep putting more and more money into a lousy business. ... Charlie and I are always suspicious that inflation will regain some of the momentum it had a couple of decades ago. We always think it's in sort of remission ... Inflation is always a factor in calculating the kind of business we want to buy. But it isn't like it crowds out all other factors. It's always been with us. See's Candies has done fine during an inflationary period because it doesn't have huge capital investments to make in current dollars."

INFLATION AND BUSINESS RISK (BERKSHIRE)

2009 MEETING (03:56:45)

WB: "I think the worst situation that could occur for our insurance businesses would be if we ran into so much inflation that people got very, very unhappy with anything that they had to buy in their daily life. This applies in the utility business, but certainly in auto insurance too. Customers express their outrage at inflationary increases and say, 'Nationalize the whole thing.' That would be a huge asset that would disappear, if that occurred. I don't think that's a high probability. But if you're asking me to look at the worst-case scenario, that's probably the one I'd come up with.

"We nationalized, to some extent, the annuity business, when we went into Social Security, which I think was a good thing. But when the public gets outraged, politicians will respond. And wild inflation would be the most likely cause, it seems to me, of something like that happening in auto insurance. It's a bill most people pay every six months, or even more frequently. And if they see that bill going up and they don't want to get rid of their car, they're going to get mad. Utility customers are going to get very mad during inflation; they need to turn on the lights, and they hate to see those monthly bills going up. It's something they can't give up and it's very visible. The reaction will be to go to public representatives and say, 'Do something about this.' One thing they can do is take it over. There's a very low probability of that, but it's not nonexistent."

COMMODITIES

2007 MEETING (04:19:48)

WB: "We have no opinion on commodities. If we're in an oil stock, it's because we think it offers a lot of value at this price, but it does not mean we think the price of oil is going up. If we thought oil was going up, we could buy oil futures, which we actually did once [in 1994–1995]. But very, very seldom would we have any opinion on what any given commodity would do.

"Owning [South Korean steel manufacturer] POSCO, we just think it's probably the best steel company in the world; when we bought it, we were buying it at four or five times earnings, with a debt-free balance sheet, for one of the lowest-cost producers around. It's a fabulous company. In addition, it was a play on the Korean won, and we made 20% by being invested through a won-denominated security. So, we may occasionally be in those kind of businesses.

"What we basically like best are businesses that require very little capital, because they're the only ones that have a chance of earning really high returns on capital. You can't have huge capital expenditures year after year and a high-return business. It just doesn't work in this world. But you can find some businesses that require relatively minimal capital investment. See's Candies is not going to require a huge capital investment ... It's a small business, but it's a wonderful business. And it's a far better business, adjusted for size, than any steel or oil business is going to be. It's just not very big. We'd love to have it bigger. And we'll do our share in every way we can, as you may have noticed up here. But we do not have any bias toward businesses involved in commodities. If we had any bias, it would be against."

CM: "By and large, we're going to be investors in businesses, not commodities."

GOVERNMENT RESPONSE TO THE GLOBAL FINANCIAL CRISIS (GFC)

2009 MEETING (00:17:28)

CM: "When a government is reacting to the biggest financial crisis in seventy years, which threatens important values in the whole world, and the decisions are being made hurriedly and under pressure and with good faith, I think it's unreasonable to expect perfect agreement with all of one's own ideas. I think the government is entitled to be judged more leniently when it's doing the best it can under trouble. Of course, there's going to be some reactions that are foolish."

WB: "The government, in mid-September 2008, was facing a situation that was as close to a total meltdown throughout the financial system as I think you can imagine. You had a couple hundred billion dollars move out of money market funds in a couple of days. You had the commercial paper market freeze up, which meant companies all over the country that had nothing to do with the financial world were going to have trouble meeting payrolls. We really were looking into the abyss at that time. And a lot of action was taken very promptly.

"Overall, I commend the actions that were taken. As Charlie says, to expect perfection out of people that are working twenty-hour days and are getting hit from all sides by new information, bad information; that one weekend with Lehman going, AIG going, Merrill Lynch would've gone, in my view, unless BofA had bought it. When you're getting punched from all sides and you have to make policy and you have to think about congressional reaction and the American people's reaction, you're not going to do everything perfectly. But I think overall, they did a very, very good job ... That's the nature of an emergency. You're going to make some decisions that can later be looked back at and somebody will say, 'I could've done it a little bit better.' But, by and large, the authorities, in my view, did a very good job. And all banks aren't alike by a long shot. In our opinion, Wells Fargo—among the large banks particularly—is a fabulous bank and has some advantages the others do not have. But in a time like that, you're not dealing in nuances."

GOVERNMENT REGULATIONS

2019 MEETING (03:50:52)

WB: "Insurance is regulated primarily on a state basis, but insurance has been regulated ever since we went into it ... Regulation can be a pain in the neck, generally, but on the other hand, we don't want a bunch of charlatans operating in the insurance business. And insurance actually lends itself to charlatans because you get handed money and you give the other guy a promise. I like that there is regulation in the insurance business or the banking business. It doesn't mean it can't drive you crazy sometimes, but those businesses should be regulated. They are too important. Anytime you can take other people's money, and they go home with a promise and you go home with the money, I don't mind a certain amount of regulation."

CM: "In banking, you're using the government's credit because you have deposit insurance; there's an implicit bargain. You can't be too crazy with what you do with the money. That's perfectly reasonable. I absolutely believe that we should have a regulation system that involves supervision of risk-taking by banks. It got particularly bad in the investment banks at the peak of the real estate crisis, and there's only one word for the behavior—it was disgusting. And it was pretty much everybody. It's hard to think of anybody who stayed sane in that boom. They felt the other guy's doing dumb things, I've got to do it, too, or I'll be left out. What a crazy way to behave. So sure, there's some intervention, but there probably has to be."

WB: "You want a Food and Drug Administration (FDA). You'll be unhappy with how they do it, if you're in the business and all that—I find any kind of regulation to be irritating. But nevertheless, it is good for the system. And actually I would say that a number of regulators have been really quite sensible about regulation. You don't feel that way when you're being told how to run your business. But, as Charlie says, you wouldn't want to be a bank that ran in an unregulated system where anybody could come in and do all kinds of things that would actually have consequences that drew you into the problems that they created themselves. We had the Wild West in banking long ago, and it produced a lot of problems in the 19th century."

GLOBAL STANDARD OF LIVING

2009 MEETING (03:35:53)

WB: "There's always a lot of things wrong with the world. We live with it and we deal with it. But the beauty of it is this [capitalist] system works very well. I don't have the faintest idea what's going to happen in business or markets in the next year or two. But over time, people will live better and better in this country. Today, we have about 35,000 people here. That was almost 1% of the population of the United States in the first census in 1790. If we had had this room filled back in 1790 with 35,000 citizens of the United States, they would've been just as smart as we are ... They would've lived in a country with the same fertile soil, same temperature, same minerals. They were just as able as we are, but they weren't turning out anything like we turn out today. Just look at how we live compared to those people several hundred years ago. We have had a system that works. It unleashes human potential.

"China went a long time without a system that unleashed potential. Now, they've got a system that's unleashing human potential. We haven't reached the end of that road, by a long shot. We're just starting, basically. We will have bad years in capitalism. It overshoots in markets. It gets overcome by fear and greed and all of that sort of thing. But if you look at the 19th century, we had a civil war, we had fifteen years or so of bad economic times spread out through that century, and we had six panics, as they called them in those days. In the 20th century, we had a couple of great wars, we had plenty of recessions, we had the Great Depression. We have these interruptions in the progress of our society—but overall, we move ahead. And we not only move ahead, we move ahead at a pretty damn rapid rate: in the 20th century, we have had a seven-for-one improvement in living. And we did that with slavery [at one time]. We didn't let women vote for 130 years or thereabouts. We were wasting human potential, and we still are, but we were doing it more so for centuries.

"We do keep moving forward, in kind of fits and starts. Right now, we're sputtering somewhat in terms of the economy. But there is no question, in my mind, that there is enormous human potential. Every year we meet, you can name a bunch of problems. But the opportunities will win in the end. Your kids and grandchildren will live better than you. We will find more ways, and easier and better ways, to do things that we haven't even dreamt of yet."

CM: "Now that I'm so close to the age of death, I find myself getting more cheerful about the economic future, which I'm not going to be here to enjoy. What I find really cheerful is that we are plainly going to harness the direct energy of the sun. We're going to have electrical power all over the world. That's going to enable overpopulated countries to turn seawater into fresh water. It's going to eliminate a lot of the environmental problems, while preserving more of the hydrocarbon resources for future needs as chemical feedstocks. I see a final breakthrough that solves the main technical problem of man, and you can see it coming right over the horizon. MidAmerican Energy and [Chinese car-maker] BYD will be participating in it. So, I think it's a huge mistake to think only about your probable misfortunes. You should also think about what's good about your situation. And what's good about our situation now is the main technical problem of mankind is about to be fixed. If you have enough energy, you can solve a lot of your other problems."

GEOPOLITICAL RISK (TAIWAN SEMICONDUCTOR)

2023 MEETING (02:16:02)

WB: "Taiwan Semiconductor is one of the best-managed and important companies in the world. I think you'll be able to say the same thing ten or twenty years from now. I don't like its location, and I've re-evaluated that. I don't think it should be any place but Taiwan, although they will be opening chip capacity in this country. Actually, one of our subsidiaries in Alleghany is participating in their Arizona construction activities. There's no one in the chip industry that's in their league, in my view ... They're marvelous people and a marvelous company, but I'd rather find the marvelous people and the marvelous competitive position in the United States. I feel better about the capital deployed in Japan than in Taiwan. I think that's the reality. And I've re-evaluated that in the light of certain things that were going on. Charlie?"

CM: "My view is that Warren ought to feel comfortable if he wants to."

EMPLOYMENT/LAYOFFS AND CREATIVE DESTRUCTION

2009 MEETING (04:04:44)

WB: "Business conditions can change such as to necessitate temporary or permanent layoffs ... There are some businesses that may permanently contract, and you have to face up to that in terms of layoffs. There are other businesses that have severe cyclical-type contractions, and they are going to face significant layoffs ... Nobody gets any joy out of it. Generally, you probably do it a little too late, because you keep hoping the business will bounce back. But if the business changes in a material way, you'd better change your business model, or somebody else will—and then you'll even have more changes facing you.

"On balance, we hope we get into businesses that don't face those kind of problems … In the textile business, in the end, we laid off everybody. It had contracted enormously before we got there and we tried all kinds of things, but we finally gave up. Capitalism is creative destruction, and sometimes, you're on the short end of that."

CM: "Some of our businesses have a shared-hardship model, where they don't layoff, at least not yet. The businesses with that model tend to be very strongly placed economically. I guess it shows Benjamin Franklin was right, when he said, 'It's hard for an empty sack to stand upright.' So, we're all over the map on that, and so is all of industry. I do think an ideal model would be a business so strong that it could operate in the shared-hardship mode instead of the layoffs."

WB: "But a lot of operations don't lend themselves to that very well, either … In some cases, you basically have to close down whole plants, that's just the nature of it. You really can't operate every plant at 50% and have it work as effectively as shutting down the least-productive plants."

CM: "In a world where you sometimes have to amputate a limb to stay alive, you can't expect that every business can stay exactly as it is."

PART ELEVEN:
See's Candies, Coca-Cola, and Consumer Brands

"We were pretty damn stupid when we bought See's. We were just barely smart enough to buy it. And if there's any secret to Berkshire, it's the fact that we're pretty good at ignorance removal. The nice thing is we have a lot of ignorance left to remove."

"I have a friend who says, 'The first rule of fishing is to fish where the fish are. And the second rule of fishing is to never forget the first rule.' We have got good at fishing where the fish are."

"It's not a great business when you have to have a prayer session before you raise your prices a penny; you are in a tough business then. And I would say you can almost measure the strength of a business over time by the agony they go through in determining whether a price increase can be sustained."

"The ideal asset is a royalty on somebody else's sales during inflation, where all you do is get a royalty check every month, and it's based on their sales volume."

INTRODUCTION

IN EARLY 1972, BUFFETT AND MUNGER COMPLETED THE ACQUISITION OF See's Candies. Over the ensuing decades, they have reflected on the lessons learned from See's about the value of a great business and dominant consumer brands. As Buffett has said, this insight led to one of his most notable investments: the purchase of ~$1.3 billion of Coca-Cola shares in the late 1980s and the early 1990s, a position Buffett has left untouched subsequently (he hasn't sold a single share in 35 years). In this section, Buffett and Munger explain what has attracted them to these businesses.

One example, to quote Buffett, is the immense value of accruing mind share with billions of people globally: "There are some industries that are never going to have barriers to entry. In those industries, you better run very fast because there are a lot of other people who are going to be looking at what you're doing and trying to figure out your weakness or what they can do a little bit better. A great barrier to entry is something like Coca-Cola. If you gave me $20bn or $30bn and told me to try and knock off the Coca-Cola Company with some new cola, I wouldn't have the faintest idea how to do it. There are billions of people around the world with something in their mind about Coca-Cola, and you're not going to change that with $20bn." (I discussed this topic in more detail at TSOH Investment Research—see "There Aren't Many See's Candies".)

SUBJECTS AND MEETINGS FEATURED

COCA-COLA DIVIDEND POLICY

1995 MEETING (02:26:46)

WARREN BUFFETT: "As it relates to altering Coca-Cola's dividend policy, it depends how they would utilize the cash, what they could use it for. ... I commend managements that have a wonderful business for utilizing cash in those wonderful businesses, or in businesses they understand that will also have wonderful economics, and for getting the rest of the money back to the shareholders. Coca-Cola, in my book, is doing exactly the right thing with its cash when it uses all the cash that it can, effectively, in the business to expand in new markets and that sort of thing. But beyond that, it pays a dividend, which distributes cash to shareholders, and then it repurchases shares in a big way, which returns cash on a selective basis to shareholders, but in a way that benefits all of them.

"You will benefit from us not paying dividends as long as we can use every dollar retained to produce more than a dollar of value, and of market value over time. That's the yardstick by which the decision is made, and it's the yardstick, I think, by which Coca-Cola's making the decision, too. And I think that they deserve great credit for exercising the discipline to quit using cash when they've run out of the opportunities to use it well."

LESSON LEARNED FROM SEE'S CANDIES

1997 MEETING (03:41:32)

CHARLIE MUNGER: "See's Candies was the first time we really stepped up for brand quality, and it was a very hard jump for us. We'd been used to buying dollar bills for 50 cents. If they demanded an extra $100,000 for See's Candies, we wouldn't have bought it. And that was after Warren had been trained under the greatest professor of his era [Ben Graham] and had worked ninety hours a week, absorbing everything in the world. We just didn't have minds well enough trained to make an easy decision right. They didn't ask for the extra $100,000 and we did buy it. And as it succeeded, we kept learning. That shows that the name of the game is continuing to learn. Even if you're very well-trained and have some natural aptitude, you still need to keep learning."

WB: "If we hadn't bought See's, and experienced subsequent developments that made us aware of other things, we wouldn't have bought Coca-Cola in 1988. You can give See's a significant part of the credit for the profit we've got in Coca-Cola. You may say, 'How could you be so dumb as not to be able to recognize a Coca-Cola?' Well, I don't know. It just made us start thinking more.

We saw how decisions we made in relation to See's played out in the marketplace. We saw what worked and what didn't work. And it made us appreciate what worked, and to shy away from things that didn't work. It definitely led to Coca-Cola. We've had the good luck to buy some businesses in their entirety that have taught us a lot.

"It's worked in the other direction too—I was in the windmill business, pumps, and second-level department stores. And I found out how tough it was; you could apply all kinds of energy to them and it didn't do any good. It made a great deal of sense to figure out what pond to jump in. What pond you jumped in was probably more important than how well you could swim."

2002 MEETING (04:56:02)

WB: "We have not done as well moving away from the West [expanding to the eastern U.S.] as Charlie and I hoped for when we bought See's. We've done way, way better in terms of the overall result, but it has been interesting to us. Bear in mind, no one really makes money with boxed chocolates through their own retail outlets in the United States except for See's. There's only one pound per capita of boxed chocolates, roughly, sold in the United States. So, it is not a big business.

"Hundreds and hundreds of firms, including some that were a lot larger than See's, have failed. Russell Stover makes very good money selling through a distribution channel that is different, but nobody's found a way to do it in stores. We've found a way to do it in the West. We have not found a way to do it elsewhere. And it's very irritating that we can't figure out a way because it's so successful when it works, as it does in the West ... It is a very tough business in this country because Americans just don't buy much boxed chocolate. They're always happy to get it as a gift, but you don't normally walk down the street or walk in a mall and buy it for yourself. It's usually a gift or it's usually at holiday time.

"So, we don't do as well as you might think we would when we get to very successful malls that are located in other parts of the country. We have opened holiday kiosks at fifty stores at Christmas time around the country, away from our natural territory. And we make some money out of that, but we wouldn't make money if we were there year-round. We've been thinking about it, I guarantee you, for thirty years because it's a terrific business where it works ...

"We're not going to go through any distribution channel at See's. You're already getting a bargain at our retail prices and we're not going to go through any other distribution channel at See's that's going to discount ... We'll buy things from Costco, but we're not going to sell a product where the price is part of the integrity of the product—we're not going to sell it through a distribution system like Costco where discounting is basic to their whole approach. Costco is a wonderful operation, and See's is a wonderful operation, and never the twain shall meet."

2003 MEETING (01:46:16)

CM: "I think there's some mythology in this idea that I've been this great enlightener of Warren Buffett. He hasn't needed much enlightenment, but we both kept learning all the time, so that the men we were five years earlier were less sensible than the men who ultimately were there. And See's Candies did teach us both a wonderful lesson.

"If See's Candies had asked $100,000 more, Warren and I would've walked; that's how dumb we were at that time. And one of the reasons we didn't walk is that, while we were making this wonderful decision to not pay a dime more than $25 million, [Munger's friend] Ira Marshall said to us, 'You guys are crazy. There are some things you should pay up for. You're underestimating quality.' And, Warren and I, instead of behaving the way people do in a lot of places, listened to the criticism. We changed our minds. That is a very good lesson: the ability to take criticism constructively. Think of all the money we made from accepting that one criticism. If you count the indirect effects from what we learned from buying See's, you can say Berkshire's been built, partly, by learning from criticism. Now, we don't want any more today."

WB: "I had learned investments, and got enormous benefit out of that learning, from a fellow who concentrated on the quantitative aspects, Ben Graham. He didn't dismiss the qualitative aspects, but he said you could make enough money focusing on quantitative aspects, which were a more sure way of going at things and would enable you to identify the cigar butts. He would say that the qualitative is harder to teach, to write about, it may require more insight than the quantitative—and besides, the quantitative works fine, so why try harder? And on a small scale, there was a very good point to that. But Charlie really did emphasize the qualitative much more than I did when I started ... It makes more sense to buy a wonderful business at a fair price than a fair business at a wonderful price. Of course, we've learned by what we've seen. It's not hard when you watch for fifty years to learn a few things ... Overall, we kept moving in the direction of better and better companies, and now we've got a collection of wonderful companies."

2011 MEETING (01:26:47)

WB: "If you have a wonderful product that requires very little capital to grow, and to do more dollar volume, as will happen with inflation even if you don't have unit growth, and it doesn't take much capital to support that growth, that is a wonderful asset to have in inflation … Anything where additional capital is not required to finance inflationary growth.

"The worst kind of businesses are those with tons of receivables and inventories and all of that. And in dollar terms, if their volume stays flat but the price level doubles, and they need to come up with double the amount of money to do that same volume of business, that can be a very bad asset.

"Take See's Candies. It was doing $30 million of volume when we bought it, and it sold 16 million pounds of candy at $1.90 per pound. Now, we're doing well over $300 million of business. It took $9 million of tangible assets to run it when it was doing $30 million in sales, and it takes about $40 million of tangible assets at $300 million in sales. So, we've only had to plow back $30 million into a business that's made us, probably, $1.5 billion pre-tax during that period. And if the price of candy doubles, we don't have any receivables to speak of. Our inventory turns fast. We don't store it or anything like that. We gear up seasonally and the fixed assets aren't big, so that is a much better business to own than a utility business if you're going to have a lot of inflation."

CM: "And what's interesting about it is that we didn't always know this."

WB: "And sometimes we forget it."

CM: "That's true, too. But it shows how continuous learning is absolutely required to have any significant achievement at all in the world."

WB: "I've said in the past that I'm a better businessman because I'm an investor and I'm a better investor because I'm a businessman. There's nothing like actually experiencing necessity. Particularly in the 1970s, when inflation was gathering strength, and the early 1980s, you would see this absolutely required capital investment on a very big scale that really wasn't producing anything commensurate in the way of earnings.

"I wrote an article for *Fortune* called 'How Inflation Swindles the Equity Investor' back in 1977. The ideal asset is a royalty on somebody else's sales during inflation, where all you do is get a royalty check every month, and it's based on their sales volume. You came up with some product originally, licensed it to them, and you never have another bit of capital investment. You have no receivables, no inventory, and no fixed assets. That kind of business is real inflation protection, assuming the product maintains its viability. So even though we are going into some very capital-intensive businesses, part of that reflects the fact we can't deploy the amount of capital we have in a whole bunch of See's Candies. We just can't find them. We would love to, but we can't find them in that quantity. So we are not doing as well with capital when we have to invest many billions a year, as we would if we were investing a few millions a year. There's no question. That's true in investments and operating businesses. There is a real disadvantage to size, and we just hope that problem grows."

2014 MEETING (01:48:48)

WB: "See's not only has provided us with earnings used to buy other businesses—so we've added lots of earnings power *through* See's [distributable earnings/ free cash flow from See's used to fund other investments], beyond the earning power we've added *at* See's —but it also opened my eyes to the power of brands. You could say we made a lot of money in Coca-Cola partly because we bought See's. I'd understood brands to some degree, but there's nothing like owning one, seeing the possibilities with it as well as the limitations, to educate yourself about things you might do in the future. In 1972, we bought See's, and in 1988, we bought Coca-Cola. If we had not owned See's, I would not be surprised if we wouldn't have owned Coca-Cola later on."

CM: "There's no question about the fact that its main contribution to Berkshire was ignorance removal, and it's not the only big contributor. If it weren't for the fact that we were so good at removing our ignorance, step by step, Berkshire would be practically nothing today. What we knew originally wasn't enough. We were pretty damn stupid when we bought See's. We were just barely smart enough to buy it. And if there's any secret to Berkshire, it's the fact that we're pretty good at ignorance removal. The nice thing is we have a lot of ignorance left to remove."

2017 MEETING (00:31:07)

WB: "We sort of know a great investment idea when we see it. It would tend to be a business where, for one reason or another, we can look out five, ten or twenty years and decide that the competitive advantage that it has at present will last over that period. It will have a trusted manager who will not only fit into the Berkshire culture, but who is eager to join the Berkshire culture. And then it will be a matter of price. When we buy a business, we're essentially laying out money now based on what we think it will deliver over time. The higher the certainty with which we make that prediction, the better we feel about it.

"You can go back to a kind of a watershed event, which was a relatively small company, See's Candies. The question when we looked at See's in 1972 was, 'Would people still want to be both eating and giving away that candy in preference to other candies?' ... We had a manager we liked very much. We bought it for $25 million, net of cash, and it was earning about $4 million pre-tax. It must be close to $2 billion, pre-tax, that we've since taken out of it. But it was only because we felt people would not be buying, necessarily, a lower-priced candy. It does not work very well if you go to your wife or girlfriend on Valentine's Day—I hope they're the same person—and say, 'Here's a box of candy, honey. I took the low bid.' We made a judgment about See's Candies that it would be special in 1982 and 1992, and fortunately, we were right on it. We're looking for more See's Candies, only a lot bigger."

CM: "But it's also true that we were young and ignorant then. The truth of the matter is that it would have been very wise to buy See's Candies at a slightly higher price. But if they'd asked for it, we wouldn't have done it, so we've gotten a lot of credit for being smarter than we were."

WB: "If it had been $5 million more, I wouldn't have bought it. Charlie would have been willing to buy it. Fortunately, we didn't get to the point where we had to make that decision. Charlie would've pushed forward when I probably would've faded. It's a good thing that the seller [Charles B. See or 'Candy Harry'] came around. He was not interested in the business. He was more interested in girls and grapes, actually. He almost changed his mind. Well, he *did* change his mind about selling. I wasn't there, but [fellow investor] Rick Guerin told me Charlie went in and gave an hour-long talk on the merits of girls and grapes over having a candy company. This is true, folks. The fellow sold to us; I pull Charlie out in emergencies like that."

CM: "We were very lucky that, early on, we had the habit of buying horrible businesses because they were really cheap. It gave us a lot of experience trying to fix these unfixable businesses as they headed downward toward doom. That early experience was so horrible, fixing the unfixable, that we were very good at avoiding it thereafter. So, I would argue our early stupidity helped us."

WB: "We learned we couldn't make a silk purse out of a sow's ear. So, we went out looking for silk after that."

CM: "But you have to try it for a long time and fail, to have your nose rubbed in it, to really understand it."

2017 MEETING (00:47:21)

CM: "I think that a life properly lived is just learning, learning, learning all the time. I think Berkshire gained enormously from these investment decisions, like See's Candies, by learning over a long, long period. Every time you appoint a new person who's never had big capital allocation experience, it's like rolling the dice. I think we're way better off having done it so long. But the decisions blend, and the one feature that comes through is continuous learning. If we had not kept learning, you wouldn't even be here. You'd be alive probably, but not here."

WB: "There's nothing like the pain of being in a lousy business to make you appreciate a good one."

CM: "Well, there's nothing like getting into a really good one that's a very pleasant experience and it's a learning experience. I have a friend who says, 'The first rule of fishing is to fish where the fish are. And the second rule of fishing is to never forget the first rule.' We have got good at fishing where the fish are."

WB: "Yeah, we bought a department store in Baltimore in 1966 [Hochschild Kohn]. And there's really nothing like being in an experience of trying to decide whether you're going to put a new store in an area that hasn't really developed yet enough to support it, but your competitor may move there first. You have to decide whether to jump in. And if you jump in, that kind of spoils it. Now you've got two stores where even one store isn't quite justified. You learn how to play those business games by trying. What you really learn is which ones to avoid. If you just stay out of a bunch of terrible businesses, you're off to a very great start; we've tried them all."

2019 MEETING (05:02:05)

WB: "We've probably had a dozen or so ideas over the years to expand See's. We used to really focus on it because it was a much more sizable part of our business. In fact, it was practically our only business aside from insurance. We've had ten or twelve ideas, and some we tried more than once; as we got a new manager, they tried them again. The truth is none of them really work.

"The business is extraordinarily good in a very small niche. Boxed chocolates are something that everybody likes to receive, or maybe give it as a gift. But relatively few of the people go out and buy to consume themselves. If I leave a box of chocolates open at the office—we've only got twenty-five people—it's gone, almost immediately. If I take it as a gift to somebody, they're happy to get it. And if you leave the box open at a dinner party, they're all gone. But those same people that so readily grab it when it's right in front of them do not walk out to a candy store very often and buy it just to eat themselves. It's very much a gift product. It does not grow worldwide.

"It's very interesting. Last time I checked, people in the West prefer milk chocolate, people in the East prefer dark chocolate. People in the West like big, chunky pieces. People in the East will take miniatures. We've tried to move it geographically many, many, many times. When it works it works wonderfully. But it doesn't travel that well. If we open a store in the East, we get enormous traffic for a while and everybody says, 'We've been waiting for you to come.' And then we end up with a store that does X pounds per year when we need one and a half X in the same square footage to make terrific returns. And we've tried everything because the math is so good when it works. Overall, chocolate consumption generally doesn't grow that much."

CM: "We failed in turning our little candy company into Mars or Hershey for the same reason that you fail to get the Nobel Prize in physics and achieve immortality. It's too tough for us."

WB: "But we put $25 million into See's, and it has since given us well over $2 billion of pre-tax income, which we've used to buy other businesses. If we were the typical company and had bought See's, and tried desperately to use all the retained earnings within the candy business, I think we'd have fallen on our face. All these formulas you learn, or having a strategic plan to use all the capital—some businesses just work in a fairly limited area. Others really play out.

"Dr Pepper might have a 10% or 12% market share in Dallas, and then you go to Detroit or Boston and it's less than 1%. Dr Pepper has been around since the time that Coke was founded in 1886—it's amazing how certain things travel and certain things don't. You mentioned Hershey. Cadbury doesn't do that well here and Hershey doesn't do that well in the UK. Here we are, we all look alike. But somehow, we eat different candy bars. It's very interesting to observe. ..."

CM: "I once told a very great man at dinner after he'd written a very great book, 'You know, you're never going to write another great book like that.' He was deeply offended. I've read his four subsequent books and I was totally right. To write one great book is a lot to do in one lifetime. People aren't holding back on you when they don't do more. It's hard."

WB: "You ought to make the most of the first one you got. I would've blown the chance to buy See's, but Charlie said, 'Don't be so cheap,' basically. And we still got it at a pretty good price. "

CM: "It's amazing how much we've learned over the years—and if we hadn't, the record would be so much worse. At any given time, what we already knew was not going to be enough to take us to the next step. That's what makes it difficult. Think of all the people who have tried to take one extra step and have fallen off a cliff."

THE HISTORY OF COCA-COLA'S U.S. DISTRIBUTION

1997 MEETING (04:33:05)

WB: "Coca-Cola has been very intelligent about using their capital to fortify and improve their bottler network around the world. They've done a terrific job. That was a neglected area for a long time.

"The bottling thing's kind of interesting. [Coca-Cola COO] Don Keough had a lot to do with this, and [Coca-Cola CEO] Roberto Goizueta had plenty to do with it, too, obviously. Back in the late 1880s, [business tycoon] Asa Candler essentially bought the whole Coca-Cola Company for $2,000 in a series of transactions. That may be the smartest purchase in the history of the world. Then in 1899, a couple of fellows from Chattanooga, Tennessee came down. And in those days, soft drinks were primarily sold over the counter to people in drug stores. But there was a little bottling going on; these fellows came down and said, 'Bottling has a future—you're busy on the fountain side of the business, why don't you let us develop the bottling system?' I guess Mr. Candler didn't think much of bottling. So, he gave them a contract, in perpetuity, for almost all of the United States, for $1, and gave them the right to buy Coca-Cola syrup at a fixed price forever.

"Asa Candler, who had scored with his $2,000 [Coca-Cola purchase] in a rather big way, managed to write what certainly looks like one of the dumbest contracts in history. And, of course, as the years went by, and particularly around World War II with the price of syrup—the primary ingredient, in terms of cost, was sugar, and sugar went wild during and after World War II in price—here was a guy that, in effect, had contracted to sell sugar at a fixed price forever. He'd also given these people perpetual rights and so on. In those days, they sold the sub rights to bottler contracts, and those were usually the distance that a horse could go in a day and come back.

"The Coca-Cola Company was faced, over the years, with a problem of having the bottling system, which soon became the dominant system for distribution of Coke, being subject to contracts where there was no price flexibility and where the contracts ran in perpetuity. And, of course, every bottler on his death bed would call his children and grandchildren around, prop himself up and croak out in his last breath, 'Don't let them screw with the bottling contract.' So, the Coca-Cola Company faced this for decades, and they really couldn't do much about that bottling system for a long time. Roberto Goizueta and Don Keough and some other people spent twenty-five years getting that rationalized. It was a huge, huge project, but it made an enormous difference over time in the value of the company.

"That's what I mean when I talk about intellectual capital, because you know you aren't going to get results on that in a day, week, month, or year, if you set out to get that all rationalized. But they decided that to get the job done, they had to do this. And that took capital. ... But they used capital beyond that to repurchase shares in a big way. It's been very smart. They are repurchasing shares, probably, as we talk. And that's fine with me."

CM: "The Coca-Cola Company is one of the most interesting cases in the history of business. There's just lesson after lesson after lesson in the history of the Coca-Cola Company."

EVALUATING COCA-COLA

1998 MEETING (01:35:40)

WB: "With Coca-Cola, the bottling transactions are incidental to a long-term strategy which, in my view, has been enormously successful to date, and which has more successes ahead of it. But in the process of rearranging and consolidating the bottling system, and expanding to relatively undeveloped markets, there have been, and there will be, a lot of bottling transactions. Some produce large gains, some produce small gains. I ignore those in my evaluation of Coke. The two important elements in Coke are unit case sales and shares outstanding. If shares outstanding go down and the unit case sales advance at a good clip, you are going to make money over time in Coca-Cola. There have been transactions where people have purchased rights to various drinks, and when you see what is paid for 100 million-unit cases, and then you think maybe Coke will add 1.5 billion cases a year, that's a real gain in value. It's a dramatic gain in value. And that is what counts, in terms of the Coca-Cola Company. If you think they will sell some multiples of their present volume fifteen or twenty years from now, and you think there'll be a lot fewer shares outstanding, you've gone about as far as you need to go. But I would pay no attention to asset gains. I would take those out of the picture."

2003 MEETING (03:28:21)

WB: "Ever since I described Coca-Cola as an 'Inevitable', I talked about it in terms of the probabilities that they would dominate the soft drink market and not lose market share, that they would grow over time. It's happening year after year; I don't think the global market share of Coca-Cola products has ever been higher than it is now, and I don't see anything that changes that in the future. It is a huge distribution system that has been getting into the minds of more and more consumers since 1886, when John Pemberton, at Jacobs' Pharmacy in Atlanta, served up the first one. It is in the minds of people, the product is all over the world, and there'll be more people and it will be in their minds more firmly. And over time, they should make a little more per drink. So, I don't know how in the world anybody would successfully dethrone Coca-Cola."

COCA-COLA: MARKET SHARE AND MIND SHARE

1999 MEETING (02:10:19)

WB: "It's in Coke's interest to have prosperous countries around the world. They will benefit from increased prosperity, increased standards of living, throughout the world. I think people's preference for Coca-Cola products will do nothing but grow. What I am concerned about is share of market and then what I call share of mind. In other words, what do people think about Coca-Cola now compared to ten to twenty years ago? What are they going to think about it ten to twenty years from now? Coca-Cola has a marvelous share of mind around the world. Almost everybody in the world has something in their mind about Coca-Cola products—and overwhelmingly it's favorable. Try to think of three other companies like it. I can't do it, in terms of that ubiquity of good feeling about the product.

"We want a lot more unit cases sold and we like the idea of fewer shares outstanding over time. I'll be giving that same answer ten or twenty years from now. And I think they'll be a lot more unit cases sold then ... Right now, we own 8.2% of Coca-Cola, and we'll probably own a larger percentage ten years from now, because they'll have probably repurchased some stock. The P/E ratio of Coke, like virtually every other leading company in the world, strikes us as being quite full. That doesn't mean they're going to go down. But it does mean that our enthusiasm for buying more of these wonderful companies is less than it was when the P/E ratios were substantially less. Ideally, those are the kind of companies we want to buy more of over time. My guess is there's a reasonable chance, at least, that sometime in the next ten years, we buy more shares of either Coke or Gillette or American Express or some of those other wonderful companies we own. We do not like the P/E ratios, generally. But, again, that does not mean they're going down. It just means that we got spoiled in terms of how much we got for our money in the past. And we hope that we get spoiled again."

CM: "If what matters to you is what you think Coca-Cola is going to look like in ten years or even further out, you don't really pay much attention to short-term economic developments in this country or that, currency rates, or any other such things. They don't help you in making the ten to fifteen-year projection, and that's the one we're making. So, we have tuned out all this noise."

WB: "It's hard to think of a better business in the world, among big businesses. There are obviously companies that are starting from much smaller bases that could grow faster. But it's hard to think of a much more solid business."

2012 MEETING (04:20:10)

WB: "There are some industries that are never going to have barriers to entry. In those industries, you better run very fast because there are a lot of other people who are going to be looking at what you're doing and trying to figure out your weakness or what they can do a little bit better. A great barrier to entry is something like Coca-Cola. If you gave me $20 billion or $30 billion and told me to try and knock off the Coca-Cola Company with some new cola, I wouldn't have the faintest idea how to do it. There are billions of people around the world that have something in their mind about Coca-Cola, and you're not going to change that with $20 billion."

THE WALT DISNEY COMPANY

1996 MEETING (03:38:41)

WB: "I would say that by far the most important person at Disney in the last twelve years has been CEO Michael Eisner. If you know him and what he has done in the business, there's no one [who compares] ... Eisner has been the 'Walt Disney,' in effect, of his tenure. He knows the business. He loves the business. He eats, lives, and breathes it. He has been, in my view, by far the most important factor in Disney's success. Now, they face competition. The big money is in the animated films and everything that revolves around that, because you go from films to parks to character merchandising and back. It's a circular sort of thing, which feeds on itself. There's going to be plenty of competition. You've seen what MCA and Universal are going to do in the parks in Florida. And you know what DreamWorks is going to do in animation. And now, you've got new technology in animation, through Steve Jobs at Pixar. There's a lot of things going on in that field.

"So the question is, ten years from now, what share of mind—they call it share of market, but it starts with share of mind—what place in the minds of billions of children around the world, and their parents, does Disney have, and their characters, relative to other organizations and other characters? It's a competitive world, so there will be people fighting for that. I would rather start with Disney's hand than anyone else's by some margin. And I would rather start with Michael Eisner running the place than anyone else, by some margin. That does not mean that it can't become a much more competitive business. People look at the video releases of *The Lion King* and they salivate—30 million copies at $16 or $17, you can figure out the manufacturing cost, it gets your attention. And it gets your competitors' attention. But going back, if I thought the children of the world were going to want to be entertained ten or twenty years from now, and I had my choice of betting on who is going to have a special place in the minds of kids and their parents, I think I would bet on Disney. And I would feel particularly good about betting on them, if I had the guy who has done what Eisner has done over those years presiding in the future."

CM: "It helps to do the simple arithmetic. Suppose you have a billion children of low-to-middle income twenty years from now. And suppose you could make $10 per year per child, after taxes, from your position. It gets into very large numbers. I don't know about your children and grandchildren, but mine want to see Disney. And they want to see it over and over and over again. They don't want to see Katzenberg, in terms of the trade name."

WB: "It's a pretty good trade name. When you think about names around the world, it's very hard to beat Coca-Cola, but Disney's a very, very big name. And to Charlie's point, they want to see them over and over again, and it's kind of nice to be able to recycle *Snow White* every seven or eight years. You hit a different crowd. It's kind of like having an oil field, where you pump out all the oil and sell it, and then it all seeps back in over seven or eight years."

PRODUCTS THAT TRAVEL WELL

2000 MEETING (04:16:11)

WB: "With any business that's been around in the United States a long time, there's probably more opportunity, potentially anyway, around the rest of the world ... We love the idea of products that will travel—but some travel well and some don't. It's an incredible world that way. ... We're always interested in geographical expansion, whether it's in the United States or into other countries. It's just not as easy as it looks. But when the chance to do it comes, then you ought to just pound and pound and pound."

COCA-COLA BOTTLERS

2002 MEETING (02:42:11)

WB: "Certain Coca-Cola bottlers became quite leveraged. They have a business that's a solid, steady business, but it's not one with abnormal profitability. So, it can take leverage, in the sense that it won't be subject to huge dips, but it also is a business where it's very tough to increase margins significantly. So, if most of the money goes to debt service, that is something that you have to take into account when you value the equity. It's a fairly capital-intensive business; on average, the bottlers probably spend between 5% and 6% of revenues on capital expenditures just to stay in the same place. And in a business that, before depreciation, interest, and taxes, makes maybe 15 cents on the dollar, having five or six cents go to capital expenditures is a pretty healthy percentage. It's just the nature of the bottling business. It's a reason why I basically like the syrup business better than the bottling business. It's less capital-intensive. On the other hand, I think that the bottling business is a perfectly decent business. It isn't a wonderful business because it's very competitive.

"On any given weekend, the big supermarket or Walmart in town is going to be featuring one or the other of the colas, and it's going to be based on price.

And it has become something where a lot of people will switch from one to another, based on price. And that makes it a tough business for bottlers. But it's a decent business.

"In terms of the Coca-Cola Company itself, its bottlers are going to do perfectly OK over time. They've got to earn enough money to be able to sustain that kind of capital expenditure and earn a cost of capital. And if they get in trouble because they pay too much for another bottler, it gets tough to make the math work. In the end, there's no question the Coca-Cola Company needs a successful bottling group in order to prosper as a syrup manufacturer. But the profitability of bottling will allow that. And the capital requirements at Big Coke, as it's called, are relatively minor, so most of the money they make can be used to pay dividends or repurchase shares."

PRICING POWER AND INFLATION

2005 MEETING (00:53:44)

WB: "We like buying businesses where we feel that there's some untapped pricing power. Back in 1972, when we bought See's Candies, I think it was $1.95 a pound. And they were selling 16 million pounds of candy a year, making $4 million pre-tax against our $25 million purchase price, which I very foolishly refused to budge on, and which would have cost us a lot of money. But one of the questions we asked ourselves, and we thought the answer was obvious, was if we raised the price $0.10 a pound, would sales fall off a cliff? And the answer, in our view at least, was no, there was some untapped pricing power. It's not a great business when you have to have a prayer session before you raise your prices a penny; you are in a tough business then. And I would say you can almost measure the strength of a business over time by the agony they go through in determining whether a price increase can be sustained … You can learn a lot about the durability of the economics of a business by observing the price behavior."

2011 MEETING (03:09:00)

WB: "The businesses that will perform best during inflation are the ones that require little capital investment to facilitate inflationary growth and which have strong positions that allow them to increase prices with inflation. At See's Candies, the value of the dollar since we bought that business has probably fallen at least 85%. That business sells 75% more pounds of candy than it did when we bought it, but it has ten times the revenues and it doesn't take a lot more capital. Any business that has enough freedom to price to offset inflation without huge investment to support it will do well."

2015 MEETING (02:37:51)

WB: "The best businesses during inflation are usually the businesses you buy once and then you don't have to keep making capital investments subsequently ... A brand is a wonderful thing to own during inflation. See's Candies built their brand many years ago. We've had to nourish it as we've gone along, but the value of any strong branded good increases during inflation. Gillette bought the entire radio rights to the World Series in 1939, and, as I remember, for $100,000. Think of the number of impressions they made on minds in 1939 dollars for $100,000; they were getting in the minds of young guys like myself—I was eight or nine—and they did it in those dollars. If you were going to go out and try out and have similar impressions on millions of minds now, it'd cost a fortune. Part of that is due to inflation, part of it's due to other things. But it was a great investment, which could be made in 1939 dollars that paid off, in selling razors and blades, in 1960, 1970, and 1980 dollars. So, that's the kind of business you want to own."

COCA-COLA'S STOCK PRICE

2006 MEETING (01:49:09)

WB: "Coca-Cola is a fabulous company. Coca-Cola will sell over 21 billion cases of various products—Coke more than anything else—around the world this year, and it goes up every year. The stock in 1998 sold for over $80 a share when the earnings were $1.50 a share, and the earnings then were not as good a quality as the earnings now ... It strikes us as a really wonderful business that sold at a very silly price some years back. You can definitely fault me for not selling the stock. I always thought it was a wonderful business, but clearly, at fifty times earnings, it was a silly price. But we like it; we'll own it ten years from now, in my view."

COCA-COLA COMPENSATION AND STOCK OPTIONS

2014 MEETING (00:13:13)

WB: "I did talk to Coca-Cola CEO Muhtar Kent and I informed him that we were going to abstain. I told him that we admire, enormously, the Coca-Cola Company, and we admire the management. And we thought the compensation plan, although it was very similar to a great many plans, was excessive ... Immediately after the vote, I publicly announced we had abstained, and gave the reasons that we thought the plan was excessive. I think in terms of having an effect on Coca-Cola's compensation practices, as well as maybe having an effect on some other compensation practices, that was and is the most effective way of behaving for Berkshire. We made a very clear statement about the excessiveness of the plan—and at the same time, we in no way went to war with Coca-Cola. We have no desire to go to war with Coca-Cola, and we did not endorse some calculations that were wildly inaccurate.

"For those of you who would really like to know how to think about calculating dilution, Coca-Cola has regularly repurchased shares that are issued through options. The share count has come down just a small bit, although not anywhere near as much as if they hadn't issued as many shares. But Coca-Cola has a plan that involves 500 million shares. And they say in the annual report that they expect to issue these over approximately four years ... That's a lot of shares.

"Let's assume Coca-Cola is selling around $40 a share and that all the options are issued at $40. And when they're exercised, we'll say that the stock is at $60. At that point, there has been a $10 billion transfer of value; $20 per share times 500 million shares equals a $10 billion transfer of value. When that is done, the company gets a tax deduction, and at the present tax rates, that would result in $3.5 billion less tax. So, if you take $20 billion of proceeds from exercise of the options [500 million × $40 per share], and add $3.5 billion of tax savings, Coca-Cola receives $23.5 billion. And if they buy the stock at $60 a share, they would buy 391,666,666 shares. In effect, the Coca-Cola Company, net, would be out a little over 108 million shares [500 million shares minus 391.7 million shares]. That's on a base of 4.4 billion shares. The dilution, assuming all the proceeds from the option exercise and the tax refund were used to buy shares, would be 2.5% [108 million ÷ 4.4 billion]. I don't like dilution, and I don't like 2.5% dilution—but it is a far cry from the numbers that were getting tossed around."

RETAIL BARGAINING POWER

2006 MEETING (04:17:49)

WB: "I think it's clear that Procter & Gamble is a consumer powerhouse. And Gillette, in its field, has about as strong a consumer position as anybody will ever have. In blades and razors, stronger than most of the P&G brands, as strong as they may be. And I do think the big retailers are becoming—and more so all the time—brands of their own. So I think the struggle between the manufacturers of brands and retailers will go on and on, and become more intensified. If I were on either side of that equation, I would want to be strengthening my hand. And I think the future of both Gillette and P&G are better as a combined enterprise than they would have been as a separate enterprise. And I think that's particularly true because of the strengths of the Walmarts and the Costcos of the world."

CONSUMER BRANDS

2008 MEETING (02:52:55)

WB: "I would say most of the big food companies are good businesses in that they earn good returns on tangible assets. If you own important, branded products in this country—Wrigley's, Mars, Coca-Cola, See's Candies, or a number of the Kraft brands—you have good assets.

"It's not easy to take on those products. Coca-Cola will sell 1.5 billion eight-ounce servings of its product around the world today. There's something in everybody person's mind virtually around the globe about Coca-Cola. Since 1886, it's a product that has been associated with happiness and good value in terms of refreshment and all that. It's just about impossible, in my mind, to take on a product like that. It clearly satisfies people in a huge way everywhere on the globe.

"Kraft has Kool-Aid in the powdered soft drink business; I don't think I'd want to take on Kool-Aid, but I'd rather have Coca-Cola. RC Cola has been around a long, long time, but it isn't going to go anyplace. That is very, very difficult. They say that a brand is a promise. There's a promise involved in picking up a Milky Way or a Coca-Cola, as to what it's going to deliver to you.

"Richard Branson came over ten years ago, a fellow with a famous airline, and he came out with something called Virgin Cola. And I thought that was kind of an unusual promise to have in a product; I never could quite figure that one out, what the promise was. But whatever it was, it didn't work. And there have been hundreds of colas over the years. But in the end, who is going to buy some substitute cola for a penny or two less than a can of Coca-Cola? The same thing with See's Candies, Kool-Aid, or whatever it may be.

"So we feel pretty good about branded products when they're runaway leaders in their field. The specifics of which one we buy may depend on how we feel about the price. It certainly will make a difference how we feel about the price, the management, and some other factors. But if you buy in with good branded products and you don't pay too much, you're probably going to do OK. On the other hand, you're not going to get super rich because the attributes that I've just laid out are pretty well recognized."

KRAFT/CADBURY DEAL

2010 MEETING (03:30:34)

WB: "I didn't like the Cadbury decision or the pizza decision [deal announced in early 2010 by Kraft to acquire confectioner Cadbury, along with the decision to sell its pizza business to Nestlé]. But we've made our share of dumb deals at

Berkshire. So I've gotten more tolerant of other people. Incidentally, the fact I think it's a dumb deal doesn't for certain make it a dumb deal, but I think the odds are it was. In fact, I think the odds are that both deals were dumb.

"The pizza deal was particularly dumb in my view ... They announced they were selling the pizza business for $3.7 billion; they didn't sell it for $3.7 billion, that's what the other guy paid. What they got was about $2.5 billion. That was a terribly tax-inefficient deal ... They didn't reference what pizza was earning beforehand; I think Nestlé said it was earning $280 million pre-tax, but that was referring to the previous year. When they talked about the Cadbury earnings they were buying, they were talking about next year. And when they talked about the pizza earnings they were selling, they talked about last year. In 2009, pizza earned $340 million pre-tax. So they got $2.5 billion for $340 million of pizza earnings that were growing as fast or faster than the Cadbury earnings and where the sales were growing as fast or faster. It really didn't make sense ... If it was me, I would have voted to keep pizza and not buy Cadbury. I expressed myself, and I don't do that too often, but we owned a lot of Kraft ... I just hated to see them give up a significant portion of those businesses to buy Cadbury at what I felt was a very fancy price."

CM: "I think generally, at the top of American businesses, people think they know too much about strategy. And they tend to hate the tough competitive conditions in the business they're in, and to yearn for some business where it's less difficult. You remember when Xerox bought Crum & Forster, an American insurance company, one of the dumbest acquisitions in all time? The reason Xerox did that is they didn't have any tough Japanese competing in the insurance business. They were really tired of facing the tough competition they had in the business they were in. I think it's quite typical to dream, if you're in business, that something that's a little different, no matter how much you pay for it, will make your troubles less."

WB: "And you will have an absolute army of lawyers, investment advisors, public relations people, all of whom will have a strong economic interest in having you push ahead on deal after deal after deal, regardless of how the shareholders come out. It's just the way it works."

KRAFT/HEINZ DEAL

2019 MEETING (01:06:26)

WB: "When we originally owned about half of Heinz, we paid an appropriate price. We actually did well. We had some preferred redeemed and so on. But we paid too much money for Kraft. To some extent, our own actions drove up the prices. Now Kraft Heinz, the profits of that business are roughly $6 billion pre-tax on $7 billion of tangible assets; that is a wonderful business. But you can pay too much for a wonderful business. We bought See's Candies, and we made a great purchase as it turned out. We could've paid more. But there's some price at which it wouldn't have worked. The business does not know how much you paid for it; it's going to earn based on its fundamentals. And we paid too much for the Kraft side of Kraft Heinz.

"The profitability has basically been improved in those operations over the way they were operating before. But you're quite correct that Amazon itself has become a brand. Kirkland, at Costco, is a $39 billion brand. All of Kraft Heinz is $26 billion. It's been around on the Heinz side for around 150 years, and it has spent billions and billions of dollars advertising their products. They go through tens of thousands of outlets. And here's somebody like Costco, it establishes a brand called Kirkland. It's now doing $39 billion, more than virtually any food company. And that brand moves from product to product; it is terrific when a brand travels ... Kirkland operates through 775 or so Costco warehouses. The retailer and the brands have always struggled as to who gets the upper hand in moving a product to the consumers. And there's no question, in my mind, that the position of the retailer, relative to the brands, varies enormously around the world.

"In different countries, you've had 35% or 40% private-label market share in soft drinks. It has never got anywhere close to that in the United States. But certain retailers have gained some power. In the case of Amazon, Walmart, Costco, Aldi, and some others, they've gained power relative to brands. Kraft Heinz is still doing very well, operationally, but we paid too much. If we paid $50 billion, it would've been a different business. It'd still be earning the same amount. You can turn any investment into a bad deal by paying too much. What you can't do is turn any investment into a good deal by paying little, which is sort of how I started out in this world. But the idea of buying the cigar butts that are declining or poor businesses for a bargain price is not something we try to do anymore. We try to buy good businesses at a decent price. And we made a mistake on the Kraft part of Kraft Heinz."

CM: "It's not a tragedy that out of two transactions, one worked wonderfully and the other didn't work so well. That happens."

WB: "The operations of Kraft Heinz have been improved by the present management overall. But we paid a very high price for the Kraft part. We paid an appropriate price for Heinz."

PART TWELVE:
GEICO and U.S. Auto Insurance

"We do not like having a huge umbrella over an industry. We want the most efficient companies to be the ones that do well and the less-efficient ones to have plenty of problems."

"The auto insurance business ought to be studied in business school because it essentially refutes so many of the things they're currently teaching."

"Picking some extreme example and asking my favorite question—'What in hell is going on here?'—is the way to wisdom in this world."

"The thing to do is just keep trying to think things through and not do too many stupid things. Sooner or later, you have a lollapalooza, as Charlie would say."

INTRODUCTION

ON A SATURDAY MORNING IN JANUARY 1951, WARREN BUFFETT LEARNED about the insurance business from Lorimer Davidson (who became GEICO's CEO in 1958). As Buffett later noted, what Davidson told him that morning had an immediate impact on how he thought about the business: afterwards, he promptly invested more than 65% of his net worth into GEICO. Fast forward forty-four years, to 1995, when Berkshire paid ~$2.3 billion for the 49% of GEICO that it didn't already own. As highlighted in this section, Buffett and Munger have taken numerous investing and business lessons from GEICO, as well as from the history of industry peers like State Farm.

But it became apparent in the late 2010s that GEICO had started to lag certain competitors, most notably on rate setting at Progressive due to data/telematics. As you will see, that disadvantage took many years before it became a notable headwind at GEICO; the problem, as seen in the early 2020s, is that it has also taken a long time for an effective response to be found at GEICO (as of late 2024, they are still working to address these challenges). This has offered an important lesson on how even a well-positioned business with significant competitive advantages can come under real pressure if it misses key developments and technological changes within its industry. (For more on this topic, see "GEICO: The Gecko Stumbles" at TSOH Investment Research.)

SUBJECTS AND MEETINGS FEATURED

ADDITION OF GEICO TO BERKSHIRE

1996 MEETING (01:32:41)

WARREN BUFFETT: "GEICO is a huge plus to Berkshire. We owned 50% of it before, and we've benefitted from our GEICO investment in a big way since 1976. We paid a good price for GEICO, but it is a terrific company. It has outstanding management. It has a low-cost method of distribution, which is very difficult for people to [compete with]; everybody wants to have that, but very few come close. Management is focused on bringing costs down even further and widening that competitive moat. I personally think that, just from what I see, GEICO's growth rate is likely to be greater in the future versus where it has been in the past.

"I think there are some advantages to it being part of Berkshire, in that there are costs attached to bringing new business on the books, and we care not at all about reported quarterly earnings. GEICO was relatively insensitive to those before, and that's a compliment when I say that. But they had more pressure on them in respect to reported earnings than they will have as part of Berkshire. And I think there's some really big opportunities, in terms of what can be done with GEICO as part of Berkshire. So, I think five years from now, you'll be very happy we own 100% of GEICO. I think you will see that, as marvelous a company as GEICO was as an independent company, it will maybe flourish even a bit more in Berkshire. Not because we bring anything to the party; management will continue to run it autonomously. But there are some advantages for it in being part of Berkshire."

MANAGERIAL FOCUS AT GEICO

1996 MEETING (03:04:16)

WB: "GEICO has 2% of the U.S. auto insurance market. We have 2.5 million policyholders, but there are over 100 million in the country. There is such an opportunity here that it would be diversionary to go into other countries. There's been a firm that was very successful in England that introduced a somewhat GEICO-like operation about ten years ago. And they did very well. They are now encountering more competition and their results are falling off somewhat. But there's a huge potential for GEICO in this country. I would not want GEICO management to be going off in other directions when there's so much to be done here. Three percentage points on our growth rate here, for example, would be $75 million of premium volume. And that, in turn, would keep compounding over time.

"There's too much to do here before we set up some start-up operation around the world. And there are actually various problems in a lot of jurisdictions to run a GEICO-like operation, although I wouldn't say that prevails every place. There could be opportunities. But the opportunity here in this country is huge. And the management of GEICO is focused. I love focused management ... GEICO actually started fooling around in a number of things in the early 1980s, and they paid a very big price to do it. They paid a direct price, in terms of the cost of those things, because they almost all worked out badly. And then they paid an additional price in the loss of focus on the main business. That will not happen with the present management. [CEO] Tony Nicely thinks about nothing else but carrying the GEICO message to the 97.5% of people who are not policyholders. And that will work very well for us over time."

HISTORY OF U.S. AUTO INSURANCE

1997 MEETING (04:23:50)

WB: "The history of auto insurance is quite interesting; it's something that should be studied in business schools. The great insurance companies of the early 1900s—Aetna, Hartford, Travelers—had agency forces nationwide and wrote what was then more property business. They wrote a lot of fire business in those days, and, of course, the automobile came in the early 1900s. So, their orientation was to property business, but they had this huge agency force throughout the United States. There were property insurance agents representing these big companies throughout the country, and they had lots of capital. And now, in 1997, if you look at the business, probably close to 25% of the personal, auto, and homeowner's business in insurance is written by State Farm.

"State Farm was started in 1922 by a fellow in Bloomington, Illinois, with no capital to speak of, no agency force initially and started as a mutual company, no [stockholder] incentive—I mean, no stock options, no capital invested where he could become a billionaire if he built the business up. So, this company starts without any of the capitalist incentives that we are taught are essential to a business growing, and in a huge industry, becomes the dominant player—it has more than twice the market share of Allstate, the second player—against these extremely entrenched competitors with great distribution systems and loads of capital. And incidentally, State Farm, on the Fortune 500 list, has the third largest net worth of any company in the United States. Number three, from Bloomington, Illinois, with a guy who had no money in it. How does that happen? Well, I would say that's a subject worth studying in business schools. Darwin used to say that any time he got any evidence that flew in the face of his previous convictions, he had to write it down in the first thirty minutes or the mind was such that it would reject contrary evidence to cherished beliefs. And certainly, there's some cherished beliefs around business schools that might, at least, find some interesting aspects in studying how a company could become the third largest company in net worth in the country with no apparent advantage going in.

"There's another company called USAA. It has been enormously successful, has billions of net worth, loads of satisfied policyholders, the highest renewal ratio among policyholders in the country. Nobody studies that, to my knowledge, either. The people who started GEICO came from USAA. In 1936, Leo Goodwin and his wife, who had worked for USAA, started GEICO with practically no capital. Now we have about 2.7% of the market, and we'll write probably $3.5 billion of voluntary auto premiums this year.

"Catching State Farm is going to be very difficult, so I wouldn't want to predict we'll do that. I will predict that we will gain very materially in market share over the next ten years. We have got a very good mousetrap. I said in the annual report that 40% of you would save money insuring with GEICO—I didn't say 100%, 80%, or 60% because there are areas and professions where somebody else is going to have a lower price. But across the country, and for all classes of citizens, we are going to have the low price more often than anyone else. We've got that because we've got low costs and our costs are going to get lower. And we've got a virtuous circle going, feeding on itself. So, GEICO will grow a lot."

CHARLIE MUNGER: "I love your example of State Farm. Picking some extreme example and asking my favorite question—'What in hell is going on here?'—is the way to wisdom in this world. A lot of the mutual companies are now trying to demutualize, helped by a bunch of consultants and so forth. And they are not looking at State Farm, they're looking at some other model. Everybody can't be a State Farm. That place got some fundamental values into its operating mechanics, the way it selected personnel, the way it selected agents, the way it discarded agents. It was huge discipline in that operation."

WB: "Yeah, you would say somebody had to do something very right. But I don't know anybody studying what they did that was right. They don't want to because it doesn't fit the pattern. When something like a State Farm or a GEICO happens in this world, you should try to understand it. In 1948, I think two-thirds of GEICO was for sale because the fellow who had originally backed these two people from USAA died, and so they had the stock for sale. You couldn't sell it. That's how Ben Graham ended up buying it for Graham-Newman, because they [tried to sell it] for six months. They went to all the big insurance companies, and those companies, who could see this company on a very, very tiny scale offering a product for way less money and making lots of money doing it, simply couldn't shake themselves loose from the myths of the past to buy it. They could've bought the whole company for $1.2 million, as I remember. Instead, they've watched their own distribution system get their heads beaten in over the years. And all the time with these ideas from the past. So, you have to be very careful to look hard at what's really happening. As Yogi Berra said, 'You can observe a lot just by looking.'"

KEY VARIABLES AT GEICO

1998 MEETING (01:37:55)

WB: "At GEICO, the key is policies in force (PIFs) and underwriting experience per policy. And that is exactly the way we pay people there. We pay them, from the bottom to the very top, based on what happens with those two variables. We don't talk about earnings per share at GEICO, and we don't talk about investment income. We don't get off the track, because those are two things that are going to determine what kind of business GEICO is over time."

GEICO'S COMPETITIVE ADVANTAGES

2000 MEETING (03:54:20)

WB: "The auto industry has been unduly benign in the last few years. I would regard this as much more a return to normalcy. The profits in auto insurance, industrywide, have been far higher than, I think, are sustainable, and higher than I would've predicted five years ago. So the industry got very, very lucky for a while. That wasn't necessarily good for us, incidentally. We made more money than we would've otherwise made. But there was a big umbrella over the industry, too, so that less-efficient competitors still did very well. We do not find the [current] environment of lower profits undesirable at all. We do not like having a huge umbrella over an industry. We want the most efficient companies to be the ones that do well and the less-efficient ones to have plenty of problems. So, we are not unhappy about the fact that margins in the auto insurance business are going down. We think they should go down. As long as we feel that we are adding policyholders at a cost that's less than their net value to us over time, we will continue to do it. We'll love to do it. But we won't be making the kind of money, in 2000, that we made in 1999, which was not as good as what we made in 1998. As far as we're concerned, that's fine.

"Over time, we will be the low-cost producer—that is our goal. And I think we've got a lot of things going in our direction to enable us to do that. The low-cost producer in a huge industry is going to do very well over time … The GEICO equation is fundamentally good … We think we can attract business at a lower cost and then run it at a lower cost than most of the competition, if not all … We've got a very good business model … We've got a great machine at GEICO …"

2000 MEETING (04:28:10)

WB: "The sustainable competitive advantage at GEICO is to be the low-cost producer providing very good service. There will be a number of companies that provide good services, so that does not distinguish us from a great many competitors. Having the low cost is crucial. There are companies that specialize in given groups of policyholders, such as USAA, that have very good costs. So they are very, very competitive with us in their chosen area. There's another company in Los Angeles … called 21st Century Insurance, which has costs like ours. So they are extremely competitive within that geographic area. I don't think anybody is any better than us who operates nationwide. We don't operate in Massachusetts or New Jersey, but in the other forty-eight states, we will have a quote for just about anyone.

"So, in terms of a broad-based auto insurance competitor, our competitive advantage has to be low cost over time. Now, we also have to be as good as other people at distinguishing among the risks posed by different kinds of drivers. In other words, we have to be able to select people who are going to be better-than-average drivers, and we have to be able to understand who is likely to be a poorer-than-average driver. The ability … to distinguish those people would be a competitive advantage. I think that many companies tend to be fairly equal on that point. So it's really at this cost level … that there is the competitive advantage. And we have to sustain and widen that, if possible.

"The internet is going to be very important. It already is important to GEICO. It will be more and more important to the insurance industry, because with the internet you have a situation where somebody thinking about insuring a car can click to one place, find out what that rate will be, then click to someplace else and find out what that rate will be. They can shop all around without going from place to place to place and driving all over town or calling lots of agencies. They can just do it right there in their house. And that makes it very important, again, that we be the low-cost company. I think it's going to be an advantage for us, over time. For one thing, I think it makes brand very important. We want people to be thinking of GEICO as one of the possibilities to call. If you have the XYZ Company that nobody's ever heard of, nobody's going to think about clicking on them. And GEICO's brand is becoming extremely familiar to people throughout the country, and we're spending a lot of money to make it even more familiar."

2004 MEETING (03:39:30)

WB: "Virtually every American family wants to have a car. They don't want to have insurance, but they can't drive their car without insurance. So they're buying a product they really don't like very well that will cost them a significant part of their family budget. And cost, therefore, becomes very important. It's not a luxury item, it's a mandatory item. Saving significant money makes a real difference in a lot of household budgets, so the low cost is going to win. Progressive has a wonderful direct operation competing with GEICO, and we're the two that will be slugging it out over the years. It's a better system, and better systems win over time."

2009 MEETING (02:26:10)

WB: "I think it was John Dorrance at Campbell Soup, when asked whether they wasted a lot of money on advertising, who said, 'We waste half of it, but we don't know which half.' That is the nature of advertising—although we can measure it better with GEICO than most companies. We will spend about $800 million on advertising. Even though we're the third largest company, we will spend far more than State Farm or Allstate. We were spending a little over $20 million a year when we bought control in 1995.

"We want everybody in the United States to have in their mind the fact that there's a good chance they can save money by picking up the phone or going to the website and checking it out. When we get that message in people's minds, you never know when it's going to pay off later down the line ... We love spending money on advertising at GEICO. And we want to be in everybody's mind ... A brand is a promise. We're getting that promise in people's minds that there's a good chance they can save money if they check with GEICO."

CM: "If GEICO would remain more or less the same size if we didn't advertise so heavily, and if the new subscribers [policyholders] are worth more than the $800 million we're spending in advertising, then, in an important sense, GEICO is earning $800 million more pre-tax in a way that doesn't even show. That's the kind of thing we like to see within Berkshire Hathaway."

WB: "The value of GEICO goes up by far more than the earnings every year, if we keep adding these people, as Charlie says. And we could maintain, I'm sure, for a very long time our present policyholder count and probably spend $100 million a year, maybe less. But we are getting more than our money's worth for what we spend. Overall, we're getting a terrific return on it. And if I thought we could get anything like the same return by spending $2 billion next year, we'd spend it. It's a very attractive business. I don't see how you create anything like it. We are the low-cost producer. And if you're the low-cost producer in something people have to buy and [it costs] roughly $1,500, you've got a terrific, terrific business. We have durable competitive advantages."

INTERNATIONAL EXPANSION FOR GEICO

2001 MEETING (01:31:31)

WB: "When you've got a business model that works as well as GEICO has in this country, and it continues to work well and has that fundamental advantage of being a low-cost operator, we think about every possible way we can to take that idea and extend it. It's been remarkably hard to do it. The management has tried various things, ever since Leo Goodwin started the company in 1936, to take it into other areas, and those efforts have been modestly successful at certain things like life insurance, but then they got out of it. But it's an idea.

"We have 4% or so of the market in the United States. This market is huge. As we look at the drain on human resources involved in extending it into other countries—and we've looked at it a lot, and it may be something we'll do at some time—we've never felt the possible gain, considering the rigidities both in Europe and Asia, of breaking in; it's not easy to get into those markets. The cost, the time, we just felt that it would be better to concentrate those same resources in this country. It's not a question of capital at all. We'd put the money in in a second. There's a human cost to it, there's a financial cost to it. The financial cost bothers us not at all. The human cost is a real question because it gets back to Charlie's opportunity cost. We have talented managers, but we have a finite number of them. And I would rather have Tony Nicely and Bill Roberts and their crew focusing on how to gain additional market share in this country at the right rates than I would starting in a project in Europe or Asia now. But it's a very good question. It's something I can guarantee you we think about all the time and will continue to think about."

PROGRESSIVE AND TELEMATICS

2012 MEETING (00:43:35)

WB: "Progressive has probably been the leader in telematics. We have not done that at GEICO, but we would if it becomes a superior way to evaluate the likelihood of anybody having an accident. I think you have to answer fifty-one questions if you go on GEICO's website to get a quote. Every one of those is designed to evaluate your propensity to get in an accident. Obviously, if you could ride around in a car with somebody for six months, you might learn quite a bit about that propensity, particularly if they didn't know you were there. I do not see that as being a major change, but if it becomes something that gives you better predictive value about the propensity of any given individual to have an accident, we will take it on.

"We're always looking for more things that will tell us someone's likelihood of having an accident. Youth, for example—there is no question that a sixteen-year-old male is much more likely to have an accident than some guy like me who drives 3,500 miles a year and is not trying to impress a girl when he does it. That one is pretty obvious. Some things are very good predictors that you wouldn't necessarily expect to be. Credit scores will tell you a lot about driving habits, but they're not allowed in all places. We'll look at anything, but I don't see in this new experiment anything that threatens GEICO in any way.

"Our marketing is working extremely well, our risk selection is working extremely well, and our retention is working well. GEICO is quite a machine. I think we carry it at roughly $1 billion over its tangible book value; it's worth a whole lot more than that. Based on the price we paid, that figure would come up these days to something like $15 billion over carrying value. We wouldn't sell it there. We wouldn't sell it at all, but that would not tempt us in the least."

2013 MEETING (00:36:17)

WB: "Auto insurance underwriting is an attempt to figure out the likely propensity, based on a number of variables, of a person having an accident ... There are a number of variables that are quite useful in predicting that. Progressive is focusing on this Snapshot arrangement [telematics], and we'll see how they do. I would say that our ability to sell insurance at a price that's considerably lower than most of our competitors, evidenced by the fact that when people call us, they shift to us, and, at the same time, we earn a significant underwriting profit, indicates that our selection process is working quite well.

"If your selection process is wrong you're going to get terrible underwriting results. Our systems and underwriting criteria have been developed over many decades. Everybody in the business is trying to figure out ways to predict with greater accuracy the possibilities that a given individual will have an accident. Progressive is focusing on Snapshot, and we watch it with interest—but we're quite happy with the present situation at GEICO."

2013 MEETING (01:40:27)

WB: "Obviously Progressive disagrees with us, but I don't think that their selection method is better than ours. I would say I might even feel that ours is a little bit better than theirs. But every company has a different approach to it ... We are obtaining, under our selection system, a hugely disproportionate number of new policyholders compared to the growth in the market, so our rates are attractive and our underwriting results are attractive. And we continue, always, to look for further ways to refine the selection technique. But we don't do any of it lightly because what we're doing now is working very well. I invite you to compare the Progressive results with the GEICO results in the next two or three years. If we're wrong, I will be here to freely admit that we were wrong—but I don't think we will be."

2019 MEETING (03:07:38)

WB: "Progressive is a very well-run business, and GEICO is a very well-run business. For a long time, I think they will be the two companies that the rest of the auto insurance industry has trouble not losing market share to. I've always thought for a long, long time that Progressive has been very well run. They have an appetite for growth. Sometimes they copy us a little, and sometimes we copy them a little. I think that'll be true five and ten years from now.

"GEICO sells substantial amounts of homeowners' insurance through an agency arrangement. We were in the business of writing it ourselves until Hurricane Andrew, when the decision was made that in homeowners, essentially, you could lose as much in one year as you made in the previous twenty-five years. And the float isn't as large. So, GEICO places our customers' desire for homeowners' insurance with several other large and solid organizations.

"The big thing is auto insurance ... I feel extremely good about GEICO; what has been built there by Tony Nicely and his people is perfect. But Progressive is an excellent company; we will watch what they do, and they will watch what we do. And we'll see, in five to ten years, which one of us passes State Farm first."

AJIT JAIN: "The underwriting profit is really a function of two major variables: one is the expense ratio, and the other is the loss ratio. GEICO has a significant advantage over Progressive when it comes to the expense ratio, to the extent of about seven points or so. On the loss ratio side, Progressive does a much better job than GEICO does. They have, I think, about a twelve-point advantage over GEICO. So, net-net, Progressive is ahead of us by about five points. GEICO is very aware of this disadvantage on the loss ratio that they are suffering, and they're very focused on trying to bridge that gap as quickly as they can. They have a few projects in place. Sometimes GEICO is ahead of Progressive. Right now, Progressive is ahead of GEICO. But I'm hopeful that GEICO will catch up on the loss ratio side and maintain the expense ratio advantage as well."

WB: "GEICO has gained market share virtually every year since Tony took over. And I would bet significant money that GEICO increases its market share in the next five years. So, it is a terrific business. But Progressive is a terrific business. As Ajit says, we have the advantage in expenses, and we will have an advantage in expenses. They have a very sophisticated way of pricing business. The question is whether we give some of that six points back in terms of loss ratio. We are working very hard at that, but I'm sure they're working very hard as well to improve their system. To some extent it's a two-horse race, and we've got a very good horse."

CM: "In the nature of things, every once in a while, somebody's a little better at something than we are."

2019 MEETING (04:44:25)

WB: "Actually, General Motors had a company for a long time called Motors Insurance Company, and various manufacturers have tried it [selling auto insurance]. I would say the success of the auto companies getting into the insurance business is probably about as likely as the success of the insurance companies getting into the auto business. I worry much more about Progressive than all of the auto company possibilities that I can see, in terms of getting insurance business. It's not an easy business at all. I would bet against any company in the auto business being any kind of an unusual success. The idea of using telematics, in terms of studying drivers' habits, that has been spreading quite widely. And it is important to have data on how people drive, how hard they brake, how much they swerve, all kinds of things. So, I don't doubt the value of the data, but I don't think auto companies like Tesla will have any advantage in that. I don't think that they will make money in the auto insurance business."

2021 MEETING (01:25:25)

WB: "Progressive has had the best operation in recent years, in terms of matching rate to risk. That's what insurance is all about; you have to have the right rate. If you think ninety-year-olds and twenty-year-olds have an equal chance of dying, you're going to be out of business very quickly in the life insurance business. You will get all the ninety-year-old risks and the other guy will get the twenty-year-old risks. The same thing applies in auto insurance. The companies that do the best job of having the appropriate rate for every one of their policyholders is going to do very well—and Progressive has done a very good job on that. We're doing a much better job on that already, and Todd Combs has gone there. It's very interesting. Both Progressive and GEICO were started in the 1930s, and they've had the better product for a long, long time, in terms of cost. Yet here we are, eighty-five years later, and the total is 25% of the market for the two of us. That's after eighty-some-years of having a better product. So, it's a very slow-changing competitive situation, but Progressive has done a very, very good job recently. We've done a very, very good job over the years, and we're doing a good job now, but we have made some very significant improvements.

"State Farm is still the largest auto insurer, but I predict that in five years, it's very likely that the top two will be GEICO and Progressive. I don't know which order, we'll see. GEICO has done extremely well, but Progressive was better at setting the right rate. And we're catching up, I think, fairly fast."

2022 MEETING (01:21:02)

AJ: "The personal automobile insurance business is a very competitive business. Having said that, both GEICO and Progressive are two very successful competitors in this segment. Each have their pluses and minuses. There's no question, more recently, Progressive has done a much better job than GEICO, both in terms of margins and in terms of growth rate. There are a number of causes for that, but I think the biggest culprit as far as GEICO is concerned is telematics. Progressive has been on the telematics bandwagon for more than ten years, probably closer to twenty years. GEICO, until recently, wasn't involved in telematics. And it has only been over the last years that they've made a very serious effort in using telematics for segmentation and for trying to match rate and risk. It's a long journey, but the journey has started, and the initial results are promising. It will take a while, but my hope and expectation is that in the next year or two, GEICO will be in a position to catch up with Progressive in terms of telematics. And hopefully that will then translate into both growth rate and margins."

WB: "The auto insurance industry is a fascinating one to study. … It was 1903 or so when cars really got started. And it wasn't too many years after that they were turning out 2 million cars a year. So, car insurance became very important. For hundreds of years, when people thought about insurance it was ships at sea and fire where they had protective societies. Insurance as a product has been around a long time. But auto insurance, that's been pretty much the same thing since Leo Goodwin started GEICO in 1936. And we came along with a good idea and lots of big companies and all that. But the largest auto insurance company in the United States was started over in Illinois by a guy who didn't know anything about insurance, particularly, and it's a mutual company; it's not supposed to succeed in capitalism.

"If you go to business school, they teach you that a company can only succeed because you have incentives and compensation and all kinds of things. Nobody has really gotten rich off State Farm, and they are the largest insurance company. Leo Goodwin started GEICO some eighty years ago and he probably wanted to get rich. The same is probably true of Progressive as well. People wanted to get rich in Travelers and Aetna—you can name dozens and dozens of companies. Who wins? A mutual company, State Farm. In terms of present size, State Farm is still the largest company. Leaving out Berkshire, they have the largest net worth by far; I think it's $140 billion or something.

"Progressive had a very, very, very smart guy running it for a very long period of time, and they've got very smart people running it now—but their net worth is a sixth that of some people in Illinois whose name nobody knows. They've had the time to sell the same product, they advertise like crazy; we spend $2 billion a year telling people the same thing we've been telling them for seventy or eighty years. The policy doesn't change. But when we get all through, State Farm is still doing more business than anybody. And it shouldn't exist under capitalism. If you had a plan to start a State Farm today that would compete with Progressive, who would put up the capital? A mutual company that you're not going to get the profits from—it doesn't make any sense at all. Except they've got $140 billion or something of net worth. And Progressive, their net worth is around $20 billion or so. They are very, very, very disciplined in underwriting. And of course, on the investment side, their net worth dropped in the first quarter because they own a lot of bonds. They say, and practically everyone in insurance business would say, well, we own bonds because that's what people do. Here's half of the insurance business [managing investments, typically attributable to the float held as insurance premiums paid by policyholders are received months or years before claims are paid] where you do what other people do, and the other half of the business [insurance underwriting] where the company spends all kinds of time to analyze in every single way how you can segregate and properly rate the business. And basically Peter Lewis [from Progressive] sat in my office 40 years ago, smart as hell. And this guy was clearly going to be a major competitor of Berkshire's, and he knew insurance backward and forwards, very bright and everything, but he just ignored the investment side. And that is as important as the underwriting side. It is interesting how organizations function and have blind spots. Of course, Charlie and I know we've got all kinds of blind spots ourselves, so we have to be careful of criticizing other people for having them. But the auto insurance business ought to be studied in business school because it essentially refutes so many of the things they're currently teaching."

2023 MEETING (00:25:33)

AJ: "In terms of GEICO and telematics, GEICO has taken the bull by the horns and has made rapid strides in trying to bridge the gap in telematics with its competitors. They have now reached a point where, on all new business, close to 90% has a telematics input to the pricing decision. Unfortunately, less than half of that is being taken up by policyholders. The other point I want to make is that even though we have made improvements bridging the gap on telematics, we still haven't started to realize the true benefit. The real culprit of the bottleneck is technology. GEICO's technology needs a lot more work than I thought it did. It has more than 600 legacy systems that don't really talk to each other. And we are trying to compress them to fifteen or sixteen systems that all talk to each other. That's a monumental challenge. Because of that, even though we have made improvements in telematics, we still have a long way to go … Both that, and the whole issue more broadly in terms of matching rate to risk, means that GEICO is still a work in progress … It will not be until two years from now that we'll be back on track fighting the battles on both the profitability and the growth front."

WB: "Todd Combs was Ajit's choice and my choice to go to GEICO, to work on the problem of matching rate to risk, which is what insurance is all about. He arrived with exquisite timing, right before the pandemic broke out and all kinds of things changed. But Todd is doing a wonderful job at GEICO. He works closely with Ajit. But because he still has a home in Omaha, he comes back here and we get together on the weekend sometimes, too. That's been a remarkable accomplishment under difficult circumstances. He's not all the way home on addressing their issues, but he has made very, very big changes in multiple ways at GEICO."

BEN GRAHAM AND GEICO

2023 MEETING (02:18:44)

CM: "Ben Graham was a really gifted teacher, a very honorable profession. That is what has lasted. However, an interesting fact that Graham was sheepish about in his old age was that more than half of all the investment return that Ben Graham made in his whole life came from one growth stock, GEICO. At the time that he operated, there were a lot of sort of lousy companies that were too cheap, and you could make a little money floating from one to another—but the big money he made was in one growth stock, GEICO. Buying one undervalued great company is a very good thing, as Berkshire has found out again and again and again."

WB: "And Ben wrote a postscript to the 1949 edition of *The Intelligent Investor* pointing out exactly that fact, acknowledging it. He took some good lessons from it. That's the way life is; you prepare and you don't lose everything along the way, and then something comes along. GEICO came along because a banker in Fort Worth had financed Leo Goodwin, and I think the banker got three quarters of it. As I remember, it was for $1.25 million or $1.5 million. It almost fell apart because of a difference of $25,000 in the net worth delivered. This is a business that's now worth tens of billions. But he pointed out the irony in that, too. He was totally intellectually honest about the failings, but also the strengths of his approach. Charlie and I have seen that in our lives. The prepared mind, the willingness to act when you need to act … It's one or two things that make the right decision … The thing to do is just keep trying to think things through and not do too many stupid things. Sooner or later, you have a lollapalooza, as Charlie would say."

PART THIRTEEN:
Other Topics

"Think of how refreshing a board of directors meeting would be if they sat down and said, 'Now we'll spend three hours examining all our stupid blunders and how much we've blown.'"

"Derivatives often combine borrowed money with ignorance, and that is a rather dangerous combination."

"Investing: you don't have to do anything very smart, you just have to avoid doing things that are ungodly dumb when looked at about a year later; that's the trick."

"[Something may work] 99% of the time, but 83.3% of the time it works to play Russian roulette with one bullet and six chambers. Neither 83.3% nor 99% is good enough when there is no gain to offset the risk of loss."

"You can make a lot of money on Sunday. You may not get a chance very often, but any calls you get on Sunday, you're probably going to make money on."

"A banker should be more like an engineer. He is more into avoiding trouble than getting rich."

SUBJECTS AND MEETINGS FEATURED

BUFFETT'S BEST YEARS

2001 MEETING (01:57:21)

WARREN BUFFETT: "If I were working with a small amount of money, the universe would be huge compared to the possible ideas I'm working with now. You mentioned 1956–1969; actually, my best period was before that. From the end of 1950 through the next ten years, my returns averaged about 50% a year. I think they were 37 points better than the Dow per year, something like that. But I was working with a tiny, tiny, tiny amount of money. I would pore through volumes of businesses and I would find one or two that I could put $10,000—$15,000 into that were just ridiculously cheap. And obviously, as the money increased, the universe of possible ideas started shrinking dramatically. The times were also better for doing it … But if you're working with a small amount of money today, with exactly the same background that Charlie and I have, the same ideas and ability, I think you can make very significant sums—but as soon as you start getting the money up into the many millions, the curve on expectable results falls off dramatically. That's the nature of it. When you get up to things you could put millions of dollars into, you've got a lot of competition … When I started, I went through the manuals page by page. I probably went through 20,000 pages in the Moody's industrial, transportation, banks, and finance manuals. I did it twice. I looked at every business."

CHARLIE MUNGER: "A brilliant man who can't get money from other people, working with a very small sum, probably should work in very obscure stocks searching out unusual, mispriced opportunities. But it's such a small world. It may be a way for one person to come up, but it's a long slog."

WB: "Unfortunately most smart people in Wall Street figure that they can make a lot more money, a lot easier, by getting an override on other people's money or delivering services in some way. The monetization of hope and greed is a way to make a huge amount of money."

PAST INVESTMENT MISTAKES

1998 MEETING (03:22:12)

WB: "We'll start off with the fact that when I was eleven, I bought some Cities Service preferred at $38 and it went to $200—but I sold at $40, grabbing my $2 per share profit. Everything we've ever sold has gone up subsequently, but some have gone up more painfully than others. Certainly, the Disney sale in the 1960s was a huge mistake. I should have been buying, forget about holding. That's happened many times. We think that anything we sell should go up subsequently because we own good businesses. We may sell them because we need money for something else, but we still think they're good businesses, and we think good businesses are going to be worth more over time. Everything I sold in the past, that I can think of, has gone on to sell for a lot more money. And I would expect that to continue to be the case. That's not a source of distress. But I must say that selling Disney was a mistake, and actually the ad agencies have done very well since we sold them, too. Now, maybe some of that money went into Coca-Cola or something, so I don't worry about that. I would worry, frankly, if I sold a bunch of things right at the top, because that would indicate that, in effect, I was practicing the bigger fool approach to investing, and I don't think that can be practiced successfully over time. I think the most successful investors, if they sell at all, will be selling things that end up going a lot higher, because it means that they've been buying into good businesses as they've gone along."

CM: "… it is really useful to be reminded of your errors. And I think we're pretty good at that. We kind of mentally rub our own noses in our mistakes. That is a very good mental habit. Warren can tell you the exact cents per shares that he sold at and compare it with the current price. It actually hurts him."

WB: "It actually doesn't hurt because you just keep on doing things. But it is instructive to do postmortems. Every acquisition decision, that kind of thing, there should be postmortems. Now, most companies don't like to do postmortems on their capital expenditures. I've been a director at a lot of companies over the years and they've usually not spent a lot of time on postmortems. They spend a lot of time on telling you how wonderful the acquisitions are going to be, or the capital expenditures, but they don't necessarily like to look so hard at the results."

CM: "Think of how refreshing a board of directors meeting would be if they sat down and said, 'Now we'll spend three hours examining all our stupid blunders and how much we've blown.'

DERIVATIVES

1994 MEETING (00:13:44)

WB: "There was an article in *Fortune* a month ago by Carol Loomis on derivatives, and far and away it's the best article that has been written on the subject ['The Risk That Won't Go Away,' March 1994] … last year, someone asked what the big financial story of the 1990s might be, and we said we obviously don't know, but that if we had to pick a topic it could well be derivatives because they lend themselves to the use of unusual amounts of leverage and they're sometimes not completely understood by the people involved.

"Any time you combine ignorance and borrowed money you can get some pretty interesting consequences, particularly when the numbers get vague. And you've seen that with the recent Procter & Gamble announcement. I don't know the details of the P&G derivatives, but I understand, at least from press reports, that what started out as interest rate swaps ended up with P&G writing puts on large quantities of U.S. bonds and, I think, one other country's bonds. And any time you go from selling soap to writing puts on bonds, you've made a big jump. The ability to borrow enormous amounts of money combined with a chance to get either very rich or very poor very quickly has historically been a recipe for trouble at some point. Derivatives are not going to go away. They serve useful purposes, but I'm just saying that it has that potential."

1995 MEETING (01:11:15)

WB: "The use of derivatives would be dramatically reduced if the CEO had to say in the report whether he understood them or not ... There are times when there are things we would want to do—not often—that could be best accomplished by a transaction involving a derivative security, and we wouldn't hesitate to do so. We would obviously care very much about the counterparty, because that transaction is just a little piece of paper between two people. And it's usually going to cause one of the two to have to do something painful at the end of the period, which is to write a check to the other person. Therefore, you want to be sure that person will be both willing and able to write the check. We're probably more concerned about counterparty risk than most people might be.

"Derivatives often combine borrowed money with ignorance, and that is a rather dangerous combination. We've seen some of that in the last year. When you can engage in non-physical transactions that involve hundreds of millions, billions, or tens of billions of dollars, as long as you can get some party on the other side to accept your signature, that has the potential for a lot of mistakes and mischief. And if you've looked at the formulas involved in some, particularly interest rate-type derivative instruments, it is really hard to conceive of how any business purpose could be solved by the creation of those instruments. They essentially had a huge gambling element to them, in terms of engaging in a risk that doesn't even need to be created, as opposed to speculative aspects. They involved a creation of risk; not the transfer of risk, not the moderation of risk, but the creation of risk on a huge scale. It may be fortunate that in the last year, there have been half a dozen or so cases of people who have gotten into trouble, because that may tend to moderate the troubles of the future. The potential is huge.

"I've used this example before, but in borrowing money on securities, the Federal Reserve or the U.S. government decided many decades ago that society had an interest in limiting the degree to which people could use borrowed money in buying securities. They had the example of the 1920s with 10% margin, which was regarded as contributing to the Great Crash. So, the government, through the Fed, established margin requirements and said, 'I don't care if you're John D. Rockefeller, you're going to have to put up 50% of the cost of buying your General Motors stock,' or whatever it may be. And they said maybe Mr. Rockefeller doesn't need that, but society needs that. We don't want a bunch of people trading on thin margin—gambling, essentially, in shares—where the ripple effects can cause all kinds of problems for society. And that's still a law.

"But it means nothing anymore because various derivative instruments have made the 10% margin requirements of the 1920s look like what a small-town banker in Nebraska would regard as conservative, compared to what goes on. So, it's been an interesting history. Perhaps the experiences of the last year ... They've got everybody focused on derivatives, but nobody knows exactly what to do about them. If we think something makes sense and Charlie and I understand it, we may find ways to use derivatives to what we think will be our advantage."

CM: "I disapprove even more than you do, which is hard. If I were running the world, we wouldn't have options exchanges. Derivative transactions would be about 5% of what they are, and the complexity of the contracts would go way down. The clearing systems would be tougher. I think the world has gone a little bonkers. And I'm very happy I'm not so located in life that I have to be an apologist for it. A lot of these people, I feel sorry for them. They had great banks. And they have to go before people, sometimes even including their children and friends, and argue that these things are wonderful."

1999 MEETING (05:12:06)

WB: "There's a lot of potential for mischief when people can write down a few numbers on a piece of paper and nothing changes hands for a long time and their compensation, next month or this year, depends on what numbers are attached to a bunch of things that won't come to fruition for a long time, particularly when you're guaranteeing credit or anything of the sort. So, when the numbers are big in relation to the amount of profits, you want to look very carefully, because if anything goes wrong, it could go wrong on a fairly big scale, and you're not getting paid a lot for running that type of risk."

2001 MEETING (03:17:05)

WB: "We regard that area as potentially being dynamite because if you get a large group of people who, in many cases, are getting paid based on front-ending potential profits, that's a dangerous situation. You're going to find people who will crack under that, in terms of what they will do. We had a case of it in the electric utility industry a year or two ago, when Edison in California, through a subsidiary, compensated people based on projecting the profitability of the business they were putting on the books. That's Wall Street practice—it was brought to the utility industry and it produced predictable results.

"It's dangerous to pay people to make deals where you won't know the outcome for fifteen or twenty years and give them a lot of money upfront for doing it. And that's fairly standard practice in the business. I mean, it was standard practice at Salomon when I was there. As I say, people occasionally crack under that. It isn't exactly analogous, but it's worth reading Roger Lowenstein's book entitled *When Genius Failed*, because it touches on some of the problems we've described that Charlie and I are apprehensive about."

CM: "The derivatives business has the very significant problem that the accounting profession sold out. The accounting is improper. It front-ends way too much income. It's irrationally optimistic because that's the way the denizens of the field want it because it creates bigger compensation. This is intrinsically an irresponsible system. The accounting profession has failed the wider civilization ... The main problem is the whole system of accounting is wrong, it's too optimistic. It would be like going into the taxicab business with a thirty-year depreciation rate."

WB: "Or it'd be like writing very long-tail insurance, and paying a big commission upfront based on the expected profit of that insurance over a ten-year period or something, with that prepared by the guy who wrote the policy. There are certain activities that are really just dangerous in the financial world. And when you get close to that kind of situation, you just have to be very careful ... So, you can try to attack it—but it's also hard to get too far away from industry norms and still do business."

CM: "Our accounting is way more conservative than the standard derivative accounting of the country, thank God."

2003 MEETING (02:21:37)

WB: "Charlie and I think there is a low, but not insignificant, probability that sometime—maybe in three years, five years, twenty years, and very possibly never—that derivatives could accentuate, in a major way, a systemic problem that might even arise from some other phenomenon. And we think that's inadequately recognized. We think the problem will grow as derivatives get more complex and as their usage increases ... We saw it in the energy field in the last two years. It destroyed or almost destroyed certain institutions that never should have been destroyed. And we also saw, in 1998, the whole financial system almost become paralyzed, particularly in the credit markets, by the action of a firm [LTCM] which was not solely based on derivatives, but which would not have gotten into as much trouble as it did without derivatives.

"So it's a subject that no one quite knows what to do with. Charlie and I would not know how to regulate it, but we think we have had some experience in seeing the firm's specific dangers in that field, and we think we have some insight into the systemic problems that could arise. And people don't want to think about it until it happens. But there are some things in the financial world that are better thought of before they happen, even if they're low probabilities. We're thinking about low probabilities all the time; we don't want anything to go wrong in a big way at Berkshire. We therefore think about things that a good many people don't think about—simply because we worry about that."

CM: "In engineering, people put big margins of safety into systems—atomic power plants being the extreme example. In the financial world, in derivatives, it's as though nobody gave a damn about safety. They just let it balloon and balloon and balloon in usage, the number and size of trades. And that ballooning is aided by false accounting, where people are pretending to make money they're not really making. I regard that as very dangerous, and I'm more negative than Warren. I'll be amazed, if I live another five to ten years, if we don't have some significant blow-up."

WB: "They've been advertised, and sometimes in a fairly prominent way, as shedding risk for participants in the system and reducing risk for the system. They have long crossed the point where they decreased risk to the system; now they enhance risk. The Coca-Cola Company could bear the foreign exchange risk or interest rate risk that they run; but when Coca-Cola starts laying those off, and every other major company in the world does the same with relatively few players, you have now intensified the risk that exists in the system. You have not shed risk at all, you have transferred it, and you have transferred it to very few players. And those players have huge interdependencies with each other, and to some extent, central banks and all of those similar institutions are vulnerable to the weaknesses of those institutions.

"When you start concentrating risks in institutions which are highly leveraged, and who intersect with a few other institutions all bearing the same risks, all having the same motivations in the trading departments, to take on more and more esoteric things because they can book more and more immediate profits, you are courting danger. And that's why I wrote about it. It's not a prediction, it's a warning."

2004 MEETING (01:07:39)

WB: "A lot of mischief can happen with derivatives ... and the scale is absolutely huge and getting larger all the time. I know the managements of some of the companies that have big derivative activities, and they do not have their minds around what is happening. We didn't have our mind around what was happening at Gen Re Securities. We tried to get our mind around it, but we couldn't do it. And that was far from the most extensive or complicated derivative operation around.

"A lot of things correlate in the securities world that people don't expect to correlate, and the financial world operates on a hair trigger, to some extent. People want to jump the gun and move ahead of the other fellow. And when you get huge amounts of transactions, which many people only vaguely understand, you are creating a potential huge problem that may come about because of some other exogenous event that triggers defaults on a huge scale ... I would predict that sometime in the next ten years you will have some very big problems that will either be caused, or accentuated in a big way, by people's activities in derivatives."

CM: "Part of the trouble you were talking about with Freddie Mac [secondary mortgage market guarantor] came because people didn't think enough about the consequences of the consequences. That's a common error. You start trying to hedge against interest rate changes, which is a very complicated thing to do when you've got a mortgage portfolio where people have options to pay the mortgages off early. And then, under the accounting conventions, the hedges started making the quarterly results lumpy instead of nice and regular, the way all the institutional analysts like them. So then they gave us another bunch of derivatives to smooth out the returns. Well, now you've morphed into lying. It's complicated enough to start with. But when you add lying to the process, it's a Mad Hatter's tea party. And yet, this happens with eminent directors of vast financial sophistication sitting on the board. It shows that the sophistication won't save you. Somebody has to have the common sense to say, 'We're just not going there.' It's too tough."

WB: "The one thing you can be sure of is that the trader who puts on some derivatives transaction will want to mark them at a profit, either immediately or within a year or two, because he gets his bonus often based on the figures for that year ... he will be gone when the consequences fall to the firm. Anytime you have incentives, with people who are quite smart, to mismark things, you're going to get mismarks, or temptations to take on risk in an inappropriate manner."

2005 MEETING (02:07:48)

CM: "I do think a lot of the troubles that came for [secondary mortgage market guarantors] Freddie [Mac] and Fannie [Mae] came from a large use of derivative books, and from Fannie and Freddie both believing a lot of silver-tongue salesmanship from derivative traders. I think there is much wrong with derivative accounting and derivative trading operations in the United States, and I don't think the full penalties have yet been paid."

2009 MEETING (01:37:35)

WB: "After 1929, Congress decided it was very dangerous to let people borrow a lot of money against securities and that it had contributed to the Great Depression. Therefore, they said the Federal Reserve should regulate how much people could borrow against securities. It was important for society. The Federal Reserve created margin requirements, and they still exist.

"You are not supposed to be able to borrow more than 50% against your securities … Derivatives came along and made those rules a laughing stock. You have total return swaps, which means you can borrow 100% against what you own. That goes way beyond anything that existed in 1929. So, derivatives became a way around regulation of leverage in markets, which like I say, Congress felt was important and the Federal Reserve still has a responsibility for enforcing … There's a book called *The Great Crash* by John Kenneth Galbraith. It's a great book."

CM: "I think there's been a deeper problem in the derivative business. The derivative dealer takes two advantages of the customer. One, there's croupier-style mathematical advantage equivalent to the house advantage in Las Vegas. Two, the derivative dealer is playing in the same game with his own clients, with the advantage of being a better player, and having knowledge of what the clients are doing. This is basically a dirty business. You're really selling things to your clients, who trust you, that are bad for the clients. We don't need more of this kind of thing in America. We need less."

2010 MEETING (02:23:07)

CM: "I think the usefulness of derivatives has always been overrated. If we didn't have any derivatives at all, including contracts to buy and sell grain that were traded on exchanges, we'd still have plenty of oats and wheat. I think it is slightly more convenient for people to be able to hedge their risks of farming by using derivative markets and commodities. The test is not, 'Is there any benefit in derivatives?' The question is, 'Is the net benefit versus disadvantage from derivatives useful, or would we be better off without it?' My view is that, if we went back to having nothing but derivative trading in commodities, metals, currencies, safely conducted under responsible rules, and all other derivatives vanished from the earth, it would be a better place."

2016 MEETING (01:05:15)

WB: "The great danger in derivatives is if there's a discontinuity. If there's not discontinuities, you probably don't have much of a problem, assuming they get marked to market, collateralized, and so on. But if the system stops for a while you will have a lot of problems. It stopped after 9/11 for three or four days. At the time of WWI, they closed the New York Stock Exchange for many months.

They debated closing the stock exchange, very seriously, the day after October 19, 1987 [Black Monday]. There were a lot of people who wanted to close it. On that Tuesday morning, it looked like it was about to stop, but it continued. If you have a major cyber, nuclear, chemical, or biological attack on the country—which will certainly happen at some point—if you have a major discontinuity, then you'll have a lot of problems, a lot of problems. When things reopen, you will find there can be enormous gaps in things you thought were fully protected by collateral, netting arrangements, that type of thing.

"So, I regard very large derivative positions as dangerous ... It's still a potential time bomb in the system. Anything where discontinuities exist—and basically that means closing up and stopping trading markets from functioning—can be real poison in markets. Kuwait, years ago, went to a very delayed system on settlement of stock purchases, so they didn't have to settle for six months or thereabouts. It caused all kinds of problems, because, you've got an IOU from somebody for six months and if you've got zillions of those, a lot of trouble can ensue. I agree with ... general caution. I'm not in the least troubled by our Bank of America investment, nor our Wells Fargo position ... On the other hand, there are a great number of banks in the world—and if you take the fifty largest banks in the world, we wouldn't even think about probably forty-five of them."

CM: "We're in the awkward position where I think we'll probably make about $20 billion out of derivatives, just from those few contracts that you and Ajit did years ago. All that said, we're different from the banks. We would really prefer it if those derivatives had been illegal for us to buy. It would have been better for our country."

USAIR INVESTMENT

1994 MEETING (01:26:05)

WB: "USAir has a cost structure which is non-viable in today's airline business ... There isn't any question that the cost structure is out of line. I think the cost structure could be brought into line, but whether it will be is another question. Looking backwards, the answer is to avoid businesses that need to solve problems like that. That was the mistake I made ... There are enormous tensions when you need to take hundreds and hundreds of millions of dollars out of the cost structure of any business. And when you need cooperative action, all by various groups, each one of which feels that maybe they're having to give a little more than some other group, and understandably feels that way, that is an enormously tough negotiating job."

CM: "If I were a union leader, I would give Seth [Schofield, chairman and CEO of USAir] whatever he wants because he's not the kind of a fellow who would ask for more than he needs. And it's perfectly obvious that's the correct decision on the labor side. But whether the obvious will be done or not is in the lap of the gods."

WB: "It's a lot of people with different motivations, and those are really tough questions. Charlie and I have been involved in that sort of thing a few times; frequently it works out, but it's not preordained."

AIRLINES

2017 MEETING (00:57:24)

WB: "You couldn't pick a tougher industry than airlines. Since Orville Wright went up in that plane, if anybody'd really been thinking about investors, they should have had Wilbur Wright shoot him down, to save everybody a lot of money for a hundred years. Something like a hundred airlines, in that general range, have gone bankrupt in the last few decades. Charlie and I were directors for some time of USAir. People write about how we had a terrible experience in USAir. It was one of the dumbest things I've ever done."

CM: "You made a fair amount of money out of it, too. It was undeserved."

WB: "We made a lot of money out of it, because there was one little brief period when people got all enthused about USAir. And after we left as directors and sold our position, USAir managed to go bankrupt twice in the subsequent period.

"You've named a number of factors that just make for terrible economics. It's a fiercely competitive industry. The question is whether it's a suicidally competitive industry, which it used to be. When you get virtually every one of the major carriers, and dozens and dozens and dozens of minor carriers going bankrupt, it ought to come upon you, finally, that maybe you're in the wrong industry. It has been operating for some time now at 80% or better of capacity—being available seat miles—and you can see what deliveries are going to be and that sort of thing. So I think it's fair to say that they will operate at higher degrees of capacity over the next five or ten years than the historical rates, which caused all of them to go broke.

"Now the question is whether, even when they're doing it in the 80s, will they do suicidal things in terms of pricing; that remains to be seen. They actually, at present, are earning quite high returns on invested capital. I think higher than either FedEx or UPS, if you actually check that out. But tomorrow morning, if you're running one of those airlines and the other guy cuts his prices, you cut your prices, and as you say, there's more flexibility when fuel goes down to bring down prices than there is to raise prices when prices go up. So it is no cinch that the industry will have some more pricing sensibility in the next ten years than it has had in the last hundred years. But the conditions have improved for that. They've got more labor stability than they had before because they've been through bankruptcy. And they're all going to sort of have an industry pattern bargaining … They're going to have a shortage of pilots to some degree. But it's not like buying See's Candies."

CM: "No, but the investment world has gotten tougher with more competition, more affluence, and more absolute obsession with finance throughout the whole country. We picked up a lot of low-hanging fruit in the old days, when it was very, very easy. And we had huge margins of safety. Now we operate with a less advantageous general climate. And maybe we have small statistical advantages, where in the old days it was like shooting fish in a barrel. But that's all right. It's OK if it gets a little harder after you get filthy rich."

WB: "Charlie's more philosophical than I am on that point."

CM: "Well, I can't bring back the low-hanging fruit, Warren. You're just going to have to keep reaching for the higher branches."

WB: "I think the odds are very high that there are more revenue passenger miles five years from now or ten years from now. If the airline companies are only worth, five or ten years from now, what they're worth now, in terms of equity, we'll get a pretty reasonable rate of return, because they're going to buy in a lot of stock at fairly low multiples. So if the companies are worth the same amount at the end of the year and there's fewer shares of stock outstanding, over time we make decent money. And all four of the major airlines are buying in stock."

CM: "You've got to remember that the railroads were a terrible business for decades and decades and decades and then they got good."

WB: "By buying all four, it means that it's very hard to distinguish, at least in my mind, who will do the best. I do think the odds are quite high that, if you take revenue passenger miles flown five or ten years from now, it will be a higher number. There'll be low-cost people who come in. The Spirits of the world and JetBlues, whatever it may be. But my guess is that all four of the companies we have will have higher revenues. The question is what their operating ratio is. They will have fewer shares outstanding by a significant margin. So even if they're worth just what they're worth today, we could make a fair amount of money. But it is no cinch, by a long shot."

2020 MEETING (01:39:58)

WB: "You'll see in April that we net sold $6 billion or so of securities. That isn't because we thought the stock market was going to go down or anything of this order. I just decided I'd made a mistake. I made a probability-weighted decision, when we bought the airlines, that we were getting an attractive amount for our money. We bought roughly 10% of the four largest airlines. It's not 100% of what we did in April 2020, but we probably paid somewhere between $7 billion and $8 billion to own 10% of the four large companies in the airline business. For that, we were getting roughly $1 billion of earnings; not $1 billion of dividends, but we felt our share of the underlying earnings was $1 billion. And we felt that number was more likely to go up than down over a period of time, even though it would be cyclical, obviously. And we could only effectively buy roughly 10% of each of the four. We treat it mentally exactly as if we were buying a business.

"It turned out I was wrong about that business because of something that was not in any way the fault of four excellent CEOs. Believe me, there's no joy being a CEO of an airline. But the companies we bought were well managed. They did a lot of things right. It's a very, very, very difficult business because you're dealing with millions of people every day. And if something goes wrong for 1% of them, they are very unhappy. So I don't envy anybody who has the job of being CEO of an airline. But I particularly don't enjoy them being in a period like this [the Covid-19 pandemic] where people have been told not to fly. I've been told not to fly for a while ... The airline business—I may be wrong, and I hope I'm wrong—I think it changed in a very major way. It's obviously changed in the fact that the four companies are each going to borrow perhaps an average of at least $10 billion each. Well, you have to pay that back out of earnings over some period of time. You're $10 billion worse off if that happens. And in some cases, they're having to sell stock or sell the right to buy a stock at these prices, and that takes away from the upside.

"I don't know whether two or three years from now people will fly as many passenger miles as they did last year. They may and they may not. But the future is much less clear to me about how the business will turn out through absolutely no fault of the airlines themselves. Something that was a low-probability event happened, and it happened to particularly hurt travel businesses—the hotel business, cruise business, theme park business, and the airline business in particular. And the airline business has the problem that if the business comes back 70% or 80%, the aircrafts don't disappear. You would have too many planes. It didn't look that way when the orders were placed a few months ago and arrangements were made, but the world changed for airlines."

2020 MEETING (02:07:04)

WB: "We were not disappointed at all in the airlines as they were being run, but we did come to a different opinion on it. And they're the four largest U.S. airlines: American Airlines, Delta Air Lines, Southwest Airlines, and United Continental. Collectively, they probably are at least 80% of the revenue passenger miles flown in the United States. We like those airlines, but the world has changed for airlines. And I don't know how it's changed, and I hope it corrects itself in a reasonably prompt way. I don't know whether Americans will have now changed their habits or will change their habits because of an extended period if it happens that we're semi-shutdown in the economy. I don't know whether the trends toward what people have been doing by phone. I mean it's been seven weeks since I've had a haircut or put on a tie. It's just a question of which sweatsuit I wear. So who knows how we come out of this. But I think that certain industries—and unfortunately, I think that the airline industry, among others, is one of those—will be really hurt by a forced shutdown, by events that are far beyond their control.

"We would have bought other airlines, too, incidentally, but those were the four big ones. We put in $7 billion or $8 billion into it, and we did not take out anything like $7 billion or $8 billion, and that was my mistake. It's always a problem if there are things on the lower levels of probabilities that happen, and it happened to the airlines. We sold our entire stake in all four airlines. When we sell something, very often, it's going to be our entire stake. We don't trim positions. That's just not the way we approach it. Any more than if we buy 100% of a business, we're going to sell it down to 90% or 80%. If we like a business, we're going to buy as much of it as we can and keep it as long as we can. But when we change our mind, we don't take half measures or anything of the sort … We have sold the entire airline positions."

STOP-LOSS ORDERS

1994 MEETING (02:40:49)

WB: "I happened to be talking to the NYSE specialist, Jimmy Maguire. At the time, the stock was around $16,000, and he had some rather significant stop-loss orders on the books at $15,500 involving hundreds of shares … Why somebody wants to put in an order to sell something for $15,500 that they don't want to sell at $16,000 is beyond me. The idea of people using stop-loss orders with Berkshire tells me that we've got some people in who are using it as a trading vehicle of some sort, or have some totally non-investment-type calculations in their mind … The stock did go down and hit $15,500; I think it was close to 300 shares, which is $4.5 million of stock. Somebody decided, apparently, that they wanted to sell something at $15,500 that they could have sold for $16,000. The lower it went, the better they liked the sale. It has always struck me as like having a house that you like, you're living in, it's worth $100,000, and you tell your broker, if anybody ever comes along and offers $90,000, sell it. It doesn't make any sense to me."

PUT OPTIONS

1994 MEETING (02:49:07)

WB: "We wrote puts on five million shares, as I remember, of Coke sometime in the early fall last year. ... I think the premium was $7.5 million dollars, and they were priced around $35 per share ... It's not something we're really very likely to do. I was happy to do it, and in that particular case, we made $7.5 million. If we like something well enough to write a put on it, we're probably better off buying the security itself ... On balance, I don't think it's as useful a way to spend my time as just looking for securities to buy outright."

AMERICAN EXPRESS

1995 MEETING (01:25:16)

WB: "We own just under 10% of American Express. They're in a number of businesses, but by far the most important factor in American Express's future will be the credit card. That is a business that has become—and will forever, probably, become—ever more competitive.

"I think I met Ralph Schneider [co-founder of Diners Club] in the late 1950s. American Express entered into the credit card business out of fear; they were worried about what the credit card was going to do to their traveler's check business. The traveler's check business originated back in 1890-something, I believe. That was, in turn, building off the old express business where, I think, it was Henry Wells and William Fargo, who would chain themselves to express boxes as they delivered them to the West. They decided that maybe issuing traveler's checks would be a little easier than carrying all this stuff around. So, the traveler's check evolved out of the express business, and the credit card business at American Express arose out of fear particularly of Diners Club at the time; they were all terrified of Diners Club, which got the jump on everybody. And they became enormously successful with it.

"The American Express card had a terribly strong position in the travel and entertainment part of the card business. The banks entered in on a big scale, and Visa's been enormously successful. So, the card has a strong franchise in certain areas, like the corporate card ... The card has a significant franchise, but it doesn't have the breadth of franchise it had many years ago. For a while, it was 'the' card. Now it's 'the' card in certain areas, but nothing like as broad as before.

"It has certain very important advantages and economic strengths, but it has some weaknesses. You have to assess those in deciding where it'll be in 2000 or 2005. We think the management of American Express thinks well about the question of how you keep the card special in certain situations. And they've reacted to the merchant backlash for higher discount fees in an intelligent way. So, we'll see how it all plays out. The real key will be how the card business does over time."

1996 MEETING (02:37:03)

WB: "American Express has slipped from where they were twenty years ago in the credit card business. I think they may have taken their customer a little bit for granted for a while. CEO Harvey Golub is very focused on correcting that and has made some progress. But the credit card business is a very different competitive struggle now than it was twenty or twenty-five years ago. Interestingly enough, American Express backed into the business because they were worried about what was going to happen to their traveler's check business, originally. And they saw Diners Club come along. They saw the inroads being made, so the credit card was a reactive move. For a while, they really dominated the field. And, of course, they still dominate the travel and entertainment part of it. But credit cards are going to be a very competitive business over time; American Express needs to establish special value for its card in some way or it will get more commodity-like. It's not an easy business. They've got a strong franchise, but it is not what it was twenty years ago, relative to the competition."

2019 MEETING (04:29:17)

WB: "Everybody's a competitor, including Apple. It just instituted a card in conjunction with Goldman Sachs. There will always be, in my view, many, many competitors in the business. Banks can't afford to leave the field. It's a growing field. They build up receivables on it. But I wouldn't think of the credit card business as a one-model business any more than I would think of the car business as essentially being one model. I mean, Ferrari is going to make a lot of money, but they're going to have just a portion of the market.

"Amex is growing around the world with individuals and with small businesses. You just saw the contract with Delta—which is probably an ideal partner—that runs for nine or ten years. The billings go up per capita, the coverage spreads. They're going to have loads of competition, and they always will. But J.P. Morgan took on the Platinum Card—it was a competitor—and the Platinum Card had the highest renewal rates that they've had. And they increased the price, I think, from $450 to $550 during a competitive battle, and retention improved, and new business improved, and 68% or so of new business was millennials. It is not an identical product with anything else. And as a premium card, it has a clientele which is large. It may be X% of the market, it may be three-quarters of X%, whatever it may be. It isn't for the person that likes to have five cards and look every day at which one provides the most rewards that day or in what gas stations or something of the sort. But it's got a very large constituency that has a renewal rate, a usage rate, that's the envy of everybody else in the industry. So, I like our Amex position very well."

CM: "No, I think we own the world as long as the technology stays the same. I have no opinion about technology."

WB: "The technology is not the whole thing—fortunately. If you look at credit card usage, there are a lot of different things motivating different people to use different various types of payment systems. And there's a lot of them that are growing. There are some of them that are marginal. And American Express is an extraordinary operation. I think next year, our share of the earnings of American Express will be equal to the cost of our position. We'll be earning 100% on what that position cost us, and I think it will grow. And I think the number of shares will go down and our interest will go up without us laying out a dime."

CM: "As you say, we own the world if it doesn't change. I'm talking about WeChat."

WB: "Well, even if it changes some. The world has changed a lot, and you can talk about all kinds of competitors. ... But American Express, the power of that brand, intelligently used, going into the credit card business, where they entered much later than Diners Club and Carte Blanche, but came to dominate the luxury end of the business—it's a fantastic story, and I'm glad we own 18% of it."

THE MOVIE BUSINESS

1996 MEETING (04:12:19)

WB: "Charlie was a lawyer for 20th Century Fox in the old days. He saw a little how Hollywood operated, and it kept us out of buying any motion picture stocks for thirty years. Every time I'd go near one, he'd regale me with a few stories of the past. It's a business where people can trade other people's money for their own significance in their world. That is a dangerous combination. If I can buy significance in my world with your money, there's no telling what I'll do."

CM: "Part of the business reminds me of an oil company in California. It was controlled by one individual. And people used to say about it, 'If they ever do find any oil, that old man will steal it.' The motion picture business, only about half of it that has normal commercial morals."

WB: "Yeah, we're not applying that to Disney."

CM: "No."

WB: "Disney's done an extraordinary job for the shareholders. And they make real money out of movies. Most movie companies make money for everybody associated with it, but not a lot has stuck to the shareholders."

2023 MEETING (03:38:38)

WB: "It's not good news when any company—in this case Paramount—dramatically cuts its dividend. The streaming business is interesting, because people love being entertained on a screen or a phone, whatever it may be. But there are a lot of companies doing it, and you either need fewer companies or higher prices. You need higher prices or it doesn't work. And you don't lock people in when you get them to join up for the streaming period when your serial runs. You can keep them on for a while, but you can't lock them up. We'll see what happens.

"I had a gasoline station when I was twenty-one, and we had one competitor; he determined our profit because we looked at his price every day. If we cut the price, he'd match it, and we couldn't raise the price; in the end, he did twice the gallonage, so he won. There's just basic business problems you see with certain industries that you don't see with others.

"Disney was unique in its animated offerings in the 1930s and 1940s, and they wrote the stuff off at first showing and then they rejuvenated it every seven years, and that was fine. But this is a different world; the number of eyeballs and the time spent watching are not going to increase dramatically, and you've got a bunch of companies that don't want to quit. Who knows what pricing does under that? Anybody who tells you what they know what pricing will do in the future is kidding themselves."

CM: "I think the movie business is one tough business. That's my view."

WB: "The talent and the agents will make money. The theaters are now doing 70% of the business they did before the pandemic. Big hits have enormous grosses, but you can't reduce the supply. People only have two eyeballs and so many hours in a day, and they have more choice than ever before … Talent will always get paid. And when you essentially are packaging that talent one way or another, and you need to get higher prices, and you've got a lot of strong companies that don't want to quit, that's an interesting equation."

CM: "If you think the movies are tough, try to invest in a New York show on a conventional stage. There, they think a breach of faith to let the person who put up the money to ever get any money back. I don't like those businesses."

THE NEWSPAPER BUSINESS

1995 MEETING (02:38:34)

WB: "I used to love the newspaper business in two respects: I loved the economics and I loved the activity. The love of the activity has not diminished. The economics are still exceptionally good compared to virtually any business in the world, but they aren't quite as good as they were fifteen years ago. What seemed almost the most bulletproof of franchises is still an exceptionally good business, but it isn't quite as bulletproof as ten or twenty years ago. If you're talking purely economics, I can't think of many other businesses that, if I just owned one asset over my life, I would rather own than a newspaper in a single-newspaper town. But I wouldn't have quite the feeling of absolute certainty that I would've had ten or fifteen years ago."

CM: "I think it's obvious the newspaper proprietors are getting a touch of paranoia for the first time. They worry about the electronic revolution and they worry about the fact that young people don't read. It's not as much fun going to newspaper conventions as it used to be."

WB: "They're still making exceptional money, that's the interesting thing."

CM: "But I've heard you say a dozen times, people don't seem to care what floor they're on, just whether the elevator is going up or down."

WB: "That's right—people feel better on the second floor of an elevator that's just come from one than they do when they're on the 99th floor coming down from 100. It's particularly the case where they've been in a business where the profits were automatic, because they start questioning whether they really have the ability to make a lot of money, absent this favored position. And that's not something they've had to dwell on before. So, it can make them uncomfortable. They're all screaming about newsprint prices … If you compare being in the newsprint business over time to being in the newspaper business, it's a joke. Newsprint prices, you can graph them from any point, ten to twenty years ago, the price of advertising has gone up more … Believe me, it's better to be in the newspaper business than the newsprint business."

1996 MEETING (02:15:57)

WB: "At one time, daily newspapers in single-newspaper towns were probably as attractive, economically, as any business you could find. A large percentage of advertisers had very little choice, in terms of using them as an advertising medium. People had less options in the way of learning what was going on around them, other than the daily newspaper. So, they started from a position of extraordinary strength. They still have a very strong position … but they do not have the exclusive advantages, in many cases, that they had fifteen or twenty years ago.

"People have more ways of obtaining information. Information can be processed electronically and delivered at far lower cost than people dreamt of twenty years ago. So, all of those things eat away at it a little bit. It's still a very fine business, but I don't see anything that will reverse those trends. I don't think they will necessarily accelerate. If the only thing you owned in life was a daily newspaper in a single-newspaper town twenty years ago, you would feel slightly less secure today than you did at that time—but you'd still be a lot better off than owning virtually any other business."

2010 MEETING (03:02:14)

WB: "The money to run good newspapers has come from advertising, and they've become less useful to advertisers. They were the only game in town for a long, long time. They are not the only game in town now. And what a difference that makes if you're selling something … The world has really changed, in terms of the essential nature of newspapers. Back when Charlie and I talked about them in 1965 or 1970, there was probably nothing that looked more bulletproof than a daily newspaper where the competition had melted away. But it's a form of distributing information and entertainment that has lost its immediacy in many cases. Think about how stock market quotations were thirty or thirty-five years ago. You looked in the paper to see what stocks had done or to find sports scores. Its primacy has withered away, and the advertisers weren't there because they loved the publishers. They were there because it was a microphone to talk to everybody in town, and they had to talk to everybody in town. The newspaper becomes less valuable as the advertisers float away, and advertisers float away as the subscribers diminish."

CM: "The independent newspapers—due to the accidents of history, as they became dominant in their individual town—for decades had impregnable economic strength. And by and large they behaved better because they were so strong. They were called the Fourth Estate. They were really a branch of the government; they helped keep government honest. If you take this state in which we're located [Nebraska], *The Omaha World-Herald* has been a very constructive force, net, over a long period of time. As those dominant franchises have weakened and weakened, it's not been good for the country. I think we're losing something that we have no substitute for. And I think it's very sad and I don't have the faintest idea what to do about it."

WB: "The advertiser doesn't need you the same way they did ten or fifteen years ago, so your ability to price evaporates in them. Charlie and I met Lord Thomson [Roy Thomson, Canadian newspaper magnate] in 1970 or so, and he owned the paper in Council Bluffs, right across the river. He was a jovial fellow, and he was very happy to see us. We said to him, 'Lord Thomson, we noticed you own the paper in Council Bluffs. Have you ever been there?' He said, 'I wouldn't dream of it.' And then I said, 'Well, you seem to increase the advertising price of your paper every year and your poor advertisers, what can they do about it?' He says, 'Nothing.' And then I said, 'In that case, how do you decide how much to increase prices, since it's totally at your discretion?' And he said, 'I tell my managers to price to make 40% pre-tax; above that, I feel I may be gouging.' Those days are gone."

BUSINESS OWNERS/SELLERS

1995 MEETING (03:11:32)

CM: "We frequently find owners of entire businesses have schizophrenia. They want to sell their business for a little more than it's worth, taking stock, so they don't have to pay any taxes. And then they want the stock to be in the kind of business that will make just one dumb acquisition—theirs—and thereafter will guard the stock like gold, making no more dumb acquisitions.

"Needless to say, the world is not that easy. Over time, we've made acquisitions that were fair on both sides, and, averaged out, they've worked well for Berkshire. And I think a company that behaves that way is giving the best long-term value to the private owner who wants to sell. You do not want to sell your business for stock to a firm that likes issuing stock."

SMALL COMPANIES (DELTA DUCK CLUB/ATLED)

1995 MEETING (03:33:39)

WB: "We don't look at small companies anymore. We assume there are a reasonable number of opportunities as you work with smaller amounts of capital because it's always been true. Clearly, you run into companies that are less followed as you get smaller. And there's more chances for inefficiency when you're dealing with something where you can buy $100,000 of it in a month, rather than $100 million ... If you're working with very small amounts of money, there almost always is some significant inefficiency someplace. When I started out, I went through all of the Moody's and the Standard & Poor's manuals page by page. It was probably 20,000 pages, but there were a lot of things that popped out, and none of them were in any brokerage report or anything of the sort. They were just overlooked. You could find out about them, but nobody was going to tell you about them. And my guess is that continues to be true, but not on anything like the scale it was then."

CM: "I remember when you were young you bought one membership in some duck club that had oil under it. When you get down to one duck club membership, you're really scavenging for cigar butts."

WB: "It was the Delta Duck Club. It was founded by a hundred guys who put in $50 each, except two of them didn't pay, so there were only ninety-eight shares outstanding. They bought a piece of land in Louisiana, and one time somebody shot downward instead of upward, and oil and gas started spewing out of the ground. So, they renamed it Atled—Delta spelled backwards—which illustrated the sophistication of this group. A few years later, at $3 a barrel oil, they were taking $1 million a year in royalties out of the place. The stock was selling at $29,000 a share; it had about $20,000 a share in cash and it was earning $7,000 a share after-tax, about $11,000 pre-tax, and it was a long-lived field. I use that sometimes as an example of efficient markets—is that an efficient market? Paying $29,000 for $20,000 of cash, plus $11,000 of royalty income at $0.25 cent gas and $3 oil? I don't think so. You can find things out there. I'll give you hunting rights on all my duck clubs in the future."

THE BANKING BUSINESS

1996 MEETING (04:33:23)

WB: "It's a business that can be a very good business, when run right, as the Bank of Granite or Illinois National Bank proved. There's no magic to it. You just have to stay away from doing something foolish. It's a little like investing: You don't have to do anything very smart, you just have to avoid doing things that are ungodly dumb when looked at about a year later; that's the trick … We like banking if we've got somebody in charge who is going to run them right."

THE TOBACCO BUSINESS

1997 MEETING (01:34:58)

WB: "We have owned tobacco stocks in the past; we've never owned a lot of them, although we may have made a mistake by not owning a lot of them. I've had people write me about whether we should do it or not. We own a newspaper in Buffalo, it carries tobacco advertising. Charlie's a director of a sensational warehouse chain called Costco. They sell cigarettes. We are part of the distribution chain with a 100% owned subsidiary in *The Buffalo News*. So, we have felt that if tobacco stocks were attractive as an investment, we would invest in tobacco stocks. We decided some years ago that we didn't want to be in the manufacture of chewing tobacco. We were offered the chance to buy a company that has done sensationally well subsequently, and we sat in a hotel in Memphis in the lobby and talked about it, and finally decided we didn't want to do it."

CM: "But it wasn't because we thought it wouldn't do well, we knew it was going to do well."

WB: "We knew it was going to do well. Now, why would we take the ads for those companies, or own a supermarket or a convenience store that sells their products, and not want to manufacture them? I really can't give you the answer to that precisely. But I just know that one bothers me and the other doesn't bother me. And I'm sure other people would draw the line in a different way … They haven't been on a boycotted list with us; overall, we were uncomfortable enough about their prospects over time that we did not feel like making a big commitment in them."

CM: "I think each company, each individual, has to draw its own ethical and moral lines, and personally, I like the messy complexity of having to do that. It makes life interesting. I don't think we can justify our call, particularly. We just have to draw the line somewhere between what we're willing to do and what we're not, and we draw it by our own lights."

WB: "We owned a lot of bonds of RJR Nabisco, for example, some years back. Should we own the bonds and not own the stocks? Should we be willing to own the stock but not be willing to own the business? Those are tough calls. Probably the biggest seller of cigarettes in the United States is Walmart, just because they're the biggest seller of everything. They're huge. Do I find that morally reprehensible? I don't. If we owned all of Walmart, we'd be selling cigarettes at Walmart. But other people might call it differently, and I wouldn't disagree with them."

EFFICIENT MARKETS THEORY (EMT) AND ADVANCED MATH IN FINANCE

1998 MEETING (00:11:49)

WB: "Keynes said that most economists are most economical about ideas; they make the ones they learned in graduate school last a lifetime. You spend years getting your PhD in finance and you learn theories with a lot of mathematics in them that the average layman can't do. And you become sort of a high priest. You get an enormous amount of yourself, your ego, and even professional security, invested in those ideas. It gets very hard to back off after a given point. I think that to some extent that has contaminated the teaching of investing in the universities."

CM: "I would argue that the contamination was massive. But it's waning. The good ideas eventually triumph."

WB: "I've always found the word 'anomaly' interesting. It's something academicians could not explain, and rather than re-examine their theories, they simply discarded any evidence of that sort as anomalous. I think when you find information that contradicts previously cherished beliefs, you have a special obligation to look at it quickly. Whenever Darwin found anything that contradicted some previous belief, he knew that he had to write it down almost immediately because the human mind was so conditioned to reject contradictory evidence, that unless he got it down in black and white very quickly, his mind would simply push it out of existence."

CM: "One of these extreme efficient market theorists explained Warren for many, many years as an anomaly of luck. And he got the six sigmas—six standard deviations—of luck, and then people started laughing at him because six sigmas of luck is a lot. So, he changed his theory. Now Warren has six sigmas of skill ... The one thing he couldn't bear to leave was his six sigmas."

2009 MEETING (00:23:28)

WB: "We are looking to put out cash now to get back more cash later on. You mentioned I don't use a computer or a calculator. If you need to use a computer or a calculator to make the calculation, you shouldn't buy it. It should be so obvious that you don't have to carry it out to tenths of a per cent. It should scream at you. If you really need a calculator to figure out the discount rate is 9.6% instead of 9.8%, forget about the whole exercise. Just go onto something that shouts at you. Essentially, we look at every business that way. ... We do not sit down with spreadsheets and do all that sort of thing. We just see something that obviously is better than anything else that's around and that we understand—and then we act."

CM: "I'd go further. I'd say some of the worst business decisions I've ever seen are those that are done with a lot of formal projections and discounting back. Shell Oil Company did that when they bought the Belridge Oil Company. They had all these engineers make these elaborate figures. The trouble is you get to believe the figures. It seems the higher mathematics, with more false precision, should help you—but it doesn't. The effects, averaged out, are negative when you try to formalize it to the degree that you're talking about. They do it in business schools because, well, they've got to do something."

WB: "There's a lot of truth to that. If you stand up in front of a class and say, 'A bird in the hand is worth two in the bush,' you're not going to get tenure. If you're in the priesthood, it's very important to look, at least, like you know a whole lot more than the people you're preaching to. If you're a priest, and you just hand down the Ten Commandments and say, 'This is it,' and we all go home, it just isn't the way to progress in the world.

"The false precision that goes into saying that this is a two-standard-deviation event or a three-standard-deviation event, and therefore we can afford to take this much risk and all that, it's totally crazy. You saw it with Long-Term Capital Management in 1998. You've seen it time and time and time again. And it only happens to people with high IQs. If you have a very high IQ, and you've learned all this stuff, you feel you have to use it. The markets are not that way. The markets of mid-September last year, when people who ran huge institutions were wondering how they were going to get funding the next week, you can't calculate the standard deviation that arises at.

"It's going to arise much more often than people think; markets are made by people who get scared and get greedy. They don't observe the laws of flipping coins, in terms of the distribution of results. It's a terrible mistake to think that mathematics will take you a long place in investing. You have to understand certain aspects of mathematics, but you don't have to understand higher mathematics. Higher mathematics may actually be dangerous and it will lead you down pathways that are better left untrod."

Y2K CONCERNS (THE YEAR 2000)

1998 MEETING (00:33:54)

CM: "I find it interesting that it is such a problem; it was predictable the year 2000 would come."

WB: "It is fascinating, when you think about it, that a whole bunch of people with 160 IQs could build up such a problem, but here we are—and that's why we stick with simple things."

LESSONS FROM LONG-TERM CAPITAL MANAGEMENT (LTCM)

1999 MEETING (00:16:04)

CM: "What was interesting about [LTCM] is how talented the people were—and yet, they got in so much trouble. I think it also demonstrates that the general system of finance in America involving derivatives is irresponsible. There's way too much risk in all these trillions of notional value sloshing around the world. There's no clearing system as there is in a commodities market. And I don't think it's the last convulsion we're going to see in the derivatives game."

WB: "It's fascinating. You had sixteen extremely bright people at the top. The average IQ would probably be as high or higher than in any organization you could find, among their top people. They individually had decades of experience and collectively had centuries of experience in the sort of securities in which LTCM was invested. And they had a huge amount of money of their own up, and probably a very high percentage of their net worth in almost every case. So, here you had super bright, extremely experienced people, operating with their own money—and, in effect, on that day in September, they were broke. To me, that is absolutely fascinating.

"There was a book written, *You Only Have to Get Rich Once* [by Walter Gutman]. It's a great title; it's not a very good book. But the title is right, you only have to get rich once. Why do very bright people risk losing something very important to them to gain something that's totally unimportant? The added money has no utility whatsoever. The money that was lost had enormous utility. And, on top of that, reputation is tarnished and all of that sort of thing.

"The gain/loss ratio, in any real sense, is just incredible. It's like playing Russian roulette. If you hand me a revolver with six chambers and one bullet and you say, 'Pull it once for $1 million,' and I say, 'No.' And then you say, 'What is your price?' The answer is there is no price. There shouldn't be any price on taking the risk when you're already rich—particularly, of failure and embarrassment and all of that sort of thing. But people repeatedly do it.

"Whenever a really bright person goes broke that has a lot of money, it's because of leverage. It would be almost impossible to go broke without borrowed money in the equation. At Berkshire, we've never used any real amount of borrowed money. If we had used it somewhat more, we'd be really rich. But if we'd used a whole lot more, we might have got in trouble some time ... What's two percentage points more in a given year when you run the risk of real failure? But very bright people do it, and they do it consistently, and they will continue to do it. As long as explosive-type instruments are out there, they will gravitate toward them. And particularly, people will gravitate toward them who have very little to lose, but who are operating with other people's money.

"One of the things, for example, in the LTCM case: in effect they found ways to get around the margin requirements. Risk arbitrage is a business that Charlie and I have been in for forty years in one form or another. Normally, that means putting up the money to buy the stock on the long side and shorting something against it where you expect a merger or something to happen. But through derivatives, people have found out how to do that with essentially putting up no money, just by writing a derivative contract on both sides. There are margin requirements that the Fed promulgates that, I believe, still call for 50% equity on stock purchases. But those requirements do not apply if you arrange the transaction in derivative form. These billions of dollars of positions in equities, essentially, were financed by the people who wrote the derivative contracts. And that leads to trouble. It works 99% of the time, but 83.3% of the time it works to play Russian roulette with one bullet and six chambers. But neither 83.3% nor 99% is good enough when there is no gain to offset the risk of loss."

CM: "There is a second factor that makes the situation dangerous: the accounting for actively engaging in derivatives, interest rate swaps, etc., is very weak … It's favored by people who are sharing in the profits from trading derivatives; naturally, they like liberal accounting. You have an irresponsible clearing system and irresponsible accounting—this is not a good combination."

WB: "It's GAAP accounting, but it front-ends profits. If you front-end profits and you pay people a percentage of profits, you're going to get some very interesting results, sometimes."

2006 MEETING (03:53:15)

WB: "I mentioned the LTCM crisis. We were getting calls on Sunday from people that had portfolios which were in trouble … You can make a lot of money on Sunday. You may not get a chance very often, but any calls you get on Sunday, you're probably going to make money on. Things are really screwed up if you're getting calls on Sunday. And all you have to do is make sure that you're the callee and not the caller on Sunday … You never get in a position, obviously, where the other fellow can call your tune. You have to be able to play out your hand under all circumstances. But if you can play out your hand, and you've got the right facts, and you reason by yourself, and you let the market serve you and not instruct you, you can't miss."

PHARMACEUTICAL INDUSTRY

1999 MEETING (01:37:06)

WB: "If we could buy a group of leading pharmaceutical companies at a below-market multiple, I think we'd do it in a second. We had the opportunity to do that in 1993 and we didn't do it, so we blew it. Clearly, the pharmaceutical industry, as a whole, has done very well. And it has some of the threats that you enumerated, in terms of regulation and so on. But every industry has some problems. And the pharmaceutical industry has enough going for it that the threats you named should not cause, in my view, the securities to sell at a depressed multiple, which they did … As a group, I think they're good businesses. I do think it's very hard to pick the winner. So, if I did buy them, I would buy a group of the leading companies."

CM: "I would argue the pharmaceutical industry has done more good for the customers than almost any other industry in America. It's just fabulous what's been invented in my lifetime, starting with all the antibiotics that have prevented so much death and so much family tragedy. I think the country has been very wise to have a system where pharmaceutical companies can make almost obscene amounts of money. I think we've all been well-served by the large profits in the pharmaceutical industry."

2008 MEETING (04:23:59)

WB: "Unlike many businesses, when we invest in something like the pharma industry, we don't know the answer on the pipeline. It will be a different pipeline anyway five years from now. So, we don't know which of Pfizer, Merck, or Johnson & Johnson will come up with a blockbuster commercial drug a few years from now, and we don't try to assess it. What we do feel is, if we have a group of those companies bought at reasonable prices, that, overall, pharma will do well. Maybe not quite as well as in the past, but they're doing something enormously important. It should offer chances for decent profits over time. But we do not pick one by one. I could not tell you what's the number one pipeline of Johnson & Johnson or Sanofi. So I think in that area, a group approach makes sense, which is not the way we would go at banks or something of that sort. I do think if you buy a group of pharma stocks at a reasonable multiple, you will probably do OK five or ten years from now. I would not know how to pick the specific winner."

CORPORATE TAXES, PHILANTHROPY, AND CONTRIBUTION

1999 MEETING (02:57:21)

WB: "We gave about $2.6 billion to the federal government last year in income taxes. We may have paid more in federal income tax than any other U.S. company. We paid more than GE or Microsoft, both of which have market caps that are three times our size ... I would argue that to the extent GEICO, for example, is a more efficient way of delivering personal auto insurance than its competitors are, and that, if 15% is a fair indication of how much GEICO is saving people, on $4 billion of premium volume, that there is something more than $600 million that consumers save by a more efficient way of distribution, which has been honed to a fine art by GEICO management.

"Really, delivering the goods and services that people want in an economical way is a very important part, I think, of the contribution that any company makes to society, as well as the taxes they pay and their corporate philanthropy. We are not big believers in giving away the money of the owners of Berkshire, acting as their representatives and giving away their money to philanthropy. It's their money ... We do not think corporations, generally, should be passing out money to the pet charities of the CEO. We don't do it at Berkshire."

CM: "I applaud the questioner's yearning for an answer to the question of, 'Isn't there something more in this game than making and piling up money?' and 'Shouldn't we be thinking about what we owe in return and what's going to go back in return?' In the Munger case, I think 100% is going to go back in return, for a reason different from that of the Buffett case. There's a saying: 'How much did old Charlie leave?' And the answer is, 'I believe he left it all.' In essence, it all has to go back one way or another. You can't take it with you, that's the iron rule of the game. And I do think it's important to think about what you do for other people and what example you set with your own life or your own corporate life. And I do think that Berkshire stacks up pretty well in that respect. And in due course, when we get into gargantuan charities bearing the name Buffett, my guess is that'll be done pretty well, too. This is likely to be a pretty good run."

INDUSTRY CONSOLIDATION

1999 MEETING (04:28:52)

WB: "I don't think consolidation usually solves many problems. If you have two lousy businesses and you put them together, you end up with one big, lousy business, usually. I am not a big fan of consolidation where the theory is that you have two very mediocre businesses and you're going to wring the costs out of one. It just doesn't work that way in my experience."

COSTCO

2000 MEETING (00:58:07)

CM: "American Express made a deal to put their cards into Costco, and I think that is a very intelligent thing to have done. It's a very aggressive place that does a lot of interesting things."

WB: "Charlie is a director of Costco. Costco is an absolutely fabulous organization. We should have owned a lot of Costco over the years and I blew it. Charlie was for it, but I blew it."

2001 MEETING (03:59:28)

WB: "There will always be a battle between brands and retailers. To the extent people trust Costco or Walmart more than or as much as they trust the brand, then the value of having the brand moves over to the retailer from the product itself. And that's gone on for a long, long time, even back to A&P in the 1930s. A&P, I believe, was the largest food retailer in this country, and they were also a big promoter of private label brands. And they felt they could convince the consumer in the 1930s that their brand meant more than having Del Monte or Campbell's or whatever it might be in the different categories. People thought they were going to win that war for a while. I don't know all the variables that went into A&P's decline, but it was dramatic. It was a great American success story for a while, and then it was a great American failure."

CM: "The muscle power of the Sam's Clubs and the Costcos has gotten very extreme. A little earlier this morning, when I was autographing books, a very good-looking woman came up to me and said she wanted to thank me. And I said, 'For what?' And she said, 'You told me to buy this pantyhose I'm wearing from Costco.' I'd evidently made some previous comment about how amazing it was that Costco could get Hanes to allow a co-branded pantyhose in the Costco stores. That wouldn't have happened twenty years ago."

WB: "She must've been pretty desperate if she was consulting with you on where to buy pantyhose."

2011 MEETING (03:26:46)

CM: "Costco is a business that became the best in the world in its category, and it did it with an extreme meritocracy and an extreme ethical duty, self-imposed, to take all its cost advantages as fast as it could accumulate them and pass them onto customers. And, of course, that created ferocious customer loyalty. It's been a wonderful business to watch, and, of course, strange things happen when you do that long enough.

"Costco has one store in South Korea that will do over $400 million in sales this year. These are figures that can't exist in retailing, but, of course, they do. And so that's an example of somebody having the right managerial system, the right personnel selection, the right ethics, the right diligence, etc. That is quite rare. If once or twice in a lifetime you're associated with such a business, you're a very lucky person.

"The more normal business is like, say, General Motors, which became the most successful business of its kind in the world and wiped out its common shareholders, what, in the last year or two? That is a very interesting story, and if I were teaching in a business school, I would have Value Line-type figures that took people through the entire history of General Motors. I would try and relate the changes in the graph and in the data to what happened in the business. To some extent, they faced a really difficult problem: heavily unionized business, combined with great success, and very tough competitors who came up from Asia, Europe, and elsewhere. That is a real problem. To prevent wealth from killing you, your success turning into a disadvantage, is a big problem in business. There are all these wonderful lessons."

WB: "Charlie and I were on a plane recently that was hijacked. The hijackers picked us out as the two dirty capitalists that they really had to execute. But they were a little abashed about it. They didn't really have anything against us, so they said that each of us would be given one request before they shot us. They turned to Charlie and said, 'What would you like as your request?' Charlie said, 'I would like to give once more my speech on the virtues of Costco, with illustrations.' And the hijacker said, 'Well, that sounds pretty reasonable to me.' And he turned to me and said, 'And what would you like, Mr. Buffett?' And I said, 'Shoot me first.'"

DYING BUSINESSES

2000 MEETING (02:09:19)

CM: "I think it's the nature of things that some businesses die. It's also in the nature of things that, in some cases, you shouldn't fight it. There is no logical answer, in some cases, except to wring the money out and go elsewhere."

WB: "That's very tough for managements—in fact, they almost never face up to that. It's very, very rare. And it's logical that it'd be rare. In a private business, you can understand why people face up to it. In a public company, if you take the equation of the manager, he or she may be far better off ignoring that reality than accepting it."

INVESTMENT BANKERS

2000 MEETING (02:50:20)

CM: "I think our culture is very old-fashioned. In other words, I think it's Ben Franklin and Andrew Carnegie. And what I think is amazing about Berkshire is how well these very old-fashioned ideas still work. Can you imagine Andrew Carnegie calling in a compensation consultant or an investment banker to tell him whether he should buy another steel mill?"

WB: "The idea of asking investment bankers to evaluate the businesses you're going to buy, that strikes us as idiocy. If you don't know enough about a business to decide whether to buy it yourself, you'd better forget it. It does not make sense. You bring in somebody who's going to get a very large check if you buy it, and a very small check if you don't, that displays a faith in human nature that would strain Charlie and me."

COMPETITIVE IMPACT FROM THE INTERNET

2000 MEETING (03:03:34)

CM: "Will the internet, by making competition much more efficient, make business generally harder for American corporations, meaning more competitive, lower returns on capital? My guess would be yes."

WB: "My guess would be yes, too. I would say that, on balance, for society, the internet is a wonderful thing. For capitalists, it's probably a net negative."

CM: "So, all of you can be happy that the progress of the species will affect your economic futures for the worse."

WB: "The internet, if you analyze it, you have to think it's much more likely that it will reduce the profitability of American business than improve it. It will improve the efficiency of American business, but all kinds of things improve the efficiency of American business without making it more profitable. And I think that the internet is likely to fall into that category. So far, it's improved the monetized value of American business. But that will eventually follow the underlying economics of what the internet does. And I think it's way more likely to make American business, in aggregate, worth less than compared to what it would've been otherwise."

CM: "By the way, that's perfectly obvious and very little understood."

FINANCIALS AND BANKS

2001 MEETING (03:08:48)

CM: "We are especially prone to get uncomfortable around financial institutions."

WB: "We're quite sensitive to risk in banks, insurance companies, or GSEs in the case of Freddie and Fannie. We feel there's so much about a financial institution that you don't know just by looking at the figures, that if anything bothers us a little bit, we're never sure whether it's an iceberg situation or not ... We have seen enough of what happens with financial institutions that push one way or another, that if we get some feeling that that's going on, we just figure we'll never see it until it's too late. So we bid adieu and wish them the best without any implication that they're doing anything wrong. It's just that we can't be 100% sure of the fact they're doing things we like. When we get to that situation, it's different than buying into a company with a product or a retail operation. You could usually spot troubles fairly early in those businesses. You spot troubles in financial institutions late. It's just the nature of the beast."

CM: "Financial institutions tend to make us nervous when they're trying to do well. That sounds paradoxical, but that's the way it is."

WB: "Financial institutions don't get in trouble by running out of cash in most cases ... A financial institution can go beyond the point of solvency even while they still have plenty of money around."

2001 MEETING (03:28:14)

WB: "When you run a highly leveraged finance business and you run into funding difficulties, they compound on you very quickly. Confidence is a real coward; it runs when it sees trouble. And in a finance business, you're constantly faced with refinancing old obligations, you have commercial paper and all of that, so there's no honeymoon period when you get in trouble in the finance business ... It can strike anywhere when confidence disappears."

2002 MEETING (01:13:12)

WB: "I would not characterize all banks as the same ... They are not a homogeneous group. We own stock in a couple of banks, and we think those institutions are somewhat different than other businesses ... What you're trying to do is look at all the cash a business will produce between now and judgment day, and discount it back at a rate that's appropriate, and then buy it a lot cheaper than that. And, whether the money comes from a bank, an internet company, or a brick company, the money all spends the same.

"I think that a good many banks have sold at very reasonable prices. We bought all of a bank in 1969 in Rockford, Illinois [Illinois National Bank & Trust]. Charlie and I went and looked—we must have looked at half a dozen banks in a three-year period. We trudged around and we found some very oddball banks that we liked. They were characterized by very little risk on the asset side and very cheap money on the deposit side. Even Charlie and I can understand that. And low prices, incidentally, too. Then they passed [amendments to] the Bank Holding Company Act in 1970 and they killed off our chances to do anything further in buying all of banks. We will own bank stocks from time to time in the future.

"We've also seen all kinds of banks ruined. I think it was [investment banker] Morris A. Schapiro who said, 'There are more banks than bankers.' And if you think about that a bit, you'll see what I mean. There have been a lot of people who have run banks in a very injudicious manner, but that's made for opportunities for other people ... I wouldn't look for a single metric like relative P/Es to determine how to invest money. You want to look for things you understand, and where you think you can see out for a good many years, in a general way, as to the cash that can be generated from the business. Then, if you can buy it at a cheap enough price, it doesn't make any difference what the name attached is."

CM: "I would argue Warren and I have failed to properly diagnose banking. I think we underestimated the general good results that would happen because we were so afraid of what non-bankers might do when they were in charge of banks."

WB: "There are a number of banks over the last five years that have earned over 20% on tangible equity. You would think that would be difficult for an industry to do, dealing in a commodity like money … you would think those kinds of returns, in a world of 6% long-term interest rates, wouldn't have occurred, and you'd think it would be hard to sustain. We have been wrong in the sense that banks have earned a lot more money on tangible equity than Charlie and I would have thought possible. Now, I think, to some extent, they've earned those high returns on tangible equity because they stretched out equity much further than was the case twenty or thirty years ago. They operate with more dollars working per dollar of equity than people thought was prudent thirty years ago. But however they've done it, a number of banks have earned very high returns on equity in recent years. And if you earn high enough returns on equity and you can keep employing more of that equity at the same rate—that's also difficult to do—the world compounds very fast. Banking as a whole has earned at rates on tangible equity well beyond, I think, what much more glamorous businesses have earned in recent years."

CM: "We didn't diagnose it as it actually turned out, and even worse, we haven't changed."

WB: "And even worse than that, we won't."

2005 MEETING (03:17:43)

WB: "Financial companies are more difficult to analyze than many companies. If you take the insurance business, the biggest single element that is very difficult to evaluate, even if you own the company, is loss and loss adjustment expense reserve. And it has a huge impact on reported earnings in any given period … We carry $45 billion of loss reserves. If I had to bet my life on whether $45 billion turned out to be a little over or a little under, I'd think a long time. You could just as easily have a figure of $45.5 billion or $44.5 billion—and if you were concerned about reporting given earnings in a given period, that would be an easy game to play.

"In a bank, it basically is whether the loans are any good. I've been on the boards of banks where I've gotten surprises. It's tough to tell. If you're analyzing something like WD-40 or See's Candies, or our brick business, they may have good or bad prospects, but you're not likely to be fooling yourself much about what's going on currently. With financial institutions, it's much tougher. Then you throw derivatives on top of it, and no one probably knows, perfectly, or even within a reasonable range, the exact condition of some of the biggest banks in the world ... It's just a more dangerous field to analyze. It doesn't mean you can't make money in it, but it's difficult."

CM: "Where you've got complexity—which by its very nature provides better opportunities to be mistaken and not have it come to notice, or to be fraudulent and have it not be found out—you're going to get more fraud and mistakes than you are if you're in a business where you shovel sand out of the river and sell it by the truckload. And just as a business that sells natural gas is going to have more explosions than a business that sells sand, these major financial institutions, by their nature, are going to have way more problems. That will always be true, and it's true when those institutions are owned by governments. In fact, some of the worst financial reporting in the world is done by governments and institutions like government banks in China. So, if you don't like the lack of perfect accounting in financial institutions, you're in the wrong world."

2008 MEETING (03:16:44)

WB: "I don't think you should make a categorical decision about banks. So much depends on the character of the institution, which will probably be a reflection, to a great degree, of the type of CEO you have ... We owned a bank—the only bank Berkshire's ever owned in its entirety—in Rockford, Illinois, run by a fellow named Gene Abegg. It wouldn't have made any difference if it was a super-regional or a regional or a small-cap bank or a mid-cap bank, there's no way Gene Abegg could run anything other than a super-sound bank.

"You should know something about the culture of the management and the institution to make a firm buy decision on a bank, and that's hard to do for 99% of the banks. We own Wells Fargo, U.S. Bank, and M&T up in Buffalo. In all three cases, I think I understand the DNA of the institution, in terms of how it behaves. That doesn't mean those places are immune from problems, but it does mean they're immune, in my view, from what I would call institutional stupidity. I would not say that all banks are immune from that. ..."

CM: "So many of our very large banks have sort of cast a pall of disgrace over the whole industry, and that has undoubtedly pounded down the stocks of some small banks that there's nothing wrong with. So I think you're prospecting in a likely territory. It has some promise."

2009 MEETING (01:19:40)

CM: "I don't get too excited about these oddball things that happen once every fifty years. If you're reasonably prepared for them and you're dented a little on the bottom tick, and other people are suffering a lot more, and unusual opportunities are coming to you that you don't see under other conditions, I don't think we deserve any salt tears. Take Wells Fargo. I think Wells Fargo is going to come out of this mess way stronger. The fact that the stock at the bottom tick scared a lot of people, I think that will prove to be a very temporary phenomenon."

WB: "Wells Fargo actually ticked below $9 a share at a time when spreads on business were never better, when deposit flows were never better, when their advantage in relation of costs of funds versus other large banks had never been better. I had a class meeting, and it was the only time they've ever got me to name a stock. Somebody with a cell phone checked the price and it was below $9, and I said, if I had to put all of my net worth in one stock, that would've been the stock. The business model is fabulous. When would you get a chance to buy something like Wachovia, which had the fourth largest deposit base in the United States? It's a great business opportunity. Unless they have to issue a lot of shares, which they shouldn't, Wells Fargo will be a lot better off a couple of years from now than if none of this happened ... Why anybody sells Wells Fargo at $9 when they owned it at $25 and the business is better off, is one of the strange things about the way markets behave. But people do it. They get very affected by looking at prices ... They let the price tell them how they should feel, and that's kind of crazy in our view. We think you should look at the business just like you'd look at an apartment house or a farm. They let the fact that a quote is available every day turn into a liability rather than an asset."

2011 MEETING (01:37:04)

WB: "Wells Fargo and U.S. Bancorp are both among the best large banks, if not the best, in the country ... U.S. banking profitability as a whole will be considerably less, in my view, in the period ahead than it was in the early part of this century. A very important reason is that the leverage will be reduced, and that's probably a good thing for society. It may be a bad thing for individual banks that could use leverage intelligently, but the trouble was that they all thought they could use leverage intelligently, and the actions of one or more that were unintelligent about it had consequences for everybody. So even if return on assets are as good as some years ago, there will be less assets per dollar of common equity than before, which means returns on common equity will be less.

"We still think Wells Fargo and U.S. Bank are very good operations and very decent businesses. They're not as attractive as when leverage ratios could be higher. In terms of the troubles in banking, I think you've seen, by far, the worst in the past ... Banking is a very fundamental business—but as [CEO] John

Stumpf said a few years ago at Wells Fargo, 'I don't know why we keep thinking of new ways to lose money when the old ones were working so well.'

"Banks periodically go crazy ... You've got cheap money and the federal government behind it, although the federal government has never had to pay out anything in terms of the FDIC. The FDIC has handled 3,800 bank failures since it was established on 1 January 1934 ... that has not cost U.S. taxpayers a penny. It has all come from FDIC assessments on other banks. It's been a mutual insurance company. If you just keep out of trouble on the asset side, banking is a very good business because you get your money so cheap and because of the implicit federal guarantee, and you do get to leverage up to a fair extent, and America's been a pretty good place to lend money. So I like our positions. Both those companies are very well-run institutions, but they were up to 25–30% on returns on tangible equity; that's not going to get repeated in the future, and it shouldn't be."

CM: "We might add that M&T Bank, which most people never talk about, is headed by a really sensible fellow [CEO Bob Wilmers], and it's been a wonderful investment for us."

WB: "If you get the M&T annual report, the first part of the letter is about M&T specifically, but the second part is about the American financial economy in particular, and I would really recommend you read that. Bob is a very smart guy and he has a lot of good observations. He expresses quite a dislike for the fact that a market system creates a reward system where money sort of disproportionally flows to people who work with money, and that tends to attract a disproportional number of people with lots of ability; he thinks at least some of them might be better deployed elsewhere. It's an interesting read. The other I would recommend is [CEO of J.P. Morgan] Jamie Dimon's letter. It's a tour de force, in terms of describing the banking scene and the economic scene. He has some real insights in there about some very important subjects. It's a letter I think everybody could learn a lot from reading, as they could from the letter by Wilmers."

CM: "For people who like an element of morality in business, Wilmers sounds like an Old Testament prophet. He doesn't like that all the really big banks are making so much money out of trading, because he says you're really trying to outsmart your own customers, and he'd rather serve them in a culture of deserved trust in both directions. It's hard to think he's totally wrong."

2013 MEETING (02:30:03)

CM: "I'm a little less optimistic about the banking system, long term, than Warren is. I would like to see something more extreme, in terms of limiting bank activities. I do not see why massive derivative books should be mixed up with deposits that are insured by the country."

WB: "I'm with Charlie on that."

CM: "The more bankers want to be like investment bankers instead of bankers, the worse I like it. I don't want to say more. I get in enough trouble on the subject already."

2016 MEETING (01:50:12)

WB: "The public policy since 2008–2009 has been to very much toughen up capital requirements in a variety of ways for banks, but it has specifically been designed to make very large banks less profitable relative to smaller banks. And you can do that by increasing capital requirements. You can change the math of banking, and the attractiveness of banking, totally, through capital requirements. Obviously, if you said every bank had to be 100% equity, it would be a terrible business. You couldn't possibly earn any money that was significant on capital. And if you let people operate with 1% capital ratios, they can make a lot of money and they will cause the system all kinds of trouble. So, since 2009, the rules have been tilted against the larger banks primarily through capital requirements. That just means returns on equity go down, but returns on equity were awfully high prior to that. So it hasn't turned it into a bad business, it's turned it into a less attractive business than earlier."

2023 MEETING (02:45:06)

WB: "The situation in banking is similar to what it's always been, that fear is contagious. And historically, sometimes the fear was justified and sometimes it wasn't … The banking system has changed so much over the years, and we did something enormously sensible, in my view, when we set up the FDIC. As many as 2,000 banks failed in one year back after World War I. Bank runs were just part of the picture—and if you have people worried about whether their money is safe in the bank and all of a sudden they withdraw it, you can't run an economy very well. So, the FDIC was very logical.

"But here we are, in 2023, and we actually see the FDIC pay off at 100 cents on the dollar to everybody, or to make it available on all demand deposits, and yet you still have people very worried. That just should not happen. So, I think the messaging has been very poor. It has been poor by the politicians who sometimes have an interest in having it poor. It's been poor by the agencies. And I'd say it's been poor by the press. You shouldn't have so many people who misunderstand the fact that although there may be a $250,000 limit on FDIC, the FDIC, the U.S. government, and American public have no interest in having a bank fail or to have deposits actually lost by people.

"We had a demonstration project the weekend of Silicon Valley Bank [which failed after a bank run in March 2023] and the public is still confused. It's something to have a law that became effective in 1934 not be understood about something as important as the banking system … If people think that deposits are sticky anymore, they're living in a different era. You can press a button, you don't have to get in a line and wait for days and have the teller counting out the money slowly in gold. You can have a run in a few seconds. So the way it hasn't been addressed properly is a problem, and who knows where it leads. But you will have to have a punishment for the people who do the wrong thing.

"If you take First Republic, you could look at their 10-K and see that they were offering non-government guaranteed mortgages in jumbo amounts at fixed rates, sometimes for ten years before they changed to floating. That's a crazy proposition … You don't give options like that, but that's what First Republic was doing in plain sight. And the world ignored it until it blew up. And some stock in these banks that was held by insiders was sold, and who knows whether they had some plan that was innocent or if they started sensing what was coming.

"The directors do have the ability to hold the CEO accountable. If the CEO gets the bank in trouble, both the CEO and the directors should suffer. The stockholders of the future shouldn't suffer; they didn't do anything. It teaches the lesson that if you run a bank and you screw it up, you're still a rich guy, the world goes on. That is not a good lesson to teach people who are holding the behavior of the economy in their hands. There's work to be done—and it's not a difficult problem, we've just screwed up the answer and the communication of it."

CM: "I'm so old-fashioned that I kind of liked it better when banks didn't do investment banking. That makes me very outmoded in the modern world … A banker should be more like an engineer. He is more into avoiding trouble than getting rich. They could do fine that way."

2023 MEETING (02:58:29)

WB: "If you follow sound banking methods, a bank can be a perfectly decent investment. In fact, in 1969, we had $19 million invested in [Illinois National Bank & Trust] and $17 million invested in our insurance companies. If the Bank Holding Company Act of 1970 hadn't been passed, we might have ended up owning a lot of banks instead of a lot of insurance companies. But they passed the Bank Holding Company Act, and we had to divest that bank in ten years."

CM: "By the way, that bank never had a bad debt. It never had an unnecessary cost. It made nothing but money with no risk. You never present it to any deposit insurance risk or the government. It was a lovely, sound, constructive institution in this community. Any person willing to deserve credit could get credit. And we were forced out of it."

WB: "We were going to buy more banks. And if we bought more banks, we probably wouldn't have been as big in insurance—but the law changed, we divested, and we've done OK in insurance. But banking was more attractive to us. It was bigger and there were more targets. And you could run a perfectly sound bank … We would've found more banks, but we were precluded from doing that.

"Recently, we sold bank stocks when the pandemic broke out, and then we sold some more in the last six months. We don't know where the shareholders of banks are heading. I've got my personal money at a local bank and I'm probably above the FDIC limit; I don't worry about that in the least. But in terms of owning banks, events will determine their future and now you've got politicians involved.

"A lot of people don't really understand how the system works. And I would say that we've had something less than a perfect communication between various people and the American public. The public is probably as confused about banking as ever, and that has consequences. Nobody knows what the consequences are because every event starts recreating a different dynamic. You don't know what has happened to the stickiness of deposits. That changes everything. So, we're very cautious in a situation like that, about ownership of banks. We do remain with one bank holding, Bank of America. I like Bank of America and I like the management. And I proposed the deal with them back in 2011, so I stick with it. But do I know how to project out what's going to happen from here? The answer is I don't, because I've seen so many things in the last few months, which really weren't that unexpected to me, but which confirmed my belief that the American public doesn't understand their banking system."

SHORTING STOCKS

1999 MEETING (02:57:21)

WB: "It doesn't make a difference whether anybody shorts Berkshire Hathaway … It does not hurt us in any way, shape, or form … What counts is intrinsic value. If we increase Berkshire's value at a reasonable rate, the shorts will have to figure out how to eat three times a day."

2001 MEETING (04:07:07)

WB: "Short selling is an interesting item to study because it's ruined a lot of people. It is the sort of thing that you can go broke doing … It's tempting. You will see way more dramatically overvalued stocks in your career than dramatically undervalued stocks. It's the nature of securities markets to occasionally promote various things to the sky, so that securities will frequently sell for 5–10× what they're worth, and they will very, very seldom sell for 20% or 10% of what they're worth. Therefore, you see these much greater discrepancies between price and value on the overvaluation side. So you might think it's easier to make money on short selling. All I can say is that it hasn't been for me.

"It is a very, very tough business because of the fact that you face unlimited losses, and because of the fact that people who have very overvalued stocks are frequently on some scale between promoter and crook. That's why they get there. They also know how to use that very valuation to bootstrap value into the business, because if you have a stock that's selling at $100 that's worth $10, obviously it's to your interest to go out and issue a whole lot of shares. And if you do that, when you get all through, the value can be $50. In fact, there's a lot of chain letter-type stock promotions that are sort of based on the implicit assumption that the management will keep doing that. And if they do it once and build it to $50 by issuing a lot of shares at $100 when it's worth $10, now the value is $50 and people say, 'Well, these guys are so good at that, let's pay $200 or $300' and then they could do it again and so on. It's not usually quite that clear in their minds. But that's the basic principle underlying a lot of stock promotions.

"If you get caught up in one of those that is successful, you can run out of money before the promoter runs out of ideas. In the end, they almost always work. Of the things that we have felt like shorting over the years, they would work out very well eventually if you held them through. But it is very painful, and in my experience, it was a whole lot easier to make money on the long side. I had one arbitrage situation when I moved to New York in 1954, that involved a surefire-type transaction, an arbitrage transaction that had to work. But there was a technical wrinkle in it and I was short something. And for a short period of time it was very unpleasant. In my view, you can't make really big money doing it because you can't expose yourself to the loss that would be there if you did do it on a big scale."

CM: "Being short something, which keeps going up because somebody is promoting it in a half-crooked way, and you keep losing while they call for more margin—it just isn't worth it to have that much irritation in life. It isn't that hard to make money somewhere else with less irritation."

2006 MEETING (04:34:42)

WB: "Over the years, I've probably had a hundred ideas of things that I thought to short, and I would say that almost every one of them turned out to be correct. And I would bet that if I'd tried to do it, I probably would have lost money ... If somebody's running something that's semi-fraudulent, they're probably pretty good at it. If they succeed and you go in at X and the price goes to 5X, all you're hoping after a while it that it goes to X again or something of the sort. It's a very tough psychological game to play … I would never put any money with a short fund; not because I would think it would be ethically wrong, I just think they're unlikely to make money."

CM: "That would be one of the most irritating experiences in the world; to figure out something is crooked and foolish and so forth, and then to short it at X and have it go to 3X. Now you're watching all these happy crooks splashing around in your money while you're meeting margin calls. Why would you want to go in hailing distance of an experience like that?"

INDEX FUNDS

2002 MEETING (00:54:42)

WB: "In terms of buying an index fund, I would just take a very broad index. I would take the S&P 500 as long as I wasn't putting all my money in at one time … I would be very careful about the costs involved because all they're doing for you is buying that index. I think people who buy index funds, on average, will get better results than the people who buy funds that have higher costs attached to them, because it's just a matter of math. If you have a very high percentage of funds being institutionally managed—and a great many institutions charge a lot of money for doing it and others charge a little—they're going to get very similar gross results but different net results.

"I would pick a broad index, but I wouldn't toss a chunk in at any one time. I would do it over a period of time, because the very nature of index funds is that you are saying, I think American business is going to do reasonably well over a long period of time, but I don't know enough to pick the winners and I don't know enough to pick the winning times. There's nothing wrong with that. I don't know enough to pick the winning times. Occasionally, I think I know enough to pick a winner, but not very often. And I certainly can't pick winners by going through the whole list and saying, this is a winner, this isn't, and so on. So, the important thing to do, if you have an overall feeling that business is a reasonable place to have your money over a long period of time, is to invest over a long period of time, and not make any bet, implicitly, by putting a big chunk in at a given time.

"There's no single metric I can give you, or that anybody else can give you, in my view, that will tell you this is a great time to buy stocks or not to buy stocks. It just isn't that easy. That's why you go to an index fund, and that's why you buy over a period of time … If you are buying an index fund, you are protecting yourself against the fact that you don't know the answers to those questions but that you think you can do well over time without knowing the answers to those questions, as long as you consciously recognize that fact."

2004 MEETING (02:23:30)

WB: "If you accumulate a low-cost index fund over ten years with fairly regular sums, I think you will probably do better than 90% of the people who take up investing at a similar time."

CM: "I would agree with that, totally. It's awkward for us sitting here at these annual meetings, where we have a sampling of some of the most honorable and skillful stockbrokers around who have done a wonderful job for their own clients and their own families. But the stockbroking fraternity, in toto, can be guaranteed to do so poorly that the index fund is a better option."

2008 MEETING (02:22:32)

WB: "Under the conditions you name, I'd probably have it all in a very low-cost index fund; might be Vanguard, somebody I knew was reliable and where the costs were low. And because you postulated that you're not going to become a professional investor, I would recognize the fact that I'm an amateur investor … and then I'd forget it and go back to my life."

CM: "It's in the nature of things that you aren't going to have a whole lot of screamingly successful professional investors. You've got a great horde of professionals taking croupiers' profits out of the system, most of them by pretending to be professional investors, and that is in the nature of things, too. But if you don't have any rational prospects of being a very skilled professional investor, of course you should compromise on some simple thing like an index fund."

WB: "You will not get that advice from anybody else because nobody gets paid to give you that advice. You will have all kinds of people telling you how much better they can do for you than that, how if you just give them a wrap fee or commissions, that they will do better—but they won't do better … In the end, you will have a perfectly decent return over a thirty- or forty-year period by doing what I suggest. Why should you expect more than that when you don't bring anything to the party? The salesman will tell you that you'll get it, but you won't."

CHINESE STOCKS

2022 MEETING (03:36:28)

CM: "There's no question that the government of China has worried the investors from the U.S. who invest in China, more in recent months and years than in earlier periods. There's been some tension, and it's affected the prices of some Chinese stocks, particularly internet stocks. Just in the last day or two, the Chinese leader has sort of reversed course on that, he said he went too far and he's going to pull way back and so on. So, we're having some hopeful signs. But yes, there are more difficulties dealing with their regime in China than there are in the United States, and it's different. It's a long way away, and they've got their own culture and their own loyalties and so on. The reason I invested in China is I can get so much better companies at so much lower prices, and I was willing to take a little political risk to get them ... Other people might reach the opposite conclusion, and everybody is more worried about China now than they were two or three years ago. That's just the way it is."

IPOS

2004 MEETING (04:04:24)

CM: "It is entirely possible that you could use our mental models to find good things to buy among IPOs. There are a zillion IPOs every year, and buried in those IPOs, I'm sure there are a few cinches that a really intelligent person could find and pounce on. But the average person buying IPOs is going to get creamed."

WB: "An auction market, prevailing in the stock market, will offer up extraordinary bargains sometimes, because somebody will sell 0.5–1% of a company at a price that may be 25% of what it's worth, whereas in negotiated deals, you don't get that. An IPO situation more closely approximates a negotiated deal. The seller decides when to come to market in most cases. And they don't necessarily pick a time that's good for you. So, I think it's way less likely that if you scan a hundred IPOs, you're going to come up with something cheaper than scanning a hundred companies already trading in the auction market. It is more of a negotiated sale. And negotiated transactions are very hard to get bargains from ... You're way more likely to get incredible bargains in an auction market. It's just the nature of things. You'll make better buys in an auction market."

HOUSING MARKET/RESIDENTIAL REAL ESTATE

2005 MEETING (01:17:26)

WB: "At the high end of the real estate market in some areas, you've seen extraordinary movement. I've referred to this before, but twenty-five years ago or so we saw the same thing in farmland in Nebraska, Iowa, and the surrounding areas. People were worried about the fact that inflation was out of control in the late 1970s, before Volcker did his stuff, and people were fleeing from cash. And one of the ways they gave vent to that fear was to rush into farmland. There was a farm about thirty miles north of here that sold for $2,000 an acre in 1980. And a few years later, I bought it from the FDIC for $600 an acre. You can say, how can you go crazy about farmland? It's going to produce about forty-five bushels an acre of soybeans, about 120 bushels an acre of corn. And there's no way you could dream about it tripling, or the internet causing corn yields to go up, or something of the sort. But people went crazy on it. And the consequences were huge, in terms of lots of banks failing in this area, banks that had gone through the Great Depression. But people just went a little crazy.

"I don't know where we stand in terms of the residential housing cycle in that it has different behavior characteristics, simply because people live in the houses in a great many cases. So, it will not behave, necessarily, the same as other markets. But when you get prices increasing at far, far greater rates than construction costs or inflationary factors, sometimes there can be some pretty serious consequences ... I would say that residential real estate, probably, has increased in price at a rate quite a bit faster than the general inflation rate."

CM: "But if you get to Laguna, California, or Montecito, California, or the better suburbs of Washington, D.C., you have a real asset price bubble ..."

WB: "I sold a house a few months ago in Laguna for $3.5 million. It sold the first day, so I probably listed it too cheap. But that house, the physical house, would probably cost $500,000 or thereabouts. So, in effect, the land went for $3 million, implicitly, and the land is probably on the area of 2,000 square feet ... basically, I think that land sold for about $60 million an acre."

CM: "One of the Berkshire directors lives adjacent to what I regard as a pretty modest little house, which sold for $27 million recently. These are houses that look right at the ocean, and there isn't a great deal of available shoreline in California, and there are a lot of people. But you have some very extreme housing-price bubbles going on. And you would think there might be a real possibility that it could go in the other direction someday."

WB: "At $27 million, I'd rather stare at my bathtub."

2005 MEETING (01:42:09)

WB: "There's no question that lending terms have become easier and easier as prices have increased; now, that is absolutely counter to how people think about lending in general. Generally, the more the asset class becomes inflated, the less a prudent banker will lend. But of course, in this country, now you have mortgages intermediated in a way that the person buying the mortgage—I'm thinking of Freddie Mac and Fannie Mae—does not need to care about what kind of financial transaction the purchase is. All they have to do is look at the guarantee, and they look at that rather than whether somebody's put any money down, or anything of the sort. So I think you've had easy financing facilitating a boom in real estate prices."

CM: "It's obvious that the easy lending on houses causes more houses to be built and causes housing prices to be higher, probably, in the new field. Eventually, of course, if you construct enough of anything, you can have a countervailing effect. If you build way too many houses, you'd eventually cause a price decline."

WB: "I'll give you a fanciful illustration. Let's just assume that Omaha had a totally constant population and nobody could build any more houses, but every year, everybody sold their house to their neighbor. So, first year, everybody sold their $100,000 house to their neighbor, and they both switched houses, and that was fine. And then the next year, they agreed to do it at $150,000. And you'd say, well, how could that be? Well, we all go to Freddie or Fannie and get our mortgages guaranteed for a larger amount, and somebody in New York or Tokyo or someplace would buy the Freddie or Fannie paper. And we'd have an influx of $50,000 per household. We'd all have the same number of houses. We'd all be living one family to a house. And we'd have marked up our houses, and we now have a bigger mortgage, but we'd have $50,000 more income that year just to service a little higher mortgage. And we'd do the same thing the following year for $200,000 and so on. Now, that would be very transparent, and people might catch on to the fact there was something funny going on in Omaha. But you can have an accidental aggregation of behavior that somewhat leads to the same effect. If you keep marking up something, and in the process, the payment for the marked-up price comes from someone else who feels they are bearing no risk because they've got the government guarantee in between, the money can just flood in and everybody feels very happy for a long time. We don't have anything like the fanciful thing I've set forth, but we have certain aspects of that going on in the economy."

CM: "I do agree with that. You have varied Ponzi effects in various parts of any modern economy. And they're very important and they're very little studied in economics."

2006 MEETING (01:25:51)

WB: "You have to go back thirty or forty years to find volumes in manufactured housing as low as it's been in the last couple of years. There have been years where 20% of the new housing product in the United States was manufactured housing. Last year, leaving out FEMA demand, it was probably 7% of new housing starts. So, the percentage of the total new housing stock that has been manufactured housing in recent years has really been very low, while the houses are considerably better quality than in earlier years … The houses were mis-sold four or five years ago in a huge quantity because you had manufactured housing retailers selling the houses to people who shouldn't be buying them, taking the loans, and securitizing them, where somebody in an insurance company someplace lost significant sums of money. You had an abuse of credit in the field and there's a hangover from that, and it's taken a long time for that hangover to work its way through … The terms got very lax for a while, and we're bearing the consequences of that now … Clayton Homes' position is very strong. And their record is so much better than anybody in the industry that you have to look very hard to find number two."

CM: "I think manufactured housing is going to get a lot better and take a lot more of the market. It may take a considerable period, but that is so logical that I think it will eventually happen."

WB: "The industry has to think through—and they've made a lot of progress on this—the logical way of financing these things; what's the way to make sure the person who buys it really has an asset that's in excess of their loan value five to ten years down the road? Very little consideration was given to that five years ago. It was just a question of putting together the papers, selling the loans on Wall Street, and letting somebody else worry about it later on. Clayton did a way better job than other companies in that respect, but those were the industry conditions that existed then. But I think Clayton could easily be the largest homebuilder in the United States in future years because we will be a big part of an industry that, as Charlie says, should be doing more volume."

CM: "I also think some of the sin that was in the manufactured housing finance a few years ago shifted into the finance of the stick-built houses. There is a lot of ridiculous credit being extended in America in the housing field. It had a horrible aftermath in the manufactured housing sector, and my guess is there will be some trouble in the stick-built sector in due course."

WB: "Dumb lending always has its consequences and usually on a big scale, but you don't see it for quite a while … A developer will develop anything he can borrow the money against. It's that simple. And when the lending institutions pour the money out for something, it will get built … I think that has happened in conventional housing here in recent years."

CM: "Yes, and some of this dumb lending is being facilitated by contemptible accounting. The accounting profession has not stopped compromising its way into terrible behavior."

2015 MEETING (00:09:54)

WB: "When we can, we try to get Clayton customers an FHA loan, because that's the best loan for them to get. But, as I say, most of our borrowers are below the 620 FICO score. And it's true that 3% or so will lose their homes in a year. It's true that 97% of those people will have a home where their average principal and interest payment is a little under $600 a month, and that takes care of having a two-, perhaps three-bedroom house, well equipped.

"Clayton has behaved, in my book, extraordinarily well … I'm proud of Clayton management. I'm proud of the fact they put, this year, maybe 30,000 people in homes at a very low cost, a very good home. And a very high percentage of those people are going to have those loans paid off, probably in twenty years, and have a home that has been a real bargain, basically."

CM: "I don't know a lot about the mortgage practices at Clayton, but I know we've sold an enormous number of houses and we have a big share of the total market in manufactured [about 50%]. It's a very constructive thing. Personally, I've always wondered why manufactured houses don't have a bigger share of the market. It's such an efficient way of creating quite usable houses. Clayton is a very productive part of the economy—but we can't make lending to poor people who buy houses 100% successful for everybody. We wouldn't be running the business right if the foreclosure rate was zero. Too many people who deserve credit wouldn't get it."

WB: "The big causes of default are the loss of a job, death, and divorce. And, that happens with high-priced houses as well, but it happens more often with people that are living closer to the edge. I don't think that's a reason to deny them a house, and particularly when it turns out so well for so many … People want to live in those houses, and I think they deserve the right to."

BYD

2009 MEETING (02:49:59)

CM: "Although its founder is only forty-three years old, BYD is not some early-stage venture capital company. BYD is one of the main manufacturers to the world of the rechargeable lithium battery. It achieved that position from a standing start at zero under the leadership of the founder, Wang Chuanfu. They went on into cell phone components and developed a huge position. Then, finally, not satisfied with having worked a couple of miracles, Wang Chuanfu decided he would go into the automobile business. As nearly as I can tell, [he had] zero experience in automobiles. And from a standing start at zero and with very little capital, he was rapidly able to create the bestselling single model in China. And that's against competition that was Chinese joint ventures with all the major auto companies of the world, technological marvels with way more capital, and so on.

"This is not some unproven, highly speculative activity. What it is, is a damn miracle. And Wang Chuanfu has hired 17,000 engineering graduates. Those engineering graduates are selected from 1.3 billion people in China. And he's hiring at the top of the classes. So you get a remarkable aggregation of human talent … This is a very talented group. And these lithium batteries are totally needed for the future of the world. We need them in every utility company in America and in the world. We have to use the direct power of the sun, and we can't do that without marvelous batteries. BYD is in the sweet spot on that stuff. I know it looks like a miracle, and it looks like Warren and I have gone crazy, but I don't think we have.

"That car you're going to see in the annex, I think they make everything in that car except the glass and the rubber; there may be a couple of small exceptions. That's unheard of. Whoever went into the automobile business and made every part, and made a bestselling automobile? This is not normal; it's very unusual. I regard it as a privilege to have Berkshire associated with a company that is trying to do so much that's so important for humanity, when you get right down to it. It may be a small company, but its ambitions are large … I'll be amazed if great things don't happen here. Given the size, I don't think it can be all that important to Berkshire, financially—but I have never, in my life, felt more privileged to be associated with something than BYD."

2009 MEETING (03:14:01)

WB: "It's very hard to imagine that we won't find more things to do in China over time. There will, perhaps, be opportunities to buy businesses there. We would've bought more than 10% of BYD if we could've, but that's all that they wished to sell us. So, we hope that comes about."

HARLEY-DAVIDSON

2010 MEETING (01:24:30)

WB: "I don't know whether Harley-Davidson equity is worth $33 or $20 or $45. I have no view on that. I kind of like a business where your customers tattoo your name on their chest or something. But figuring out its economic value, I'm not sure even going out and questioning those guys with the tattoos that I'd learn much from them. But I thought I knew, and I think I was right, that Harley-Davidson was not going out of business and that 15% was going to look pretty damned attractive [Berkshire bought $300 million of unsecured notes in February 2009].

"Now, we could probably sell those bonds at 135 or something like that. I knew enough to lend them money, but I didn't know enough to buy the equity. And that's frequently the case. We love buying equities, but we love buying the Goldman preferred at 10%. Now, let's say Goldman, instead of offering me the

10% preferred and warrants said, 'You can have a 12% preferred, non-callable,' I might have taken that instead. There's a tradeoff involved in all these securities. And obviously, if I think I can make very good money, as we did on Harley-Davidson, with a very simple decision—just a question of, 'Are they going to go broke or not?' as opposed to tougher decisions, 'Is the motorcycle market going to get diminished significantly? Are margins going to get squeezed?', all of that—I'll go with a simple decision."

CM: "Generally speaking, I think very often when you're looking at a distressed situation and buy the bonds, you should have bought the stock. You're looking in a promising area."

WB: "Ben Graham wrote about that in *Security Analysis* in 1934; in the analysis of senior securities, the junior securities usually do better, but you may sleep better with the senior securities. As Charlie points out, we have $60 billion of liabilities to people in our insurance operation that, in some cases, extend out for fifty years or more. We might have very significant amounts of money in stocks, but we are running this place so that it can withstand anything. A couple years ago during the crisis, we felt very good about where that philosophy left us; we could do things at a time when most people were paralyzed, and we'll keep running it that way."

RATING AGENCIES

2010 MEETING (03:21:51)

WB: "The ratings agencies have had, and still have, under current conditions, an incredibly wonderful business. It takes no capital at all, the pricing power is significant, and certain parts of the world feel they need rating agencies. A certain part of the world is also very mad at rating agencies. Many feel the rating agencies let them down when the rating agencies, essentially, succumbed to the same mania, in effect, that prevailed throughout the investment world, and, really, the political world, the media, etc. They couldn't see a world where residential housing, countrywide, would collapse. The incentive part of it, there may have been some small aspect that played. I just think it's very hard to think contrary to the crowd.

"On the other hand, there is, obviously, a backlash against rating agencies. There may be legal remedies. But if the whole structure around them does not change in some dramatic way, it's a darn good business in that you can't shop pricing in the rating agency business. We have never paid any attention to ratings for bonds at Berkshire. We don't think we should farm out, outsource, investment judgment. If we can't do it ourselves, we just don't do it. We're not going to rely on somebody else's opinion, whether it's a rating agency or anybody else.

So, it's not a business we rely on, but we do recognize that if the model doesn't change, it still remains a phenomenal business."

REDUCING EXPECTATIONS

2011 MEETING (02:12:54)

WB: "I advise people to buy index funds, actually, if they're not going to be active in investments. If you've got a day job, and you want to just put money aside over time, I think the average individual will do better buying an index fund consistently over time than almost anything else available to them. It will never be regarded as a great investment, but it will be a perfectly satisfactory investment. If I personally had a choice between an index fund and Berkshire at present prices, I would rather own Berkshire. I wouldn't be unhappy if you told me I had to leave all my money in an index fund for the rest of my life—but I like Berkshire better."

CM: "I like it a lot better, and I'd be very unhappy if I had to own an index fund. My ambitions are larger. I don't think the average return of a skilled investor over the next fifty years is going to be as good as it was over the last fifty years. So, I think reduced expectations are the best defense any investor has, and after that, I think Berkshire is a pretty good bet."

WB: "Charlie's big on lowering expectations."

CM: "Absolutely. That's the way I got married; my wife lowered her expectations."

WB: "And he lived up to them."

HENRY SINGLETON AND TELEDYNE

2013 MEETING (01:52:22)

CM: "Henry Singleton was a genius who could play chess blindfolded just below the grandmaster level and never got less than an 800 on any complicated math or physics exam. I knew him. He lived in my community. But he started as a conglomerate where he was very interested in reporting higher earnings all the time so he could keep the daisy chain going. And when he managed it on the way down, he bought in the stock relentlessly and very logically, like a great chess player should. But he managed those companies on a way more centralized basis than Berkshire has ever operated. And in the end, the great bulk of the enterprises, he wanted to sell to us. By that time, he was ill and he really wanted to sell to us. And of course, he wanted Berkshire stock. And we basically said, 'Henry, we love you and we'd love to buy your businesses, but we don't want to issue Berkshire stock.' So, I don't think you should get the idea that just because he was a genius he did it better than we did."

WB: "He played the public markets way better. We're not interested in doing that, actually."

CM: "No, we're not."

WB: "He was incredible in that, and he made a fortune for shareholders that stayed with him. But to some extent, he looked at the shareholder group as somebody to be taken advantage of, and he issued stock like crazy. I'll bet he did at least fifty acquisitions ... He was playing the game of the 1960s, and we actually have never wanted to get in that game. He promoted the stock. He had the Litton Industries background on it, and it was a game that worked wonderfully if you didn't care about how it ended up. We have not played that game. In terms of wanting to get Berkshire stock, he essentially was going into the third stage of first issuing overpriced shares, then buying it back very underpriced, and then he was going to—"

CM: "—sell it to us for more than it was worth."

WB: "Exactly."

CM: "It was the wrong stock. He was an enormously talented man, and that cool rationality was to be admired—but I like our system better. We're more avuncular than Teledyne was."

MEMORABLE INVESTMENTS

2019 MEETING (00:45:34)

WB: "One time, I bought one share of stock in the Atled Corp. Atled had ninety-eight shares outstanding and I bought one; not what you call a liquid security. And Atled happened to be the word 'delta' spelled backwards. A hundred guys in St Louis had each chipped in $50 or $100 or something to form a duck club in Louisiana, and they bought some land down there. There were a hundred of them, but two of them defaulted on their obligation to come up with the $100, so there were ninety-eight shares out. They went down to Louisiana and they shot some ducks. But apparently somebody fired a few shots into the ground and oil spurted out. And I think the Delta duck club field is still producing.

"I bought stock in it forty years ago for $29,200 a share. It had that amount in cash, and it was producing a lot, and they sold it. If they kept it, that stock might've been worth $2 million or $3 million a share, but they sold out to another oil company. Actually, I didn't have any cash at the time. I went down and borrowed the money. I bought it for my wife. ... The loan officer said,

'Would you like to borrow some money to buy a shotgun as well?' Charlie, tell them about the one you missed."

CM: "I have two that come to mind. When I was young and poor, I spent $1,000 once buying an oil royalty that paid me $100,000 a year for a great many years. But that was once in a lifetime. On a later occasion, I bought shares of Belridge Oil, which went up thirty times rather quickly. But I turned down five times as much as I bought. It was the dumbest decision of my life. So, if any of you have made any dumb decisions, look up here and feel good about yourselves."

PRIVATE EQUITY

2019 MEETING (01:18:27)

WB: "If you leveraged up investments in common stocks, and you figured a way so that you would have staying power through any market dips, you'd have extraordinary returns. In my investing lifetime, if an index fund did 11%—well, imagine how well you would've done if you'd leveraged that up 50% whatever the prevailing rates were over time. So, a leveraged investment in a business is going to beat an unleveraged investment in a good business a good bit of the time.

"But ... the covenants to protect debtholders have really deteriorated in the business. And of course, you've been in an upmarket for businesses. And you've got a period of low interest rates. So, it's been a very good time for it. My personal opinion is, if you take unleveraged returns against unleveraged common stocks, I do not think what is being purchased today and marketed today would work well. But if you can buy assets that will yield 7% or 8%, and you can borrow enough money at 4% or 5% and you don't have any covenants to meet, you're going to have some bankruptcies. But you're going to have better results in many cases.

"It's not something that interests us at all. We are not going to leverage up Berkshire. If we'd leveraged up Berkshire, we'd have made a whole lot more money, obviously, over the years. But both Charlie and I have seen some really extraordinarily high-IQ people destroyed by leverage. We saw Long-Term Capital Management (LTCM), where we had people who could do math in their sleep, math that I couldn't do working full time at it during the day; they were really, really smart people working with their own money and with years and years of experience of what they were doing. And it all turned into pumpkins and mice in 1998. Then, we saw some of those same people, after that happened, go on and do the same thing again. So, I would not get excited about so-called alternative investments. You can get all kinds of different figures. But there's probably at least $1 trillion committed to, in effect, buying businesses. And if you figure they're going to leverage them, two for one on that, you may have $3 trillion of buying power trying to buy businesses in the U.S. market, which may be something over $30 trillion now, but there's all kinds of businesses that aren't for sale.

"So, the supply-demand situation for buying businesses privately and leveraging them up has changed dramatically from what it was ten or twenty years ago. And we have seen a number of proposals from private equity funds, where the returns are really not calculated in a manner that I would regard as honest. If I were running a pension fund, I would be very careful about what was being offered to me. If you have a choice on Wall Street between being a great analyst or being a great salesperson, salesperson is the way to make it. If you can raise $10 billion in a fund, and you get a 1.5% fee, and you lock people up for ten years, you and your children and your grandchildren will never have to do a thing, even if you are the dumbest investor in the world."

CM: "I think what we're doing will work more safely … What I don't like about a lot of the pension fund investments is I think they like it because they don't have to mark it down as much as it should be in the middle of the panics. I think that's a silly reason to buy something, because you're given leniency in marking it down."

WB: "Yeah. And when you commit the money—often in the case of private equity—they don't take the money, but you pay a fee on what you've committed. And you really have to have that money to come up with at any time. Of course, it makes their return look better, if you sit there for a long time in Treasury bills, which you have to hold, because they can call you and demand the money, and they don't count that. They count it in terms of getting a fee on it, but they don't count it in terms of what the so-called internal rate of return is. So, it's not as good as it looks."

CM: "Warren, all they're doing is lying a little bit to make the money come in."

WB: "That sums it up."

BOOK RECOMMENDATIONS

1994 MEETING (01:17:12)

CM: "I very much enjoyed Connie Bruck's book, *Master of the Game*, which was a biography of Steve Ross, who headed Warner and was later CEO of Time Warner. She's a very insightful writer and it's a very interesting story. I am rereading a book I really like, which is Carl Van Doren's biography of Benjamin Franklin (*Benjamin Franklin*); I had almost forgotten how good a book it was. We have never had anybody quite like Franklin in this country, and never again."

1994 MEETING (03:29:49)

WB: "There's one chapter in *The General Theory* [by John Maynard Keynes] that relates to markets, the psychology of markets, and the behavior of market participants; aside from chapter eight and chapter twenty of *The Intelligent Investor* [by Ben Graham], you'll get as much wisdom from reading that as anything written in investments … I would recommend reading that. Keynes and Graham, from vastly different starting points, came to the same conclusion at about the same time in the 1930s as to the soundest way to invest over time. They differed some on their ideas on diversification. Keynes believed in diversifying far less than did Graham. Keynes started off with the wrong theory, I would say, in the 1920s and essentially tried to predict business cycles in markets, and then shifted to fundamental analysis of businesses in the 1930s, and he did extremely well … So, I would advise you to read that. There are some letters Keynes wrote to co-trustees of life insurance societies, colleges, and so on, that I think you'd find interesting too."

1996 MEETING (04:16:13)

CM: "I'm almost ashamed to report this. I've gone back and picked up the part of biology I should've picked up ten to fifteen years earlier. It's a total circus, what they figured out over the last twenty or thirty years in biology. Take Richard Dawkins with *The Selfish Gene* and *The Blind Watchmaker*, these are marvelous books … I had to read *The Selfish Gene* twice before I fully understood it. There were things I believed all my life that weren't so. It's wonderful when you have those experiences. We always say, 'It isn't the learning that's so hard, it's the unlearning.'"

WB: "On investment books, I'd recommend the first two books Phil Fisher wrote, *Common Stocks and Uncommon Profits* and *Paths to Wealth Through Common Stocks*. They're very good books. John Train's *The Money Masters* is an interesting book. I obviously recommend *The Intelligent Investor*, chapters eight and twenty are the ones you really should read. All of the important ideas in investing, really, are in that book, because there's only about three ideas … One is to think of investing as owning a business and not buying something that wiggles around in price. The second is your attitude toward the market, which ties in with that; that's covered in chapter eight. If you have the proper attitude toward market movements, it's enormously helpful in securities. And the final chapter is on the margin of safety. Don't drive a 9,800-pound truck over a bridge with a 10,000 pound capacity; go find a bridge with 15,000 pounds of capacity."

1998 MEETING (00:46:37)

CM: "I have recently read a new book twice, which I very seldom do. And that is *Guns, Germs, and Steel* by Jared Diamond. It's a marvelous book. And the way the guy's mind works would be useful in business. He's got a mind that is always asking why, why, why, why. And he's very good at coming up with answers. I would say it's the best work of its kind I have ever read."

WB: "I read something to the effect of *The Quotable Einstein* [edited by Alice Calaprice]. It's a lot of his commentary over the years, and it's great reading. *Fermat's Last Theorem* [by Simon Sing] is also a very interesting book."

1999 MEETING (04:39:16)

CM: "Robert Hagstrom sent me his latest book on Warren Buffett, *The Buffett Portfolio.* I was flabbergasted to find it not only very well written, but a considerable contribution to the synthesis of human thought on the investment process. I would recommend that all of you buy a copy of Hagstrom's second Buffett book.

"Another book that I liked very much this year was *Titan* [by Ron Chernow], the biography of the original John D. Rockefeller. That's one of the best business biographies I have ever read. It's a very interesting family story, too. It is just a wonderful, wonderful book. I don't know anybody who's read it who hasn't enjoyed it.

"The third book is sort of a revisitation of the subject matter of the book I recommended a year or two ago called *Guns, Germs, and Steel,* which was a physiologist's view of the economic history of man. It was a wonderful book, and much of that same territory has now been covered by an emeritus history professor from Harvard, David Landes, who just knows way more economics and science than is common for a history professor. And that gives him better insight. His book is a takeoff on the title from Adam Smith, and the title is *The Wealth and Poverty of Nations.*"

WB: "If you haven't read Katharine Graham's autobiography, *Personal History,* it is a terrific book. It's an incredibly honest book. And it's a fascinating story. It's a life that's seen all kinds of things in politics, business, and in government. It's a great read.

"A book that came out in the investment world that I would certainly recommend is *Common Sense on Mutual Funds,* by Jack Bogle. Jack is an honest guy, and he knows the business. If mutual fund investors listened to him, they would save billions and billions of dollars a year. He tells it exactly like it is."

2000 MEETING (03:21:40)

WB: "Probably the most representative book on my views is the one that Larry Cunningham has put together [*The Essays of Warren Buffett*], because he essentially has taken my words and rearranged them. And what he has put together there best represents my views. We've got twenty years of annual reports or soon the internet, plus articles in *Fortune,* all kinds of things. I like to think that I laid out those views better than somebody who's rewriting them. But I'll let you make that decision. But I do think Larry's done a very good job of taking a number of those reports and rearranging them by topic in a way that makes it a lot easier to read than trying to go through year after year."

2002 MEETING (01:43:45)

CM: "The two books that I recommend this year were both sent to me by shareholders who thought I might like them, and boy were they right. The first is *Ice Age* [by John and Mary Gribbin], which is a description of the history of glaciation in the last few hundred-thousand years and how they figured out what had happened and why it had happened. I think it's the best book of scientific explanation I have ever read.

"The other book is *How the Scots Invented the Modern World* [by Arthur Herman]. That's a subject that's always interested me, how a tiny, poor, little population of Celtic people had such a huge favorable impact on the world, starting from poverty. And it's related to the Irish, who were a similar ethnic strain with a different religion. It is a marvelous book."

WB: "I'll recommend a book which may sound a little self-serving about the Berkshire managers. Robert P. Miles has brought out a book [*Warren Buffett's Berkshire Hathaway*] that tells about the people who are handling your capital … Bob has done a good job of interviewing them and I would encourage you to read about them. I think you'll like your investment better after you read about the managers."

2004 MEETING (01:24:57)

CM: "One book I really like is *Deep Simplicity* by John Gribbin. It's a perfectly marvelous book. And of course, that's a great title, *Deep Simplicity.* That's what we're all looking for."

WB: "I've been reading *A Short History of Nearly Everything* [by Bill Bryson]. It's very impressive to read about people pondering how to figure out the weight of the Earth or something in the 18th century. You would think that minds that could do that would do very well in financial matters. But, if you remember, Isaac Newton spent a significant part of his life trying to turn lead into gold. And he might have made a good stockbroker, but it didn't do much for him financially."

CM: "He lost an enormous chunk of his net worth in the South Sea Bubble. He invested in an absolute crooked mania and he was the smartest man in the world. IQ points alone won't do it."

2008 MEETING (03:25:28)

CM: "I would teach [young individuals] to avoid being manipulated to their disadvantage by vendors and lenders using the standard tricks of the vendor and lender trade—and you couldn't start with a better book than Robert B. Cialdini's *Influence*. Bob's a shareholder and is here somewhere in this audience. He's got a new book called *Yes* [co-authored with Noah J. Goldstein and Steve J. Martin]. There's two books I suggest you add to your class."

2011 MEETING (02:46:25)

CM: "I hate to admit this because I've ignored high-tech all my life, but I actually read *In the Plex* [by Steven Levy] about Google, and I found it very interesting. Here I am at my advanced age, and I find it interesting the way people have created these engineering cultures, which are quite peculiar and different from most of what we have at Berkshire. Will I ever make any use of this? I doubt it. But I certainly enjoyed learning it. And if I enjoy learning it, I regard it as important, because I think that's what you're here for: to go to bed every night a little wiser than when you got up."

2015 MEETING (03:04:38)

WB: "If you read Adam Smith [*The Wealth of Nations*], along with Keynes, Ricardo, and Fred Schwed's *Where Are the Customers' Yachts?* you will have a lot of wisdom … *Where Are the Customers' Yachts?* contains an incredible amount of wisdom in very few pages, it's very entertaining. But if you want to not only get a lot more wisdom but appear more erudite, you should also read *The Wealth of Nations.*"

CM: "Adam Smith is one of those guys that has really worn well. I mean, he is rightly recognized as one of the wisest people that ever came along. And, of course, the lessons that he taught way back then were taught again when communism failed so terribly, and places like Singapore and Taiwan and China, and so forth, came up so fast. The productive power of the capitalist system is simply unbelievable, and he understood that fully and early."

FEEDBACK AND DISCONFIRMING EVIDENCE

2002 MEETING (02:24:44)

WB: "Charlie and I have made big mistakes because, in effect, we have been unwilling to look afresh at something. That happens. But I think the annual report is a good feedback mechanism. Reporting on yourself, and giving the report honestly, whether you do it through an annual report or some other mechanism, is very useful. A partner who is not subservient, and who himself is extremely logical, is probably the best mechanism you can have.

"On the contrary, I would say the typical corporate organization is designed so that the CEO's opinions and biases and previous beliefs are reinforced in every possible way. Having staff surround you that know what you want to do means you're not going to get a lot of contrary thinking. If they know you want to buy a company, you're going to get a recommendation; whatever your hurdle rate, they're going to come back with whatever they feel that you want. And if you arrange your organization so that you basically have a bunch of sycophants cloaked in other titles, you are going to leave your prior conclusions intact, and the board is not going to be much of a check on that. I've seen very, very few boards that can stand up to something that's important to the CEO and just say, 'You're not going to get it.'

"All of us in this room want to read new information and have it confirm our cherished beliefs; it is built into the human system. That can be very expensive in the investment and business world. I think we've got a pretty good system. And I think that most of the systems in corporate America aren't very good at avoiding falling into the trap you're talking about."

CM: "I think it also helps to be willing to reverse course even when it's quite painful. As we sit here, I think Berkshire is the only big corporation in America that is running off a derivative book. And we originally made the decision to allow the Gen Re derivative book to continue, and it's a very unpleasant thing to do to reverse that decision, yet we're perfectly willing to do it. Nobody else is doing it, and yet it's perfectly obvious, at least to me, that to say that derivative accounting in America is a sewer is an insult to sewage."

WB: "The truth is that derivative accounting is absolutely terrible in this country, and there are a lot of companies that will not want to face up to what would be involved if they got out. You're seeing derivative accounting unwound at Enron in a major way, and believe me, it's not being unwound at a profit, except to the extent that the bankruptcy court lets them disaffirm certain contracts. There was no place where there was as much potential for phonying numbers at a place like Enron than the derivatives. They were marking-to-model; you give a bunch of traders the ability to create income by putting numbers down on a piece of paper that nobody can really check and it will get out of control. So we decided, finally, to bite the bullet on it, and we're getting out of it ... You couldn't devise a worse system. And, in the end, we didn't want to be in the business when we got in it, and we are now in the process of getting out. But you don't get out fast in something like this. It's a little like hell: easy to get into and very hard to get out of."

APPENDIX:
The Right Way To Run An Insurance Company

IN 1967, WARREN BUFFETT WROTE THE FOLLOWING IN HIS PARTNER letter: "Berkshire Hathaway [B-H] is experiencing and faces real difficulties in the textile business. While I don't presently foresee any loss in underlying values, I similarly see no prospect for a good return on the assets employed in the textile business." As Alice Schroder recounted in *The Snowball*, Buffett had concluded that "his most important task that year was to find something new which he could hitch the broken-down nag of Berkshire to before its 'substantial drag' on his performance became intolerable."

One potential answer Buffett had kept an eye on involved Charlie Heider, a friend and board member of National Indemnity (NICO), which was headquartered a few blocks from Buffett's office in Omaha (NICO was a property-casualty insurer that specialized in commercial auto and general liability insurance). Buffett and Heider had discussed NICO, with particular emphasis on one notable peculiarity about its CEO, Jack Ringwalt: "For fifteen minutes every year, Jack would want to sell NICO. Something would make him mad. Some claim would come in that irritated him … So Charlie and I discussed the phenomenon of Jack being in heat once a year for fifteen minutes. I told Charlie if he ever caught Jack in this particular phase to let me know."

When Heider called in February 1967, Buffett was ready to act; he asked Ringwalt how much he wanted for NICO, and Jack responded with $50 per share—"$15 per share more than Warren thought it was worth." But Buffett paid up to get the deal completed—and with that, Berkshire Hathaway's expansion into the insurance business began (the acquisition price was $8.6 million).

TWENTY-FIVE YEARS AT NATIONAL INDEMNITY

Fast forward to the 2004 Berkshire Hathaway shareholder meeting, nearly four decades after the NICO deal was finalized. During the annual meeting, as well as in that year's shareholder letter, Buffett discussed the financial results reported at NICO over the prior quarter century (1980–2004).

The first set of data is NICO's annual written premiums. As you can see, business volumes were very volatile from 1980 to 2004. After declining in the early 1980s, written premiums increased six-fold in two years, from ~$62 million in 1984 to ~$366 million in 1986 (as Buffett wrote in the 1986 letter, "The trends in NICO's traditional business ... suggest how gun-shy other insurers became for a while"). Over the next thirteen years, written premiums saw a cumulative decline of roughly 85%, from ~$366 million in 1986 to ~$55 million in 1999. This was a period of seemingly unending headwinds for NICO, with premiums declining in eleven of those thirteen years. Finally, in 2000, NICO's fortunes reversed once again: in 2004, five years after NICO's written premiums had bottomed, they exceeded $600 million—up more than 10× from the 1999 lows.

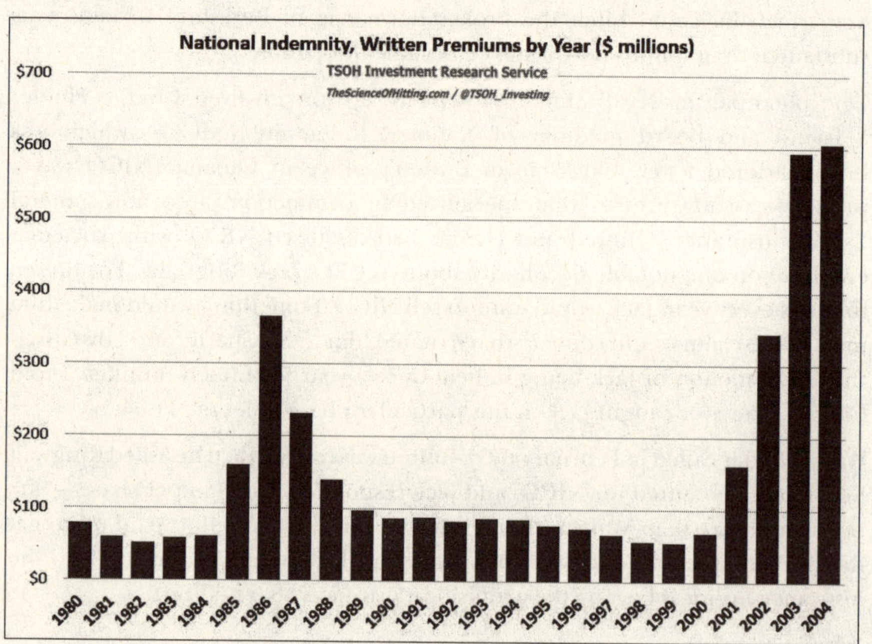

This outcome was by design; at NICO, sound underwriting was the primary goal, not premiums growth. Of course, every insurer wants sensible underwriting. But that objective, at times, clashes with the incentives of certain stakeholders—for example, employees who are more worried about keeping their job. At NICO, when the business declined ~85% over thirteen years, the number of people required to service the remaining business also declined significantly. This brings us to the discussion at the 2004 meeting, which highlighted the crucial role culture and incentives played at NICO. Here's Buffett discussing the premiums volatility highlighted above:

"I don't think there's another insurance company in the world that has a record like this. In the 'hard market' of the mid-1980s, we got up to $366 million. And then we took it down—not intentionally, but just because the business became less attractive—all the way from $366 million down to $55 million. Now, the market became more attractive in the last few years, and it soared up to almost $600 million. I don't think there's a public company in America that would feel they could survive a record of volume going down like that, year after year after year after year. But that was the culture of NICO ... We don't worry about premium volume."

As suggested earlier, that's an understandable conclusion from the perspective of a long-term business owner. The question is how to impart a similar way of thinking among the employees, whose jobs depend upon their ability to generate business (written premiums). Back to Buffett:

"If the silent message had gone out to employees that unless you write a lot of business you're going to lose your job, they would have written a lot of business. NICO can write $1 billion of business in any month if it wanted to, all it has to do is offer silly prices. If you offer a silly price, brokers will find you in the middle of the ocean at four in the morning. You cannot afford to do that. What we've always told people in our insurance businesses, and specifically at NICO, is that if they write no business, their job is not in jeopardy. We cannot afford to have an unspoken message to employees that if you don't write business, your job may be lost."

As Buffett explained, NICO never had layoffs during that difficult thirteen-year period ("other people would have, but we didn't"). The number of employees naturally fluctuated as a result of attrition, but nobody was let go at NICO due to insufficient production (volumes). Over time, that led to significantly reduced output per employee, along with a much higher expense ratio (up ~1,500 basis points, from ~25% in 1986 to ~40% in 1999).

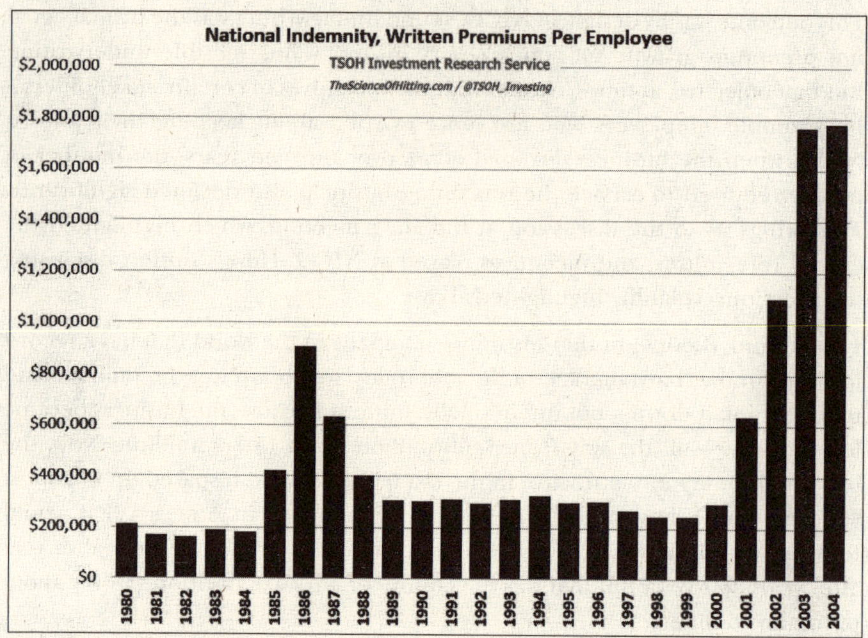
National Indemnity, Written Premiums Per Employee
TSOH Investment Research Service
TheScienceOfHitting.com / @TSOH_Investing
$2,000,000
$1,800,000
$1,600,000
$1,400,000
$1,200,000
$1,000,000
$800,000
$600,000
$400,000
$200,000
$0
1980
1981
1982
1983
1984
1985
1986
1987
1988
1989
1990
1991
1992
1993
1994
1995
1996
1997
1998
1999
2000
2001
2002
2003
2004

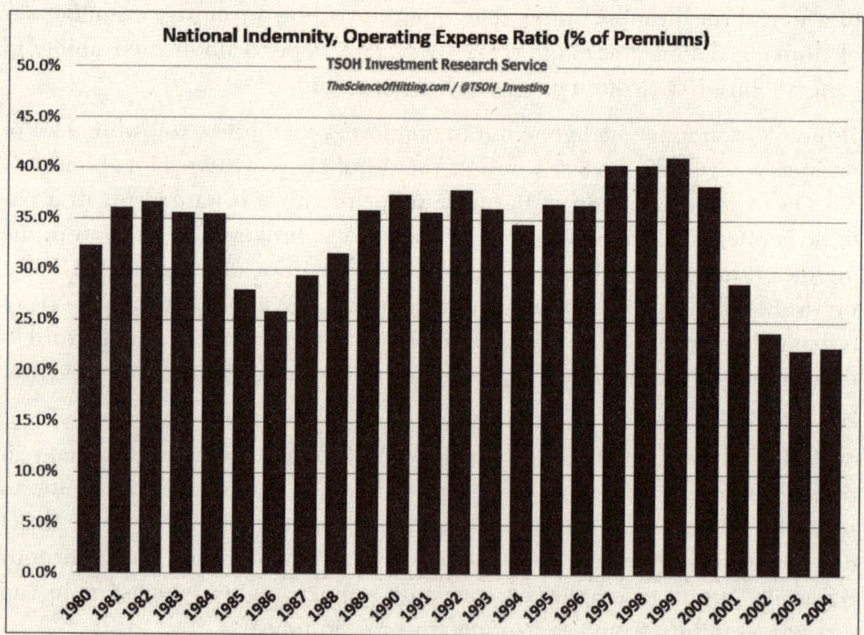
National Indemnity, Operating Expense Ratio (% of Premiums)
TSOH Investment Research Service
TheScienceOfHitting.com / @TSOH_Investing
50.0%
45.0%
40.0%
35.0%
30.0%
25.0%
20.0%
15.0%
10.0%
5.0%
0.0%
1980
1981
1982
1983
1984
1985
1986
1987
1988
1989
1990
1991
1992
1993
1994
1995
1996
1997
1998
1999
2000
2001
2002
2003
2004

As Buffett keyed in on, this was a critical trade-off/decision to be made by NICO: "Some companies would feel that having [a significantly higher expense ratio] would be intolerable—but what we feel is intolerable is writing bad business … If you get a culture of writing bad business, it's almost impossible to get rid of. We would rather suffer too much overhead than to teach employees that, in order to retain their jobs, they needed to write any damn thing that came along, because that's a very hard habit to get rid of once you're hooked on it … I think we're almost the only insurance company in the world—certainly public—that sends the absolutely unequivocal message to our people that they will never be laid off because of a lack of volume."

Where this story gets really interesting is when we look at the bottom line. The following two charts show the underwriting profitability at NICO during the 25-year period from 1980 to 2004; the first is measured as a percentage of written premiums and the second is measured in dollars. As you can see in the first chart, NICO was consistently writing profitable business during this 25-year period (even during the 1990s when it struggled to maintain its prior year volumes, let alone grow). Despite the headwind on written premiums, the insurer managed to keep its head above water by focusing on writing good business above all else ("we made money in virtually every year").

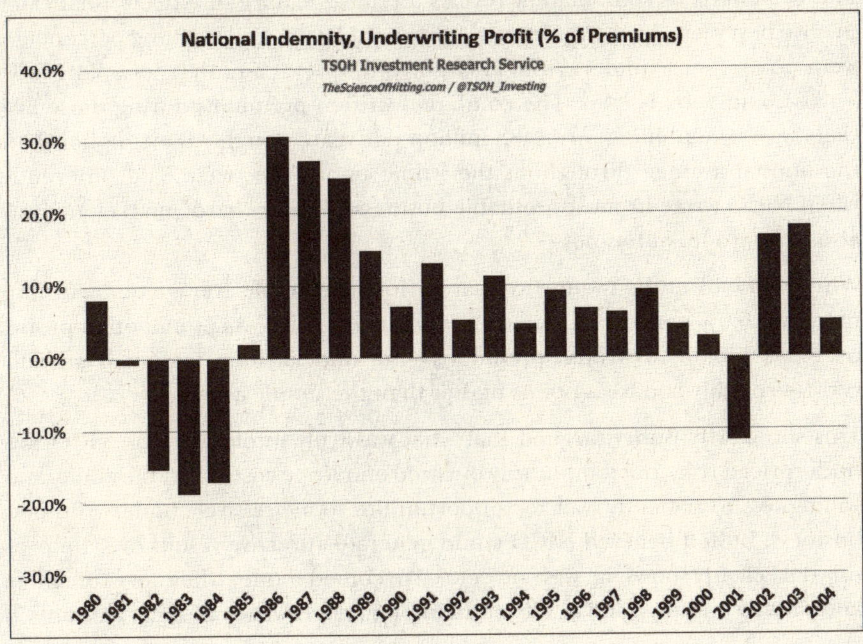

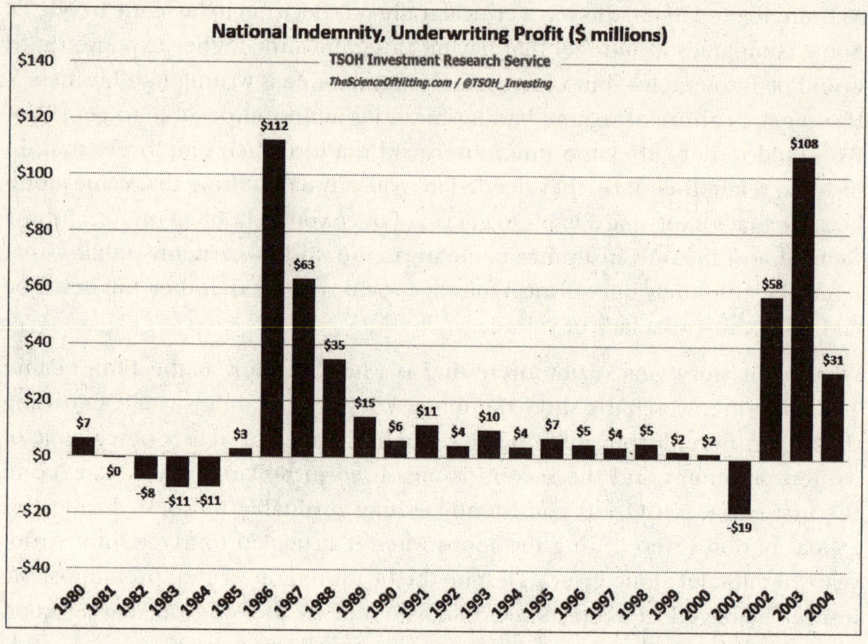

The two charts in combination reveals a crucial feature of NICO's financials: the five best years during this period, measured by the underwriting percentage, were 1986 (~31% underwriting margin), 1987 (~27%), 1988 (~25%), 2003 (~18%), and 2002 (~17%). The combined written premiums during those five years was ~$1.94 billion, or ~$388 million per year—roughly 150% higher than the annual average throughout the whole twenty-five years. Said differently, when NICO wrote its most profitable business (during "hard" markets), it was also writing a lot of business.

When you look at the twenty-five-year period, the simple average underwriting margin is 6.6% per year. But on the cumulative results—$444 million in profits on $3.84 billion in written premiums—the underwriting margin is actually 11.6%—roughly 500 basis points higher than the simple average.

This shows why Buffett argued that what was truly intolerable for NICO was underpriced risks, not temporarily outsized employee costs. With the ability and willingness to patiently wait for opportunities to aggressively underwrite new business, Buffett believed NICO could generate attractive results over time; as this data clearly shows, he was correct. ("We coined money when we wrote huge amounts of business, and made a little money when we wrote small amounts.")

CONCLUSION

In response to Buffett's long explanation of NICO's results over the past twenty-five years, Munger said the following: "The main thing is that practically nobody else does it—and yet to me it's obvious it's the way to go. There's a lot in Berkshire like that. It's just a little different from the way other people do it; it's partly the luxury of having a controlling shareholder of strong opinions ... It would be hard for a committee, including a lot of employees, to come up with these decisions."

At NICO, Berkshire appreciated the role of incentives. There was a disconnect between the short-term interests of the employee and the employer, and NICO directly addressed that through its words and actions/policies. Of paramount importance, they didn't waver when times got tough (and for long periods). It may be "just a little different"—but it mattered hugely over time.

Among public companies, I'd argue a willingness to accept significant and sustained short-term pain as a necessary cost of long-term prosperity is the exception, not the rule (as Tom Russo calls it, "the capacity to suffer"). At Berkshire Hathaway, the culture and incentives at the subsidiary companies are deliberately structured to encourage this (it helps that Berkshire Hathaway, by nature of its diversification, isn't beholden to the near-term prospects in any given business or industry). In the short term, the value of that advantage can be difficult to quantity or pinpoint (imagine running a similar exercise to this one in 1999 instead of 2004); but as NICO's twenty-five-year track record clearly shows, it shines clearly in the fullness of time. As a long-term investor, this is what I'm searching for. On the rare occasion when it's found, it should be treated accordingly.

Here's Buffett with the final word: "NICO was a no-name company thirty years ago operating through a general agency system which everybody said was obsolete. It had no patents, real estate, copyrights, nothing that distinguished it, essentially, from dozens of other insurance companies ... But they have had a record almost like no one else's because they had discipline; they really knew what they were about. And they've stayed with that—in fact, they've intensified it over time. And their record has left other people in the dust. If you went to Wall Street with that record alone in 1990 or 1995, they'd say, 'What's wrong with you?' The answer is nothing's wrong with it. You put your finger on having the right incentives ... You can't run an auto company without layoffs; you can't run a steel company this way. But this is the right way to run an insurance company. And that's why cookie-cutter approaches to employment practices, bonuses, all that, are nonsense. You have to think through the situation that faces you in a given industry with its given competitive conditions and its own economic characteristics."